D1120978

RELUCTANT WITNESS

To my old friend
Bruce Jennings: great
conversationalist, friend,
soundingboard and student of
philosophy, history, and Jim Brennan
engineering! All best
Brian H. Maloney

RELUCTANT WITNESS

Memoirs from the last year

of the European

airwar

1944-45

by James J. Mahoney

(1917-1998)

and

Brian H. Mahoney

© 2001 by Brian H..Mahoney All rights reserved

No part of this publication may be reproduced,stored in a retrieval system,or transmitted,in any form or by any means, electronic, mechanical, photocopying, recording, or otherwise,without written prior permission of the author,with the exception of short passages cited in critical reviews.Contact the author through Trafford Publishing.

The cover portrait was one of the first efforts in oil by a young Frederick P. Walkey at Rackheath.He went on to study then teach art and had a distinguished career as a commerical portraitist.

During an extended period of bad weather in 1944, Lt. Col. Mahoney had asked Walkey and a handful of artistic others to spend some of the 467th's discretionary funds on art supplies in London and set up class for idle air-crews. Walkey insisted that Mahoney sit for him; this stunning outcome (from two sessions of less than an hour each) has graced the Mahoney household ever since.

Patty Mahoney, the colonel's youngest, detailed in 1999 by her brother Brian to find the artist, made *one phone call* and through a couple she knows in Boston discovered that she was 'one degree of separation' from the artist's younger wife, Sharon. Within 36 hours of her 'assignement,' Patty had Brian in contact with the Walkeys.

The economical statement on page 463 is from <u>Memoirs of the Second World War</u> by Winston S. Churchill, ©1948, 1949, 1950, 1951, 1953, ©1958, 1959 by Houghton Mifflin Company, all rights reserved. Their permission for its use is gratefully acknowledged.

National Library of Canada Cataloguing in Publication Data

Mahoney, Brian H., 1953-
  Reluctant witness

Includes bibliographical references and index.
  ISBN 1-55212-875-X

  1. Mahoney, James J., 1917-1998. 2. World War, 1939-1945--Aerial operations, American. 3. World War, 1939-1945--Personal narratives, American. I. Mahoney, James J., 1917-1998. II. Title.
D790.M33 2001   940.54'4973'092   C2001-911149-5

TRAFFORD

This book was published *on-demand* in cooperation with Trafford Publishing.
On-demand publishing is a unique process and service of making a book available for retail sale to the public taking advantage of on-demand manufacturing and Internet marketing.
On-demand publishing includes promotions, retail sales, manufacturing, order fulfilment, accounting and collecting royalties on behalf of the author.

Suite 6E, 2333 Government St., Victoria, B.C. V8T 4P4, CANADA
Phone   250-383-6864   Toll-free   1-888-232-4444 (Canada & US)
Fax   250-383-6804   E-mail   sales@trafford.com
Web site   www.trafford.com   TRAFFORD PUBLISHING IS A DIVISION OF TRAFFORD HOLDINGS LTD.
Trafford Catalogue #01-0275   www.trafford.com/robots/01-0275.html

10   9   8   7   6   5   4   3   2   1

table of contents

part I: the memoirs

part II: 'apocrypha'

Maps

About photographs in the book

Period photos are mostly official USAAF images via James Mahoney and treated here and elsewhere as 'in the public domain.' For those few by him or his contemporaries, copyright claim is made by the estate of the late James J. Mahoney.

Photos taken in 1999 are by the younger author, subsumed under this book's copyright.

Foreword by

Brigadier General Robin Olds, USAF (Ret.)

Aviation buffs and historians will find these recollections a fascinating and detailed accounting of aerial warfare over Hitler's Third Reich. James J. Mahoney tells his tale with close attention to factual detail, taking us through the daily grind of mission preparation and performance with a patience borne of endless repetition. In prose at times droll, methodical and marked by measured emotion, but always dignified, he recounts his vivid memories of action in that long ago war. Yet his son Brian tell us his father was frustrated by his inability to "...capture what it felt like, and how it affected him."

There is a deeper level to these reflections, one perhaps not seen by the narrating father or his probing son. Who do I think I am to delve deep into the context of a man's experiences, to explain that which he himself sought to understand for the many days of his long survival? Simply, with sympathy and heartfelt admiration, I would offer to shine a little light on the important questions posed by the son.

To start by saying "I was there," would be fatuous at best. Yes, I was there—same time, same place, same war—but with a vast difference. Jim Mahoney flew *bombers*. I flew *fighters*.

One morning in September 1944, our squadron of P-51 Mustangs was ordered to escort a group of B-24s to a target in Germany. Nothing in our briefing led us to expect that this would be other than a routine mission—as much as flying missions over Hitler's Germany might be called 'routine.' The only unusual thing in our orders was the instruction to rendezvous with our assigned 'box' of bombers at the Initial Point (or 'IP'), where they turned onto their bomb run. We arrived at the proper place at the specified time. Large formations of B-24s filled the sky as they churned their way south toward their target. The day was beautiful... puffy clouds below, visibility unlimited, sky relatively calm.

By this time in the aerial war, each bomber had emblazoned on its vertical stabilizer an identifier—a square, triangle or circle enclosing a large letter of the alphabet. The geometric figure identified one of the three 8th Air Force *divisions*, the letter designated a particular one of the dozen or more *groups* within the division. Although there were typically hundreds of bombers in the daily strikeforce, it ordinarily took but a few moments to identify the bombers for whom we were assigned fighter escort responsibility.

But this day something was wrong. Our assigned box was nowhere to be found. Thinking I had made an error in timing, I turned my sixteen fighters toward the tail-end of the bomber stream to look for our B-24s. Just as we took up a northerly heading, all hell broke loose some distance up ahead. Those explosions and hideous black plumes could only be bombers under heavy enemy fighter attack, We poured on full throttle as I called out a warning on the frequency we shared with the heavies, then switched to our own channel.

Seconds seemed like minutes as we pulled close to the scene of the attack. We came abreast of the remaining B-24s and piled into what Luftwaffe fighters we could see, but they broke off their attack upon our arrival. I fired a parting burst at one of the last F-W 190s as they dove away, but doubt I even scared him. The more important matter at hand was to form a protective shield around the few surviving B-24s as they plowed on toward the target. The sky behind us was bright with explosions and filled with parachutes. Burning debris marked the falling remnants of once beautiful aircraft. The bombers made their drop and turned for home.

The trip back to England was gut wrenching. Many of the cripples we escorted must have known they would not make it even as far as our advancing armies in France. I had to watch helplessly as the lone Liberator I was with suddenly burst into flames, gave a lurch, fell off on one wing, and exploded as it plunged toward the earth. Only two chutes emerged from the stricken bird. I was horrified. That bomber was my 'Big Friend.' I had been talking to him, letting him know I would stick by, encouraging him, steering him around flak-defended towns. Now this. For the first time in combat I had to choke back tears of rage and sorrow.

That evening I was ordered up to Division Headquarters to give a first-hand account of what had happened. It wasn't easy. The people there had reason to wonder whether my squadron had blundered, leaving the B-24s unprotected. After some time at the plotting board and careful discussion of routes and timing, it was somewhat grudgingly admitted that the bombers had committed a navigational error which put them in jeopardy far from the main stream of their strike force. This was later confirmed by the B-24 survivors, not that the information made me feel any better. I was told that some forty-two B-24s did not return.

Flying back to my own base that night I thought of those 420 Americans, of their friends at their bases in England, and of the parents, wives and families back home. By this time I had been fighting for some six months and had become hardened to combat and to losses. But this was different. Those of us in fighters had options and could fight back. How could the bomber guys go at it, day after day, knowing the odds of survival were only even at the best, and that there was nothing they could do except brave it out, praying that the gods of chance would somehow let them make it? I shuddered and gave thanks for my own circumstances.

Two weeks later I was involved in a nearly identical situation, but if possible, even worse. Just short of Berlin, 52 B-17s under heavy enemy fighter attack went down in the space of seconds. Again the Luftwaffe had achieved surprise and again I had to be a witness as we fought amid and beneath the carnage of that battle.

One hundred bombers equals one thousand men. One thousand bombers, ten thousand men. Can we see into their hearts and minds as they faced each day; can we understand what drove them to such desperate acts of bravery? No two men are exactly alike; each contends with private fears and doubts in his own fashion. While all are buoyed by the camaraderie shared with their fellow warriors, few consciously consider the source of that determination and personal zeal, that sense of responsibility to persevere in the face of violence and uncertainty. Most adopt an 'it may happen to him, but not to me' attitude, yet all quickly learn to live *from day to day.*

What is the basis of this bravery?

I contend it is far more than the individual psyche. Acting in concert with his fellows, driven by the needs of his society, facing the uncertainties of the moment, each man acts within the bounds of his beliefs and with the courage of his convictions. His bravery and determination in the face of the unknown is a tribute, not just to himself, but to generations of his forebears who set for him the very highest standards of behavior and of devotion... to service, to one's country, and to one's fellow man.

As did the majority of us in those bygone times, Jim Mahoney accepted his personal responsibilities without question. It followed naturally from one's belief in the right or wrong of it. Hitler was wrong, we were right. It was that simple. This is in sharp contrast with our experience in South East Asia over a quarter of a century ago, and the political quagmires that characterize today's situation.

For the warriors themselves and for those who were never there, my thoughts on what it felt like and how it affected each man: to be there felt like hell.   You put each yesterday as deep into your subconscious as you could. Then suddenly, when it was all over and the world celebrated, you realized that for you there *would* be more than just one tomorrow, that the future stretched ahead, and that there was a life to be lived. Thoughts of the recent past didn't belong, and couldn't be allowed to affect today and tomorrow. You went on *changed,* facing life with a deep self-assurance borne of having survived harsh reality, and reverence for those who paid the ultimate price to preserve the life you now enjoyed.

To Brian Mahoney, who struggles with these large questions, and to his late father, who I have come to know and admire through his thoughtful writing, I offer this anonymous verse written in the days following the American Civil War:

To the Valiant

To set the cause above renown
To love the game beyond the prize
To honor as you strike him down
The foe who comes with angry eyes.

To count the life of battle good
And dear the land that gave you birth
And dearer yet the brotherhood
That binds the brave of all the earth.

-Robin Olds, May 2000

Acknowledgments

Both authors have been privileged to enlist the aid of many helpful contributors to this effort over three decades; hopefully they will be forgiven for any omissions here.

Gladys Russell (now Ellis), Dad's remarkable secretary at the Norwich Pharmacal Company for many years and his discreet first collaborator, transformed his dictation and loping longhand into the earliest typed drafts, at over 150 flawless words per minute.

In his endless revisions, Dad was guided by the feedback of draft readers Bill Jovanovitch and Noel Rubinton.

Colonel Albert J. Shower, the consummate officer and gentleman, and his delightful wife Char, welcomed me into their home like a son and endured hours of questions broad and narrow. Similarly, *Witchcraft* crew chief the late Sergeant Joe Ramirez and his loving Josie entertained, regaled, informed and encouraged me.

Veterans of the 2nd Air Division of the Eighth Air Force, most from the 492nd and 467th Bomb Groups, were generous with their time in face-to-face, written, or telephone interviews. Their patience in all cases, and their willingness to dig up particular information in several instances, allowed me to chase details further than I would have dreamed possible, more than half a century after the events described. I list them here alphabetically and with no mention of rank, with which they seem graciously comfortable at reunions and in correspondence. They are Dick Bastien, Bob Cash, Melvin Culross, the Allen Herzbergs, Fred Holdredge, Clarence P. Kurtz, Roger Leister, Bob McKenzie, Robin Olds, Harry Orthman, John J. Taylor, and Fredrick P. (and Sharon) Walkey.

A small group of those who served with Dad in *both* groups held intimate reunions almost annually from 1958 until just three years ago. Two of them, Ernie Haar and E. J. 'Alex' Alexander, not only treated me royally when I visited them in Florida, but they continued to answer my endless questions about pilot and bombardier lingo, practice and protocol over a period of many months. They and their wives, Emile (recently deceased) and Mary, reminded me again what impeccable taste my parents had in their choice of lifelong friends.

Jean and David Hastings dropped everything for two memorable and intensely productive days in the Rackheath environs. David's acumen, boundless energy and dedication to a handful of well served causes, especially the 2nd Air Division's Memorial Room, are only exceeded by this couple's charm and hospitality.

Susan Loth Wolkerstorfer, Deputy Commentary Editor for the Minneapolis-based Star Tribune, attempted to bring my punctuation and writing 'style' into at least the last half of the 20th century. Craig Hulvey advocated strongly for the reader by advocating the simple declarative sentence. Bryan Harrison 'empowered' me cybernetically. World-citizen Heidi Birgfeld, used to answering my questions about the *political* wind, also helped with a report on *weather*. Gary Gillard, generous with his myriad competencies, scanned images, chauffeured, caught errors, coached and coaxed during production stages, and served as an astute and resilient sounding board. My boyhood friend John Tredwell,

Captain for American Airlines, gave me a little bit of ground school regarding basic instrumentation.

For treating this *parvenu* like a colleague, sharing tips, leads and the occasional pint, I am grateful to a variety of experts—aviation researcher-author Martin Bowman, serious amateur historians of the Mighty Eighth Perry Watts and Andy Wilkerson, and Ms. Yvonne Kinkaid on the library and research staff of the Air Force History Support Office at Bolling AFB. The grandfather of the *genre*, Roger Freeman, allowed use of the wonderful station maps.

My niece Erin Mahoney, by her contribution to research for the timeline in the appendix, fulfilled one of my secret wishes: that this work would reflect the hands of *three* generations.

Both of my parents' sole-surviving siblings, Francis X. Mahoney and Elizabeth McKenna Logan, have supplied helpful fact and flavor for the biography and stories in the 'Apocrypha' section of the book.

All four of my siblings have been steadfastly supportive in ways practical and emotional. Jerry, recently retired as a USAF Colonel and the longest-seated military judge in US history, has prevented a handful of gaffes in this civilian's account of *res militaria*. His wife, Maj. Karen Mayberry, USAF, suggested sources for military information and assisted him in the OCR scan of Dad's typescript. Patty deftly disposed of a pesky research project with that miraculous 'small world' élan she inherits undiminished from Dad. Mark made useful organizational and formatting suggestions. Our step-mother Polly has put me up and put up with me, over four extended visits, so that I could do research in Dad's handsome library, which she has dubbed 'the War Room.'

The spirit of my mother, the late Mary McKenna Mahoney—diminutive, feisty and hilarious—suffuses this entire work. She spurred her husband to find words for his experiences and share them with his kids and the world, and emboldened her youngest son to push his way into a reluctant father's painful memories while he was alive, then edit him purposively after his death.

Body and soul have been nourished and supported in this venture by Bruce Rashbaum MD, Ray Milefsky, Wheaton and Eileen Griffin, Mary Partlow, Stan Bliss, Sean Favretto and Rick Molnar. Between them and the project itself, I have enjoyed knowing and feeling, day by day over the duration of this project, that I was doing exactly what I was supposed to be doing.

No doubt style in places is still stilted, sentences such as this one run on too long, and errors remain, despite the best efforts of all the foregoing individuals. For myself and my father, I thank each of them for helping to make this book, at long last, a reality.

-Brian H. Mahoney

No combat soldier's personal experience, as a tiny subtext of the fundamental insanity of war, has any structure at all, beyond a dry chronology of events. But personal accounts of war, no matter how flawed, have compelling and universal human interest as windows on the best and worst in our nature. In bringing to a wide audience his written account of his personal experience as a combat aviator and leader, I inherit from my father a paradox. It is this: one can succeed spectacularly in authoring engaging autobiography and in contributing importantly to the historic record, while remaining frustrated in all attempts to forcefully convey *how it felt.*

Among my father's never-articulated motivations for midwifing his written account over some thirty years, I now recognize the most disquieting, relentless and prime: his own need to make sense of what he and his contemporaries experienced. These veterans experienced much, and intensely, in a relatively brief and chaotic period. His own survival particularly defied comprehension. As a bomb squadron commander, he once had the experience of sending seven of his crews on a mission from which *none* returned. He had transitioned from the most ill-fated of B-24 groups to one of the luckiest, and in a stroke his chances of surviving a combat mission improved *seven times.* He was in intimate proximity with several men who 'got it,' but his own skin was never broken.

Quietly and privately for much of

his long postwar life, my father ruminated over his thirteen months in combat. He was fabulously successful at boiling artificially isolated episodes—such as the many vignettes which follow—down to digestible, comprehensible, atomistic 'war stories,' each with a beginning, a middle, and an end. Narrator and audience take an undeniable if fleeting comfort in their rehearsal, refinement and repetition. It is the nature of war stories to get better over time. But to the end, and through every iteration of the collection as a whole, he was dogged by its inability to capture for himself or us just what it felt like, and how it affected him.

My father had another unspoken but undeniable motivation: respect for the fallen, and a felt moral compunction, as survivor and witness, to make their experience and sacrifice a dignified part of the record.

In collaborating with my late father to present this book, I share several of his goals, and bring a few of my own. I have a lot more to say about his motivations in this, 'my' introduction, than he did in his, which comes later in the book. I cannot assure myself, and will not try to persuade the reader, that he would have agreed with all of my analysis. For that matter, I expect that he would have taken issue with entire parts of my contribution, such as the biography to be found in the appendix, where I offer what the historical record and the reader's curiosity require, but he in his modesty would have omitted: evidence of the character, experience and position of James J. Mahoney, which qualified him so well to hold our ear.

In his introduction, my father eschews the academic or statistical approach, applying himself to telling tales of enduring human interest. "I'm not interested in impersonal data such as numbers of bombs dropped, shots fired, gallons consumed, etc." In taking upon myself the exercise of researching and documenting some of that more quantitative stuff, I have come to understand and even embrace my father's strong ambivalence as a *reluctant witness*. He wanted to spare himself and his family from having to stare at the maimed, the dead, the devastated. He would have loved to seal off his experience of the bloodbath in an isolated time and space, and knew firsthand the paradox inherent in 'fighting for peace.' But against every inhibition to telling his story, he knew the importance of leaving the non-combatant and the succeeding generation, enjoying the (relative) *Pax Americana,* with a vigorous, vivid impression of the horror of war and, if possible, a *practical* reverence for peace.

I am grateful to have been spared the carnage, grateful for the substantial peace and prosperity hard-won by the earlier generation. But for us who were *not* in combat, the 'impersonal data' that he feared for its abstracting and reductionistic power, judiciously applied, can make the history much more real. The statistics and researched claims I contribute to this work are deliberately developed to draw the engaged reader into my own strong ambivalence. At times I surrender to a macabre fascination with history's monumental terribleness, as much as the record will support and imagination can conjure, but then I always recoil to the safe present to contemplate the lessons for which such dear tuition has been paid. History's voyeurs require the statistics, but for history's protagonists, these are but the palest surrogates of what was experienced.

Jim Mahoney abhorred individuals and institutions which he perceived as glorifying 'his' war or any other. He was of a type which many of my fellow 'baby boomers' have described: reticent to talk about his war experiences generally, and tight lipped about the more horrific things in particular. His personal style formidably compounded the task of getting him to talk. He was reserved but not stand-offish, modest and quietly self-confident in a way easily mistaken for self-effacing, and as poker-faced as the Sphinx. In total, it made for an enticing, unaffected enigma.

For many in my generation, 'the war' was unexamined background noise—so recent and familiar that we all reached young adulthood before realizing that our received impressions were more form than substance. My father's G.I. footlocker, his US Army Air Force issue leather-and-wool gunner's mitts and A-2 jacket, a knitted drab olive cap and a .50 caliber ammo box, were all pressed into practical service in the Mahoney household. The simple salesman's model black 1946 Ford two-door sedan that our parents nursed along for 17 years was affectionately named 'The Bomber.' And it went without saying that *everyone's* dad had been 'in the war.' My brothers and sisters thrilled when every so often he would project some of his 16mm Kodachrome films of his bases in England and of bomber operations, but seeing these alongside the family movies, we had no inkling how singular and extraordinary they were. Taking his two Army blankets and his perfectly serviceable duffel bag away with me to summer camp in 1965 was quite unremarkable.

So this impressionable son's early interest in planes and cameras is hardly surprising, and these, before I developed an overarching interest in WW II history, turned me into my father's most persistent interviewer. Suppertime was often a setting for my 'interrogations.' Typically I had to soften him up with a series of specific and direct questions, and be satisfied with his short and succinct answers. In time, as he realized that my interest was not passing or merely polite, he gave more expansive answers, often entailing remarkable anecdotes. I relish my memory of one occasion from my high school days. My kid sister Patty and I, still 'in the nest,' were at the supper table with our parents. A line of my questioning had provoked Dad to tell of one of his narrow escapes with death. Riveted though my attention was, I could not help being distracted by Mom's facial expression, which went from high astonishment to higher indignation. "Jim Mahoney! I have been married to you for *twenty eight years,* and you *never* told me that!" Stunned, defensive, and not at all apologetic, he said, "You never *asked!*"

Even in later years, for all of the questions I had put, there was always more to be 'mined' from him. In every retelling, along with the familiar story would emerge details and nuances that were fresh, and which unfailingly whetted more appetite than they sated. I still have incredulous moments like my mother's. Was it by some conscious or willful withholding that my father never told me, in so many words, that he was actually the second in command (Deputy Group Commander) at Rackheath? (I was in my twenties when I finally got it from my first more-than-casual reading of the 467th BG's beautiful post-war book.)   Likely, it was simply that he had no 'system,' such as ranking things by their significance, for tracking what he had and had not yet divulged. I have lately come to a companion realization: my 'debriefing' over the years was also without organizing scheme, and, sadly, committed only to the flawed record of my memory.

Just sitting down and telling it all in chronological order was never a practical option. A thoroughgoing telling of ten minutes of combat action might require years of careful speech. A worthy audience will have questions about every detail of man, machine and motive.   Truly satisfying answers will each require reference to some other context—one containing, contained by, or intersecting the 'main' one. Disparate contexts overlap and intersect to define the context in question, leaving us to despair of finding any 'real' beginning or end. We have to settle for an interesting middle, defined by all of the loose strands running out from it in every direction.

As Dad's sons came of draftable age, Vietnam increasingly shaped the conversation in terms of personal morals and global views. To this day, my father's generation and mine share a fatigued *détente* over the interminable strident arguments, the inconclusive comparisons and contrasts of 'your war' and 'our war.' Together we argued the paradoxes of the 'good war' and civil war as a form of 'free determination.' Together we suffered somberly the loss of a relative national innocence. It remains the defining national conversation of the post-WW II America, and informs the present work of father and son.

If he had not already had a broader historical perspective on the relative importance of his own experience to the historical record, my father must have come to the realization in the 1960s, when a succession of now prominent researcher-historians of 'The Mighty Eighth' began beating a path to his door and citing him as a source in their books. He was uniquely placed to speak authoritatively on a range of events and subjects. Privately, he began writing early drafts of his 'war stories' in the late '60s, keeping the effort hidden from all but his office secretary until the spring of 1973. He asked a one-time bombardier of his, who had become a principal in one of the prominent publishing houses, to consider it for publication. He also unceremoniously left a 330 page carbon-copy sitting on his desk in the family room, as if 'leaking' it. Per his plan, I discovered it after supper on a weekend trip home from college—and read it cover to cover in a single all-night sitting. At breakfast the next day, Dad, who never missed a thing, could not hide his pleasure at my obvious lack of sleep. We did not beat around the bush: I told him that it was an extremely compelling piece, if a bit chaotic in the presentation, and that he certainly should refine and publish. He allowed that his publisher friend Jovanovitch had politely said as much, and had encouraged him to 'work with a ghost' and then come back.

Over the next twenty years, the existence of the typescript was neither a secret, nor much discussed—Dad did not want to work with an assistant writer, but fitfully and quietly applied himself to improving the work. After his retirement in 1980, he turned more attention to it and to the methodical cataloging of his extensive photos, papers and films of the period. By 1993, I had become impolitic with my impatience, and was rewarded for asking him outright if he would let me help him with 'the book.' I did not have a specific time frame in mind when I offered to 'take six months off' to help him kick it out. To my surprise and relief, he accepted the offer. Unfortunately, we both acted as if he would live a lot longer; the collaboration never even got scheduled.

During what we all knew were his last few weeks, Dad and I never discussed the typescript. He left no instruction in his papers. In settling the affairs of his estate later, we found no other area of unfinished business; quite the opposite. When I later began probing in his terrifically organized files, I became convinced that he knew someone would pick it up, and that he intended to make it as easy as possible for them. The long evolution of his manuscript, various detailed source notes and references, an index to the various electronic versions, his extensive correspondence files: all had been left 'ready in wait' with the most deliberate care.

When I finally made the natural decision, early in 1999, to 'drop everything' and write this book, I still frequently had days in which I forgot that my father was no longer a phone call away. His death the previous September, following five months of illness, still seems out of character to his widow and five children. Readers, having come to appreciate the miracle of how he repeatedly beat the Reaper during the war, will agree: it seems strange that something as mundane as *multiple myeloma* should have taken this vigorous and keen giant at a mere 81 years.

I should not have been surprised that this project would be, among other things, a grieving exercise for me. But I was still unprepared for the overwhelming feelings I experienced, sopping wet astride my touring bicycle under an ancient oak tree in the hamlet of North Pickenham, England in early June 1999. I was alone on a pilgrimage to the spare remnants of USAAF Station #143, to which the ill-fated 492nd Bombardment Group was assigned in the Spring of 1944, my father in command of one of its four bomb squadrons. Knowing that only three of over 250 buildings remained, I wondered at my strange attraction to a small derelict complex being used for storage by a country auto mechanic, several hundred yards distant from the airfield. When the East Anglian rain abated enough for me to consult my accurate period map of the base, I realized that this had been my father's office, the headquarters block.

This entire project has been marked by numerous such remarkable episodes of serendipity and coincidence in which my siblings and I recognize, with comfort and amusement, that Dad's legendary precociousness in the 'small world department' has charmed this effort.

The man his children knew was larger than life, very rarely demonstrative and not very approachable, but also fair, wise, capable and solid. Only through this writing has he afforded us a candid and intimate window to the soul of the young leader who became our father.

       This wonderful picture of the young lieutenant colonel has been made more substantial and vivid over the past two years as I have met, interviewed and corresponded with men of every rank who served with my father. Scores of unsolicited personal testaments to his leadership qualities and admirable character have been pressed on me at reunions and in letters. Many of these men were at pains to impress upon me that they had 'only' been enlisted men 56 years ago, but that their respect for him had a solid foundation which transcended rank and, it would seem, the passage of years. In more than a few instances, I have been explicitly instructed to not dismiss any of this as sentimental kindnesses extended by old lads to a grieving son of one of their own.

       For my brothers and sisters, I humbly receive this long-craved closeness, which comes late and indirectly, with a wistful gratitude.

Under a lowering Norfolk sky, a derelict airfield tower looks over crops growing in what was Rackheath's airfield, 55 years earlier.

"Allied air power was decisive in the war in Western Europe. Hindsight inevitably suggests that it might have been employed differently or better in some respects. Nevertheless, it was decisive. In the air, its victory was complete. At sea, its contribution, combined with naval power, brought an end to the enemy's greatest naval threat—the U-boat; on land, it helped turn the tide overwhelmingly in favor of Allied ground forces. Its power and superiority made possible the success of the invasion. It brought the economy which sustained the enemy's armed forces to virtual collapse, although the full effects of this collapse had not reached the enemy's front lines when they were overrun by Allied forces. It brought home to the German people the full impact of modern war with all its horror and suffering. Its imprint on the German nation will be lasting."

-Summary, Unites States Strategic Bombing Survey (USSB), Conclusions

Dedication by

the Son

Preparing 'my' parts of this book over a 24 month period, with travel around the US, England and Europe, has been a personally satisfying and important odyssey. In bringing forth my late father's 'war stories,' I have been the privileged conduit of his marvelous personal account. I have, for my siblings, received the warm recollections of scores of veterans who served with our father. I have walked the remnants of his Norfolk runways. I have explored and contemplated the physical spots, softened and disguised by overgrowth and blessed peace, where he lived and worked in those momentous days.

In all of this, I have been inestimably aided by the existing body of reference literature on the Eighth Air Force in England. In the last thirty five years, a handful of researcher-authors (mostly British), and hundreds of cooperating veterans of the Mighty Eighth have steadfastly applied themselves to collecting the statistics, the records, the photos and the first hand accounts, rescuing the substance and order of a phenomenal story from certain historical obscurity. This steady flow of painstakingly researched, lovingly presented titles, taken as a whole, presents the drama of a society pitching industrial might, unity of purpose, and citizen soldiers in unprecedented numbers, against an infamous foe, amidst the strife and caprice of horrific total war.

In ways practical and moral, the people of still-grateful England have encouraged the research efforts of my countrymen and theirs. The citizens of East Anglia still harbor an unabashed gratitude to 'the Yank,' which finds expression in many ways. Stained glass windows consecrated to Americans who served and sacrificed, hang in dozens of quaint country churches and ancient urban cathedrals. Along a hundred roadsides over which lumbering and deadly bombers once struggled into the air, one encounters dignified and impeccably maintained memorial markers. In the Norfolk seat, Norwich, the The Second Air Division Memorial Library, endowed and subscribed by English and American contributions, houses a definitive collection of 8th AF literature, displays and artifacts, serving serious researcher, veteran and student equally well. In the pubs, a generation and a half on, the American who is found out to be a 'son of the Eighth' will protest in vain when he tries to settle his own tab.   On D-Day or V-E Day, ceremonies solemn, decorous and sincere are still, fifty-six years on, the order of the day.

Many veterans of 'The Eighth,' especially in recent years, have shared their piece of the story as published memoir, as oral tradition, or as scrapbook or diary entrusted to family or an appropriate collection.

The collective memory of the generation that experienced it all is now flickering out. But by making the horror and excitement vivid, the statistics and strategies sensible, and the means and events of the air war clear, all of these *stewards of the story* have honored the ground and air crews and a rendered a great service to this and coming generations.

It is to all of these *stewards,* my father in their ranks, that I thankfully dedicate my effort. They have helped build an important literature and *preserved the memory.* Here we find our heritage, and, may God so help us, dearly-bought lessons for the taking.

BHM February 4, 2001

Author's Note

This book is unusual; it would be misleading to say that I am my father's co-author, for we only *discussed* collaborating on 'his book' while he was alive. It would have been inappropriate to 'ghost' write it posthumously, as much of what I felt compelled to include is not his, and should not be passed off as such. Respect for him and his story requires that I take separate responsibility for the elements I have introduced. I can only guess and hope that most of what I have done here to 'present his war stories' would not have disappointed him, and that none of it offends his contemporaries or the truth.

This is a book within a book: my father's text is framed like a heart at the center of my supportive book. His work is the substance of this project, and readers who choose to go right for it, only reverting to my sections as needed, do so with my happy approbation.

While I have stylistically edited, retitled, and in some cases consolidated some of the original 53 developed chapters of my father's writing, I have not taken any liberties with his tone or the points he makes. I have not 'put any words in his mouth.' I have footnoted his chapters as needed to expand upon technical or historical points which will be of interest to the general reader, and in the few instances where my research has uncovered the inevitable factual error in Dad's account.

All footnotes to my father's text, and *all* elements outside of those chapters, are *my* work; I take full responsibility for its factual accuracy, and ask the reader to hold James Mahoney blameless.

At least two of the stories here have appeared, prior to my editing, in the newsletters of the bomb group associations.

As my goals for this project go a bit further than his did, I have developed several items meant to augment and support my father's work. Specifically, I include a glossary and other reference items tailored to establish the historical context which will make his story sensible to a wide audience in his, mine and following generations. I have undertaken the documentation and corroboration of a handful of his unusual claims: he was well-positioned to observe the sometimes grisly business of questionable, under-examined policy revealing itself in operational orders or unpapered practice. As much as possible, I have undertaken to research those situations or episodes which have not appeared in the literature or have been presented without due authority and force. They go against the popular, received view, and deserve the treatment. In a few instances, my father was too close to his own story to see this; in others, he realized that his more extraordinary claims entailed a burden of substantial proof which, as time went on, he seemed less inclined to meet.

My *Apocrypha* section, with its own introduction and explanation, puts me in the narrator's chair but uses Dad as the prime historical source for stories humorous and profound. It follows the *Memoirs.*

Aside from some stylistic improvements, his storytelling itself needs no help. Indeed, I would not presume to improve on the master raconteur. Family and friends who were privileged to hear him tell his stories will scrutinize this book closely, hoping to recognize in it the voice that held them spellbound. It is my sincerest hope that they are not disappointed: I take my stewardship of these stories *very* seriously.

       Dad's motivations and mine for this work are as telling for their differences as for their overlap. His introduction and dedication, distinct from mine, remain intact in the core of the book with his vignettes. Our acknowledgments, bibliography and references are combined.

-BHM

At 52°40' N latitude, predawn comes early in June. This 4:40 a.m. view along the 30° alignment of the main runway at Rackheath runs another half mile to the horizon. This one portion is still intact at its full 150' width but the rest has been narrowed to one lane for farm equipment. Postwar motorway construction created a demand for runway rubble as fill material throughout East Anglia, and returned most of the land to agriculture.

part I

the memoirs

the Father's

Introduction and Dedication

This is a collection of stories
derived from my service with two bomb groups of the
Eighth Air Force in England during World War II. My
first Group, the 492nd, suffered the unenviable
distinctions of having the shortest combat life and the
highest loss rate of any group in the Eighth. My second,
the 467th Bomb Group, to which I was transferred after the
demise of the 492nd, had the second lowest loss rate, and
by war's end had achieved the enviable distinction of
being the most effective of the forty four bomb groups in
the Eighth Air Force.

Because records of those hectic
days are scattered, not always complete, and sometimes of
questionable accuracy, what follows is mostly from
memory and cannot be considered an historical accounting.
The incidents, situations, and people described are all
real. To avoid the possibility of embarrassment or pain to
those who survived some of these actions, and the families
of others who did not, I have used invented names in some
instances and intentional distortion in others to make
them less identifiable.₁ With the passage of time and
diminution of memory, undoubtedly there is also some
distortion that is *un*intentional. I'm sure that's the case
where memory served up only the salient points of some
incidents, and license was taken in filling in the cracks.²

I'm not interested in impersonal
data such as numbers of bombs dropped, shots fired,
gallons consumed, etc. Such numbers have been
adequately covered elsewhere in historical accounts. My

interest is in the air crewmen, their experiences, and their reactions to them. For a couple of pertinent numbers on the aforementioned losses of my first group, the 492nd, I call upon the plaque at the U.S. Air Force Academy dedicated to that group. We went overseas with 70 ten-man crews, 700 combat personnel. The plaque indicates that in our eleven weeks of combat we suffered 530 KIA (killed in action), and 58 MIA (missing in action). Recently, the United States Air Force Historian has written, "The 492nd Bomb Group sustained the heaviest losses in the shortest period of any Bomb Group in U.S. military history."

The stories that follow are obviously those of a survivor. My children, and now grandchildren, call them my 'war stories.' We'll never know the untold stories of those who did not return. It is to them I dedicate this effort.

James J. Mahoney
Hamilton, NY   1997

1. A sequestered key, linking the fictional names to the actual historical names, is on deposit with the 2nd Air Division Memorial Library, Norwich, England. It will be opened on January 1, 2010, serving the needs of history while also honoring the sentiment expressed here by my father.

I have taken the liberty of revealing true identities in a few instances where other published accounts have already named the individuals involved, and use of this device might tend to confuse rather than corroborate the record.

All instances where a fictional name is used, or where I have substituted the actual name for my father's fictional one, are indicated by footnote.

2. Despite my father's apologia, and the reality that he was writing more as memoirist than historian, several of his claims *are* of a greater historical interest than he may have appreciated. He remained characteristically modest regarding his qualification and placement to make these.

I have taken great pains to research and document particular episodes or claims which run counter to the received or 'official' account, in hopes that the full value of his 'story,' its contribution to historical record, can be realized.

Claims made in *my footnotes* to the JJM text, and in all parts of the book outside his text, are presented as researched and documented *history*.

This was the day we'd so long dreamed of and talked about. The war in Europe was over. We had dropped our last bomb and were now heading home! There should have been great elation, but crews waiting to board their planes were as somber as that gray overcast East Anglian day. We should have been looking ahead to family and home, but instead, were reflecting back on experiences we'd never forget, and running down a mental roster of faces which would never be seen again. It was mildly reminiscent of graduation day, when the long anticipated joy of receiving a diploma was unexpectedly overshadowed by the sorry realization that we were leaving classmates and campus behind, possibly forever.

While waiting for the 'stations' and subsequent 'start engines' signal flares from the tower, I'd gone to a nearby hardstand for a final visit on English soil with the surviving members of my original 859th Squadron Operations staff. We'd been more fortunate than the other three squadrons of our original 492nd Bomb Group, having lost only "Smitty" (Capt. John W. Smith, KIA) our Squadron Navigator. We had finished the European war together with the luckier 467th, from whose airfield in Norfolk we were about to depart.

Major John J. Taylor (Jay), originally the Squadron Operations Officer, who'd become its commander when I moved up to group, had survived a harrowing experience. His plane had blown up over the North Sea, leaving him badly burned and in the frigid water for a couple of hours before rescue by an RAF Air/Sea Rescue boat. Only Jay and three others of the eleven aboard survived the explosion, the parachuting, and the sea.

Capt. Edwin J. ("Alex") Alexander, the Squadron Bombardier, was shot down on the last Berlin mission. He bailed out over East Berlin, was picked up by the Russians, and returned to us several weeks later via Moscow, Yugoslavia, and Italy. Alex suffered only some additional scarring to his already football-battered nose when he took a rifle-butt across the face from his Russian captor who supposedly mistook him for a German paratrooper.

Capt. Frank Green, Assistant Operations Officer, and I were the only ones to come through the whole affair unscathed—at least to the eye. What we had survived together!

Our conversation flashed-back to the beginnings of our short-lived 492nd. Like many other 8th Air Force Bomb Groups, an Anti-submarine Squadron had served as cadre to our group. We had been the 12th Anti-Submarine Squadron operating out of Langley Field, Virginia, escorting convoys and hunting U-boats along the East coast since the start of the war. When the Navy took over our aerial patrol duties, we were sent to Alamogordo, New Mexico, where we expanded to bomb group strength and started training for an overseas assignment.

Our anti-sub pilots had hundreds of hours of multi-engine experience, but those sent in with new crews to bring us up to group strength were mostly fresh out of B-24 transitional training schools, who had very little time in that plane, and not much in other types. It soon became apparent that with the amount of training we'd have to give these inexperienced crews, we'd never make our scheduled date for overseas departure. Our Commander, Lt. Col. Eugene Snavely, explained our problem to the Training Command general, who withdrew the green crews and replaced them with others, most of whose pilots had just finished tours as *instructors* at B-24

Transitional Training Schools and were due for combat assignments. Many were captains and first lieutenants. With their experience, the completion of our training was greatly simplified and accelerated. As a result, we were told that we were the first heavy bombardment group to pass our P.O.M. (Preparation for Overseas Movement) inspection and depart for overseas ahead of schedule.

From our staging area at Herington, Kansas, we flew the 'Southern Route' to England: West Palm Beach; Trinidad; Fortaleza, Brazil; Dakar and Marrakech in Africa; Valley, Wales; and our destination, North Pickenham, England.

The leg from Trinidad to Fortaleza was over densely foliated tropical forests and the Amazon. Occasionally we would see a swath cut through the greenery and intermittent reflections of sunlight off the shiny metal skin of a predecessor plane. These crash sites were usually totally inaccessible. The blemishes in the jungle would soon be overgrown, the crews probably never retrieved.

After crossing the south Atlantic on an overnight hop to Dakar, we flew North along the Atlas mountains up to Marrakech. This leg, too, was punctuated with crash scenes, plainly visible because of the lack of vegetation. Because of the harsh mountain and desert-like terrain, many of these crews were as inaccessible as their brethren in the jungle. (We were to learn on our return home via the 'Northern route,' that the overland legs, from Goose Bay, Labrador to Gander, Newfoundland, then to Dow Field in Bangor, Maine, also had a distressing string of intermittent crash scenes. An Air Transport Command navigator once ventured that you could navigate the land portions of both routes by merely following the carcasses of fallen planes.) Thankfully, our 70 planes flying individually all made the trip to North

Pickenham without loss or accident, another first for the 492nd.

Because word of our unusual pilot experience level and our two 'firsts' preceded us, great things were expected of us by the staffs of the 14th Wing and the 2nd Division to which we had been assigned. Even the senior, combat-experienced groups could not approach our pilot experience level. It was April, 1944, and their original and experienced crews were long gone— either shot down, or sent home upon completion of a tour. They were now operating with relatively inexperienced replacement crews. Most of those came directly from the transitional training schools where our pilots had been teaching. When it came time to participate with other groups in aerial exercises, the tightly held formations of our senior pilots were in sharp contrast to those flown more loosely by the less experienced pilots of surrounding senior groups. This was soon to change. As our original crews left us by virtue of being shot down, transferred, or finishing a tour, our experience level dropped dramatically with the great influx of replacement crews, and our formations loosened.[1] Upon arrival we were the longest on pilot experience, but we were also the shortest on combat experience. As with all fledgling groups, we were 'stood down' for a couple of weeks of orientation and training for all air and ground personnel.

After a couple of weeks of instruction and observing the operation of sister groups in our wing, the 492nd received a field order to prepare and fly our first mission. As with other groups, German radio welcomed us to the fray and promised that their fighters would be up to greet us, a promise they surely kept.

But that was a very long year ago; everything had changed. Frank, Alex, Jay and I were shaken from our reverie when the stations and taxi flares were fired from the Rackheath tower. The 467th, and our small band of survivors with it, were being sent back to the States, with no inkling of what lay ahead for our finely-tuned and highly effective bombing outfit.

1. Melvin Culross, interviewed in September 1999, was a member of one of the 49 replacement crews that flew combat missions with the group. His impression at the time of his relatively late arrival at North Pickenham (July 1st, 1944), was that the 492nd could have had better cohesion, flown tighter, and put in more practice flying. It is his view that the relatively loose command style of Group CO Eugene Snavely, and a bit of cockiness among the crews might have been factors in their operational fate.

Original-crew members, radio operator Bob Cash (shot down on his second mission, the 2nd Politz raid) and pilot Ernie Haar, could not be more vehement in their pride over the tightness with which the original crews flew, or more emphatic about the very high state of experience and the *esprit de corps* of the 492nd upon arrival overseas.

This author does not see a disagreement here, but rather a corroboration of his father's observations about how quickly things changed. It was *despite* the tightness of the original crews that the 492nd suffered such rapid and deep loss; the later looseness observed by Culross was emblematic of the chaotic infusion of replacement crews at the rate of *one every 44 hours*. That Colonel Snavely and his staff may not have been up to the superhuman challenge of rapidly integrating very green replacements into his highly experienced cadre of originals is no indictment of their abilities.

2. Getting Oriented

Back in the States, orientation flights upon arrival at a new base were short and simple. Our bases were very large, in remote areas, and easily distinguishable from the air. Not so here, where scores of small look-alike air fields were crowded into that tight little East Anglia corner of England.[1] The traffic pattern of every field infringed upon that of at least one other. Most were immediately adjacent to a stereotypic quaint village with church steeple, marketplace, rail line, and the river or canal running through. It was easy to become confused and lost, particularly when visibility was so often limited by the poorest flying weather any of us had ever experienced. There was always a lot of 'weather' around—mostly unpredictable, changeable, and bad for flying. Fortunately, our British Allies, after long-suffering with their weather, had devised multiple navigational aids such as radio 'bunchers' and 'splashers' which were helpful in good weather, essential in bad. They also pioneered Loran, Shoran, 'G-boxes' and other electronic navigational devices for use over the UK and also over distant target areas on the Continent. Without these, weather would have disallowed many of the missions we flew.

The most important part of our indoctrination into the 8th Air Force's way of doing business was a thorough understanding and application of the lead-crew bombing procedure. It was uncomplicated and logical. The group's air formation usually consisted of three air squadrons in a V-formation. The lead plane of the lead squadron served as group leader, and carried the group command pilot, who was responsible for the mission. Similarly, each squadron had its lead crew and command pilot. On the right wing of every leader was his deputy. A deputy took over if the leader, for any reason, was unable to carry out his role.

The bombardier in the group lead plane did the bombing for the whole group. When they saw his bombs drop, other bombardiers in the group formation 'toggled-out' their bombs. Obviously, this put the burden on the command pilot and lead crew to get the bombardier to the target, and on him to put the group's bombs on the target. In this collective effort, he hit or missed for the whole group, and could become an instant hero or goat!

The next step up from the group formation was the wing. Its formation comprised the three groups of the wing flying in-trail. The leader of the lead group assumed the role of wing leader. Similarly, the five wings of our division lined up in-trail to make the division formation. Again, the leader of the lead wing became the division leader. The ultimate step up from the air division formation would be the 8th Air Force, encompassing all three of its air divisions. That number of planes (in some instances nearly 1200) under a single command could be very unwieldy. The noteworthy maximum effort was Christmas Eve 1944, when the Eighth sent over 2,000 bombers, from all three divisions, to the same target area at the same time.[2]

There were a few other instances when all three divisions were deployed to the same general target area, but as I recall, each remained under its own command. Most of our missions were to strategic targets and were sent out in division strength. Occasionally, each wing was given a separate target. Our few tactical missions, in support of ground troops, involved smaller targets usually calling for attack by only a squadron, or even a flight.

Another important subject of in-theatre indoctrination was communications. With the enemy just across the water, monitoring the whole gamut of our radio frequencies, voice communication had to be limited and discreet—even when using low powered transmitters designed for short range use.[3] On missions, radio silence was a must for all but command pilots. We didn't want to give the Germans any more information on our plans than they already had from tracking us on radar. More important was the necessity for keeping our air channels open for vital communications. Even with just the command pilots using those channels, they often became crowded. With every one of the hundreds of planes in the division formation having transmission capability on many channels, it could be bedlam. I recall missions when so many panic-stricken planes were calling for air/sea rescue assistance simultaneously and over-riding each other's transmission, that none were able to provide

James Mahoney (back row, center) poses with Prytulak's crew.

the ground station with adequate fix information. Within the 467th, we minimized our problem by wiring the transmitter switch in the 'off' position in all but the lead crew planes. In an emergency, a wing crew could break the wire easily and transmit, but after the mission they had to justify that broken wire. The group command pilot's radio operator maintained constant communications with ground headquarters and sent via encoded Morse Code messages indicating progress of mission by 'check points,' time and place of bomb drop, and preliminary visual estimate of bombing results.

We were also given a brief course on the principal tool of our trade, the bomb, in its many types and sizes. Bomb fuses were of particular interest, with timing delays controllable from one 20th of a second to 24 hours after impact. The largest bomb we carried was the 2,000 pounder. We could carry four of them in a B-24.

Experienced personnel from senior sister groups of our wing gave us cram courses on flak and the latest enemy fighter tactics. Particular emphasis was given to having each gunner cover his own sector of the sky, and not be distracted by what was happening in other areas, about which he could do nothing. When a gunner did call a fighter attack in his sector, the natural reaction for everyone in the plane was to look in that direction and leave all others visually unguarded. The Jerries knew this and frequently sent a small diversionary force at us from one direction, and then had their major force come in unnoticed from the opposite one. It was not easy for a gunner (or any of us) to keep his eyes scanning his quiet empty segment of the sky when a three-ring circus was going full blast in another.

There wasn't much that could be done to defend against flak. 'Chaff' (bundles of metal foil strips), and later in the war, air-borne radar-jamming equipment, were sometimes helpful in interfering with radar-directed German anti-aircraft guns, but never silenced them. A mission route could be laid out to minimize exposure to known, fixed emplacement flak battery locations, but in the target areas, where they were most heavily concentrated, you were completely vulnerable. Once on the bomb run, you could not take evasive action. Your only reason for being there was to put bombs on the target. Altering your course could throw your bombs off target, defeating your objective and allowing the flak batteries to achieve theirs. Before and after the bomb run, formation leaders were at liberty to take evasive action.

After a couple of weeks of instruction and observing the operation of sister groups in our wing, the 492nd received a field order to prepare and fly our first mission. As with other groups, German radio welcomed us to the fray and promised that their fighters would be up to greet us, a promise they surely kept.

1. On the rare clear day over WW II Norfolk, a pilot at 20,000 feet could see 20 or more airfields at at time.   The Appendix features a map showing the 40 USAAF heavy bomber bases operational in England as of D-Day.

2. When the clouds finally broke after giving a critical one week of cover to Generalfeldmarschall Gerd von Rundstedt, airpower lent its mighty shoulder to turning the tide of the Battle of the Bulge.   Readers will find a WW II Timeline in the Appendix.

3. My father was fond of recounting the story of an early morning pre-flighting while he was attending the Army Air Force School of Applied Tactics in 1943.   His conversation with the tower was abruptly interrupted for several seconds by a crystal clear conversation between a Luftwaffe fighter pilot and his wingman, at least 3,200 miles distant from Orlando. It is an a instructive example of freakish atmospheric 'skips' of presumably low-power radio transmissions over very great distances.

3. Mission Preparation

In 1944, I was impressed by the efficiency with which a long and complex teletype-printed Field Order could be transformed, in a matter of a few hours, into an aerial armada. Having gone from school directly into the military in 1940, I had no basis for comparing the overseas military organization with a civilian corporate organization. Now, after many years, having worked for three sizable corporations, and having served as a management consultant to many more, I have come to appreciate that the Eighth Air Force was the most efficient large organization I've ever observed.

Our personnel were intelligent, well informed, well disciplined, conscientious, and dedicated. They knew that lives depended on their efforts, and they knew whose lives they were. They worked the job until it was done, and done correctly. There were no eight-hour days, no weekends, no holidays, and except for the occasional forty-eight hour pass, no vacations. Most days were 10 to 12 hours and longer for many—particularly those working on the planes up on the line. There were no time clocks, no wives and kiddies to go home to, no radio, bowling, ball games, etc. Under peacetime working and living conditions, those same men wouldn't have come close to accomplishing what they did then.

It is still almost incredible to me how in the space of only 10 to 12 hours, plans could be originated and carried out for the deployment of more than a thousand four-engined planes (virtually equal in size to the entire present-day US commercial fleet) on a split-second schedule to attack multiple targets on the Continent. That was the end result of the over-all planning at higher headquarters, and the execution of those plans by the division, wings, and bomb groups.

The bomb group was the smallest self-sufficient combat unit in the Air Corps. There were usually three groups to a wing, four or five wings to a division, and three divisions in the 8th Air Force. Two of those divisions, the 1st and the 3rd, flew the B-17 Flying Fortress. The 2nd Air Division to which we were assigned flew B-24 Liberators.[1]

A bomb group encompassed two distinct and very different populations. Of about 3,000 personnel on base, roughly 700 (70 ten man crews) were 'flyboys' and the remainder, excepting a few command and staff flying personnel, were non-fliers, or 'paddlefeet.' The paddlefeet were the permanent party. They had been there since the start-up of the base, and would be there for the duration of the war. They had time to form friendships on base and in local villages. They kept our planes flying and made the base and its equipment run. They worked hard and long, but never heard a shot fired in anger, except from an infrequent intruder.

The 'flyboys' were the transient element of the group. Their stay to complete a tour[2] was only three or four months—slightly longer in the winter, when the weather made some days unflyable. On average they were younger than 'paddlefeet', carried more rank and stripes, and earned more pay by virtue of their flight assignments and the risks involved. With the exception of some involvement with operations, intelligence, and medical ground personnel, their contacts were mostly with other 'flyboys.' There were so many who 'got it' so early in their tour, that those 'Poor Joes' weren't really known by anyone on base, and sadly became just another statistic.

In final analysis, probably the greatest difference between paddlefeet and flyboys was fear. 'Flyboy' was in constant fear of being killed. 'Paddlefoot' had no reason for such fear. Despite their different situations, there was no rivalry, resentment, or lack of respect between the two groups. One might liken the situation to boxing. The paddlefeet were in the corner doing all they could and cheering for their man out there taking the punches.

It was different when we first arrived overseas. During our long training period at home, our original crews had become well known by all. When we experienced our early combat losses, those who went down were not just crews, they were friends also. As time wore on and our original crews had either gone down or finished a tour and gone home, we were operating with all replacements. There was hardly time for anyone to get to know them very well. We didn't have time and some weren't very anxious to become involved with them personally, knowing that many would not return one day. As Spivvy, my Flight Surgeon (Capt. Seymour E. Spivack, M.C.) put it with graphic indelicacy, "I'll band-aid them, give them physicals and short-arms, but that's it!" Nonetheless, every crewman lost, no matter how little or briefly known, left a mark somewhere on the base. But, if we were to continue to do our jobs and serve well the crews we still had, we could not allow ourselves to become preoccupied with crews lost.

At the group level, the key to mission preparation was the briefing team. A new briefing team was designated each day, 'in business' just for that day's mission. The briefing officer, a pilot from the group operations staff or any of the four squadron operations staffs, led the team. The first echelon of his team consisted of a pilot, bombardier, navigator, and intelligence officer, who were also drawn from the group and squadron staffs. Other members of the team represented all the other activities on the base that serviced the crews and their planes. With the team throughout its planning and briefing of the mission was the command pilot, who would be responsible for the group's performance in the air from takeoff until return.

Most days, the group was on 'alert' status and 'standing by' for a mission assignment to come in on the teletype. This usually occurred in the early evening hours. On those days, mostly in winter, when the weather over the United Kingdom was unflyable, or that over the Continent wouldn't allow visual or even radar bombing, we were 'stood down.' In the hard-hit 492nd Bomb Group there were a couple of occasions when we had been so badly battered on consecutive days, unable to put up even a modest effort, that were 'stood down' to lick our wounds, human and mechanical.

The communications room would notify the briefing officer when the mission field order (FO) started coming in on the teletype. He and his first-echelon team members and the command pilot would gather around the staccato-clattering machine to watch the mission unfold. The FO was lengthy, was received in sections, and might take hours to be completely transmitted. As each section was finished, a copy of it would be given to the team member responsible for that phase of the mission. Some sections, such as that for the target, had to be sent to the Secret Room for decoding. If parts of the incoming order were unclear or questionable, we had a special phone line to wing and division on which we could 'scramble' our conversation and discuss our problem without fear of interception. Only the briefing officer had a complete copy of the field order. Because it was classified 'SECRET,' he was responsible for its security, and was supposed to wear a sidearm and/or be guarded by an MP until mission return.

In the tranquil surroundings of our little corner of England, it was not easy to maintain a high level of security consciousness continually and one tended to become casual in treating classified material. In that regard, we were brought up short very early one morning at the 467th when the 'Old Man' and I were called out of our beds by a panic-stricken briefing officer. His field order was missing! At about 2 a.m. he had stopped by the mess hall for a cup of coffee, and slipped the clipboard holding the FO under the driver's seat cushion of his jeep. When he came out a few minutes later it was gone. We joined his frantic search and sweated it out for a while, before finally calling wing and division. They were so upset that they joined in the sweating-it-out agony, and forgot to chew us out until later.

After what seemed to be an interminable period, but was probably less than an hour, and serious consideration had been given to canceling the entire 2nd Division mission, a staff sergeant walked into our Ops Block and handed over the missing FO. He identified himself as a CIC (Counter Intelligence Corps) agent. He told us he'd come to our base a week earlier on some trumped-up transfer orders for a routine clandestine checkup of our security procedures in general, and potential risks with Communists and homosexuals on our base. He told us we had none of the latter, but two of the former.[3] One we knew about. Sgt. Irving Miller was an open and avowed Communist and one of our best non-coms. The other, an officer, was a surprise to us. His assignment was not in a security sensitive area, but we were advised to keep an eye out for any extra-curricular activities on his part.

After decoding, folders relating to the target section were pulled from the hundreds of target file in the Secret Room. The target folder contained a wealth of information gathered mostly by British Intelligence. It had aerial and sometimes ground photos, detailed maps, and specific information about the parts, functions, and war importance of the target. It gave the location, size and numbers of fixed and mobile flak batteries in the area and their effective radius of destruction. The maps and photos gave not only the 'vertical' perspective of the target as it would appear from directly overhead, but also 'approach' views as would be seen from various distances These were very helpful in enabling the bombardier to pick up the target early and fine-tune his equipment well before the bomb release point.

The FO spelled out the IP (the Initial Point of the bomb run) at which time the bombardier started working with the pilot to lock the bombsight into the automatic pilot and take over flight control of the plane until 'bombs away,' the MPI (Mean Point of Impact) around which the formation's drop should cluster, and the AP (Aiming Point), just short of the MPI. The fractional delay of the total formation's drop, after they saw the leader's bombs fall, was the reason for setting the AP just short of the MPI.

In terms of activity during a mission, the bombardier had the least to do until we reached the IP, but those few minutes from there to the target were our *raison d'etre*. If not successful, we'd have to go there again. The bombardier's function was truly the *sine qua non* of the mission.

The briefing team navigator was concerned with the many aids available to flying the route —radio, radar, dead reckoning, etc. The route to the target was laid out to include turns intended to deceive the enemy as to our real destination and at the same time avoid flak battery locations en route. The route home did not have to create deception, just avoid trouble and get us there as quickly and safely as possible.

Numerous other sections of the FO went to appropriate members of the team. The intelligence member covered the description of the target and its location, and the type and amount of resistance we were likely to encounter, both fighters and flak. The ordnance member and his people, responsible for for transporting and installing the numbers, types, sizes and fuse settings of bombs called for in the order, frequently had the tightest time schedule. The armament section of the FO seldom varied. It usually prescribed the same mix of armor-piercing, tracer, incendiary, and ball ammo in our guns. The radar section had to double-check the navigational, bombing, and counter-measure radar equipment on the planes selected for the mission. Automatic cameras, which followed the drop of the bombs to target, had to be installed in specific planes, hand held cameras in others. Flak suits, chaff, flares and miscellaneous supplies had to be delivered to the planes.

The operations member of the team met with the four squadron operations representatives and selected from lists of 'standby' crews those who would be called upon for the mission. Each was assigned a specific position in the group's aerial formation. The names of the chosen crews, already alerted, were given to the squadron orderly who would be responsible for waking crews at the appointed hour, seeing to it that they got to the mess hall on time.

Crew selection hinged on many considerations. Among them was the actual or potential need for radar navigation and/or radar bombing due to anticipated weather conditions at the target. Only a limited number of crews were trained in the use of this highly sophisticated equipment; only a few planes had the requisite equipment.

Alerted crews had been told the day before that they'd probably be routed out of the sack at 2 to 3 a.m. and they'd better roll in early. With double daylight saving time in the summer it didn't get dark until after 11 p.m., and got light before 5 a.m. This made for difficult sleeping. They were told also not to partake of any alcoholic beverages. In the Officers' and Enlisted clubs, red lights were turned on over the bars to indicate our 'Mission On' status and remind the alerted crews not to drink. Before hitting the sack, crewmen spent considerable time going through their highly individual rituals in preparation for the following day: selecting layers of clothing; penning a hopefully-not-final letter home; confidential 'if I don't come back' instructions to a friend, and maybe a few prayers. No personal items were to be carried on missions, just dog tags. No billfolds, non-GI watches, jewelry, etc. Such items were hidden in footlockers, entrusted to friends, or put in a paper bag for safekeeping at the equipment room when drawing flight gear after the briefing.

Each crewman hid an evasion photo on his person. If you were shot down and succeeded in contacting the underground in an occupied country, they could help you evade capture with forged papers, but not with the ID photo to go with them. The Germans saw to it that no film or photo-processing capability was available to citizens of occupied countries. Part of our new crew orientation was a stop at our photo lab to have an 'evasion photo' taken. There, from a limited inventory of continental-style civilian jackets, shirts, ties, berets, etc., we tried to make them all look like a Pierre or Hans. Because our supply of civilian attire was so limited, it was jokingly rumored (and possibly true) that the Germans could tell what group you came from by the clothes worn in your ersatz ID photo.

These ID photos were of poor quality, intentionally. In earlier days it was learned that supplying crews with good quality photos became their undoing in attempted evasion. The Germans recognized that the photo paper we were using was of noticeably better quality than what they were using for ID photos in the occupied countries. We then started using a lesser quality paper. Some rumored it was German paper captured in North Africa, others that it was stolen from the Germans by the French Underground.

Even if the enemy never fired a shot at us, high altitude bombing missions would still have been long, tedious, and very uncomfortable. Aside from the Germans and their weather, our principal adversaries were the cold and the low atmospheric pressure at bombing altitude which required the use of oxygen and caused other discomforts. At our bombing altitudes of 20,000 feet and above, the thermometer was usually in the minus 50 degree Fahrenheit range, and I've seen 70 below. Our planes were not heated, nor were they pressurized. To suit up against that cold we wore layers of everything—socks, underwear, trousers, shirts and gloves. The mix was to some extent a matter of personal choice. Each crewman eventually arrived at a compromise between multiple layering for warmth, and the flexibility and mobility needed for his airborne activity. Manual dexterity was essential to all, but pilots and bombardiers especially, needed to be able to flip myriad little switches, and press the right tiny buttons quickly and unerringly, even with heavily mittened fingers.

Before electrical suits, we wore fleece-lined leather everything—boots, pants, jackets, helmets, and gloves. The electrical suit eliminated much of that bulk and weight, but to depend solely on electrical heat could cause big trouble when the suit's or plane's electrical system malfunctioned. The fine calfskin electrical gloves were a major advantage over the layers of silk, cotton, and wool we had worn under the fleece-lined leather gloves. The electrical boots gave the pilots a much better feel of rudder pedals, but unlike the fleece-lined leather, did not fit over GI shoes. They would hardly sustain you for much of a hike through the Fatherland in the event of a bailout. Chances were that if you did bail out wearing the rather loose-fitting electrical boots, they would be jerked off your feet anyhow by the jolt of your chute opening. I took my GI shoes and tied them by the laces to my parachute harness.

The improvement of our equipment made our stay at altitude slightly more tolerable, but it could never be considered comfortable. We still had some frostbite cases, usually fingers and toes and mostly belonging to gunners, who occupied the most exposed positions in the plane. One of the most annoying effects of the cold was that we couldn't drink or eat on a mission. There was no container that could keep a drinkable liquid from freezing up there, hence, nothing to wet the palate from breakfast until coffee-and-doughnut time after the mission. That was at least seven hours, and could be as much as thirteen. The only 'food' items carried on board were Hershey bars and Milky Ways. Both became as hard as rock and brittle as glass. They were eaten at the risk of cracking your teeth.

On one mission return, after letting down to 10,000 feet and removing the oxygen mask to light a cigarette, I tried to bite into a Milky Way. I stopped when I heard an ominous cracking noise that didn't sound like chocolate—even frozen chocolate. I took the candy from my mouth and there was the full-sized porcelain cap belonging to what had once been an upper front tooth. It was a memento of my my final polo game in the cavalry. I had taken a mallet across the face, which removed that tooth and the two downstairs opposing it, and mashed my once more prominent nose to what it is today. Our base dentist wasn't equipped to refit the damaged cap or make a new one, so I was sent to London for major repairs.

We started wearing our oxygen

masks at 10,000 feet. At 20,000 feet, nearing our bombing milieu, the weight of the air and its oxygen content are half of that at sea level. A properly fitted mask was not uncomfortable provided you were clean-shaven, but the rubber was cold against the skin. Every crew station had an oxygen outlet. In addition, there were a number of 'walk around' portable oxygen bottles which also served in the event of oxygen system failure. The moisture you

Liberators of the 467th making a drop from one of their characteristically tight formations.

exhaled turned to ice inside the mask and had to be cleared periodically; beyond the annoyance, ice interfered with the function of the microphone built into the mask. I preferred the throat-mike which wrapped around the Adam's Apple, obviating the icing problem. For some reason, it also picked up my dull voice better than the mask mike did.

Beside the shortage of oxygen, there were other physiological effects of lower atmospheric pressure on the body. The body, with less air pressure against it, is subjected to some infinitesimal expansion. Shoes laced comfortably snug at sea level could become uncomfortably tight at altitude. The same held true for other bodily constrictions such as belts and collars. More surprising and initially embarrassing were the effects of lower pressure on gases within the body. They expanded and demanded relief. Any air on top of the liquid in the bladder would slowly try to expand to twice the volume it occupied on the ground, exerting pressure on the liquid. Here was an unexpected demand for relief, from a department you thought you had taken care of a short time ago. Other gases expanded and sought escape from your body via one end or the other. Rising to altitude, a burping and flatulating crew could offer a fair rendition of the Anvil Chorus, if barely audible over the din of the four Pratt & Whitneys. An infrequent but painful side effect of altitude was the unseating of fillings. Even when teeth had been reasonably expertly filled, some air could have been trapped between the tooth and the filling. After some time at altitude, that air also would try to double the space it occupied at ground level and unseat the filling in the process. This happened suddenly and painfully. My first time, my instinctive reaction was to clamp down on the large filling to reseat it in my molar. After returning to the ground, I found that this resulted in a reverse and equally painful experience. I learned that the best solution was to allow the popped filling to stay that way until return to ground level, then clamp it back in place. Low pressure at altitude did have one temporary benefit. If you had a cold or sinus problem, the nasal passages opened up allowing drainage and relief. But that lasted only as long as you were up there, and the congestion returned with a vengeance upon landing.

Our planes were also affected by altitude. Just as we needed to supplement our oxygen, so too the engines required superchargers to cram more of that thin air into their combustion chambers. And as you rose into the ever colder air, the metal of the plane was subjected to increasing contraction and gave off a variety of crackling noises. Control cables shrank a bit too, making the manipulation of rudders, elevators, and ailerons a wee bit stiffer.[4] Bombsights were fitted with electrically heated covers. On the ground, machine guns had to be cleaned, oiled, then wiped bone-dry to prevent any lubricant from congealing and 'freezing' the gun. A round was always kept in the chamber ready to be fired and free-up any balky part.

Inasmuch as Uncle Sam did not provide toilet facilities in our bombers, each crewman had to provide for himself. I carried a bomb fuse can, a sturdy water-tight canister with a screw-on top, about the size and shape of a tennis ball can. I wedged this under my seat so that it wouldn't roll around when we hit rough air. A failure to anchor his can securely produced some interesting results for Carl Johnson on one of my early missions with his lead crew. As was my custom, I was riding in the co-pilot's seat while serving as command pilot. This was before the days of heated suits and we were wearing layers of clothing under fleece-lined leather, which made even the simpler of bodily eliminations very difficult   We had completed our assembly and were enroute to Holland when fuse cans became busy throughout the plane. Carl had the need for his, but couldn't find it. He had placed it under his seat but it had rolled to some inaccessible place. I took over the controls while he searched with obvious exasperation and discomfort. Finally he picked up his flak helmet from next to his seat, the only container of any size or sort within reach. At best, the whole procedure was ridiculous and frustrating —to be tightly strapped in your seat trying to move aside a layer of armor suiting, unzip the cumbersome fleece-lined leather, unbutton and wade through several thicknesses of clothing, and accomplish the task with a minimum of misdirection, or exposure to the elements at 50 below!

Carl's   effort   was   complicated

further by the large circumference of the unwieldy helmet. He was swearing so into his oxygen mask that it vibrated and exhausted steam from the edges.   Finally with his delicate mission of the moment accomplished, he looked around for someplace to put the helmet.   Eventually he placed it gingerly on the floor beneath his seat, hoping it wouldn't spill.   Several minutes later—just long enough for a skim of ice to have formed—we got our first greeting of flak.   I put on my helmet, took the wheel, tapped Carl on the shoulder and signaled him to don his tin hat.   He had forgotten his prior use of it until he pulled it down over his head, breaking the thin layer of ice and giving himself an unwelcome shower.   Carl became the spitting image of that common depiction of old man winter, icicles hanging from every part of his face and oxygen mask.   As he brushed them off angrily, others would form.   The crewmen on the flight deck were convulsed with laughter and went on interphone to describe for the others what had happened.   Those close enough to do so snuck up to the fight deck to take a look at their gallant leader enshrined in golden icicles.   Later, en route home, as we reached lower altitudes and warmer temperatures Carl started to thaw out.   He was beside himself as he dripped incessantly.   That the rest of us gagged with laughter did not improve his disposition.

Few who have ever flown in the military have not had a bout with air-sickness.   The motion causing it can be any combination of rough air, poor piloting, or one's location in the plane.   The tail is where the whiplash effect of the plane's movement is greatest, and airsickness is most likely to occur.   Rough air could bounce the tail gunner around, as could the continual rudder or elevator movements of an inexperienced pilot, especially in formation flying.   Those who were prone to air-sickness or concerned about bowel problems carried an assortment of self-styled 'whoopee bags.'   Chronic and serious cases were grounded, but those usually had been detected in training, long before they got to us.   Air-sickness was a regrettable side effect of our operation, but not a valid reason for a crew to abort a mission.

The carrying of personal weapons on a mission was a matter of personal choice. I don't recall any official position on this question; some carried a .45 caliber automatic pistol in a shoulder holster. Others felt that after bailing out over enemy territory you were more likely to be shot if you were armed than if you were not. Originally I took the latter position, but changed my thinking after reported instances of bailed-out airmen being attacked with pitchforks or shotguns, and being hung by irate German civilians. At Bernburg, at least one of my squadron crewmen was lynched by angry crowds pouring out of air raid shelters after the bombing ceased. The lead crew pilot that day, Lt. Bernie Harding, and some others of my crews were saved from a hanging-party mob by a Luftwaffe corporal who happened on the scene, drew his pistol on the crowd and insisted that he take our crewmen as prisoners of war. We felt that in the presence of the Wehrmacht or the Luftwaffe you could expect to be treated according to the mandates of the Geneva Convention. With the Gestapo or angry civilians, I felt that I might have at least some chance with a .45, so I started wearing one.

I also kept a six-inch switchblade knife in a knee-pocket of my coveralls, but not as weapon. I wanted to be able to cut the shroud lines of my chute in the event I got hung up in a tree or entangled under the canopy in water. One other personal item I took along was a very battered small leather pouch containing a crucifix that had belonged to my grandmother, given to me when I left for flying school with the admonition that I carry it whenever I left the ground. I hadn't done so before coming overseas, but in the war zone I figured I should use all the help I could get, from any source. It certainly was not a compromise with security in the event of my capture.

When some of my surviving crew members were released from Stalag Lufts after the war, I learned that at their interrogation center at Frankfurt am Main, the Luftwaffe had very complete files on senior officers of the Eighth Air Force. When taken there, Bernie Harding was shown papers from the file they had on me, which included home address, flight training, some military assignments, and clippings from Boston and New York papers, including wedding write-ups! He said they knew a lot more about me than he did.

Another section of the FO described the size and makeup of the division effort, and when and where the formation would be assembled. The division formation consisted of a representation from each of the five wings, which in turn were composed of formations from each of their three groups. The lead position in the division formation was rotated among the wings, just as the lead position in each of the wings was rotated among its component groups. This rotation was usually maintained and allowed us to know in advance, not the date or target, but the sequence in which we'd be called upon to furnish wing and division leads. This allowed us to do some advance planning on the scheduling of our lead crews and command pilots.

Among our lead crews we had a variety of experience levels and skills. When it was our turn to lead the wing, we selected from our more seasoned crews, and when we led the division we used our most qualified. At the 467th Group, our command pilots were similarly designated. The commanding officer, the air executive (deputy group commander) and the group operations officer rotated our division leads. We were also in the rotation pool for wing leads along with the four squadron commanders. For group leads, we added squadron operations officers to the pool. The FO also told how many planes we were to put up, what time our assembled group should join our wing and in what position, and the wing join the division on the DAL (Division Assembly Line) at a precise time, direction, altitude, and location.

As sections of an FO were parceled out, there was a ripple effect all over the base, which buzzed through the night, right up until the planes took off. The second echelon members of the Briefing Team gathered in the Ops Block to learn the mission's requirements of their activities. They represented just about everything that went on at the base and required as much time as we could give them to have everything in place by 'start engines' time. The largest effort of the team members was that required of the group engineering Officer. He usually had with him representatives of the four squadron engineering sections. They were the ones who had to provide the planes. After knowing the number needed, they had to know the special equipment requirements: e.g. radar navigation; radar bombing; radar counter measures, etc. We had only a few planes so equipped. They would then have to give a list of the selected planes to all the other servicing activities, for installation of their equipment as called for in the FO. They would also have to hold in reserve a few planes ready to go in the event of mechanical problems developing with some of the original selection. The list was also given to the squadron operations officers to assign crews to specific planes.

Communications was another important subject. We received extensive and explicit instruction on the assignment of frequencies, VHF channels, etc. Communication of airborne radio operators (via Morse Code) with ground headquarters was clear cut and relatively easy. The multiple VHF channels for voice contact from the plane to the ground and to other planes was comparatively complex. All planes had a five channel VHF set with which they could talk with the tower, other planes in the group, our division fighters, air/sea rescue, and a locator station. Lead planes had an additional VHF set for talking to other groups in the wing and division, fighters from the other two divisions of the 8th Air Force, the weather scouts, etc.

Another very important section of the FO dealt with ordnance. It listed the number, types and sizes of bombs to be carried, and their fuse settings. We had a great variety in our bomb dump. The general purpose (GP), high explosives (HE) ranged from 100 up to 2,000 pounds. We also carried fragmentation, incendiary, and smoke bombs. The latter we used only in lead planes, to provide an immediate visual signal of that plane's bomb release. Maximum B-24 payload was 8,000 lbs. This could be four of the big ones, or an infinite variety of various smaller ones.

The type and mix of bombs was not always the same for all planes on the same mission. For example, those scheduled to pass over the target first might drop HEs followed by incendiaries. HEs would blow the target apart, making it more susceptible to the fires the incendiaries could start. A notable mixup in that sequence occurred on the famed original Ploesti raid. Confusion en route had some incendiary-carrying planes reach the target before those carrying the HEs. Result: the blasts of the latter blew out some of the fires started by the former!

The most un-favorite bomb with the crews was the anti-personnel cluster fragmentation bomb. This was not attributable to an altruistic concern for the personnel on whom we would be dropping them, but to the danger posed for us in carrying and dropping them. Individual explosive sticks were bundled together in a cylindrical shape. After release from the plane, a small explosive charge blew the bundle apart, spreading the sticks in all directions. When they touched anything, including each other or one of our own planes, these 'bump and boomers' blew up and had the same effect as flak on any nearby planes. We tried to spread out and flatten our flying formation when we dropped these, because the low Squadron would have risked picking up some 'flak 'of our own doing if we flew in standard formation. There was also fear that if enemy flak happened to hit one of these bundles when still in the bomb bay, it would start a chain reaction like a string of firecrackers, which could blow the plane apart. I have not heard of that actually happening, but it may well have, and there would have been no one left to tell about it. Our other bombs were not so affected by flak.

The FO also gave the intervalometer settings to be used. This established time spacing between the release of individual bombs from the plane, as opposed to 'salvo,' when all the bombs were released at once. With an interval setting, you could achieve a longer bomb pattern on the target. The length and breadth of the target determined the intervalometer setting chosen. The FO specified bomb fuse settings. Each bomb carried a nose and a tail fuse. Either could trigger the bomb. We usually fused at a 20th of a second in both fuses, but this could be varied greatly. It was assumed that bombs striking the average surface would penetrate 4 to 6 feet in the 20th of a second before detonation.

When we bombed railroad marshaling yards, we found that slave labor crews would have filled in the craters, salvaged some rails and ties out of our mess, and have a track or two in operation in a relatively short time. As a counter-measure, we started using variously delayed fuses in some bombs. The longer delayed fuses would allow bombs to dig in deeper and just sit there. When we first did this, the Germans probably thought them to be duds. Then while their crews were busily repairing the damage, periodically one of our 'duds' would let go and seriously interrupt their repair efforts.

A sprinkling of delayed fuses (up to as long as 24 hours) increased enormously the effectiveness of attacks on rail and other fixed installations. We felt sorry for the slave laborers that may have been blown to bits by our 'duds', but, *c'est la guerre*. Interestingly, one of our photo-reconnaissance pilots was reported to have almost suffered the same fate. He was making a low pass to secure close-up damage photos of a target we had bombed the day before, when one of our delays exploded just ahead of him. He made it home, but not unscathed, victim of another form of 'friendly fire.'

The armament crews delivered ammunition to the planes. Every plane had twin .50 caliber machine guns in each of its four turrets, and a single .50 at each waist window. The ammunition belts called for in the FO were usually the same mix and sequence. Of every five shells in the belt, two were ball, and one each, tracer, incendiary, and armor-piercing. The armorers also brought the flak jackets and flak helmets to the planes. The jacket was an olive drab colored canvas vest containing little pockets of metal plates which, hopefully, would resist or deflect flak fragments. The helmet was a regular GI helmet from which spaces had been cut on the sides to allow for our headphones. Hinged armored flaps covered the headphones and buckled down with a chin strap. All of the personal equipment—metal hardware, the chute, layers of clothing, etc.—added about eighty pounds to our own weight.

The armament crews also delivered to the planes boxes of 'chaff' bundles. These thin strips of aluminum foil bundled together, were cut in varying lengths to correspond with the wavelengths on which German radar-directed flak batteries operated. Breaking the paper band and scattering the strips rendered enemy radar ineffective. On days of solid undercast, when the enemy couldn't see us and had to rely on radar to direct their guns, the chaff appeared to help sometimes. On occasion, chaff appeared to detonate proximity-fused flak shells, which were designed to explode when they neared metal.

Armorers also supplied the flares. All planes carried double red star flares to signal emergency. The lead planes carried a quantity of the group's designated colored flares, which it fired continually during assembly to identify itself to our planes as they climbed individually to join the formation. In the case of the 467th, ours was a red/green two star flare, fired at 20 second intervals until all the group's planes were in close proximity. During the mission, the lead plane also fired flares to signify the IP as he turned toward the target. On this signal, following planes opened their bomb bay doors. Upon return to base, any plane with wounded aboard or in mechanical difficulty, could fire its two-star red flares to achieve priority in landing.

Bombsights had to be taken from the vault, delivered, installed, and tested in those planes designated to do the bomb aiming. The bombsight was the most secret piece of equipment on the base[5] and was handled accordingly. Its electrically heated cover was removed at the start of the bomb run. Within the bombsight was an explosive charge which could self-destruct our secret weapon. It could be detonated manually if landing in enemy or neutral territory, and by the force of impact in a crash.

The Radar Section was another group on base responsible for highly technical equipment. In designated planes they installed their machines for the radar navigators and radar bombardiers. In others, RCM (radar counter-measures) transmitters were installed for that specialist operator. His job on the mission was to pick up the frequencies on which German radar was operating, tune his transmitters to those frequencies, and jam them.

The photo section installed automatic cameras immediately behind the bomb bay of one plane in each squadron, typically the lead plane. They were electrically operated and began taking pictures with the release of the first bomb and continued to do so at a specified interval (usually 3-5 seconds) until after the bombs hit the ground. These SAV photos (strike attack vertical) were the basis for early interpretation of our bombing effectiveness. Smaller hand-held cameras were also given to waist gunners in selected planes to photograph actions and scenes of possible interest. These produced some surprisingly useful and high quality results in the hands of gunners who had little photographic training other than the mechanical operation of the camera itself.

The tower operators needed a list of crews, the number on each's airplane, and the precise order and time of taxiing and takeoff. This information also had to be given to the Tower's remote unit, the 'caravan.' This was a black and yellow checkered circus-like four wheeled van. Having no automotive power, it had to be towed to its position to the immediate left of the starting end of the runway in use. From there, flight control people in the caravan led control takeoffs with signal lights, and even with hand signals as they were just a few yards away from the pilots. This allowed us to get our planes in the air without the use of radio. The caravan was in constant telephonic touch with the tower, and had radio capability, if needed. The tower was also responsible for the deployment of crash equipment.

There were also many service units on the base involved in mission preparation and support. There were the mess halls, the MPs to provide extra security for the briefing rooms, the motor pool to move the crews from mess halls to briefing rooms and then out to the planes at the hardstands. The equipment room had to know not only how many crewmen would be on the mission, but also, the general area of the mission so as to provide the crews with appropriate escape aids: maps, money, blood chit, etc. Toward the end of the briefing,the medics and chaplains in turn offered final sick-call and prayer.

While all the feverish night time preparation was going on, aircrews were trying to get some sleep, much needed for the day ahead. For many, if not most, that was difficult. Visions of what had been seen, and might be seen again, could toss and turn even the most stout-hearted. Wakeup time depended, of course, on takeoff time. Most often it was around 3:30 a.m. Emissaries from the squadron orderly rooms stumbled along dirt paths through the blackout with their hooded flashlights, and did their best to awaken the right crewmen from among the rows of cots in the darkened huts. Even their correct selections were met with growls, and their occasional errors with howls of quickly chosen unkind expletives.

Wakeup came first for the lead crew officers and command pilots. In the 467th, we roused them 40 minutes before all others. They were given a brief preview of the target, studied the target photos, and practiced with them on the bomb trainers. They then went to the mess hall at about the time the other crews were arriving there. A head-count was taken of all crews there. After mess and a latrine stop, it was into the trucks and up to the main briefing room. The briefing team had the maps, charts, and Balopticant (opaque projector) all set for the big show.

The briefing officer took over the stage in front of the large curtained situation map of the

UK and the Continent. After a few introductory remarks, the curtain was drawn back and the route and target revealed. Reactions to these unveilings were quite predictable. A 'Noball' mission (attack on German missile launching site in nearby France) drew sighs of relief—this meant a 'milk run,' with full credit for a mission. A ride into the 'Fatherland' drew moans and groans; the deeper the distance into Germany, the longer and louder the reaction. The intelligence reps had plotted all the known flak battery positions along the route. These were mostly the large caliber fixed emplacement guns. They also indicated spots for likely reaction from the lighter caliber mobile 88mm guns. In turn, each of the first echelon briefing team members gave his information, instruction, and advice to the crews. Meteorologist 'Cloudy' Lindstrom gave his latest bad news, a time hack was given to coordinate all watches, and then the command pilot did what he could to inspire the crews. Frequently, but not always, the group CO, deputy CO, or operations officer would add a word of encouragement before the chaplain gave his offering and prayer. The medics at the back of the room were then available for anyone feeling physically unfit for the mission. This happened with surprising rarity. Crew pride was strong, and one would have to be really sick to let his crew down at that point. I usually took one of their plentiful supply of benzedrine inhalers to clear my nasal passages and fight off any drowsiness. The Catholic chaplain said a prayer and gave Communion to those attending his get-together.

We then broke up into multiple special briefings for pilots and co-pilots, navigators, bombardiers, radio operators, gunners, and when involved, radar specialists. After these, all converged on the equipment room and lockers for their flight gear and parachutes, and to deposit personal items for safekeeping until return.

We were issued four escape

packets. Two were rigid plastic boxes, curved like hip flasks and sized to fit into the trouser hip pockets. These contained an interesting and imaginative assortment of miniatures. One held a variety of concentrated food items: two small cans of cheese, caramel candy, cookies, a large number of dextrose tablets, chewing gum, etc. The other had non-edibles: a hacksaw blade, compass, sewing kit, razor and blades, toothbrush and paste, matches, pain pills, halzone tablets, and an inflatable plastic pouch with drawstring which served as a canteen. The halzone tablets were to be added to a pouch of water to make it safe for drinking. Supposedly, you could live for a couple of weeks with what you had in your back pocket. The contents of these packets had been selected based upon the extensive experiences of downed Allied airmen. For example, the razor was found to be essential because at that time all males in Germany and the occupied countries were clean shaven. To be unshaven or in torn clothing was a dead give-away.

The third packet was also pocket size, but made of a flexible rubberized waterproof material and sealed airtight. It contained maps of the area over which that day's mission was to be flown. They were designed for finding your way on the ground and showed key topical features, roads, railways, waterways, villages, etc. They were printed on silk, in color, and were waterproof. The fourth packet was of the same material and size as the third, and contained currencies of the countries over which the mission was to be flown. I never opened one, but the amount of money was said to be substantial, and supposedly counterfeit. These four packets were given to each crewman before the mission, and were to be returned unopened upon its completion.

There was another personal escape item with which the airman was equipped. Each had been given a trouser fly button which could serve as a compass! It looked like a regular GI metal fly button, but was made in two pieces snapped together. You could unsnap the top piece, invert it, and lay it on top of the bottom half and it would 'float' and indicate north.   It was up to the individual to replace one of his regular GI fly buttons with this bit of ingenuity before his first mission.

Next came the Mae West (inflatable flotation life preserver worn about the neck and shoulders) and the parachute. The Mae West had attached to it a packet of yellow dye marker to make one more locatable in the event you wound up in the water. There were several options in parachutes. Gunners and others who had to fit into tight spaces or move around a good deal, wore just the parachute harness and carried aboard the parachute pack which snapped on to the harness when needed. On some, there were two solid metal rings on the harness and two snap buckles on the pack. Unfortunately, some less-than-brilliant Air Corps supply person had also ordered the reverse combination: snap buckles on the harness, and solid rings on the pack! More than once a crewman was found en route to a plane with the unworkable combination of solid rings on both the harness and the pack. This necessitated stocking both kinds.

The regular parachute, with harness and pack attached, came in two versions also, seat pack and back pack. Both made moving around, especially in tight places, slow and difficult. I found the back pack less cumbersome, but it didn't fit as well as the seat pack when worn with a flak jacket, so the latter is what I wore on missions. Also drawn from the equipment room were six large first-aid kits per airplane. These were part of the plane's regular equipment, and stateside they were always left in place. But on our bases in England they were being tampered with because each contained several syrettes (small volume syringes) of morphine. We physically checked everyone on base to see if we had any users. We didn't, so they must have been taken for a drug market—we heard that London had a sizable one. We safety-closured the zippers on the kits, and the co-pilot had to sign for them and return them unopened. Finally, each crewman with his large canvas bag of gear started for the trucks outside to be delivered to his plane at its hardstand just off the perimeter strip.

1. Some Third Division groups were originally equipped with B-24s, but by September 1944 they were only flying 'Fortresses.' 8th AF command recognized the operational drawbacks of mixing two airplane types within a division—logistical, operational and training considerations did not easily mix or interchange. The Liberator could carry a heavier load further and cruised 30 mph faster, but was not stable at the Fortress's higher and safer operational ceiling.

General Doolittle preferred the Fortress to the Liberator; had the war in Europe continued much longer, he intended to implement a changeover to the B-17 within the 2nd Air Division.

2. When T/Sgt. Michael Roscovitch became the first 8th AF combat crewman to complete a tour (then 25 missions) on April 5, 1943, the chance of a crewman surviving 20 missions *was less than 50%*. His last was the fledgling 8th's 50th mission. By July 31, 1944, when Lt. Dave O'Sullivan's crew in 'Irishman's Shanty' became the first crew of the 492nd to complete a tour, a tour was 30 missions, and the odds across the 8th *were* that you *would* complete it. By the end of the air war in Europe, 35 missions were required to complete a tour. Within the hardluck 492nd, however, odds were reminiscent of the earlier times. In 66 missions (1602 sorties) over its 89 days of combat, only *six* of the 119 crews which flew combat in the group, completed tours.

Counting 70 original and the 49 replacement ten-man crews that arrived in time to fly combat missions with the group before it was stood down, and noting the 588 combat casualties (530 KIA, 58 MIA), a combatant stood a *5% chance* of completing a tour with the group, a *49% chance* of being killed or missing in action.

One's chance of completing a tour in this ill-fated group was on a par with that of being MIA, and one was *ten times* more likely to be KIA than to complete a tour before higher command pulled the plug on the original 492nd. Many went on to finish tours with other groups at more normal rates of attrition.

The risk of becoming a casualty on any single sortie in the 492nd was 3.67%. If a crewman had survived *14 missions,* he was beating the odds. The 60 who flew 30 defied odds of 19-to-1 or worse.

3. With regard to the homosexuals, I infer my father's 'wink' as he recounts this datedly naive assertion. Many times he remarked that the Service was a great societal 'leveler;' that all types were thrown together in concerted effort. As is seen elsewhere in the text, he was a worldly commander, and in hindsight would not have considered the 3,000 men under his command to

be a statistically unrepresentative section of American society of the day.

The demographics of the original famous Kinsey Report (1948), except for its over weighted inclusion of an imprisoned cohort, was a close functional match for the US Army of WW II.   Applying accepted, conservative present-day analysis, it is likely that there were *at least* 150 homosexuals under his command at any given time.

4. The B-24, although of later design than the Boeing B-17, was not fitted with power assisted flight controls.   Under normal circumstances, the Liberator had to be muscled about by comparison.   Under marginal conditions—overloaded takeoff, flying near the plane's service ceiling, or with wing, control surface or engine damage, the heavily loaded Davis wing demanded finesse as well.   While this advanced design allowed for the Liberator's higher speed and payload, it was 'twitchy' and prone to stalling at low attack angles and vulnerable to mechanical failure if damaged in the area of the main-gear wheel-well.

5. The Norden bombsight was not fully declassified until 1986, when the computing head of one was finally put on display at the National Air and Space Museum in Washington.   It was a mechanical-analog computer which integrated with aircraft instruments and bombardier inputs to account for all of the relevant factors in bomb aiming—ground speed, drift angle, height above target, even presumed winds between.   Once the plane was set up on the bomb run, actual control of the aircraft was given over to the bombardier, who flew the plane on course using the Norden.   Developed in the 1930s, this technological marvel emboldened advocates of the Strategic Daylight Bombing Doctrine to boast that we could "...put a bomb in a pickle barrel" from high altitude.   The less sophisticated Sperry bombsight of the day was more common in other theatres and arguably as good or better for low altitude tactical bomb aiming.

4. Into the Wild Blue

        Weather had tremendous impact on our operations. Another significant factor was our geographic latitude in East Anglia, 52°40' north. That same latitude on this side of the pond would put our base near Goose Bay, Labrador, about 760 miles north of New York City. That gave us about eighteen hours of daylight for mid-summer missions, six in the winter. Most of our winter missions took off and landed in the dark or near darkness. Of course, winter was when we had our worst weather.

        Darkness complicated every phase of our activities and presented many occasions for non-combat losses. Collisions during morning assemblies in the dark increased as did landing accidents upon return in the dark. Stragglers limping home in the dark risked misidentification by coastal anti-aircraft batteries and numerous times fell victim to 'friendly fire.' Crews that flew their missions in the winter had a tougher row to hoe than those who did theirs in the summer.

        Even stumbling in the early morning dark through the woods from Nissen huts to the mess halls, then being trucked to the briefing room and later to hardstands with the benefit of only 'blackout lights' could be adventurous. At the hardstand, preflighting the bird and donning flight gear in the dark entailed more stumbling around and nasty words for cantankerous GI blackout flashlights. The one plus for operations in the dark: flare signals were much more visible.

        When the 'stations' flares were fired from the tower, everyone consulted the preflight checklist for his particular position, stowed his chute, flak-suit, and other equipment and went to his take-off position.   Crew positions for take-off, landing, crash landing, and ditching were all the same: pilot and co-pilot were strapped in their seats; seated behind them on the flight deck, facing aft, were all the others whose assigned stations were forward of the bomb bays. The gunners in the rear of the plane were seated against the rear bulkhead of the bomb bays, also facing aft.

The engines had been checked just recently by the ground crew, so that when 'start engines' flares were fired from the tower, you cranked up in turn #3,#2,#4, and #1, gave each a quick check of the magnetos and a run-through of the prop feathering mechanism. During the dark when 'taxi' flares were fired, the flight engineer opened the top hatch, climbed out, sat on top, and used his flashlight to read out the number of each plane as it rolled by on the perimeter strip. He had to know when it was his plane's turn to take its place in the lineup as prescribed in the 'taxi plan.' Planes too, were running under blackout orders.   Taxiing and take-off were accomplished with wing-tip running lights only.   The flight engineer kept his vantage point during taxiing so as to help the pilot avoid other planes, and running off the peri-strip into the mud.[1] Upon arrival at the starting end of the runway, he withdrew into the flight deck and buttoned up the hatch

Even preparing something as seemingly simple as a taxi plan was a fairly complicated affair. A 'formation plan' was drawn first showing the exact position of each crew in the aerial formation with the number of the plane it would be flying. This established the sequence in which the planes would take off in order to make up the lead squadron formation upon reaching assembly altitude, then the second and third squadrons. The sticky part then was to match the takeoff order with the hardstand locations of the planes with an order of taxiing which fed half of the planes into the runway from one side of the perimeter in alternation with half on the other side. Each pilot had to know when to leave his hardstand and enter the lineup on the peri-strip; more importantly, those on the peri-strip had to know where to stop and let someone into the lineup ahead of them.

The first plane to take off was our assembly ship, 'Pete The POM Inspector.' 'Big Pete' as we called him was an old war weary B-24 from which we had removed all armor, turrets and other war gear so that it was lighter and faster than any of our combat-active craft. He was highly decorated with brightly colored disks over his entire surface, replete with little flashing lights all over, like a Christmas tree, which made him stand out like a sore thumb in the dark early morning sky. Following Big Pete on takeoff was the group leader, then his deputy, the leader and deputy of the high squadron, and then those of the low squadron. After the leaders, the wing planes took off in the same order in which they had taxied, and in which they would join the formation. They climbed individually in the blackness to assembly altitude (typically 22,000 feet) where they took their briefed formation positions. When group assembly was completed, Big Pete returned to his hardstand, and his minimum crew to their sacks.

Upon arriving at the take-off end of the runway, the planes dropped flaps to takeoff setting, took to the runway 15 seconds after the plane feeding in from the opposite side, and started takeoff down its side of the runway thereby avoiding the propwash of the plane ahead, and minimizing it for the one behind on the opposite side of the runway. Takeoff power settings were roughly 90% of the total power available from the engines. That other 10% was available for emergencies, and when used was known as pushing the throttles 'to the firewall.' Once he cleared the ground, the pilot tapped his brakes to stop his wheels before retracting them. The concern was that spinning tires would throw water and dirt into the wheel wells after retracting, which would ice-up at altitude, and interfere with the next lowering of wheels.

At a safe altitude, wing flaps were retracted, power settings established, props synchronized, and trim tabs set for the long climb on a race track course between two radio beacons. A clear indication of the experience of a multi-engine pilot was the ease and speed with which he performed these steps. At takeoff power, the engines whined and sounded an irregular beat. The experienced pilot could remove that 'beat' by ear, synchronizing the two inboard engines first, then successively each outboard to its inboard engine. The less experienced pilot might try to synch the inboards by ear then the outboards by eye, as the beat between adjoining engines was not only audible, but also visible through the propellers. At nighttime he could see the beat with a flashlight and make adjustments.

Interestingly enough, when at night we heard a plane overhead with a pulsation to its props, we knew that it was a German intruder. Like us, the RAF always synched their props, but the multi-engine Luftwaffe planes that visited us did not. The only explanation I ever heard, that absolutely perfect synchronization could be destructive to the plane, seemed implausible. It was likened to troops marching over a bridge being ordered to 'break step' so as not to set up harmonic vibrations which could set the bridge in destructive oscillation. Although the beat of non-synchronized engines became very annoying after a while, I never heard of it causing any inefficiency or damage.

For the climb during formation, each group had its own set of radio beacons. These sets were not very far apart. All of the Eighth's bomber and fighter bases (and many RAF Stations) lay within a 100 mile diameter circle covering a large part of East Anglia.

Our bomber bases alone held over 3,000 four engine bombers. In an area about the size of Greater New York City, you could have a thousand or more bombers forming up at the same time. On the rare clear days when you could see dozens of other planes from your own and other groups going through the same procedure, this was a reasonably safe and monotonous 45 minute process. In the dark or in clouds at any time, this could be a hair-raising undertaking. Mid-air collisions were not unheard of; near-misses were frequent. The most likely cause of collisions and near ones, was the difficulty of gauging the velocity and direction of winds aloft. The pilot could keep his nose pointed directly at the radio beacon, but a stiff cross-wind could still blow him far off course, into somebody else's race track. Anyone who completed a tour in the Eighth Air Force experienced other planes crossing very close, felt the bumps from running over somebody else's fresh propwash, or even saw debris spinning down from a collision.

During formation, the crew at their stations kept a watchful eye not for the enemy, but for other of our own big birds bent on a collision course. At the 10,000 foot level we went on oxygen and a designated gunner went into the bomb bays and pulled nose and tail safety pins from the bombs. There were claims that American bombers dropped a high percentage of duds because we had too many safeties on our bombs. Occasionally, photo interpreters felt that the number of bursts they could count in target strike photos was not commensurate with the number of bombs dropped. True or not, if we dropped 'duds,' we wanted to make sure that it was the bomb's fault and not ours, so in the 467th the gunner had to save the arming pins and turn them in upon mission return, or the crew would not get credit for the mission. After the gunner pulled the pins, there were still safety vanes, or 'spinners,' on both nose and tail fuses. After a free fall of four or five hundred feet, these would spin off, totally arming the fuses and the bombs.

As the planes approached assembly altitude, they looked for Big Pete's blinking lights. Behind him was our group leader, firing our identifying two star red/green flares every twenty seconds. Following him were the deputy group leader and the leaders and deputies of the high and low squadrons in a skeleton formation. Very often new crews had difficulty finding their leader. In heavy cloud, so did the experienced ones. When we could anticipate such conditions, one of us from the group staff would join the assembly procedure in our P-47 fighter 'Little Pete.' We could move around quickly in our assembly area, locate our lost souls, fly in close and herd them into the fold with hand signals.

Assembly complete, Big Pete returned to base. Little Pete hung around a while to lend a hand when needed in the subsequent wing and division assemblies, then returned home. The group leader circled the group, expanding or contracting the circle as needed to facilitate his entry into the wing formation at the specified time, altitude, location, and heading. At that point radio silence was frequently broken by the three group leaders in order to effect a successful wing assembly. The radio call sign of our 96th Wing was 'Lincoln.' The 467th Group was 'Lincoln Green' and the other two Groups were 'Lincoln Red' and 'Lincoln Blue.' We rotated the wing lead among the three groups. The wing leader became 'Lincoln Leader' and the other two kept their call signs. The wing leader maneuvered his formation in circles or by making 'S' turns so as to be in a position to take his place in the DAL (division assembly line) on schedule.

This was a sight to behold, one I never got over. With changes in aerial warfare, nothing like it will ever be seen again. Five wings, totaling sixteen groups of 25 to 30 planes each, folded into an elongated string of vee formations; large ones made up of successively smaller ones. Even more unforgettable were those few occasions when the other two divisions of the Eighth would be going out at the same time and heading, each of them with an equal number of their B-17s. From the ground, the sight of a thousand-plus bombers, each with four droning engines, turned all heads upward.

At about the time we were heading out, our 'Little Friends' were just crawling out of their sacks and their crew chiefs warming up their P-51s and P-47s. They would rendezvous with us later, hopefully before the Luftwaffe did. Some might fly high cover (usually over 30,000 feet) hoping to catch and tangle with the Jerries in their assembly area. Others would be assigned to provide us with close cover, flying just a couple of thousand feet above us and in position to intercept a German diving down to attack. Depending on the distance of our mission and the operating range of their equipment, we might have one set of escorts going in and be met by another set as we returned from the target.

Heading out over the water at briefed altitude and on the course of the first leg of the mission, things settled down. The apprehension of the assembly procedure was behind us. Our next worry was the reaction of the enemy. Shortly after landfall over any part of Adolf's *Festung Europa,* you could expect flak. Eventually you would learn that the greater the importance of your target to the enemy, the denser, blacker, and more lethal was this acknowledgment of your presence. You knew that on every mission you were almost sure to get flak; sometimes you even had a pretty good idea where it was going to start. But when it came, it always startled. It was just downright offensive that somebody was shooting at you, trying to kill you.

With time and exposure you learned a lot about flak—how to distinguish the smaller from the larger stuff, the predictor, or *tracking* (single gun) fire from *barrage* fire (from a battery of guns); the *time-fused* shells which detonated at a specific interval after leaving the gun, from the *proximity-fused,* triggered by passing near metal. When flak came up, there was no place to hide. "There are no foxholes in the sky" was the airman's retort to infantry detractors. You could crouch down a bit in your seat, but like the head-in-the-sand ostrich, you were just kidding yourself. The plane's sheet metal surrounding you might stop a BB, but nothing that the Krauts were throwing up!

At this point, the wing crews were busy trying to stay in reasonably tight formation on the leader, but not so tight so as to be require constant 'sawing on the throttles' to make minute speed adjustments or climbing all over the controls in a vain effort to immediately mirror every minor move of the leader. This was not an aerobatic show. Pilots would save that concentration for the bomb run, where it was essential for a good drop that all planes were in tight on the leader and making a simultaneous release.

With altitude gain, the pilot would also be gradually adjusting his mixture controls to reduce fuel consumption, but not to a point that would over-heat the engines. To impress some of us young pilots with the importance of mixture control, I recall an old-time engineering officer once started his discourse with the mildly startling statement that air-cooled engines are really liquid-cooled. The more fuel used (the richer the mixture) the cooler the engine runs, and conversely, the leaner the mixture, the hotter the engine. There's a considerable range between the two and it takes some experience and understanding of engine instruments to attain the optimum setting for engine efficiency and fuel conservation.[2] It was not unusual, on a long mission, to have some experienced pilots use as much as 200 gallons less than others in the same formation. It was not so much that Uncle Sam could not afford a few extra gallons of 100 octane gas at 11 cents each, but later in the mission after picking up some battle damage, you might just need those extra gallons to save your neck and get home. Also, too rich a mixture could carbon-up the engines and make the ground crews pretty unhappy.

Other members of the crew were in place, alert to their sectors of the sky and ready for whatever the Krauts had in store for us. Possible exceptions to total readiness were the flak suit and helmet. They were so cumbersome that those who were in a position to don them quickly waited to do so until the first sighting of flak. The gunners in the turrets had to put them on before entering those tight spaces. Like most pilots, I put on the vest before strapping into the pilot seat, but reserved the heavy and uncomfortable helmet until the initial flak burst.

Lead crew pilots had the easiest piloting jobs in the formation. The more senior and skillful ones could set up the automatic pilot to fly smoothly 'hands off' at prescribed mission speed, altitude, and heading. This made the wing crews' job much easier, and lessened the whipping around of those farthest out in the formation. They really appreciated good leaders. For division, wing, and group leaders, who had plenty of vertical and lateral space between their formations, there was no reason not to be on automatic pilot and give the poor wingmen a good ride. Of course, there were emergency conditions under which you had to override or cut off the auto-pilot and fly by hand. The lead crew navigators were busy with their charts and sophisticated navigational gear (Shoran, Loran, G-Boxes) and handing periodic position reports to the radio operator for code transmission to the folks back home sweating us out. The bombardier didn't have much to do but sit and worry. Like the field-goal kicker in the closing seconds of a tied Super-Bowl game, he was ignored all day, then at the last minute was called upon to decide the success or failure of the whole operation.

The command pilots of the division, wings and groups were all busy with multiple radio communications. Lead crew ships were equipped with a second VHF set for contacting a number of other sources of information, such as Weather Scouts, not available to the wing ships. In the combat zone, there was no longer the same need for radio silence; the enemy knew where we were and probably had a good fix on where we were headed. We learned later, that with his radar locations along the length of the coasts of Germany and the occupied countries, he could spot us during assembly, and as we headed out, know our strength and the general area of our interest. He then speculated on our specific targets and started initial deployment of his fighters. As we proceeded, his information increased and his speculation narrowed. We sometimes split off our formation to separate targets to confuse their defenses and force redeployment of their fighter forces.

Command pilots checked with each other frequently to confirm position reports. The checks were more frequent whenever undercast interfered with viewing ground check-points or German radar jamming of our navigational devices was particularly effective. Of continual interest to us were the reports from weather scouts up ahead. They gave us their best visual assessment of the route and target area cloud conditions we would encounter. At one time, the division would send a senior command pilot to fly as a passenger in a fast twin engine plane over the route and target area. He went out well in advance of the bomber stream, and would contact us on his way home, when we were going in.

One day, one of our division's group commanders (I'll call him Jones) was riding in a

Mosquito weather ship, and on his way back from the target area saw our 2nd Division planes going in, and decided to take a good look at how well his group was flying its formation. He sidled in for a close look—too close, because a Mosquito looked very much like an Me.210, and some of his own gunners opened fire. Jones pulled out in a hurry, got on his group's frequency and screamed, "Stop your firing! This is Colonel Jones, your Group Commander, in the Mosquito! Stop firing! Stop firing!" A pregnant pause ensued, broken by some wag responding in a calm voice, "We know, we know," followed by another short burst of fire!

Later, a regular scouting force was established consisting of experienced bomber command pilots and fighter pilots. They flew P-51s in pairs. The bomber pilot led, navigated, observed and reported on the weather and the fighter pilot on his right wing 'flew cover' and scanned the skies for possible attackers. In the event of trouble, the fighter pilot took the lead. I had many useful reports from the Weather Scouts, and one day, a very unusual one. I was wing lead on a mission that called for us to just skirt the northern edge of the flak-laden, heavily industrialized Ruhr, known as 'Flak Alley.' My navigator had been complaining that the winds aloft appeared to be much stronger than briefed and were pushing us south of our briefed course. Our navigational radar was being jammed, and we were over a solid undercast and couldn't check our position visually. The navigator had given the pilot several correctional headings but still felt unsure of himself. I checked with the other two group leaders and found that their navigators were having the same problems and felt that mine was doing the best he could under the circumstances. Then unexpectedly another voice came in on our wing channel calling, "Lincoln Leader, this is Nuthouse." I'd never heard that call sign before, nor could I find it in my communications folder. I suspected it might be a German cutting in on our communications but responded anyway with, "Go ahead Nuthouse, and verify." I then gave a letter from that day's code and asked him to respond with the matching one. He responded with an incorrect one, and added, "You are almost 20 miles south of your course." Using language I can't and probably shouldn't remember, I told him what course he might take. I didn't need any navigational advice from the Luftwaffe. Then another voice came in "Lincoln Leader, this is Stormy 2. Nuthouse is for real, and when he says you're off course, believe him." I knew that Stormy 2 was my Weather Scout contact for the day, but I hadn't talked to him yet. I then asked him for verification, and he flunked also! Was this another German? I puzzled and wondered because that second caller's voice had a bit of a familiar ring. Could it be Frank Elliot, who I'd heard had recently left one of the other Groups in our Wing to go to the Weather Scouts? If so, why would his 'verify' also be wrong? When we were in Flying School together at Maxwell Field before the war, one of Frank's roommates was Joe Barrett from Ossining, New York. I took a chance: "Stormy 2, give me the last name of Joe from Ossining." With a smile in his voice he came back "Barrett... and you must be Jim from Rackheath. Believe me, Nuthouse is legit and accurate." I made a course correction, which we subsequently learned was the right thing to do, and barely avoided the heavy flak area.

In a phone conversation with Frank the next day, he couldn't explain how both he and my new friend 'Nuthouse' didn't have the same daily code I had. He did explain that Nuthouse was a new 9th Air Force radar installation in Belgium used primarily for directing P-47 dive bombing attacks in the Aachen area. They also monitored 8th Air Force frequencies, and Frank had had a couple of occasions to use them to pinpoint his position. He found that they had great range and were very accurate and obliging. We weren't sure how Nuthouse knew who I was, and where I was supposed to be. They certainly didn't have our flight plan. They must have picked up on my call sign by hearing my conversations about our navigational problems with the other two group leaders on our wing channel, and knowing that we were headed for trouble over the Ruhr, assumed that we were meant to be north of it.

We had scheduled times and points for rendezvous with fighter escort. When we had close cover escort we could make a visual rendezvous. They would be just a couple of thousand feet above us and off to one side, close enough that we could see their group markings on propeller spinners, cowls, and tails. High cover escort would be ten thousand feet or more above us; usually we couldn't even see them, and we made our rendezvous via radio. Once the bomber and fighter leaders confirmed rendezvous there was very little contact between them, even in the presence of enemy fighters. They did their thing and we did ours. We seldom had to tell them enemy fighters were around. They usually knew where and in what numbers, and warned us. In earlier days when we were sometimes operating near or beyond the range of our fighters, and they were fewer in number, our calls for 'Little Friends' were more frequent and urgent. When our rendezvous was late or failed altogether, our fighter-channel transmitters became red hot also.

Most of their activities were distant from us. I never saw a dogfight or even one of our planes chasing one of theirs. You could see contrails high above where a lot of the action was, but couldn't tell who was doing what to whom. Our Little Friends did a great job trying to protect us, but even when they accompanied us in great numbers, they could not be expected to eliminate attacks on us entirely.

The Luftwaffe pilots were skilled, daring, and persistent. They could attack from any direction, with a number of different types of planes, firing bullets, shells, and rockets. Sometimes we were warned that they were in our area. Other times, our first hint would be a 'bogie' (un-identified aircraft) call from a gunner. A closer look changed the call to 'bandit' (enemy aircraft). Unlike flak, fighters were quiet. Muzzle flashes of their guns, particularly the cannon, were very visible and frightening, but their noise could not be heard over the noise of our own engines unless one of their projectiles hit. Strangely, my most vivid memory of a fighter attack was one in which the attacker didn't even fire a shot. It was in late '44 over northern Germany and turned out to be only the second reported sighting of what was later identified as the new rocket-engined ship, the Me.163. He made three successive 12 o'clock-high passes within fifty feet of us, at a closing speed of about 1,000 miles per hour! He passed below, turned on his propulsion, looped high overhead, and down he came again. He did this twice, apparently more interested in the maneuverability of his craft than taking a shot at us, unless perhaps his guns were jammed. We'd never seen a plane like this, nor had we been advised by intelligence of its existence. Our initial reporting of the incident brought several intelligence types up from London for additional in-depth interrogation.

The 12 o'clock-high attack wasn't the only one used against us, but probably from the enemy position the most effective, and from ours, the most fearsome. The rate of closure with an attacking F-W 190 or Me.109 was nearly 800 miles per hour—fast enough to give him only a few seconds to fire, and less time for our guns to return it, because his cannon had much greater range than our .50s. You could see his machine guns sparkle, but it was the intermittent flash of his cannon that got your attention. You couldn't help but admire the skill and guts of those head-on attackers as they came right at your nose, then after firing, split-S'ed under you and headed down. Some even rolled on their back, then fired and split-S'ed out, exposing their under-side armor to deflect our gunners' shots. One day an attacker mis-judged a bit and took half the tail off of one of our squadron leaders. I looked at the 12 o'clock-high attacker with some admiration, but also with a strange and strong ambivalence. On the one hand I hoped that he was a helluva good pilot and wouldn't ram us, on the other hand I hoped just as hard that he was a lousy shot and wouldn't hit us with his projectiles.

As if the incoming Jerries weren't trouble enough, one's own top turret gunner added to a pilot's misery. The muzzles of those twin .50s were just a couple of feet above the pilots' heads, separated only by the plane's thin aluminum skin. When they let go, their muzzle blasts shook everything nearby. Your head vibrated and dust and debris fell from little niches and insulation overhead. One day I thought I'd caught a piece of flak in my lap. It turned out to be a package of bobby pins! Some Rosie-the-Riveter at the Ford Willow Run plant must have left it up there when she took her lunch break.[3]

Fighter attacks and patches of flak not withstanding, we chugged along on our appointed task of the day. We could not deviate from our target and the course laid out to get us there. The course consisted of a number of legs designed to steer us around known heavy flak areas as much as possible and also to confuse the enemy as to the location of our target. Each leg was a straight line of flight between two checkpoints. These had to be reached at precise times, and reports made to headquarters. The final leg to the target was the 'bomb run,' and it began at the IP (initial point of the bomb run). The compass heading for the bomb run was chosen in consideration of a number of factors. The direction of the wind over the target was very important. By attacking directly into the wind you reduced your ground speed, allowing the bombardier more time to fine-tune his sight and increase the accuracy of his drop. Of course, it also gave the flak batteries more time to improve their aim. During one attack, on the oil facility at Merseburg, fantastic headwinds aloft reduced the ground speed over the target to a ridiculous 20-30 miles per hour! The bomb run was excruciatingly long, the flak guns had a field day, and loss of our bombers was very heavy.

Another factor to be considered was the shape of the targets, particularly industrial targets. They were usually rectangular or square in shape and flying diagonally across them gave the best bomb coverage. One exception aroused our curiosity because of the angle of attack and aiming point given in the field order. The target was a very large, long, and rectangularly shaped manufacturing plant in Germany. At the south end, separated by a couple of hundred yards, was a much smaller square building. Observed from the air, the target resembled an exclamation point. The angle of attack given was straight-across rather than diagonal, and more surprising, the aiming point was the little building, not the big one. When we checked our target folder closely we found that the small one was the power plant for the big one. Presumably, if we knocked out the little one the big one would be idled. But why not try to take them both out with a diagonal approach, per our usual routine? Reading farther into the folder we found the reason for the kid-glove approach. The owner of the plant and the maker of the planes we were flying were one and the same—the Ford Motor Company.

After making the turn at the IP things got busy. Pilots had to tighten-up the formation. Bomb bay doors were opened. Lead bombardiers got over their bombsights and started conferring with the pilot and pilotage navigator for inputs such as ground speed and wind drift affecting the plane's movement over the ground. Once he had these entered, he locked his bombsight in with flight control of the plane and the rest was automatic. The bombsight 'flew' the plane, and when those cross-hairs met over the target, the lead plane's bombs released. All others in the formation, seeing the drop, toggled theirs out immediately.

No matter what else was going on in the sky, 'bombs away' over-rode all, at least for the moment, followed by a sense of great relief. It was the sole reason for our being there. You hoped that you made a good drop and wouldn't have to come back. The plane gave a sigh, greatly relieved by the tons of weight loss, and surged upward. The universal feeling was that we'd been on government time up to this point but now we were on our own, so let's close those bomb bay doors and get the hell out of here!

Frequently, a plane or two might have a 'hung' bomb, one that didn't release. Someone had to put on an oxygen walk-around bottle, go into the bomb bay and try to kick or otherwise knock it out, a very uncomfortable and risky task with the bomb bays open. Failing in that, you had to bring it home and re-safety-pin it before landing.

The end of the bomb run leg of the mission was not the point of bomb release, but some distance beyond at the RP (rally point). There the leader did a sweeping turn into the next leg, giving any who had fallen behind a chance to cut the corner and catch up. This was frequently a time for calling the roll by the leader to find out who was gone, and who was beat up and still around, if not for long. You could advise the cripples of possible correctional steps for plane malfunctions, navigational advice for what might be a solo ride home for them, and what the other undesirable options might be, including safe haven in neutral Sweden or Switzerland. There wasn't much else you could do for them except to wish them luck.

After the target you were by no means home free. Exit routes from north German targets were often over the North Sea. While flak barges along coastal areas were not as intense a threat, the over-water route did not reduce the fighter attacks. The Luftwaffe seemed to always have a fresh supply of Jerries on hand. Those who had hit you before the target could land, refuel, rearm, and come up again to deliver a parting shot. The hornets were even angrier, now that we had bombed their nest.

Once we cleared the coast of Europe, we started our letdown. That was the longest and happiest leg of the trip. Down at 10,000 feet the oxygen masks came off and the cigarettes and candy bars came out. Any planes with damage that might affect a safe landing were advised to head for Woodbridge or the Manston Strip, two RAF fields on the coast uniquely equipped for handling crashes (with lots of 'meat wagons' and fire engines). Those with lesser damage or with wounded aboard were given landing priority. They would identify themselves to the tower by radio and by firing red flares when they reached the landing traffic pattern. Those red flares made everyone on the tower very nervous. We had only one runway long enough to comfortably accommodate our B-24s. If a cripple cracked up on landing, he could put us out of business and we'd have to send the rest of the planes elsewhere. This was not a great solution; nearby bases were now receiving their own planes and would be delayed in accepting any of ours, many of which were low on fuel. It was breath-holding time when a plane firing red flares made his final approach.

The other planes remained in formation and underwent our rigid landing procedure designed to have a plane touch down every twenty seconds. That was an ambitious time schedule for our very tired pilots, and we didn't always make it. Finally, touchdown—that beautiful horrible squeal of rubber on the runway, which erased the last remnant of the day's anxieties.

The crews were picked up at the hardstands and returned for interrogation to the building where they had been briefed that morning. After a quick opportunity to file a physical complaint with the medics, to pick up a shot of scotch, and a welcome coffee and doughnut from the Red Cross girls, each crew sat around a table with an intelligence officer to run through their experiences on the mission. Losses and damages were covered first and in greatest detail. Flak and fighter activity were noted as were any observations of our bomb drop and firing of our guns. Any variances or inconsistencies between crew reports were cross-checked and a complete mission report for the group was prepared and sent up through channels. Eventually these were consolidated somewhere at higher intelligence levels and press reports released.

The mission was history, over but not forgotten by the crews. They looked forward to reading accounts of the mission that would appear in print media from home. Before coming overseas we read in the press and listened to the radio for the full and dramatic coverage given the early air war in Europe. It never occurred to us that it might not be accurate. Later as we read and listened to reports on actions in which we participated we became less credulous, and somewhat disillusioned. We found that once you made allowance for some understandable bias and permissible puffery, the same-day German Radio reports of our mission were more informative and accurate than newspapers, 'pony editions' of Time, etc., received much later from home. Our press had some bias for the home team, and generally overstated our accomplishments and underplayed our failures and losses.

Our intelligence people insisted that the distortion of the mission reports we furnished took place after they were given to the press. Some speculated that Elmer Davis's OWI (Office of War

Information) intervened and painted a more rosy picture for home consumption. Most blamed the press itself for reliance on intelligence reports and scuttlebutt picked up around officers' club bars in London. It was easier for the press to cover ground forces' actions from there too. The airman's gripe was that most of the press got their material from rear echelon sources and that "...there aren't many Ernie Pyles out there."

1. With its 'tricycle' landing gear, the Liberator should have afforded pilots a better view during ground maneuvers than the 'tail wagger' Fortress. In fact, the B-24s long unsloping nose, festooned with Navigator's plexiglas observation dome and forward gun turret, obstructed forward view of anything below the horizon. Wingtips were hidden by engine nacelles, and looking at the main gear wheels required the pilot and co-pilot to each lean way forward and look way back and down. The engineer's hatch was behind and above the cockpit, just ahead of the top turret, from whence he guided the pilots via interphone.

    Turns into and out of hardstands off of the perimeter strip required great precision and coordination of steering, throttles and brakes (used sparingly). A wheel off the pavement was usually a calamity. Heavily loaded mains would sink in any but frozen ground, and the notoriously vulnerable nose gear could buckle if positioned to plow earth.

2. Piston-engined aircraft engines are mechanically and operationally far more complex than jet engines. Approximately three times as many parameters must be monitored and controlled, and in WW II aircraft, very little of this was automated.

    A close comparison of the instrument panels from the multi-engine bomber of the 1940s and from modern transport aircraft, both of which are very complex, reveals that far more instrumentation then was concerned with engine conditions than now. Far more today is devoted to communication, 'avionics' and redundant systems. The old-timers had comparatively less communication and navigation equipment, little system redundancy, and no 'stand-off' weapon systems.

    One concept of appropriate 'ergonomics' had evolved by WW II: the convention of setting all of the analog gauges so that the 'normal' condition was indicated by a needle pointing straight up. A quick scan of the complete instrument panel by a pilot would catch the shaking or off-angle needle without need to 'read' every one.

3. Clarence Kurtz, a mechanic at Attleborough and Old Buckenham before North Pickenham and Rackheath, remembers finding an unwrapped, unused tampon in a remote cranny one of the Liberators in his charge, and wondering whether Rosie the Riveter was being worked too hard and not getting reasonable breaks. (Interviewed 10-1-99 in Tucson, AZ.)

5. Four Rough Ones

On the 492nd Group's first mission, to Mulhouse, France, our only losses resulted from fuel shortage. On return, two of our planes ran out of gas and crash landed in England, killing one crewman and injuring several others. Both planes were beyond repair.

On our second mission, the primary target was an oil installation at Zeitz, Germany. I was leading the high right squadron and at bomb release time the low left squadron slid directly underneath us. My bombardier quickly switched the bombsight off and held our bombs. Fortunately, nearby on our return route was our secondary target, a major oil refinery at Merseburg. It had been the primary target that day for a large effort of B-17s. We were able to drop there with very good results. Both targets were well protected with flak and at Merseburg a large number of fighters were beating up on the 17s. We were most fortunate in avoiding their attack and not suffering major flak damage.

One of our pilots did have a harrowing experience that day, the result of an unusual bit of 'friendly fire.' Three bombs dropped onto his plane from above. One hit a propeller, shattering it and forcing him to shut down that engine. Another stuck into the top of his wing, but he was able to shake it loose. The third lodged into the top of the fuselage just behind the nose turret, but he couldn't budge it. That bomb sticking up behind his nose made a frightening/comical sight for onlookers when he landed back at base. He made a safe landing and the bomb was then safetied, de-fused, and removed without incident. None had fallen far enough for their final safeties spin off and arm them, luckily. Overall, it was a good mission—good bombing of two heavily defended targets with some battle damage, but no losses or personal injuries.

Our third mission was a long one to Tutow near the German-Polish border. It was successful and uneventful. On the fourth mission, to Siracourt, France, one pilot was killed,[1] a few others were injured, excellent bombing, no planes lost, and very minor damage.

The first of the 'four rough ones' (which collectively cost our group 358 KIA and 37 MIA) was our fifth mission, to marshaling yards at Brunswick, Germany. All losses at Brunswick were to fighter attacks before and after the target. One F-W 190 came through the formation so close that our crews could see the pilot's head down on his shoulder. He was already dead, and luckily missed ramming anybody. A number of gunners 'claimed' him. One of the Me.109s, on a 12 o'clock (or head-on) attack, collided with one of our planes, knocking off his own wing and slicing off the top half of our plane's vertical stabilizers. With some difficulty and a great deal of skill, pilot, Lt. Wyman Bridges flew it home.

The next six missions were relatively uneventful. We flew excellent formations, had average bombing results, very little damage, and only one crew and plane lost. Our next two 'rough ones' were to Politz, Germany's largest synthetic oil refinery (not to be confused with the more publicized natural oil refinery at Ploesti, in Rumania). Near the Polish border in northeastern Germany on the Oder river, not far south from where it empties into the Baltic Sea, Politz was the target that proved most disastrous for our Group.

The first (and easier) of these two 'rough ones' to Politz was a long ride, eight and a half hours roundtrip. In the immediate target area there were known to be at least 430 fixed-emplacement, heavy caliber anti-aircraft guns; there were estimated to be a nearly equal number of mobile guns. The fixed guns were clustered close enough around the area that all could be brought to bear on an attacking force at the same time. (By comparison, Berlin was the most heavily defended target in Germany with some 1,100 fixed guns and very many mobile ones too. But its anti-aircraft guns were spread out over such a large area that less than a third could be

Larrivee, Pascual and Schlosser of McMurray's crew.

deployed against an attacking force at one time.) I was command pilot for our group, the third in our wing, and our wing was in the middle of the long division lineup.

The first legs of our route going in were over the North Sea, with a turn south after passing the island of Helgoland. After making landfall, we took a line of flight toward Berlin and picked up some flak skirting around Hamburg. Our plan called for a sharp left turn toward our IP when we came abreast of Politz, then a right turn at the IP to the bomb run. We expected we'd see the Luftwaffe straight ahead between us and Berlin, ready to defend 'Big B.' Instead, the largest gaggle we saw was to our left, circling over our IP and waiting for us! That was the only time I recall when there was some idle speculation about the Jerries having been tipped-off about our target. We watched some groups ahead taking a beating from the fighters. We were dreading them and the turn we'd be taking at the IP right into the middle of the flak we could see over the target area. At the IP we opened the bomb bay doors and I got on the intercom full time with Alex to ready his bombsight for taking over control of the plane. At that point we came under brief fighter attack—a mixed and seemingly uncoordinated bag of Me.109s and F-W 190s came from all directions of the clock and several Me.210s launched rockets at us from 3 o'clock level.

They did surprising little damage and abandoned us just seconds before we entered the flak zone; the worst flak I was ever to see. It was a thick carpet of scarlet flashes centered in large oily black puffs which seemed solid enough to walk on. From their experience with the planes ahead of us, the flak gunners had our altitude calculated perfectly. It was all barrage fire, and right at our level. Everybody was being peppered with shrapnel and our planes were being tossed about like falling leaves which made it difficult to stabilize the plane for locking in with the bombsight. I put on my best calm voice encouraging Alex to ignore the bedlam all around and concentrate on his Norden. I still remember his reply. "Don't give me that *calm* crap; you're up there staining your drawers just like I am!"

What made his job even more difficult was that the target was partially obscured by low scattered clouds and thick billowing white smoke across the target. The Germans had ringed the target with dozens of smoke pots, and whenever bombers threatened, they touched off the ones on the windward side and did an effective job of blanketing it. We were forced to drop into the middle of the smoke and hope we hit our AP. After clearing the flak zone, reaching our RP, and turning north along the Oder river heading for the Baltic, we were jumped again by Jerries. In short order they knocked-off two of our planes, and by the time we reached the Baltic and headed west over the Kiel Canal area we had two more nursing very serious wounds which would prevent them from making it home. The remainder made it back, all damaged to varying extents, but surprisingly no fatalities and not as many injuries as we expected. Our SAV photos, full of clouds and smoke, were inconclusive as to the damage we did to our target.   Subsequent photo-reconnaisance photos showed some damage, but not sufficient to consider the mission a complete success. The division would have to go back again.

On the second Politz mission, Major Jack Losee, Squadron Commanders of our 856th BS, led The 492nd. This time the route flown was the reverse of the first—out over the North Sea, crossing the Danish Peninsula north of Kiel, over the Baltic and down the Oder river to Politz. Our Group was hit hard by fighters over the Baltic long before reaching the target. Nine of the fourteen planes we lost never even reached the target. Losee and a few other cripples managed to reach safe haven in nearby Malmo, Sweden. That mission alone, our worst, cost us 138 KIAs and 14 MIAs.

The last of the 'four rough ones' was an attack on an aircraft factory at Bernburg in central Germany. Here again, Luftwaffe fighters were our undoing. I sent up seven planes from my squadron and not one came home. Our group's twin brother pilots, Frank and George Haag, were both on the mission—George watched his brother Frank's plane go down and explode.[2] Frank was hurt but survived as a POW. Lt. Bernie Harding, one of my lead crew pilots, was leading the high squadron, and they were all shot down. After bailing out, he and others, seized by Germans civilians, were being beaten, and one of his crew was lynched. Bernie and the others were saved by the intervention of a Luftwaffe Corporal who drew his gun on the civilians and insisted that the rights of our airmen as prisoners of war be respected.

1. See Chapter 12, 'Gilbert Baker.'

2. The Haags were in different bomb squadrons within the 492nd Bomb Group. The different services had, by this time, policies restricting brothers from being in the same combat unit, owing to a much publicized incident where five brothers serving on one Navy ship were lost at once.

JJM used to tell of another set of twins, one of whom was with him in the 467th, the other in a different 8th AF heavy bomber group. On an afternoon when the 467th was not 'on,' Dad and the he were enjoying a beer in the 'Chain and Sword' Officers' Club at Rackheath, while the twin was on a mission. In the middle of a sip, the man wordlessly dropped his glass to the bar. His face and body went slack, he turned and walked away. Dad ran after him and asked what was wrong. "My brother just got it." Dad marked the time. Returning crews from the brother's group, upon debriefing, gave that exact minute as the time when the brother's plane took a direct flak hit and exploded with complete loss of life.

6. Tough Luck Crew #1:

McMurray

A superstitious belief prevalent in ours and other groups was that there was such a thing as a tough-luck crew. Periodically a crew would come along that would run through a series of incidents—having its plane shot up, crewmen injured, etc., before being wiped out in one lethal blow. Of our original crews, several exhibited tough-luck tendencies early in their tours which qualified them for this unenviable category. One such crew was that of Lt. Dave McMurray.

Dave's crew was a motley collection of ethnic backgrounds—a couple each of Scots, Irish, and Italian, a Spaniard, and three non-descript. They were a happy lot; experienced and able, they had great respect for Dave. On most of their first few missions they came home with a variety of minor plane and crew problems, but nothing fatal. Shortly after D-Day they had the dubious distinction of being the first plane shot down over the Normandy beach-head. When the crew bailed out over the irregular and nebulous 'front line,' some landed on our side, some in the hotly contested area between Allied and German troops, and one on the German side who became a POW. Another was never accounted for. We first learned that day, and were to experience a number of times later, that every descending parachute in a frontline area was assumed by both sides to be suspending a paratrooper from the other side. Both sides shot at it.

Those landing in 'no-man's land', after spending daylight hours hidden in hedgerows and ducking fire from both sides, managed to identify themselves and reach Allied lines under the cover of darkness. One of this group was the very colorful Latin bombardier from Brooklyn, Lt. Ramon 'The Duke' Pascual.

Very handsome and dapper with his neatly trimmed mustache, The Duke was also the crew's comedian. When he bailed out, he landed in a rose arbor near a French farmhouse and was scratched a bit by the thorns. He had taken cover in a nearby hedgerow. In response to calls from American troops to identify himself, his Brooklyn accent and knowledge of the Dodgers' lineup assured the GIs that he couldn't be a German. Upon finally reaching our lines he was sent to a field first-aid station for repair of his rosebush 'wounds.' There they bandaided his scratches and awarded him a Purple Heart! McMurray assembled what was left of his crew and hitched a ride across the Channel on a LST. We picked them up at the English port and brought them home. There was much good-natured banter about 'The Duke's' medal for "...wounds received in action against the enemy." He countered by insisting that the rose bush had been put there by the Germans as an obstacle to the Allied invasion—hence it really was German action that did him in! After a period of R&R we filled the vacated crew position with a replacement and made them operational again.

The ball turret gunner on that crew had been with me longer than anyone in our entire Group. When I was assigned to a squadron at Newark Airport in mid 1941, six months before Pearl Harbor. Sgt. Pat Tracey, a good-natured, hard-working Irish-American from Bayonne, was a corporal in the armament section of that squadron. Even then he had been at his gunner trade for quite a while and was very proficient both in the maintenance of guns and turrets on the ground, and firing them in the air. Because we'd known each other so long and had more or less grown up together in rank and rating, I had a special regard for Tracey, as I believe he did for me. McMurray told me of some of the extravagant compliments Tracey made to the crew about me. By his own choice, Tracey was a ball turret gunner, which to me was the least desirable position in the plane.[1] Also, he was a little on the chubby side to be squeezing into the extremely limited confines of that turret.

On the second mission after their
return to combat, as the group returned to the field,
McMurray broke out of formation firing red flares. Smoke
was coming out of one engine and he had feathered another
on the opposite side. He was given number one priority in
landing, dropped his wheels and made a close-in approach.
We saw that his ball turret was in the 'down' position
instead of being retracted as it should have been for

Sgt. Pat Tracey

landing. When the tower called Dave on this, he quickly explained that it was jammed, nor could he communicate with Tracey, still inside it. Tracey was going to be in a very dangerous position during landing as the bottom of the turret was sure to scrape along the runway—how badly would depend upon how well McMurray could execute the landing. If he could keep the plane's weight pretty well forward during the touchdown and roll, there probably would be little damage. Should he land tail-heavy, it could be rough on Tracey.

The fire trucks and meat-wagons were readied for whatever McMurray and crew had concocted for them this time. Under difficult conditions, he made a beautiful landing with weight well forward and the turret barely touching and sparking along the runway. At the end of his roll, he pulled off onto the grass to clear the runway for our planes coming in behind him. He cut his engines and the crew scrambled out of every opening. The smoking engine was quickly brought under control, so our next concern turned to Tracey. He was the reason I went out there instead of staying back in the tower.

As the firefighters were working on the engine, we saw that the circular, heavy armor-glass window between the ball turret's two .50 caliber machine guns was shattered and had a cannon shell hole in its center. There was little doubt that the projectile that made that hole had put an end to Pat Tracey. Hoping against the obvious, we climbed into the plane and tried without success to manually open the doors atop the turret. A couple of ground-crew men with some tools pried it open. Tracey was slumped forward with only the back of his neck showing, and blood everywhere. Normally, I wouldn't be directly involved in this kind of activity. The fire fighters, crash crews, and medics were trained and fully capable of handling this situation and it was their job. Because of my concern for a long-time GI

friend, I found myself taking over where I had no business
doing so.

The smallness of the hatch opening
was such that it wasn't possible for two people to get into
position to lift Tracey out. By getting on my knees I could
put my arms down into the turret with my hands under his
armpits. It was an awkward position for lifting and it was
not going to be easy to extract about 165 pounds of Tracey
plus all that equipment. Having set myself for that weight,
I gave a mighty heave, and to the astonishment of
all—especially me—Tracey, or rather, the top half of poor
Tracey, came out of the hole easily and wound up on top of
me as I tumbled over backwards. That shell had literally
cut him in half just above the belt. At that point I quietly
turned over the rest of that job to those who should have
had it in the first place, and climbed out of the plane.
Some solicitous medics helped me wipe Pat's blood from
my clothing and hands—the first time I'd seen someone
else's blood there since I gave Red Molinsky a bloody nose
in the sixth grade! The next meal was light one, and I was
in for another of those nights when sleep was long in
coming.

Again, we added a replacement to
the McMurray crew. After a few more missions, the much
wounded crew received its *coup de grâce* from the
Luftwaffe. All were killed on the Bernburg mission.[2]
Beyond our view, it was for us the least dramatic of the
several episodes the McMurray crew provided. For them it
was the worst and last.

---

1. Official postwar analysis corroborated the counterintuitive finding of the
staff of the 467th BG late in the war, that the ball turret was the safest crew
position on a B-24. Toward the end of the European war, increasing
numbers of these were removed, making the planes lighter and faster.
Nonetheless, the grisly spectre of its failure to retract into the plane and
release its occupant, especially if there were landing gear problems, could
never have been very far to the back of the mind of a Liberator crewman.

2. Enrico Schwartz is a German researcher interested in bringing closure to the cases of still-missing American crewmen over northern Europe, and has involved this writer in the enigmatic case of the McMurray crew. It is rather singular in that the 9 bodies were never definitively identified and recovered, although one of the vertical stabilizers bearing the serial number of their plane was recovered among the substantial confusion and litter of 7 planes shot down within 15 minutes in the vicinity of Westerlegen, Germany on 7-7-44

Schwartz and his fiancée Swetlana Reimer, founders of WW II Missing Allied Air Crew Research Team, have recently succeeded in helping the family of radio operator Staff Sergeant Lawrence Nursall find the remains of his crewmates (in the crew of pilot Lloyd Herbert, 856th BS, 492nd BG) in a careful exhumation near Nienburg, Germany. They successfully enlisted the participation of archaeologists and US Army Mortuary Affairs Office in this work.

7. Tough-Luck Crew #2:

Prewitte

One of the better and more experienced of my original crews was that of Lt. Bill Prewitte. He was one of the pilots who had come to us at Alamogordo after having been an instructor pilot at a B-24 transitional training school. He was a first lieutenant with many hours in four-engine aircraft, a competent pilot, and an effective crew commander.

His early missions were reasonably uneventful. On all he turned in a good job, usually as a deputy squadron leader and later, a squadron leader. It was on his 13th mission that he first ran into real trouble. It was supposed to have been in the 'milk run' category, a rail target not very distant in France. After the target he received some heavy flak which severely damaged his plane and critically wounded his nose turret gunner. Coming back over the Channel he headed for the first air base he could find to get treatment for his gunner, an RAF station in the Dover area. He landed safely, turned his gunner over to the medics and awaited evaluation as to whether or not his plane should be flown again before repairs were made. The gunner, whose leg was nearly shot off below the knee, was transferred to a general hospital. (I learned later that it was four years before he could walk again unassisted.) The next morning we picked up the rest of the crew and brought them home.[1] We rested the crew for a couple of days, then declared them operational again with a replacement nose gunner. They flew some more missions with no exceptional problems until we were called upon for our first of two missions against the synthetic oil refinery at Politz. I was group command pilot that day, and over the target Prewitte called to tell me that he had an engine knocked out completely and some gas tanks punctured. He considered going to nearby Malmo, Sweden, as many did after being clobbered over that target, but instead decided to try to make it home. He couldn't keep up with the group formation and started a lonely, long, gradual let-down over the North Sea. About 50 miles from the English Coast he found his rate of fuel loss had worsened and he wasn't going to be able to make it to the coast. They would have to bail out or ditch. I heard him contact Air/Sea Rescue and he was vectored to a surface craft which happened to be very close. They were able to locate it then bail out. All but one of the crew jumped, and after 20 to 30 minutes were gratefully fished out of the frigid water by the RAF Air/Sea Rescue boys. For some reason, the bombardier didn't appear to have left the plane, or at least was not found.

A short time later our original 492nd Bomb Group was disbanded, and Prewitte was transferred with me to the 467th Bomb Group at Rackheath. Again we filled out his crew, this time with a replacement bombardier. Things seemed to settle down for him and his revamped crew, and we started using it again for important leads.

Because the 467th had been performing so consistently well on its missions, on a couple of occasions, when the division commander wanted to demonstrate how our division's groups prepared and assembled a mission, he sent visiting brass, touring congressmen, and correspondents to our base and asked that we run a practice mission for their benefit. While we were flattered to be his showcase, sometimes this caused disruptions we could do without—particularly the politicians and newspeople, most of whom seemed to be primarily interested in these visits as photo opportunities for home consumption.

One day division called to say that they had a brigadier visiting from Washington and suggested we run a practice mission with the general riding in the lead plane. It happened on this occasion that it was no inconvenience as we had a practice mission already scheduled. The general turned out to be a nice guy who wasn't trying to impress anybody, asked intelligent questions, and didn't even ask to have his picture taken. After a quick run-through of our ground installations and activities, we took him through the preparation of a mission. He indicated, as division had suggested, that he would like to ride in the lead plane with me. I felt his interests would be better served by flying outside of the formation so that he could observe the whole operation better. Riding in the lead plane, his view would be very limited. He and I could fly outside of the formation in our assembly ship, 'Big Pete,' listen in on the command pilot's instructions, and I could answer his questions. He agreed, so I asked Jay Taylor, the CO of the 788th Squadron, to take my place in the lead plane as group commander. Prewitte's crew was selected to lead the group. His co-pilot, Lt. Bill Clarey, was on sick leave at the time so he took along a young pilot named Lt. Richard Kenton,[2] who had arrived at the base as an individual replacement just a couple of days earlier.

The general and I took off after the group, observed the assembly of the three squadrons into group formation at altitude, and followed as they proceeded on briefed course to a target (a dye-marker dropped in the water by a preceding plane) several miles off-shore on the North Sea. Everything was running smoothly and on schedule until they reached the point where gunners test fire their weapons. I had positioned our plane above and to the left rear of the formation so that from the co-pilot's seat the general had a good view of the whole formation. When the gunners started their firing, tracers radiated out in all directions from the formation. Suddenly, to our utter astonishment, the lead plane burst into flames, dropped straight down, and exploded in a fiery ball. We had no inkling as to what had happened, so I called the deputy leader for an explanation. He replied that the 'slot' plane, flying just below and immediately behind the leader, had poured bullets from its top turret into the underside of Prewitte's lead plane. The turret was rotating 360 degrees at high speed, firing all the while. We counted six opened chutes from the flaming wreckage. I told the deputy to take over the lead, put the formation in a steep descending spiral to get to the surface, and drop life rafts. I asked that he also have his navigator give an exact position report to Air/Sea Rescue.

Having the fastest plane and no formation to worry about, I was able to reach water level first, only minutes after the chutes splashed down. Unfortunately, in our stripped-down assembly ship we had no life rafts. The most I could do was to circle as low and as slowly as I could to keep in sight the men in the water so as to help direct the dropping of rafts from the formation's planes when they arrived. The six in the water were spread out over a wide area and only three were close enough to see each other as they regularly disappeared in the troughs of the heavy sea. The deputy did an excellent job of maneuvering his formation over the survivors, making several passes and dropping plenty of rafts, some within reach of the men in the water.

We had never practiced dropping life rafts from an airplane or anticipated that we'd have to. It turned out to be a much more difficult feat than we thought. Obviously, the raft had first to be removed from its case in the plane, or it would sink immediately upon hitting the water. Out of its case, the rolled-up raft with some heavy survival equipment inside and liberally dusted with talc to keep the rubber from sticking to itself, made for a very cumbersome and slippery package to handle and drop out of a bomb bay. Some didn't unravel when dropped, hit the water and sank. I saw one inflate when dropped and explode in a cloud of talc dust as it hit the water. Another couple hit on the upside of waves and skipped a great distance from their target. Fortunately we had many planes with a lot of rafts, and eventually had one within easy reach of the cluster of three survivors, and others dropped near to the scattered three. One of the latter three turned out to be Ed Grooms, the navigator. He appeared to be unhurt. He hung on to a raft for a while, then inexplicably, let go and drifted off.

All of the survivors were burned. Taylor was in the worst shape, but it was he who was the first to respond when a successful drop of a raft was made near the cluster of three. He swam to it, inflated it and pulled it toward the others.

There was nothing further we could do from the air except to leave a flight of 24s circling the area until the Air/Sea Rescue folks arrived and took over. They had dispatched a flying boat and a speedy PT-boat from their base at nearby Great Yarmouth. When the flying boat arrived on the scene he realized the sea was much too rough for a safe landing, so he also circled until the surface boat arrived. They picked up the survivors about three and a half hours after they had bailed out.

After returning to Rackheath we kept in touch with Air/Sea Rescue for an estimated time of arrival of the rescue craft at their dock, and arranged to be there with ambulances. Spivvy and I rode over in a staff car and the ambulances followed us. The rescue boat radioed ahead that Taylor was badly burned, but not shot. The other crewmen, though burned, would make it. We had about a forty minute wait before the rescue boat pulled up to the dock. Our survivors were strapped to litters on the deck. We jumped on deck as soon as the boat bumped the dock. Taylor was conscious and lucid, and although in considerable pain, was trying to make light of it. His first words to us were, "Get me a bottle, a bucket, or something—I have to take a leak!" Spivvy replied "You stupid sonovabitch, you couldn't be any wetter than you are, or smell any worse. Never mind a bucket, just let it go!" Taylor grinned a bit, and overriding inhibitions since toilet training days, let it go. Spivvy was right about his smell and appearance. Those parts of his body which had not been covered by flying gear were badly flash-burned and emitted that characteristic unpleasant odor. His exposed areas looked like blackened toast. In some places the skin had peeled off altogether and left raw, bleeding flesh. Taylor was a pretty sorry and frightening sight. Spivvy medicated all as best he could and we took them to the 65th General Hospital.[3]

This accident occurred just a couple of weeks after the Battle of the Bulge, and like every other hospital in the UK, the 65th was overburdened with the tremendous influx of ground forces casualties. The cases they evacuated to the UK were the more severe ones. Every cot in the hospital was taken and they were crowded in only about two feet apart in the wards. Both sides of the corridors were lined with cots. Surgical crews had been working around the clock with little rest, and they were a tired looking bunch of doctors and nurses. There was much confusion and they were far behind in with ordinary housekeeping chores. In the hallway outside of a surgical area was a lineup of large metal containers, like garbage cans. Some were uncovered and contained a gruesome assortment of mangled limbs which had been separated recently from their owners. Even Spivvy found this revolting and let out a string of epithets, more in a sad tone than angry. As we waited with our crewmen for their turns through the surgical mill, blood splattered orderlies periodically emerged from the operating rooms with additional contributions for the 'garbage cans.' Had we waited much longer, I would have qualified as a patient there rather than a visitor.

We may have been a little impatient in getting attention for our wounded, and probably gave the medics a harder time than we should have. They were doing their best under unbelievable conditions. Luckily, Spivvy found a young major who had just recently joined the Army at that rank. He had been a specialist in burn therapy at Tulane Medical Center and had been inducted into service for the specific purpose of teaching to Army medics the latest methods of burn treatment. He had been assisting in general surgery when we arrived, and seemed almost relieved to have the opportunity to practice his specialty on our boys. He took over their care and we returned to Rackheath.

It was very late when we arrived back at base. The next day's field order was already in and the briefing team was working on it. I was told that interrogation of the top turret gunner proved fruitless. He was terribly upset and wasn't making much sense. The following morning we convened a board of inquiry consisting of operations and armament personnel, to meet with the gunner and the rest of the 'slot' airplane crew. The plane they flew had been grounded until the top turret and all of its equipment could be examined for possible malfunction.

When we met, the gunner, if anything, was worse than in the previous evening's session. He had had a night to reflect on the full impact of his actions and was overwhelmed by them. He had no explanation for his failure to react once things started to go awry. He was fully aware of the steps he could and should have taken to stop his guns and the turret. The problem was not lack of knowledge, but inexplicable failure to act. We soon reached a point where continued questioning was to no avail. His fellow crew members were of no help. They had only good things to say about the gunner, and were mystified by this whole episode. The conclusions of our inquiry were two and simple: the equipment was all in good working order, and the gunner was guilty of gross but unintentional errors, reasons unknown. Our recommendation was that the gunner be reclassified to a ground job and be reduced in grade accordingly. The latter action was not punitive, simply recognition that his staff sergeant rating was based solely upon his being an aerial gunner. No longer able to fill that function, he was not entitled to the grade that went with it.

We were always saddened by losses. Eventually you became inured to combat losses, realized they went with the trade, took them in stride, and got on with the next mission. But non-combat and training mission losses were different. Even though it made no difference to the victims whether they died in combat or on a training mission, the latter seemed so purposeless that it always cast a longer shadow over the spirit of the base. It took much longer to stop the rehashing of what happened to a crew such as Prewitte's than one that just fell out of the sky over Germany. His long history of misfortune had him tagged earlier by some, as another of those 'hard luck crews.' Now he had gone and proven it. His surviving gunner, Bob Mattson, with the unique distinction of twice bailing out into the North Sea with that crew, quickly recovered from his burns and injuries, as did the other crewmen and were returned home with no more missions asked of them. The other survivor of the original crew, Bill Clarey (the co-pilot who was luckily sick the day of the fateful flight), finished his tour with another crew and made it home safely. Clarey, some years later, located the Royal Navy sailor who fished him out of the water in the crew's first ditching, and they have met many times since on both sides of the Atlantic.

The talk of the incident eventually subsided and our only active link with it was Jay Taylor, still in the hospital for a long stay. The latest treatment for burns that the Tulane specialist brought with him was to strip away all of Jay's burned flesh, cover it with ointment, wrap it in layers of gauze, then cover all with casts. This ponderous scaffolding was to remain in place unchanged for four or five weeks. His hands looked like white boxing gloves—big plaster balls with wristlets extending half way to the elbows. These made his hands very heavy and, with no fingers protruding, quite useless. His head and neck down to the shoulders, were completely enclosed in a cast. This had slits for the eyes, small holes for the ears and nostrils, and a somewhat larger oval one for the mouth. He was a frightening sight, a Boris Karloff look-alike. For the first few days they kept Jay fairly well sedated so that he wasn't too unhappy with his condition. He was completely helpless. He couldn't eat, drink, or even go to the bathroom by himself. With the extreme shortage of nurses and orderlies at the hospital, we arranged for someone from the base to be with him at all meal times at least.

When they first put on the casts, Jay was badly swollen in the burned areas. As he started to repair, the swelling subsided and an increasing amount of air space developed between him and his casts. His 'boxing gloves' became loose, and when his head started to rattle around inside of his white 'helmet,' it became a real problem to feed him. The opening in the cast for his mouth was very small, he was sure to spill some of every spoonful between his neck and the cast. After several days of this he had all the airs of a walking garbage bucket. Thankfully, Jay got used to the stench, but some of our voluntary feeders began holding their noses with one hand while shoveling food into the slit with the other, a very comical sight!

Other concerns for us visiting non-medical assistants were the severe combat injury cases all around Jay. Due to the shortage of nurses, we frequently wound up performing minor medical chores for some of those unfortunate guys in nearby cots. In one cot just a couple of feet from Jay was a young armor lieutenant who had been hit in the chest with some kind of an explosive device. He had a large cavity there, and to hear him wheeze, whistle and shudder was distressing. One day when I was there, he gave his last shudder, to the relief of all around him. He was finally out of his terrible misery, and they wouldn't have to listen to that agony any more. Some of them later said that when the lieutenant was alive they realized how much better off they were than he; with him gone they started to feel more sorry for themselves again.

When they finally cut off Jay's casts, he had new pink skin like the proverbial hind end of an infant. After getting shaved and cleaned up, he looked great. There were no real scars, just some slight discoloration. After a brief recuperative period he returned to his assignment as CO of the 788th Bomb Squadron.

That would have been the end of the tragic Prewitte saga except for a telephone call I received sometime later. The call came in for our Group Commander from a Major General with one of the other divisions of the 8th Air Force. Since Col. Shower was off base at the time, the call was directed to me. The general's tone from the outset was not social or even friendly. He started by asking me to confirm his distorted version of "...shooting down and killing your own people on a training flight." I tried to explain what happened and that it was a freak accident, etc. He wasn't listening, and to my increasing irritation, went on haranguing us for "...letting this happen," and wanting to know what had we done about "the guilty gunner," still not revealing his particular interest in the Prewitte accident. I went through the whole story once more, elaborating on the good crew, half of whom were killed, the beating a squadron CO took, etc., and possibly with a tinge of sarcasm, added that unfortunately, training accidents did happen, and might have occurred even within *his* command. Not being a career officer, and never intending to become one, I'd taken enough from this chairborne general, obviously out of touch with our real world. Surprisingly he backed off, then described his connection with our accident. It was Lt. Kenton, Prewitte's acting co-pilot for that fateful mission. Kenton had come to us just a few days before as an individual replacement, and not as part of a crew. Nobody in his squadron had gotten to know him.

The general related that Kenton's father, owner and publisher of a newspaper in a small Texas town, was a good friend of his. When the family had received word from the War Department that their son was killed in a training accident they were understandably grieved and anxious to learn more about the circumstances of the accident. They had addressed a letter to our group commander asking for such information. As was customary, such letters were turned over to a chaplain for answer. The chaplain had prepared the usual letter offering condolences and explaining that the incident occurred in a theater of war, therefore details could not be given, etc. Mr. Kenton was not satisfied with that response, so he called his friend the general and asked him to intervene and get answers. He needled the general saying that if he couldn't get the answers from him, he'd use his political clout and get them from Washington. The general was passing the needle on to me and in closing, dropped an off-hand comment that he would give my name and our base phone number to Mr. Kenton and that I should be expecting a call from him. This was not the military way to handle a 'notification of kin.' The general knew it and was just getting himself off the hook with his friend by sticking us on it, and I resented it.

I had never heard of anyone getting a phone call through from the U.S. to a base in England, but the next day I had one, person-to-person from Texas. Being a newspaper man, Mr. Kenton was all questions, and wanted answers. Being a father he was understandably distraught, but also inexcusably abusive. Out of respect for his son, I kept my cool and told him what I could. He wanted the name of the gunner, which I declined to give.   What bothered me most about his attitude and questions was that he was almost saying that he could be proud of his son's sacrifice had it occurred on a combat mission, but felt he'd have to be almost apologetic for it happening on a practice mission. I wound up my end of the conversation expressing regret that we'd not had the opportunity to know his son, and that as far as we were concerned, his son died in the line of duty and his death was no less heroic because of the unusual circumstances. I'm not sure that he accepted that rationale, and were I in his shoes, I might not have either. I felt truly sorry for the man, but, what more could I say? After a while he just seemed to run out of steam and closed his end of the conversation without a "thanks" or even a "goodbye."

I thought that certainly put an end to the tragic Prewitte affair, and it did—for about thirty-six years. At Christmas time 1981, a doctor friend asked us to a cocktail party to meet his visiting mother and stepfather. The latter turned out to be the same general, my telephonic adversary during the Prewitte episode. He had long since retired from active duty as a Lt. General.[4] I wasted no time in taking him back to our phone conversation in England and made clear my feelings then (softened a bit by time) about his part in it.   He was apologetic and explained that when the Air Corps had sent him to that Texas town before the war to arrange for the construction of a training field, Mr. Kenton and his newspaper were of great assistance to him. They became friends, and when called upon, he felt obligated to do something extra for him in his quest for information about his son's death. Our conversation then turned to more current topics and we parted on more friendly terms—a very belated epilogue to that unhappy event.

1.   Interestingly, the existence of the little known 492nd assembly ship, recently corroborated by Roger Freeman with photographic evidence, has been more personally substantiated. Ernie Haar, interviewed in Florida in December 1999, told of his being sent to Bournemouth on the south coast of England to fetch Prewitte's rescued crew, in "Zebra."

2. 'Kenton' is not the real name. Please see the first footnote to JJM's Introduction and Dedication.

3. Present-day Wymonden College was the 2nd AD hospital during the war. Located 8 miles W-SW of Norwich, it has as one of its governors a prominent trustee of the 2nd AD Memorial Library, and actively maintains its linkage to the past.

4. In a phone interview on 6-14-00, J.J. Taylor identified this man as Major General Earle Partridge, who at the time of the WW II episode was Commander of the First Air Division of the Eighth Air Force. The riddle of *which* hometown denizen and friend of my parents was the step-son in-law, is not yet solved.

8. Getting Hit

Each plane attacked by the Luftwaffe fighters or flak developed its own particular set of problems, but they also had much in common. The most frequent experience with enemy activity was a slight dose of flak. When flak was distant or light, bursts could be seen, but not heard or felt. This is not to say that those sooty-black puffs were not frightening and dangerous, because they did pepper and puncture the skin of the plane and sometimes that of its occupants. Most survived this type attack and can still recall vividly the sound of flak hitting the plane like a blast of pebbles or hail striking a tin roof.

When flak was closer the dull thump of the burst could be heard and felt. Puffs from larger caliber antiaircraft guns were proportionately bigger, oilier and more lethal. The dirty deep scarlet flashes that propelled those jagged pieces of steel toward you were ominous and frightening. In GI circles this was known as "drawer-staining time." A close attack of this type would knock planes out of the sky, inevitably causing heavy damage and injuries, often death.

The effect of enemy fighters on crews was different than flak. If less common, fighter attacks were more devastating. When they engaged us, the Luftwaffe rarely went away empty-handed, and frequently decimated our formations. You could see fighters coming and knew what they were out to do. You were plenty frightened, but not startled. With flak, when unseen guns four or five miles below suddenly popped shells into your airspace, you were startled first.

While flak bursts could be both heard and felt, the fighter's machine guns and cannon were not. Tracers from his guns and intermittent red-orange flashes from his cannon were visible, but whatever noise they made could not be heard over the drone of your own engines and the very noisy return fire of the twin-fifties from your turrets. This made your first exposure to a fighter attack seem unreal and eerie. It wasn't the noisy, gun-rattling sequence you had heard on Hollywood soundtracks.

Panic can take over after receiving damage from enemy attack. Much of the damage is obvious-holes in the plane, engines burning, vibrating, or quitting altogether, oil streaking out from under cowl flaps, raw gasoline pluming from the wing's trailing edge, etc. Excited crewmen over-ride each others' transmissions on the interphone reporting damage to the plane and themselves. Some fail to respond to the co-pilot's check of all stations, maybe hurt, or even gone altogether. Pilots and flight engineer are totally preoccupied with trying to get the plane and its engines under control. Other crew members are frantically trying to put out fires, replace their failed oxygen system with walk-around bottles, patch up the plane, themselves, or each other.

In cases where the pilot judges the plane no longer flyable or safe, he pushes the bail-out button, ringing alarm bells at all stations and signaling everyone to jump out into the breeze, post-haste. Conversely, a decision to stay with a crippled plane forces a new set of problems and fears. Assuming reasonable control of the plane and some of its engines, the first order of business is survival. You will no longer have a leader to make navigational and other decisions for you. You give up the protection and comfort afforded by the group's other planes and many guns. When the power in your remaining engines will no longer sustain level flight, you assume the slow gradual descent required to maintain minimal flying speed. Trading away your hard-earned asset of altitude for speed is hard. Every airman knows that in a jamb, altitude lost is as useless as runway behind you while landing. It's a hollow feeling to watch your bomber stream become more distant above as you become a sitting duck for the Luftwaffe.

Having compensated for the obvious damage you now began to sweat-out hidden damage, some of which might show up on the gauges. Your "big-assed-boid" may not have been killed outright, but it may have received mortal wounds not yet evident. Temperatures started rising, pressures fell, and tachometers became erratic. You were not sure of electric and hydraulic power, whether or not your tires had been punctured, how long your fuel and oxygen supplies would last. The fuel system in a B-24 was complicated, with a crude and unreliable system for measuring tank levels. At the rear of the flight deck, out of view of the pilots, were vertical glass tubes like thermometers, connected to the tanks and supposedly measuring the fuel in each. As the plane's attitude changed even slightly, fuel levels in those glass columns could vary significantly. You could never be sure your readings were even close to accurate. Under stressed conditions they provided a poor basis for making life-critical decisions.

Crews faced with such decisions were given some broad guidelines. First, try to make it home. If unable to do so, try to make neutral Sweden or Switzerland to be interned. Failing that, bail out and hope to make your way to friendly hands in the underground. Best resolution of the peculiar set of problems facing an individual crippled plane and crew often demanded more of the airplane commander's judgment and leadership qualities than of his flying skills.

9. The Missing

The crews who returned from missions could usually furnish some information on those who didn't. They had seen the plane hit and go down and counted the number of opened chutes. This was helpful but not always accurate, and seldom complete. We were instructed to delay chute opening to under 10,000 feet where oxygen was sufficient—this also reduced the possibility of being attacked by German fighters, who were usually at our bombing altitude or higher. If you did follow those instructions, chances were your chute opening would not be seen from bombing altitude, so you would not be counted as a survivor. However, most bailouts did pull the ripcord immediately.

It took several days before the Red Cross passed on to us the names furnished by the Germans of our KIAs and those taken prisoner. It took about the same time to receive the names of KIAs and internees in Sweden and Switzerland. The remainder, sometimes a sizable percentage of those missing, were listed as MIAs. If they hit the ground alive in occupied countries there was a fair chance that they had made it to the underground, but we might not hear from them until the war's end. Landing in Germany afforded almost no chance of evading capture. Of the unresolved MIAs (eventually listed as 'presumed dead'), most went down over the North Sea or the Channel. The air/sea rescue (A/SR) outfits did as good a job as could be expected under extremely difficult conditions, but a high percentage of those who went down over the water were never heard from again.[1]

Once it was determined that a crew was not returning, the first step taken was to notify the appropriate squadron orderly room so that they could immediately gather the personal effects of the missing. This had to be done with some dispatch; valuables of those downed sometimes disappeared. This 'ghouling' was the most exasperating and maddening of my administrative challenges. So long as one was still around—on base and away from your hut, or even off base—your personal effects were generally safe. But as soon as you went down, your stuff became fair game for the occasional ghoul. We wanted so to catch an offender and really throw the book at him, but never did catch anyone red-handed. So too, most crewmen were hoping to nab a culprit and apply a little 'barracks discipline' before handing him over for official punishment.

Our handling of the effects of those who didn't return was frequently complicated by the

Alexander, Spivack, Mahoney, Smith and Priest with the 492nd

morbid practice of 'willing' possessions to others, and issuing IOUs in payment for gambling and other debts. After going broke with dice or cards between paydays, some gave written IOUs, and 'wills' of property to the lender. When Snuffy Briggs[2] was lost, we found that he had given three attested wills for his accordion. Not having the time or inclination to serve as executors of instant GI wills, we added to our new crew indoctrination the caveat that no 'wills' would be honored at the base; all KIA, MIA, and POW belongings would be sent home to designated next of kin.

Only a limited percentage of base pay (and no flying pay) could be designated for direct payment to family at home, so air crews received a relatively large amount of cash each month in English currency. With no banking facility on base, each man developed his own way of safeguarding his cash. Since nothing personal was supposed to be taken on missions, some left their wads with other personal effects in paper bags in the equipment room. Others entrusted their cash and valuables to a paddlefoot friend or some secret hiding place. No doubt, many of these private arrangements were never uncovered when assembling personal effects. Responsibility for picking up the trail of belongings and closing out the records fell to the squadron executive officer and his staff. Collecting the personal effects from the equipment room and the barracks bag and footlocker from the hut were the first steps. Sometimes through hut-mates or friends of the missing they learned of obligations or personal matters that required consideration. Some had established local bank accounts.

Many had down payments with local tailors for battle jackets and other custom made apparel, which could present sticky problems. A majority of officer crew members went off base on their first pass to be measured for this *de rigueur* garment, another inheritance from the RAF, later adopted by U.S. ground forces in Europe and widely known as the 'Eisenhower Jacket.' The initial measuring visit required a substantial deposit. The first fitting, six or eight weeks later, called for more good-faith money. Many never made it to the first fitting, even fewer got to subsequent fittings and collected the finished jacket. Finding receipts for deposits and reclaiming a portion was a hopeless exercise. One of our navigators was around long enough to get 'his' finished jacket, the very one on which our people claimed that at least two others had made deposits previously.

Before sealing an individual's belongings for shipment stateside, a final review was given his personal effects for removal of anything that might be embarrassing to him or distressing to his next of kin. This practice was contrary to regulations but honored the dignity of the deceased and the sensibilities of his family.

1. At the beginning, all of the AS/R work was done by the British, using their extant, highly refined fighter control system to direct boats operating out of stations along the Channel from Great Yarmouth to Portsmouth. Through the end, Americans looked to the experienced British as they acquired better life rafts, search methods and spotting and amphibious rescue aircraft. The 5th Emergency Rescue Squadron was attached to the 65th Fighter Wing of the 2nd AD and based at Boxted, then Halesworth, where they received 10 Catalina flying boats to supplement specially modified raft-dropping P-47s and a B-17. Over the time of American operations from England, the survival rate for those who ditched in the North Sea doubled—to a nonetheless depressing 45%.

2. My father had used a fictitious name for Briggs. I doubt that his fraudulent accordion beneficiaries of 57 years ago continue to carry a grudge.

10. Replacement Crews

Periodically we'd receive crews to replace those lost in combat or which had completed their tours and gone home. Some came by sea and rail, but most flew in from the States with their shiny new planes and eager, shiny young faces. This was what they'd looked forward to, being a part of the 'big league' bombing Germany. They were mostly under 21, intelligent and in good physical condition.

Almost all were fresh out of transitional training school. The pilots seldom had more than a couple of hundred hours of flying time, and not much of that in the B-24 type aircraft they'd be flying in combat. This was not a reflection on the Training Command; they just didn't have the time to give the specialized training that each combat theater needed for its particular operating conditions. Nowhere stateside could you provide training for the weather conditions under which we operated. Even totally disallowing enemy reaction to our missions, the flights themselves were much longer in duration and more intricate than those the training bases could provide.

The replacement crew's initial meeting on base was with commanders and operations officers who welcomed them, gave them the 'big picture' of the war in Europe, and spoke to the importance of each individual and crew to the overall effort of defeating Hitler, etc. As commanders, we gave a brief overview of how our group operated in concert with other groups, wings, divisions, and the entire Eighth Air Force to achieve our two major objectives: put our bombs on the designated targets and to save our own skins, in order of importance.

We also gave out information they didn't like to hear. The airplanes which they brought to the base were no longer 'theirs,' but would be pooled with all other aircraft and assigned to crews for missions on an availability basis. Also, for the first couple of weeks they would be flying practice missions every day that weather allowed. When not on practice missions they would be spending time in flight trainers and classrooms, learning our particular ways of doing things on missions and on the ground.

It was difficult for them to appreciate that additional training was needed. They felt that as a crew leaving the States they had their fill of it and were a finished product, all set for combat. To emphasize the need for more training we gave examples of how the Herrenvolk across the water took exception to what we were doing and had developed some very imaginative, effective, and lethal deterrents. We impressed upon them that the effective performance of their mission required a high degree of individual and crew discipline, beyond the airplane-related skills they had acquired.

The average replacement had not been in service very long and had been subjected to rapid changes in his way of living and doing things. The metamorphosis began with induction and donning the military uniform. He lost his identity, looked like everyone else in uniform, and began to feel an alliance with them and a distance from the civilian ranks he'd just left. The military was a great common denominator—you couldn't tell from which side of the tracks the man in uniform had come, or whether he'd been silver-spooned, white collared, blue collared, or had no collar at all.

After basic military training and subsequent training in an MOS (military occupation specialty), he was assigned to a combat crew. The individual started to re-establish his personal identity, the crew developed some esprit de corps. This process continued at such a rate that by the time a crew was assigned to us, they felt that they were a part of the best of air forces, in its best wing, group and squadron, in which they were the best crew. They were quite satisfied with themselves atop their pyramid of personal presumptions. The pilots felt that they were at least as good as any, if not the best. Because many aspects of pilot skill were difficult to measure, that feeling was not easily disproven. Performances of bombardiers, navigators, and the rest of the crew were more measurable.

A lot of self-confidence—even some cockiness—was desirable in a new crew. It was bound to erode with successive missions, so it was helpful to have a high starting point, even if unwarranted. Everyone was chastened somewhat by combat. It showed in attitude and manner, even in the face. Comparison of photos taken upon completion of a crew's training at home with those taken upon completion of their overseas combat tour, never failed to show this effect.

We tried to impress upon them that the discipline we required did not equate with subservience. It was not un-American, and was the prime requisite for team action. Boys from the South and rural areas appeared to adapt to it more readily than Northerners, particularly those from big cities. The English seemed more amenable to military discipline than we, possibly because theirs was a more deferential society in which each recognized his 'station,' and was not bothered by the notion that others might be considered superior.

Evaluating replacement crews was an important and sometimes difficult job. The records and personnel jackets they brought with them indicated only the flight and ground training to which they had been exposed individually and as a crew. The information was all quantitative and did not contain any qualitative assessment of performance. It was up to us, in our 'in-theatre' pre-operational training program, to measure their proficiency and supplement the individual and crew skills as best we could in the limited time available.

Most crew proficiencies could be measured on the ground in tests and trainers, and in the air on practice missions. Successive tests of accuracy in navigation, bombing, firing, etc., could be charted to provide a reasonably accurate picture of capability. More difficult was the evaluation of piloting ability—not the mechanics of reading gauges and flipping switches, but the manipulation of flight controls and power settings for optimal efficiency and safety of the airplane. There were infinite shadings of performance between the pilot who could quickly and smoothly trim the controls to allow the plane to fly 'hands off,' and the 'driver' or 'throttle jockey' who was constantly sawing back and forth on the controls, expending more of the plane's fuel and his own energy than was needed to do the job. Because of the intangibility of this skill, it was not uncommon for two competent instructors to rate the same pilot differently.

The even more difficult aspect of piloting to measure was judgment. How well would a pilot decide whether to land or to go around, whether to bail out or attempt a dangerous landing? How easily would he panic? Some inkling could be gotten in air checks, but most answers came after pilots had faced tough situations and made decisions.

The single most important factor in air crew evaluation, as with any group or team effort, was the leadership quality of the pilot. In the air, he was both the pilot of the airplane and commander of the crew.

On the ground he was still the latter, a point lost on many young crews. A bomber crew, like a submarine or tank crew, was operating within the same little box. Usually what happened to one happened to all. Here rank had no privileges, just additional responsibilities. The crew had to respect the leader's ability, intelligence, and courage. They were operating in a split-second arena. When he said shoot, they had to shoot, and when he said jump, they had to jump. There was no time for conferences or persuasion. A good crew recognized that their informal and seemingly un-military relationship should exist only in flight. On the ground they were supposed to resume the traditional relationship and respect that went with their ranks and ratings. That is where too many crew commanders failed.

The new crews had been together throughout training, had become 'buddies' (good) and considered theirs to be the best crew in the Air Corps (also good), but some regarded the traditional officer/enlisted relationship of the military to be 'chicken.' (not good) This *Three Musketeer* attitude of "all for one and one for all" was great so long as there was a recognized and respected leader.

It was not difficult to distinguish between pilots who were crew commanders, and those who were just airplane drivers. Every group in England (and elsewhere I'm sure) had its own disheartening list of cases where crew failures, rather than equipment failure or enemy action, had cost lives needlessly. It was not difficult to spot a weak crew commander, even on the ground- a lack of respect and response from his crew, sometimes an un-neat appearance, sloppy salute, the 'Terry and the Pirates' slouch hat, the noisy wad of Wrigley's, etc. We busted more pilots to co-pilot for failure to exercise responsibility as a crew commanders than for lack of flying ability.

There was also a round of ground orientation programs to go through, assignment of quarters, familiarization with the base, air raid and blackout rules and procedures, etc. New arrivals had to have physicals at our base dispensary before lifting a plane off our runway. They had endured many in training, but ours had one extra step. After routine checking for cavities and gum problems, dental impressions were made. When most asked the reason for this new experience, our calloused dentist answered straight faced: "When a plane burns, the only parts of the body we can identify are the teeth—even the dog tags melt." Even the ruddiest of faces blanched a bit as they left the sardonic dentist's chair.

I deferred suggesting that he develop a less harsh stock answer. His accurate response triggered within new crews some sobering thoughts about the job that lay ahead; for the cocky ones at least, that was probably a good thing.

It didn't take long to lay out the strategic bombing concept under which we operated. It was the responsibility of the lead plane to find and drop its bombs on the target. Everyone else in the formation dropped or toggled out their bombs when he did. The leader hit or missed the target for everybody. The lead plane was flown by a lead crew, but was the responsibility of the command pilot who was aboard. We also spent some time on subjects with which they had not had any experience such as radar bombing and navigation, and enemy flak and fighters. More time was spent on communications and emergency procedures. The latter covered such subjects as bailing out, evasion, crash landing, and ditching.

We'd always considered 'hitting the silk' to be a frightening but nevertheless simple expedient. You cleared the plane and "pulled that string."

No need to practice; you did it right the first time or, as the paratroopers said, you'd be "jumping to a conclusion." Combat situations called for the 'delayed jump.' This was a bit of a misnomer; there was nothing delayed about the *jump*. The delay was in opening the chute, preferably at 10,000 feet or lower for several reasons. Most important, it avoided the dreaded danger of having burning fuel from your shot-up plane ignite your parachute. It was very sickening to watch full blown chutes catch fire then plummet to earth. By delaying, you got more quickly to a safe altitude for breathing, versus floating down under a chute from 22,000 feet, subject for several minutes to the dangers of anoxia. Another consideration when jumping from a plane doing 250 miles per hour: your body was traveling at that same speed and took quite a jolt when your chute opened. By waiting until your body decelerated to the free-fall speed of 120 miles per hour, you reduced the jolt to less than half. Other reasons for delaying were to get out of the flak zone and below the arena of German fighters. It was unlikely that they would chase a falling body down, but there were reports of their having attacked and set chutes afire with incendiary or tracer bullets. In spite of all those good reasons for delaying, when the time came, not many did. As soon as the plane was abandoned, panic set in and chutes blossomed immediately.[1]

A crash landing, including ditching, involved critical and irreversible decision making. Decisions had to be made intelligently and immediately. Unless the plane responded reasonably well to flight controls, it was wise to bail out. However, the natural reluctance to jumping caused many, to their later regret, to stay with planes which were not adequately maneuverable for a safe landing. Sometimes, having wounded aboard who couldn't jump or even be bailed out by other crew members, further complicated this hard decision.

In our anti-sub days we had learned that a B-24 did not crash-land well on any surface. The wing was strong, but the underside of the fuselage would tear apart upon impact. It would not skid far on the ground or plane well on water to allow gradual deceleration. The Lib came to a very abrupt stop, tearing itself up and beating up its occupants. At Langley Field, we witnessed a deliberate ditching of a B-24 on the James River. It showed that even under the ideal conditions of calm water with a a skilled pilot at the controls of a fully functioning aircraft, it broke apart and disappeared in less than thirty seconds. This was in sharp contrast to the B-17 with its strong semi monocoque fuselage construction and low wing, which could survive crash landings very well on any surface.

The RAF provided two crash-landing strips, for their use by night and ours by day. Both Manston Strip (in Kent) and Woodbridge (close to the Channel along the Suffolk coast) had over-long grass runways constructed on an incline. Landing uphill, your run or skid on the ground was shortened, and the grass eliminated the danger of runway sparks igniting fuel. Each was equipped with an abundance of fire-fighting equipment and 'meat wagons.'

A refresher course was given on the use of the oxygen and first aid equipment we carried on board our planes. Considerable time was devoted to evasion and escape in the event of being downed in enemy or occupied territory. Crew members would have evasion photos taken and be shown how to use the supplies they'd be given on a mission to avoid capture.

'Communications' was a major subject in our new crew indoctrination program. On a mission, radio was our invisible tie to the world outside. Within the plane the intercom system linked together the members of the crew. Most of the crew remained 'on intercom' throughout the mission. The radio operator would be on and off between intercom and his CW wireless link of coded messages with ground headquarters. The co-pilot stayed on the group channel for instructions from the group command pilot and relayed them to the pilot. The pilot stayed on intercom with his crew until the bomb run when he'd switch off with the co-pilot so he could give immediate response to the group leader's instructions.

Two points stressed during instruction on the use of intercom were voice recognition and oxygen checks. At our operating altitude, you could lose consciousness in less than a minute if your oxygen supply failed. It was the co-pilot's responsibility to run frequent oxygen checks with crew members who were not on the flight deck and within his sight. The quickest and easiest way to do this was to call "oxygen check" then name in sequence each position from tail to nose—"tail," "waist," "ball," etc. Each position responded simply by two clicks of his microphone button. A failure to respond from any position brought quick action from another crew member with a walk-around oxygen bottle, as it didn't take long to die of anoxia.

Voice recognition within a crew was important to crew performance, even survival. Crises called for *speedy* communication, not formal. It was not the Hollywood scenario of "Pilot from tail gunner, enemy fighters approaching my position, sir." A quick and anonymous "Bandits at six o'clock high" did the job. When the pilot called "bail out!" there was no need for verification. Everyone knew the voice.

To impress the importance of voice recognition on my group when we first arrived overseas, one instructor, a rather pompous lieutenant colonel from a senior group, gave an in-flight demonstration. He circled our base with one of our crews while the rest of us gathered around the tower to listen to a broadcast of their intercom conversation.   The crew flying with the instructor had a tail gunner, Sgt. Red Warren,[2] well known as one of our group's leading comic characters.   Our airborne instructor made some introductory remarks to the crew on the importance of voice recognition and gave some examples. He then said he would call upon each crew member to give, in turn, a one minute discourse on any subject so that the other crew members would become familiar with his voice. The whole exercise seemed a little ridiculous, but it was his show. He commenced with "Tail gunner, I want you to start." There was a long silence. "Tail gunner, did you hear me?" "Yes sir." "Well go ahead, say something!" Another pause, then "What'll I say, sir?" Impatiently, "Anything goddammit! Tell us the story of your life!!" The plane droned on... and finally Misty drawled "Well, Colonel, Sir, at the age of five, I had my first sexual encounter..."—not the exact words he used, but the assembly around the tower howled, and the WAAF tower operators tried to shrink into the woodwork, as Red made the demonstration memorable if not effective.

Controlling plane-to-plane transmissions was a major problem.   Counting just the division, wing, and group leaders there were about fifteen command pilots operating on many of the same channels. Unless all exercised considerable restraint, communications became chaotic. Add to that as many as five hundred planes in a division formation all sharing communication channels with other planes in the group and wing, and with escorting fighters and air/sea rescue service, and the enormity of the problem is evident.

There were numerous situations which justified breaking radio silence, during assembly in the dark or bad weather in the friendly skies over East Anglia, and certainly when under attack in the less friendly ones over the Continent.   But the strong temptation of an inexperienced pilot when he became confused, lost or just scared, to clutter the air with avoidable calls for assistance, needed to be suppressed.

As if we didn't have enough communications problems of our own doing, the Germans frequently joined in on our channels. They had quite a bag of tricks. In one instance they set up a navigational radio beacon in Holland with the same frequency and call signals as the homing beacon at our base in North Pickenham. One of our pilots, Capt. Bill Earlywine, lost in foul weather, in the dark and separated from the group, homed-in on our frequency, started a let-down procedure through the clouds, talked to the tower and was cleared for landing. When he broke through the base of the clouds and recognized it was not our base, he gunned his engines, pulled up his landing gear and flaps, and headed back up amid a hail of machine gun fire from the ground. We later pin-pointed that transmission to a field near Amsterdam. Their bogus tower operators all spoke very good 'American English.'

On another occasion while I was talking to a fighter escort leader about our rendezvous, a third party came in on the channel purporting to be another bomber command pilot in urgent need of assistance. He claimed to be under heavy fighter attack at a point some distance from where we were and wanted our fighter escort to break off his rendezvous with me and go to his aid. My fighter friend challenged the caller and asked him to verify with that day's code. When no answer was forthcoming, my fighter leader friend took off on the intruder with a tirade of GI and other expletives, finishing with an angry "Krauthead!"

Other orientation subjects did not involve airplanes or air operations. We were paid in English currency ("funny money"), and it took some time and patience to correlate dollars to pounds and mysterious fractions and multiples thereof. Many poker and craps games were blown wide open by the betting of some novice who hadn't yet learned that a pound note was worth more than four dollars at that time, that a five-pound note ("bed sheet") was closer to twenty five dollars than *five*. Only in Africa had we found money changing more confusing-dollars, pounds and francs were all legal tender. In our gambling there, as much time was spent arguing current rates of exchange as dealing the cards or rolling the bones.

The local public telephone system run by the GPO (Government Post Office) also required some education. After one deposited an assortment of strange coins into a noisy metal box, the operator would ask what number you wanted. If you were lucky, after a couple of minutes and a new variety of noises you might reach your party and start a conversation, whereupon the operator would come back on the line and ask "Are you through?". In 'Yank,' this meant "Are you through talking?" (The operator was asking whether your call had gone through to the intended party.) Upon hearing the GI's anxious "No," the operator would disconnect the call with a "Sorry, I'll try again." A few of repeat performances of this misunderstanding left most inclined to pull the phone from the wall and express some nasty thoughts about the GPO.

Most would also come to acquire a bicycle, the most common form of transport on and off the base. At Rackheath we had 300 government issued bikes and over 1400 privately owned ones. The bikes were all English and presented a new, dangerous experience for Americans familiar with rear wheel coaster brakes, and unfamiliar with handlebar mounted brakes. On at least one occasion, every GI squeezed the wrong hand brake, stopping the front wheel and propelling himself 'arse over teakettle' into a hedge-row or worse. Riding off-base on the left side of the road and in the dark didn't help.

Adding to the confusion, we still kept all traffic to the right side on base. The medics told us that bike accidents were responsible for more treatments at our base infirmary than any other type of accident or ailment.

Relationships with our English allies, military and civilian, were the subject of several lectures. An uninitiated GI turned loose off base could be a menace to himself as well as the natives. He had to be told and periodically reminded that almost everything was rationed—food was sparse, pubs could not serve an unlimited number of drinks, they had to reserve some of their ration for their local, long standing patrons, etc. Or that most households did not have the cars, appliances, and conveniences that we knew at home. That there really had been a war going on over here for a few years and that everything was in short supply, and that which was available was not always up to pre-war standards. That he was more highly paid than his RAF counterpart, and it had nothing to do with superior knowledge, ability, or performance. And that he should do nothing to swell the considerable number of locals who felt that we were "over-paid, over-sexed, and over here," or the lesser number who felt that a *German* invasion might have been preferable to the *American* one.

The off-base activities of our personnel gave our medics a number of concerns, among them the rather diverse subjects of dairy products and venereal disease. Since milk was not pasteurized in England, tuberculosis was a significant problem. We were ordered (not merely cautioned) to not consume dairy products off base. On base we had powdered milk. The dairy ban never became a problem, but VD did. The men were a long way from home, most for the first time, and would be exposed to pitfalls they had never experienced. Hometown inhibitions fell by the wayside around Picadilly Circus. For some, unlikelihood of being seen or caught had more to do with behavior than moral principle or rectitude. At home gonorrhea could be treated on an out-patient basis with sulfa drugs and supposedly cured in 24-36 hours. In England, the same bug was much more virulent and required a week to ten days of hospital treatment to effect the same cure. Despite the information, warnings, and threats given, enrollment in our "Poison Ivy Club" flourished and VD consumed a frustrating and disproportionate amount of administrative and medical time.

Finally, fully oriented crews got to a chance to fly. A couple of hours were given to local orientation flights to familiarize them with approaches to our base, our navigational aids, other bases in the area, off-limits air spaces, barrage balloon locations, etc. The local geography was so different from that of stateside training bases that it was very easy to become confused, even in broad daylight and under good visibility conditions. Then came the practice missions—as many as time would allow before we had to use them on missions.

During the course of its tour, members of a combat crew would see more action than they had ever experienced in their young lives, likely more than they would in the rest of their lives. They would also develop closer, deeper and more enduring relationships than they had known pre-war or would develop post-war. Just by virtue of 24-hour togetherness on a military base they came to knew each other very well. Flight activities intensified that camaraderie, particularly when mortal fear under combat situations stripped any layers of pretense shielding real selves from intrusive eyes.

1. For the record, my father never did have to jump, and was never wounded in his 35 missions and hundreds of additional operational hours related to training and formation duties. I pressed him once on the subject of 'accidents,' and he confessed to costing the taxpayer a single-seat training aircraft at Newark before the war, when he skidded off a iced and 'socked-in' runway. But he still never had a 'bad landing,' one that he did not walk away from.

The appendix contains a list of the various aircraft types he flew.

2. My father, ever modest, had used a fictitious name for Warren. I reveal his identity in hopes that his friends and family would take more pleasure than embarrassment from a corroboration of a funny irreverence. See the first footnote to JJM's Introduction and Dedication.

11. Helluva Welcome

On the day of the Bernburg mission when my squadron lost seven crews, Sergeant Ball, the Squadron First Sergeant, had to pick up all the non-coms he could find and quickly get to almost every hut in the Squadron's living area to secure the personal effects of the seventy missing crewmen. The processing of the their effects was so time consuming that we were only half finished when replacement crews started to arrive two days later. Because of the limited space within the huts, the footlockers, barracks bags, battle jackets, etc., were simply piled up at one end to make room for the new arrivals and their belongings.

Such was the case with hut #6, not very far from mine, where the officers of two of my original crews had been living until they were lost that day at Bernburg. Lt. Carl "Dusty" Rhoads and Lt. Joe Bates and their crews were both nearing the 25th mission mark and close to going home when they went down that day flying behind Lt. Bernie Harding. Both were very capable crews and a fine bunch of individuals who we had gotten to know rather well during our training period before coming overseas. That all of Dusty's crew were KIA was even sadder: of the ten crew members, seven had left pregnant wives when they came overseas. Appropriately enough, they had emblazoned "Pregnant Pappies" on the nose of their plane.

I never really had a chance to learn the names of the two replacement crews who arrived a couple of days later, because several days after their arrival we were called upon again for a maximum effort. Contrary to our usual practice, we had to send these new crews on a combat mission before their training was completed. Both were lost that day. We were then faced with the job of processing the effects of an additional two crews out of hut #6, which then became jammed with the personal effects of 16 officers.

The next day we received two more crews from the replacement depot.   When Major Dana Smith, my Squadron Executive Officer called to tell me that they had arrived and the only available space was hut #6, I instructed specifically that the belongings of the downed crews be either processed or moved out before the new crews were taken there.   Unfortunately, it didn't happen. Later that day when walking to my hut I saw Lt. Jimmy Cole, the Squadron Adjutant, leading these eight young officers of the replacement crews toward their new quarters. I went over to greet them and continued with them and Jimmy to hut #6.

One of the pilots was introduced to me as 2nd Lt. Denny Hudson,[1]   a tall and rangy boy with a slow Mississippi drawl. He looked a little older than his age as his hair had receded to midfield, and was getting thin all the way back to the end zone. He was eager, attentive and generally of the type to whom people react favorably even at first meeting. We talked briefly as we approached the hut. Our conversation was terminated abruptly when we pushed open the door and I saw that none of the effects of the previous two sets of crews had been processed or moved. It was too late to do anything about it. We were already in and the young eager-beavers were looking for places to drop their belongings and lay claim to a cot.

All belongings of the two most recently lost crews were as they had left them. Beds were made, foot lockers closed, barracks bags underneath, gas masks at the head, etc. Those of Dusty and the previously lost ones were piled rather messily at one end of the hut. The new crews assumed that we had taken them to the wrong hut. Rather than waiting for a question, I informed them that what they saw on and around the cots belonged to the crews they were replacing. They had gone down the day before and we hadn't had time to take care of their things. This announcement pretty much wiped from their faces the eager expressions of a few moments earlier.

Things were somber enough when Hudson's curiosity got the better of him and he asked the unwanted question about the ownership of the belongings at the far end of the hut. There was no point in evading the issue, so I rather matter-of-factly responded that those were the property of the second previous occupants who had "had it" a few days earlier. They had lost their eager expressions before, and now lost some color, too.

Some time later, over a drink at the Officers' Club bar, Denny confided that it had come to be an apt 'welcome,' and his unforgettable first impression of the hard-luck 492nd.

1. My father had used a fictitious name for Hudson, for reasons unclear. See the first footnote to JJM's Introduction and Dedication.

12. Gilbert Baker

One day while scanning the personnel records of some incoming replacement crews, my attention was drawn to the rank, age, and background of one of the pilots. Gilbert Baker[1] was in his late twenties, a lawyer, and a 1st lieutenant. All of our replacement crew pilots had been coming in as 2nd lieutenants, typically twenty years old or younger. Baker had been a practicing attorney when war broke out, and as a result of ROTC training in undergraduate school, was called to active duty with ground forces. After about a year of service, he transferred to the Air Corps when accepted for flight training. Our experience with older officers going through flight training in-grade had been disappointing, consequently we were a little apprehensive about receiving them. Unbeknownst to him, Gilbert Baker had one strike against him, and he hadn't even been up to bat.

When the new crews were brought to my office for introduction and Baker removed his hat, I was reminded of the old adage, "When he checked his hat, he checked his youth." It had covered much more skin than hair. It shouldn't have, but it made me a little more concerned about the ability of this older-appearing young man to handle the job we had in store for him. But that initial meeting ended with brownie points for Baker. Reserved and quiet but not shy, he was obviously intelligent. On subsequent occasions when I saw him with his crew, I was very favorably impressed by the ease with which he handled them and the obvious respect they had for him—not the type that comes from the rank worn on the shoulder, but from recognition of demonstrated leadership qualities. This was the only kind of leadership that stood up when somebody was shooting at you.

After this batch of crews had received indoctrination training, on the ground and in the air, Baker and his crew received highest grades in every category. This was all the more remarkable because he had to overcome the same misgivings amongst the trainers as I had held. After five or six combat missions flying wing positions, he was stood down for training as a lead crew. Completing that, he was assigned to fly squadron deputy leads, then squadron leads. Again, all reports on his performance were highly favorable.

One Sunday in the late Spring of '44, under our command pilot rotation system, it came my turn to lead the group. The target was an aircraft assembly plant in France, south of Fontainebleau.[2] Although the mission could not be characterized as a pure 'milk run' because of the distance and long flight-time over enemy-held territory, we didn't expect it would be very difficult; not in the same category as a mission of equal length into Germany. At the group operations officer's suggestion, we gave Baker his first group lead.[3] I watched him and his crew closely through the pre-briefing for lead crews, the main briefing for all crews, and the special briefing for pilots. Again I was impressed by the questions asked by him and his crew and their understanding of their assignment.

Takeoff and assembly went routinely. The mission was a little unusual in that it was all daylight from takeoff to landing. The cloudless, crystal clear weather throughout was also unusual. We exited the UK at Beachy Head, flew down across the Channel, and had a magnificent view of the French countryside, including Paris in the distance. We chugged along all the way to the target without a smidgen of enemy interference. The target was readily visible, the bombardier picked it up, took over the plane and made an excellent drop. As we headed home, I couldn't help but feel that things had been going too well on this beautiful Sunday afternoon ride. Our presence was certainly known, we still had a long ride back over France, and I couldn't believe we'd continue unchallenged much longer. Since our route did not take us over any major cities, we wouldn't be drawing fire from any heavy fixed-emplacement anti-aircraft guns. I was expecting fire from the 88s of German ground forces. These versatile artillery pieces could shoot at ground targets or be elevated to shoot at us. Also, I was very much aware that our course took us well within the range of the 'Abbeville Kids'—a very accomplished Luftwaffe fighter group based in France.[4]

Finally we did receive a few bursts of light flak. It didn't last long, and nobody was knocked down or seriously hurt. All was quiet for a long period again. When the coastline came into sight and it looked as though we were home free, a shell ripped up through the floor of the flight deck, out the top of the plane, and exploded some distance above. In the total confusion, it took a few moments to figure out exactly what had happened. Ruptured skin of the plane flapped loudly around the holes created by the shell coming through the underside and exiting above. A noisy tornado of all the dust and dirt accumulated in that plane since it left the assembly plant swirled maps, papers, flight plans and shredded insulation. In sorting things out, I ascertained first that the engines were running well and the props were still synchronized. We hadn't lost any power yet. The plane was flying straight and level, and the flight controls were responding properly. Then I looked over to Baker. His chin was on his chest, which was covered with blood. His visual oxygen indicator was not blinking—he was not breathing. I leaned over the controls pedestal to get a better look at his condition, and then came to a full realization as to what had happened. When the projectile came up though the bottom of the plane, it passed between Baker's feet on the rudder pedals, between his knees, struck him below the breast bone, went out his back just below the neck, through the seat back, out the top of the plane, then exploded somewhere above. Some of the fragments showered down on us. The top turret gunner caught a couple of little ones, and the plane quite a few more. The gunner was not seriously hurt, but Baker was obviously gone.

I could have easily put my fist through the hole in his chest. Because of the very frigid temperature at our altitude, his blood soon congealed and almost stopped flowing. There was nothing that could be done for Baker, and the navigator and radio operator were administering to the gunner on the flight deck, so I got back to the pressing business of flying the plane. Baker's shoulder harness kept him from falling forward over the controls, and we decided to leave him there until we landed.

Since we knew the plane had received a number of noisy hits from the explosion of the shell, I was expecting problems might develop with the plane and advised my deputy to be prepared to take over if they should. Although the gunner didn't appear to be in serious trouble, he was hurting, uncomfortable, cold, and a bit frightened. I decided to start an early, faster and steeper let-down than called for in the flight plan to accelerate our arrival home and treatment for the gunner. When we reached lower altitudes, as expected, Baker started to thaw out and resume some bleeding. The plane, to my continuing surprise and relief performed perfectly for the rest of the flight.

When we examined the plane on the ground, we found that indeed it was an 88mm shell that went through us. It must have been time-fused to detonate at a predetermined interval after being fired. Luckily for us, that interval expired somewhere above us. Had it been impact-fused, or proximity-fused it would have exploded inside the plane and taken us all down.

When something dramatic and

shocking happened, people usually reacted quickly, with fear displacing panic, so long as the action was still going on. Later, during a quiet after-the-fact mental review of the incident, a fuller appreciation of what had happened could cause jitters which would have been a problem during the actual incident. That night (and a few times since) I 'replayed' this mission and wondered: why Baker, not me? Did that shell have his name on it from the day it was made? It traveled up through more than four miles of space being buffeted and slightly deflected by differing winds at intervening elevations—did it just happen to be nudged four feet to the right and find Baker's middle instead of mine? Four feet the other way, and Baker would be telling this story. This, of course, was a frustrating and useless exercise which had to be dismissed with acknowledgment of the simple fact that he's dead and I'm alive. I never will know why, so to hell with it!

1. This is one of my father's 'made up' names, although I suspect that it was used because JJM was not sure that he recalled the real name correctly, not because anything more serious than this man's pre-mature balding is discussed. On his key to fictitious names, paired with "Gilbert Baker" is "Donald Miller?" (Question mark *his*.)   See the first footnote to JJM's Introduction and Dedication.

2. This May 21, 1944 mission was considered an Operation CROSSBOW strike against aircraft production.

3. To clarify: My father was in the role of *Group Lead Commander* for this mission, having operational charge for the planes from the 492nd BG which operated within the 14th Wing, within the 2nd Air Division on this mission, and Baker's specially trained 'lead crew' was the one carrying him. Lead crew navigators and bombardiers were followed by the other planes in their group, unless the leader became disabled. at which time the *deputy* group lead commander, in the plane of the *deputy* lead crew, would take over.

The deputy would be flying in the same leading three-plane element, slightly behind, higher, and just to the leader's right. This deputy-leader hierarchy was reduplicated at each organizational level in the bomber formation, from squadron to division.

In this episode, my father acting as group lead commander is obviously 'flying right seat,' displacing the normal co-pilot of Baker's crew. The strident controversy around this practice is discussed at length in Chapter 15, 'The Indestructibles.'

4. JG (Jagdgeschweder) 26, known as the 'Abbeville Kids,' flew Focke-Wulf 190s and covered the Pas de Calais region and coastal Belgian airspace from their base 10 miles inland from the Channel and 130 miles SE of Dover They were resourceful and inventive adversaries, developing aggressive tactics to engage attacking bombers and their fighter escort, but their 'time was up' in the Spring of 1944 as direct combat attrition strategic targeting of aircraft manufacture and fuel targets began to pay off.

13. Deadstick

Radar was not entirely new to us. We had had some experience with a different application of it when flying anti-sub patrol trying to detect U-boats along the East Coast early in the war. Radar for high altitude bombing had been long talked about, but we'd not seen any equipment. The time did arrive when we were told to select some experienced crews to send for radar-bombing training. As was frequently the case in the military, a request to select personnel for permanent transfer was looked upon as an opportunity to unload dead wood. In my squadron we were fortunate in not having any problem crews, so I sent two very good ones, both led by captains. In the other squadrons we did have a couple of crews we wouldn't be unhappy about losing.

The pilot of one of these crews was our oldest. He had been a 1st lieutenant in the artillery, gone through flying school, served in a variety of assignments in the training command, was promoted to Captain, went through B-24 transition school, picked up a crew and was sent to us. Warren Gould[1] was a very fine officer, but, based on the couple of times I had ridden with him, his reaction time as a pilot was slower than it should have been. I felt he knew what to do, but was very lackadaisical about doing it.

Some weeks later, after Gould and the other crews had been radar-trained, they were sent to our 14th Wing headquarters station at Shipdham with their new radar-equipped planes. There they would be available to the three groups of the wing to serve as lead crews for radar bombing missions and ones where the uncertainty of target weather made it advisable to provide for such a contingency. These crews had been enlarged by the addition of a radar bombardier and a radar navigator. These radar specialists were referred to as 'Mickey'

bombardiers, and 'Mickey' navigators. Their equipment
was called PFF—the acronym derived from RAF Pathfinder
Force missions.

This augmentation of the crew, and
the addition of their specialized equipment caused
overcrowding and some dislocation of crew positions
within the plane. It also added considerable weight which
sometimes necessitated a reduction of bomb load in these
lead planes to keep gross weight within safe operating
limits. The size and mix of the PFF lead crew could vary
with the requirements of the mission. The most complex
situation was when a hoped-for visual target had a better
than even chance of becoming cloud-obscured by the time
we got there. Allowing for both contingencies meant we
flew: a pilotage navigator in the nose turret (replacing a
gunner); a visual bombardier over the bombsight in the
nose; on the flight deck, the lead crew pilot, the command
pilot replacing the co-pilot, a Mickey navigator and
bombardier; and the usual enlisted crew members at other
stations.

Such was the case one day in the
late Spring of '44. Under our command pilot rotation
schedule, it was my turn for the next group lead, so that
evening when the teletype started its ominous clattering of
the field order, the briefing officer and I were called to
the communications center. The target was oil, this time it
was in the Hamburg/Harburg area. Our mission
preparation activities were running smoothly when we
received word that weather was moving in from the North
Sea toward the target area. This put a hold on the visual
bombing plan, and division was faced with a decision as to
whether the mission should be scrubbed or we should
attempt radar bombing. Because of the large bodies of
water near the target, it should present a good image on the
radar screen, and by stretching out the intervalometer
setting for the bombs, we could cover a larger area with
them and stand a better chance of some finding their mark.

When it was decided that the mission would go 'visual,' but with radar backup, I was driven to Shipdham to fly my first lead on a PFF mission. I was almost looking forward to this new experience until I found out the crew assigned me was Capt. Gould's! I felt that I had drawn the short straw on this one and was becoming somewhat apprehensive about our chances for complete success. It was unlikely that a couple of weeks of technical training in radar bombing would have corrected the deficiencies I had seen in this crew their newly acquired Mickey specialists were both very impressive. The special briefing for lead crews, and the regular briefing of all crews went off smoothly. We were driven out to our shiny new bird full of equipment I'd never seen before. I watched with interest and increasing confidence as the Mickey boys pre-flighted their equipment.

Because of the length of our mission, the field order called for our 'Tokyo tanks' to be filled. These were internal wing tanks out near the tips, holding about 225 gallons each. The standard procedure when using these tanks was to run on main tanks for a couple of hours then transfer the Tokyo fuel to the main tanks with electrically driven pumps. There was no way of gravity feeding fuel from those tanks to the engines, or to the mains. It was the responsibility of the flight engineer to watch fuel levels and accomplish this transfer at the appropriate time.

Despite my earlier misgivings, the first phases of our mission went very smoothly. We made our takeoff, climb to altitude, group assembly, wing assembly, and DAL, all right on schedule. Our first leg was on a northeasterly heading over the North Sea which roughly paralleled the German coastline until we neared the German fortified island of Helgoland. We then turned southerly along the shipping channel leading to our target, visible in the distance. Only scattered clouds lay in our path. We had successfully avoided the barge-based flak installations offshore, but after landfall started receiving heavy land-based flak, and had to run the gauntlet to the target with no chance to take evasive action. A gaggle of Jerries was high above and ahead waiting their turn to welcome us to the Fatherland. As we closed toward the target, the intensity of alternate flak and fighter attacks increased. For some welcome reason, our Group was not receiving its fair share of enemy attention. Fighters were pounding particularly hard on the lead group of our wing, and heavy flak appeared to be taking a heavy toll on the trailing group. We were sandwiched in between.

With our bomb bay doors open and about twenty seconds from release time our virginal status was abruptly and loudly terminated by a near direct hit under our right wing. Gould was quite shaken and was letting our plane start to veer sharply off course. I had to get on the controls quickly to get us back on course and regroup the formation for the drop. It was too late to turn the lead over to the deputy. We were able to hold position until 'bombs away,' then gave way to our deputy and dropped out of formation. Number four engine was sputtering, complaining bitterly of some internal injury, but didn't quit altogether.[2] Number three was knocked out completely and a few small flames started licking out from under the cowl flaps. Luckily, by slipping the plane hard away from the fire, we were able to blow it out, then feather the windmilling prop to cut down on the drag it created. Gould reached for the feathering button on number four also, as it was vibrating a little. I knocked his hand away as I felt that with a reduced power setting we could get some good out of this engine, which we did. His was the training school reaction; feather a balky engine immediately to save it and bring it home for repair. The combat philosophy was to use the engine for all you can get out of it or there may not be a tomorrow to save it for. Probably many crews were lost which shouldn't have been when inexperienced pilots feathered engines that still had a lot of power and flight time to contribute.

As we dropped lower and farther behind the bomber stream we picked up some light flak. We took another hit on the left side which cost us some power in number two engine. The tail section took a burst which I could feel on the controls and the tail gunner

Remnants of MacArthur's fiery crash on outskirts of Norwich; no survivors

received some light wounds from it—a waist gunner helped him out of the turret and administered first aid. We established a gradual descent to maintain minimal flying speed, and disregarding the briefed exit route which would have avoided some flak areas that lay ahead, we set a direct course for home over some of those areas, hoping the flak batteries wouldn't be interested in a single cripple which had already bombed and probably wouldn't make it home anyway. Our biggest concerns at that point were remaining airborne and avoiding the Luftwaffe.

Fortunately, the Jerries didn't spot us, or if they did,were so busy with our outgoing bomber stream way above and ahead of us, that they elected to not take time out to come down and jump us. After a while we had our sorely crippled big bird settled down to a fairly steady level of performance. Engine #3 was out and feathered, #2 and #4 were giving somewhat reduced power, and #1 was groaning at a slightly elevated power setting to offset somewhat the shortfall of the other three. All told, they were probably giving us about 60 percent of normal power. We were at a minimum safe glide speed and a tolerable altitude loss rate. If everything would stay the way it was, we figured we could make it home. We did have some other problems, but none of them flight-threatening. We could see gashes in the wings which might effect our stalling speed when landing. The oxygen system in the rear of the plane was out, but the gunners were managing with walk-around bottles until we could descend to 10,000 feet. The tail gunner was now out of pain with the couple of syrettes of morphine that had been jabbed into him.

We had lost some electrical power which didn't appear to present any insurmountable problems, but we lost some hydraulic power also, and that could cause big problems for landing. We hoped we had enough pressure left in the accumulator to put down some wing flaps, and for a few applications of brakes after touchdown. The key factor in all our decisions now was the amount of fuel we had left. This didn't appear to be a problem. We figured we had plenty, even at the inefficient rate at which we were now forced to use it.

Sometime after we had departed the Continent, and were on our way over the North Sea, the very nervous flight engineer confessed that he had 'forgotten' to transfer the fuel from the Tokyos to the main tanks! Now, without electrical power, he was unable to do so. This really darkened picture. There was now a very real question as to whether we could make the English Coast. We quickly reviewed the factors leading to our original decision to try to make it home, and nervously stuck with it. In this reassessment, the inaccuracy of our fuel gauges was the most disturbing element. The consideration of our injured gunner, now deep in the arms of Morpheus, was also a factor.

Committed to a nerve-wracking flight across that frigid water, we lightened our load by tossing overboard everything loose and non-essential and broke radio silence to inform various folk back home of our predicament. We told division we were still airborne and alone, asked the dependable British Air/Sea Rescue to try to get and keep a fix on us in the event that we required their services, and notified the British coastal defenders to check their nervous trigger fingers; we'd be coming in low, late and alone, and hoped not to be mistaken for an intruder or a buzz-bomb.

We then settled down to tedious scrutiny of gauges and straining of ears to engine sounds. Those highly inaccurate fuel gauges drew the lion's share of attention and prayers. The crew made another check for damage. We had received considerable flak and in all likelihood there was more damage than we had discovered in our earlier excitement. Despite the number of holes in the wing and fuselage, there didn't appear to be any structural damage and the control surfaces were functioning normally. We didn't have electricity, but there was no need for heated suits now. Everyone was in a nervous sweat. The senses became unusually keen and over-reactive. The slightest bounce in a little rough air, and you were sure a piece of wing or tail had just fallen off. A minor sputter or pop of an engine sounded like a major explosion. The tiniest wiggle of an instrument needle out of the green (safe) zone was certainly an omen of disaster. When not focused in the cockpit, all eyes strained for a glimpse of the coast at Great Yarmouth. You had done all you could do to stay airborne, now all you could do was sweat it out and pray. Not that prayer was always the last resort, but the tangibles of staying airborne did take precedence.   When it did come to praying, it was more considered and meaningful than the habitual recitation by rote in church. The words were given thought, and all of a sudden there was a fearful realization that "...now and at the hour of our death" might be one and the same time, and imminent.

When the coast finally came into view, we had about 3,000 feet of altitude with engines running pretty much as they were when we left Germany. By the time we actually made landfall, #2 was giving about 60 percent power,' #4 about a third of its power and throwing some oil, and old faithful #1 was still putting out 110 percent. #3 of course, was still feathered. We called Shipdham to give our position and condition.   They suggested we head for the RAF emergency field at Woodbridge, especially equipped for crash landings. When I told them I doubted our fuel would get us there, they reluctantly OK'd a direct approach and landing at Shipdham.   They would ready the fire engines and meat wagons. There would be no traffic problem, as everyone else who was going to make it home from the mission already had.

About a half mile from the field we shook our wheels down, were able to get a little flap down, and were feeling somewhat encouraged about our prospects for living, when old faithful #1 started to sputter—a clear signal that it was running out of fuel. At that point we were committed to landing—there were no alternatives. We were too low to bail out. Gould became so unnerved he was more of a hindrance than a help. Earlier we had to crank in a lot of aileron and rudder trim tabs to help offset our uneven power condition in flight. Now, with virtually no power, and in a glide, the tabs were working heavily against manual control of the plane. I asked him to return the tabs to neutral, but he didn't react. Fortunately, the flight engineer responded quickly and took a heavy load off of the controls. The two partially powered engines also started coughing as we came 'over the fence.' For the last several seconds of flight we were totally without power, but fortunately in a good landing attitude; my first deadstick landing of a multi-engined airplane.

Before having time to heave a sigh of relief, we were treated to our final two surprises of the day. We had almost no brakes, and a flat tire! We feared we might not have much hydraulic pressure for braking, but had hoped we'd have more than the two brief applications we had. The flat was a complete shock, but may have been a blessing in disguise. Without it, with no brakes and no engine power, we'd not be able to intentionally ground-loop to stay within the confines of the field and would go whistling through the end of the runway to God knows where. The wobbling of the strut with the flat tire slowed us down, then collapsed, and the wing tip caught the ground and put us into a fairly flat, slow ground loop off the runway and onto the grass.

When the violent motions and crunching of metal subsided there was a momentary eerie silence. Dust shaken form obscure niches around the flight deck filled the air. Then the silence was broken as the contorted airframe started popping rivets with the sound of a BB gun. That prompted recovery from a momentary stunned condition. Everyone bolted for the nearest exit, driven by the constant fear of fire. All got out under their own power excepting the semi-conscious gunner. Another plus for the flattened position of our plane: it was easier to pass him out the waist window directly into the ambulance. A quick check revealed the landing had caused no further personal injuries, but Uncle Sam's shiny new radar plane was in need of major repair.

---

1. 'Gould' is one of the fictitious names used by my father. See first footnote to JJM's Introduction and Dedication.

2. Then and now, engines are numbered from pilot's left-to-right. WW II heavy bombers needed virtually *all* of their power to get airborne and to keep in formation, but could maintain level flight with about 70% of that. Altitude was money in the bank in situations where there was substantial power loss; putting the plane into a glide converted the potential energy of mass at one height into faster moving mass at a lower height. This is critical, because a plane stalls when it does not maintain enough airspeed over the lifting and control surfaces.

A knocked-out engine was a double liability: it went from being capable of contributing up to a third of the energy needed for safe flight, to being a 1,400 lb. burden on the remaining engines.

The ability to 'feather' the blades of a propeller, or turn them so that they knife fairly straight into the windstream, was very critical when an engine shut down. Unfeathered propellers generated tremendous drag on the plane as they converted the substantial force of the air striking their angled blades into turning force on the dead engine, which would 'windmill' and vibrate dangerously.

The pitch of the blades is controlled by hydraulically or electrically driven mechanisms in the hub. Its failure would prevent feathering, but could also result in the equally hazardous 'run-away engine' situation, where a low angle of attack on the blades in high speed air would make the engine over-rev, but not contribute useful power to flight. Spinning engines which exceed their 'red line' (maximum allowable revolutions per minute) have stressed parts and are inclined to fly apart.

Situations where most of the power comes from one side of the plane are extremely dangerous, and only the luckiest of dumb pilots from those days lived to tell about it if he 'turned into a stalled engine.'

14. Simpson's Crew

Bob Simpson[1] was an experienced pilots who came to us from a B-24 transitional training school where he had been an instructor. He was a captain, and had well over a thousand hours of flying time. He was also a very nice guy, possibly so much of one that he was not effective in establishing much discipline in his crew. On a number of occasions he was called on by his squadron CO for less than satisfactory performance. With his experience, Bob should have been a lead crew pilot. He was given a try at it, but didn't make the grade.

Simpson's crew went through its missions as a wing crew rather uneventfully, seldom getting into serious trouble, but never excelling. They were always there with their bombs, and in position. They were a lucky crew, never having had any damage to crew members and very little to the planes in which they flew. When they needed only one more mission to complete their combat tour, as was our unpublicized custom, we held off scheduling them until we were given a mission which we felt was well within the 'milk run' category. We didn't like to lose a crew anytime, and went extra length to avoid losing one on its last mission.

Because the completion of a tour was such a disappointingly infrequent event, it called for some celebrating. It usually involved official greeting upon return by the group or even wing commander, extra rations of scotch at interrogation, possibly a cake in the mess hall, a pass off base, etc. The crew usually arranged a celebration for themselves also, and if they overstayed their pass a little, official notice was not taken.

Aerial celebration of this occasion was also inherited from our senior brethren, the RAF. On returning from its final mission, an RAF crew buzzed its base, fired flares, and raised merry hell in the air and on the ground afterwards. Many 8th Air Force units picked up, and some amplified this custom.

After a couple of potentially dangerous incidents at our base, we published strict prohibitions against the aerial antics. We found that flares fired from low altitudes would reach the ground still burning and could set fire to a farmer's field, or worse, his thatched roof. But in anticipation of their aerial show, crews would still procure extra flare guns and flares surreptitiously, and instead of just firing out of the planes flare-gun port, would hand-hold the guns and fire out of waist windows, top hatch, bomb bay, etc. Hand held, a flare gun was difficult to control, especially in the hands of the uninitiated. It packed much more of a wallop than a .45 automatic.[2] Also, pilots trying to impress fellow pilots and others on the ground would sometimes exceed their own ability or that of the plane, which was not designed for aerobatics, and get into severe trouble.

On the day of Bob Simpson's last mission, after the briefing, a special point was made by his CO of reminding him that there was to be no horsing around upon return to base. Once they had their feet on the ground, they could do as they pleased and would be headed back in the States in a few days. He heard, but apparently didn't listen. Later that day when the tower received radio notification from the group command pilot that they were making landfall at Great Yarmouth, he added that Simpson was safely in the formation and was about to complete his tour. A couple of minutes later the group started its landing procedure over the base. When Simpson's turn came, he peeled off from the formation but instead of entering the traffic pattern, disappeared low over the horizon. No one was surprised: that was typical Simpson. He was planning to "beat up" on the base, put on a real "buzz job."

At least he waited until the other planes had landed and he had the full attention of all. Then, just clearing the trees, came screaming (as much as a Liberator could scream) across the field right in front of the control tower, pulled up into a chandelle and treated all to some admittedly very capable, but risky handling of a B-24. He concluded his show circling low over the field with flares firing from every opening in the plane. It was a colorful performance, confirming what was known all along, that Simpson could really fly a B-24 but was short on judgment. The show commanded the attention of everyone on and near the base, and was thoroughly enjoyed by all except for the 'brass' on the upper deck of the control tower. Suddenly a fire broke out in the bomb bay area and the plane exploded in a huge flash. That really got the attention of everyone, and spoiled the whole show.

As was surmised, and later determined, one of the exuberant crewmen fired a flare from too deep within the plane and missed a waist window. The flare probably ricocheted around and touched off a fuel tank. So this joyful celebration, in defiance of rules, became the funeral pyre of ten good men for whom this mission became their last, in more than the intended sense.

A lapse in crew discipline became its total undoing. It was a very compelling lesson for the crews and all watching. Nobody had to say "I told you so." Simpson said it for all.

---

1. This was not the individual's real name. See the first footnote to JJM's Introduction and Dedication.

2. The uninitiated should understand that the kick from a .45 is fairly substantial to begin with. Flare guns were also called VERY pistols.

15. the Indestructibles

   If you had asked our original
492nd crews to name those among us most likely to survive
the war, after his own name most would have listed Captain
John W. Smith and Lt. Col. John I. Turnbull. All who knew
them well 'knew' them to be indestructible. Both very
intelligent, each had attained prominence in sports, great
skill in his military specialty, and the high regard of
those serving with them. Both were lost on relatively easy
missions after surviving many difficult ones. Both of their
planes crashed in Belgium.

   Like every other outfit, we had our
share of Smiths. In just the officer ranks of my squadron
alone, we had a Dana, a Bill, a Herschel. When "Smitty"
was called out, John W., my squadron navigator, was the
least likely intended.

   He had been a high school chum of
movie star Van Johnson in Newport, Rhode Island. He was
graduated from Springfield College with a degree in
physical education, where he achieved acclaim in weight-
lifting, wrestling, and squash. With all of his physical
attributes, he was also unusually handsome. He was one of
those rare sorts—very much a man's man, and despite his
studied aloofness, a ladies' man. To the slight discomfort
of Smitty and the total annoyance of his wife, girls
swarmed about him

   After college, Smitty joined the
Air Corps and went to flying school. He didn't make it as a
pilot, but was kept on for training as a navigator. At that
time, lacking facilities of its own to train navigators, the
Air Corps sent them to a school in Miami run by Pan
American Airlines, where they trained navigators for
overseas flying boat service. Upon completion of that

course, he spent some time as a navigator on Pan Am overseas flights. He'd already had considerable experience when he was assigned to my crew as an navigator for long range anti-submarine patrol in early 1943. He did his job so easily and quickly that at the outset I put little confidence in the information he provided. But over time, his almost unfailing accuracy made me to accept Smitty's way of performing his job; he spent most of his air time either reading or dozing between calls for position checks and new headings. Once we were asked to rendezvous northeast of Bermuda with a large convoy heading for North Africa. We arrived at the coordinates given to us by the Navy convoy commander, and could see nothing. Smitty assured me that we were at the right spot. We circled for a while and finally called the naval escort for a position check. They gave us a radio signal on which we homed-in to their position—about thirty miles distant. Smitty was furious when I suggested that with his little sextant he couldn't expect to be a match for the octants and other sophisticated navigational gear on those ships below. At his insistence, and for the sake of my crew integrity, I called the escort commander saying almost apologetically, "My navigator has your position as - - -, and not as given to us." This was followed by a very long silence, during which I was fearful that one of those destroyers or DEs below might open up on us. Finally, their very curt vindication for Smitty: "Your navigator is correct."

When I was given a squadron, I chose Smitty to be my Squadron Navigator. His ability was soon recognized by all in the group. When it came time to start our long trek overseas via South America and North Africa, I wanted Smitty steering my course, but so did Lew Adams, our Deputy Group CO. He pulled his rank and had Smitty aboard his ship for that long flight. Their total elapsed flying time from Herington, Kansas. to West Palm Beach, Brazil, Dakar in Africa, and up to the final destination at North Pickenham, England, was almost two hours shorter than the next best time among the other 69 planes making the same trip. That was not due to higher power settings or superior piloting, but Smitty's navigational expertise.

Smitty's skills were not limited to the sextant, protractor, and other tools of his trade. He was a superb pilotage navigator. This is simply a matter of being able to locate yourself by visual reference to the ground—no instruments involved, just your eyes and a map. Sadly, this was not a common talent among navigators or flying personnel generally. Over England and the Continent, too many places looked alike from five miles up. The ability to identify your position exactly by reference to topical features was crucial to the performance of a visual bombing mission.

The 492nd Bomb Group's first mission was to Mulhouse, a small French town close to the Swiss border. It was a long haul to a tiny target. Our Group CO Gene Snavely, flying as command pilot, selected Smitty as navigator to help ensure a successful combat debut for the group. Our Wing Commander, General Leon Johnson attended our briefing, gave an appropriate welcome to our joining the war effort, and a warm send-off on our first mission. Being the newest group in the wing, we were assigned to the 'Tail-end Charley' position, following the other two groups. With the mission well underway and nearing the target area, Smitty advised Gene that the wing leader was slipping well off the briefed course and would have to make a substantial correction to make our approach as briefed. Gene relayed that information to the wing command pilot who, after consulting his own and the other group's lead navigator, insisted that he was on course. Soon thereafter, the wing leader fired his IP flares and opened bomb bay doors. Smitty protested vigorously that they had gone by the target by about thirty miles and were very close to Switzerland. Gene was in a real bind. He'd be in for a roasting if, on our first mission he failed to follow the wing lead and it proved to be right. He decided to follow the other two groups, but nervously held his bombs when they dropped theirs. After turning away from the target to the RP, with Smitty's help, he selected a target of opportunity, left the wing formation, bombed it, and came home alone. He had to get rid of that weighty bomb load if they were to have enough fuel to get home safely.

The radioed strike report received at wing headquarters from the 492nd was quite different from those of the two senior groups. The General hurried back to our base, prepared to deliver a hot reception to complement the warm send-off he'd given earlier that day. At the interrogation room, Gene and Smitty were besieged by a horde of disbelievers as Smitty pointed confidently to a small town on the map, asserting that that was where the two other Groups had laid their eggs, not Mulhouse.[1] After a tortuous half hour, General Johnson was called to the phone to learn that strike photos from the other two groups verified Smitty's assessment exactly. A little icing on our cake: our strike photos showed a fair placement of bombs on a railroad marshaling yard in France, and some on a farmer's field.

Smitty, so unique in his many positive attributes, was fittingly singular in a deficiency, evidenced on his first rough mission. A heavy dose of flak induced sudden and severe incontinence! It happened on several subsequent tough sorties. This was an agonizing as well as embarrassing experience, impossible to counter in flight or hide on return to the ground. We dubbed him our "flakometer;" it got so that we could measure the degree of difficulty of a mission by the severity of Smitty's waddle away from the plane after landing. This physical reaction, over which he had no control, happened once when he was on a mission with me. He never panicked or seemed more frightened than the rest of us. After a hard mission, it could provide some welcome comic relief, to which Smitty became resigned, even good natured.

In addition to being squadron navigator, Smitty accepted my assignment to an but essential non-military role, squadron bouncer. A non-drinker, he could always be relied upon to be in good shape during the most raucous of Officers' Club affairs. He also enjoyed the respect of all for being a great guy as well as an excellent physical specimen. One would have to be thoroughly drunk, quite stupid, or both to challenge him to a physical contest. On those occasions someone might take a larger sip than he could handle, and get out of line and become obnoxious. Rather than summon the OD (Officer of the Day) or the MPs and make a sticky situation nasty, I would ask Smitty to quietly remove the individual from the club and take him to his quarters. He did this unobtrusively, with ease, and with muscle only when required. Only once do I recall a truant having the poor judgment to return to the club after Smitty had deposited him in his quarters. This offender did it twice. When he resisted the third assist to his quarters, Smitty picked him up by the seat of his trousers and the back of his collar, walked him out the door, lifted him to a full press and tossed him a considerable distance into the bushes. There was no third return.

We lost Smitty over Belgium in the Fall of '44. He was riding as pilotage navigator in the nose turret of the lead plane. The plane hit the ground at a steep angle, was crushed and buried, but did not burn. Some American troops arriving at the scene found the other crew members' bodies, but not Smitty's. Belgians who had witnessed the crash didn't see any parachutes or crash survivors. Other crews who had watched the plane go spinning down felt sure that no one bailed out. Smitty was initially listed as MIA but later as 'presumed dead.'

Our other 'indestructible' was just as interesting as Smitty, if more widely known. The 492nd, was the direct descendant of the 104th Observation Squadron, Maryland Air National Guard. From shortly after WW I until just before our entry into WW II, the 104th had been a rather exclusive military flying club for Baltimoreans. From the time of its induction into Federal Service in mid 1941 until it ultimately became the 492nd Bombardment Group (H), it underwent many changes of station, organization, personnel, assignment, and equipment. By the time we went overseas in early '44, the only officer remaining from the Baltimore squadron days was pilot Jack Turnbull.

Jack was a well known sports figure in Maryland and beyond. In the 1930s he was an outstanding football and lacrosse player at The Johns Hopkins University. A member of the U.S. Olympic teams in 1932 and in 1936, many consider him one of the best lacrosse players this country has ever produced. After a U.S. victory at the Berlin Olympics, he was invited to Hitler's box and witnessed first-hand the dictator's infamous snubbing of Jesse Owens. Jack once mused, over our warm beer in a cold Nissen hut, "I could have reached over and strangled that sonovabich then, and we wouldn't be here now!" Well, at least Jack wouldn't have been.

Jack was not tall, but very sturdily built, strong as the proverbial ox. His features were consistent with his frame, square and rugged. He was good-looking with straight black hair, brown eyes, and a swarthy complexion. He was an engineering honors graduate, and a very able long time pilot. With all he had going for him, it was surprising that Jack, who was eight years my senior, had been able to retain his bachelorhood.

When we went overseas Jack was Group Operations Officer, and I was one of the four Squadron Commanders, one step below Jack. We were good friends and constantly needling each other. He was sure that during my "Civil War" and his "War between the States," some of his ancestors had done in some of mine.

To him I was an "Irish Mick" and to me he was "Johnny Bull Turnbull." When we learned that we were headed for England, he went on ad nauseam about the opportunities I would have to observe how a really intelligent and cultured people behaved and lived. After we got there, he was the first to complain about the GPO phone service, the poor roads, the time it took to get things done, the lackadaisical attitude of the people, etc. After being there a couple of weeks we took a two day pass and headed for London. In the train compartment with us was a local public school headmaster. Jack proceeded to give him a very hard time about the way things were and how they had deteriorated since he was last there in the thirties. I found myself siding with the headmaster and later chided Jack about our inverted Anglophile and -phobe roles.

We also had a couple of disagreements about operations. As our original experienced pilots were lost in combat or finished a tour and were replaced by greener ones, I felt that we could no longer expect the discipline in aerial formations to which we had become accustomed, picture-perfect tight from start to finish on every mission. Jack disagreed and drove hard to maintain our earlier standard. I agreed our planes had to be in tight over the target for a good bomb drop, and reasonably so in anticipation of turns to keep them from spreading all over the sky, but felt it was unreasonable to expect these young pilots to maintain a tight 'air show' formation throughout the mission. In the course of trying to do so, their constant throttle-jockeying used up too much fuel and really whipped around the poor devils at the outermost positions of the formation. By the time they did get to the target they could be exhausted enough to find it tight grouping elusive, just when it was really needed. There were many other pros and cons on the subject. A tighter formation provided a better concentration of firepower against attacking aircraft, but it also provided a more concentrated target for them and flak guns. I had seen Jerries attacking head-on, fish-tailing the rudder and spraying their bullets as they passed through a tight formation, presuming that they could get more than one. A plane that got hit and exploded in a tight formation increased the danger of taking others down with it.

During the brief interval between our arrival in England and becoming operational, we had occasion to fly with and learn from a couple of experienced Groups. We found out that even in such a well developed military machine as the Eighth Air Force, there were unresolved procedural questions. One was the seemingly simple question: where should the command pilot, responsible for the mission, ride in the lead airplane? Jack and I joined this debate on opposite sides.

Some groups had the command pilot *displace* the co-pilot and ride in the right seat. Others felt the command pilot should be an *addition* to the crew and improvised a seat for him on the flight deck between the pilot and co-pilot. When it came time for our group to establish a policy, Jack agreed with them, arguing that you'd damage the integrity of the crew, its team spirit, by dropping the co-pilot. Pilots depended on the assistance of the co-pilot, especially during takeoffs and landings, and command pilots had competing important business. Lead crews themselves were strongly opposed to displacing co-pilots, as were some of our senior people.

I led the opposition, equal in number but lighter in rank, which favored dropping the co-pilots. We dismissed the spirit and morale claims as emotional, overblown, and having very low priority in the purpose and performance of the mission. As for pilot assistance during takeoffs and landings, those were the times when the command pilot had fewest duties and could lend a hand—one invariably more experienced than that of any co-pilot. Once in formation, the lead crew pilot had it easier than any other; he could set up his automatic pilot and let it take over the flying of the plane. The poor wing-position pilots had to fly manually, jockeying throttles and controls to stay in formation, especially in turns, all the while getting bounced around in propwash and trying to see through contrails.

Sitting between and behind the pilot and co-pilot on an improvised seat, a command pilot's visibility was severely limited. He could only view an eye-level narrow band straight ahead. He had no view above, where most fighter attacks came from, none below for navigational reference. He could see hardly any of the planes in his own formation. A command pilot, by virtue of his rank and experience, was the most capable pilot on board, yet his 'sling' position gave him no access to flight controls in the event of an emergency, no direct way to correct errors of the lead pilots who, though relatively able, were still mostly young and inexperienced. The command pilot's two VHF radio command sets were beyond easy reach; one of the pilots had to change channels for him. Riding on an improvised, uncomfortable seat in very cramped quarters didn't make his already difficult job any easier. This additional body on the flight deck interfered with the functions of others and impaired the chances of all for a quick emergency exit. Further, I objected in principle to carrying more people on a mission than absolutely required for its performance. It meant risking another life needlessly, carrying extra weight, using more of the limited supply of oxygen, and required the installation of additional hookups for oxygen, heated suit, and communications not provided for in the plane's design. We didn't need any more weight. As it was, we were taking off with more than the design load for the plane, on runways shorter than called for, too often in marginal weather.

My contingent lost the argument. Snavely decided that we would fly the command pilots as excess baggage, allowing lead crew co-pilots to occupy their usual seats. In our lead airplanes we installed wide web belts between the backs of the pilot and copilot seats. The belt was about six inches wide with snap buckles at both ends. Once the pilots were seated, the belt was snapped in position trapping them there. The "monkey swing" as I dubbed it had no back, no safety belt. The slightest motion of the plane set it swinging.

I made a few missions this way and griped more loudly about it each time. Some others joined the cause. My last time flying group lead from the monkey swing may have influenced Gene's subsequent decision to let the individual bomb squadron's commander decide, and almost won some empathy from Jack.

I was riding the monkey swing, flying a group lead. We were in a target area and getting some flak. The co-pilot of the lead crew with whom I was flying tapped my headset, signaling me to switch to interphone so that he could talk to me. He told me very excitedly that our deputy leader (on the right wing) was on fire and was not leaving the formation. Because the B-24 had such a nasty habit of blowing up when on fire, we had a rule that a burning plane was to leave the formation immediately; if you did blow up you wouldn't take a couple of neighboring planes down with you. Our deputy may have hoped to put out the fire out and feared leaving the protection of the formation from the Jerries which were gathering above and ahead of us.

From my position on the swing I couldn't see any of this. I had to half-stand and lean over the control pedestal in order to look out the co-pilot's window and survey the situation. The deputy was badly on fire; it was not just an engine fire. Flames were coming out of the trailing edge and a fuel tank was likely to become involved.[2] I tried to raise the deputy on the radio without success. He was undoubtedly preoccupied with his problem and talking with his crew on interphone, and nobody was guarding our group frequency. He finally looked over and responded to my frantic signals for him to get away from the formation He was a few hundred feet below and off to our right when he blew up in a ball of fire. The blast threw us into a steep bank and I was thrown from my awkward position into the co-pilot's lap. As I tried to scramble back to my swing, another louder and closer explosion occurred. Something had torn a hole in us and the flight deck became engulfed in a torrent of flying debris and dust. When I tried to back into my swing I went head over heels backward into the well below the flight deck at the entrance to the bomb bay. I was shaken by the unexpected fall, which tangled and disconnected my headset, electric suit and microphone wires, and my oxygen line. The alert radio operator slipped down from his seat, connected a walk-around oxygen bottle to my mask, and helped me back up to the flight deck. It became apparent that a large piece of flak had come up through the plane cutting my swing neatly in half, and gone out through the top. I covered the hole in the flight deck with a flak suit, and knelt or sat on it for the rest of the flight to block out the frigid blast.

                    Adding to our confusion, some B-17s a few thousand feet above had gotten us between them and their target and were dropping their bombs through our formation. Luckily, with what the Germans had going for us already, nobody got hit from above. While we were getting flak, they were under fighter attack. We saw a couple of their planes go down, and their falling debris came uncomfortably close. One of their airmen who had fallen or bailed out, bounced off the top of our plane near the co-pilot's head with a sickening thud, then just brushed against our right vertical stabilizer before hurtling earthward. Our tail gunner never saw the hoped-for chute. We hoped he was making a delayed opening, but inwardly knew he had had it when he struck us. Stomachs drew up tight as we vicariously shared that poor guy's plummet to mother earth—every airman's silent fear.

All of this happened in a few short
minutes on the bomb run. We managed a good drop and

Lt. Col. Jack Turnbull

made it home without further damage to our airplane or
underwear. At the hardstand we checked the flight path of
the flak that severed my swing. Had I not been called upon
to leave my seat to look at our deputy, I would have been
the recipient of the grandest goose of all time.

Jack persisted in riding between the seats on the swing rather than displace the lead crew co-pilot.   Later, after the beleaguered 492nd was disbanded, Jack and I went to different groups. He became Operations Officer of the 44th Bomb Group, one of the oldest groups in the Eighth.[3]   Whenever we met at divisional meetings or Officers' Club gatherings we continued to needle each other on this subject, each insisting that the other's way of riding command pilot would one day be his undoing. Little did I realize how sadly right I would be.

Returning from a mission to Germany in August '44, Jack was leading his group when they encountered a high thin layer of clouds over Belgium. Rather than go around or above it, they opted to go through it. When they came out the other side, the formation was intact except for the leader. No one knows how or why, but in the cloud, Jack's pilot apparently fell into a spin. Jack was heard on the radio telling the pilot to "Get on the needle and ball!" They spun in and all were lost. Had Jack been in the co-pilot's seat where he could have taken over the controls, it's highly unlikely a spin would ever have happened in the first place, and if it did, with 20,000 feet under him, I'm certain that Jack could have recovered from it.[4]

It was a helluva way to win a point and lose such a good friend and nine others in the process. It seemed such an ignominious death for a man who had accomplished so much. Like Smitty, Jack proved to be not indestructible after all; we took our costly mortals' lesson bitterly.

---

1. Readers are referred to 'Neutrality' and Internment in the Apocrypha section of this book, and The Day We Bombed Switzerland for further accounts of gross navigational errors and their consequences; see Bibliography.

2. Piston driven aircraft use extremely volatile aviation gasoline, many orders more combustible than the heavier grade fuels used in turboprops and jets. A nearly-empty gas tank was especially dangerous owing to vapors. A leaking fuel line could convert the fuselage of a plane into potent bomb, easily touched off by tracer bullet, cannon shell, flak fragment or errant spark.

In the bomb bay of the B-24, amidships under the structurally critical wing spar, were myriad fuel-containing gauges, lines, valves and transfer pumps. The flight engineer used these to keep the plane balanced and to compensate for an infinitude of possible battle and mechanical damage scenarios involving multiple fuel tanks and four engines. This area was also the locus of the very flammable hydraulic oil swirl-tank/accumulator and several high pressure oxygen tanks and lines.

Armor plate, for all of its weight, was used sparingly to protect *some* crew positions from attacks at *some* angles, but most of the plane, and all of the bomb bay, had only a single skin of thin-gauge aluminum. Aircrew veterans and unforgettable photographic records attest to the the extreme vulnerability of the Liberator to conflagration or explosion.

Just sitting at its hardstand, no enemy shooting at it, empty of bombs or bullets, a WW II bomber had terrific explosive potential.

Warfare accelerates the development of materials and technologies. Self-sealing tanks became highly refined in the bloody and fiery crucible of WW II combat.

3. Colonel Snavely and Major Adams also went to Shipdam with five lead crews, all continuing the same work in the 44th Bomb Group.

4. "Get on the needle and ball" is old-school lingo for *Look at and trust your instruments,* specifically the turn-and-bank indicator, and the air speed indicator. The 'needle and ball' guided a pilot through a 'well coordinated turn,' one in which the amount of rudder was appropriate for the speed and banking of the plane. A mismatch can lead to 'slipping' (toward the side where there is insufficient rudder for the banking) or 'skidding' (if there is not enough bank to 'carve' the turn called for by the rudder).

Spatial disorientation in the absence of visible horizon or ground points, as when flying in cloud or darkness, is the norm. Yet the human inclination to 'trust the seat of one's pants' prevails and costs lives. The 1999 loss of John Kennedy, Jr., in a light aircraft he was piloting near Nantucket, has been attributed to his relative inexperience with instrument flying in conditions—fog and dusk—which required it. While instrument failure is not unheard of, old pilots get to be that way by overcoming the strong urge to trust their body sense over instrument indications.

The Liberator was a very unforgiving plane, especially with regard to stalling, and it took very little to put it into a flat spin. It seems that in cloud the pilot of that lead plane was not attentive to the instruments in the first place, then not skilled enough to use them to break the spin which resulted.

Every man I have met who knew Jack Turnbull *lionized* the man, and I am certain that no other personal wartime loss affected my father as much. While very few mortals could have recovered a B-24 from a spin, I knew my father to be an unerring judge of ability and character. When he says Jack Turnbull could have saved that crew, I believe it.

16. St. Lô Road

When Allied ground troops pushed away from the Normandy beaches in June '44, their first real barrier was the St. Lô road. The Germans were well entrenched on the south side of the road and our advance came to a halt. It was then that the Eighth was called upon for its first major ground support mission.[1] The road was to be our aiming point, and our bombs were to trail from the German frontline positions there back to the reserve and artillery positions behind. Instead of our wings flying in trail in the usual division assembly, they would fly with their groups abreast, covering a much wider area and all hitting the road simultaneously.

The ground forces had asked that we not use our larger bombs as they might create craters which would impede the progress of our advancing tanks. They also emphasized that even though our aiming point was 'the road,' their artillery would shoot up to our altitude a line of red star shells paralleling the road, and we were not to release a bomb until we crossed that red star line. We had some misgivings about those restrictions, but it was their show and we were glad to oblige.

I had our group lead that day. We were assigned a spot on the extreme right of the line, closest to the town of St. Lo. We approached and passed our aiming point and were still far short of the line of red star shells we could see up ahead. We held our bombs until we crossed that line. We knew that they would hit the ground many miles beyond the road, and probably assist some French farmers with their Spring plowing. For those of us to cross the line first, it was a milk run—not a fighter or single burst of flak in sight. For those coming later, German ground forces had time to elevate their 88s, give them a heavy dose of flak, and do considerable damage.

        This was a debacle in every way. Our ground forces, in nervous anticipation of our bombing, had pulled a long way back from the road. The Germans, remembering what Napoleon had said about never losing contact with the enemy, followed our troops' pullback with an advance of their own, crossing the road in force, and leaving our target area pretty much uninhabited. Our drop did little harm to the enemy, we missed our mark, and our bombs were too small. We learned later that bigger bombs were much more effective against well entrenched positions.

        One bomber outfit near the end of the procession of planes, dropped short, and killed a number of our troops, including General Leslie McNair. There were rumors, but I never heard an official report as to whether this drop was made by some heavy bombers from the Eighth, or some mediums from the Ninth Air Force. Reportedly what happened was that when the bomb bay doors were opened, a plane's bombs accidentally released. Because this inexplicable electrical glitch sometimes occurred at altitude, our group had anticipated the possibility and opened our doors over the Channel before making landfall at Normandy.

1. Diversion of the heavy bombers from strategic bombing, which happen almost continuously once allied troops invaded northern Europe, made the analysis of the effectiveness of the strategic bombing doctrine a forever muddled exercise.

        While medium bombers and attack bombers were proven effective at more 'surgical' (tactical) work, such as close support of ground troops and taking out bridges, fast-paced modern war often calls for a 'whatever it takes' reaction to changing needs, and for the use of specialized personnel and equipment in roles for which they were neither well prepared nor best used. In rare moments, when forgetting the greater objective of winning the war quickly and with minimum loss is forgotten, academicians, military theorists and armchair generals still wonder if 'their' side in the 'effectiveness' argument would have been conclusively proven, had the heavies never been distracted by having to bomb hedgerows, drop relief supplies, or ferry gasoline. But the men who put their shoulder to these various wheels then, and most latter day analysts now, accept that diversion of the strategic air arm for other tasks, if costly and imperfectly efficient, was necessary in most cases.

17. Sergeant Benson

Another of my squadron's original crews was that of Capt. Carl Johnson.[1] Carl was another of the B-24 instructor pilots sent to us at Alamogordo. His was one of our better lead crews—very talented in all positions. Of the enlisted crewmen, two were particularly interesting. Sgt. Anderson, the radio operator was about eighteen years old and could send and receive coded messages faster than anyone we had ever tested. He was also gifted with a unique memory. Usually, filling out the plane's log (Form 1) was the duty of the co-pilot. This was not difficult, but it was an annoying chore requiring among other things, the listing of the name, rank, and serial number of everyone on board. Anderson did this very easily, as he had memorized all of this information for the ten crew members, as well as any command pilot who had ever ridden with them. The other was one of the waist gunners of this crew, who eventually complicated many of our lives in the process of ruining his own.

Benson[2] was the classic young farm boy from a small mid-western town, who could handle a gun but not the pitfalls of big city life—especially London. He was a good soldier, so quiet and retiring that he gave the impression of being shy. With the waist gun he was quite another person. He loved to handle that weapon.

I flew overseas with this crew, flew my first command pilot mission with them, and more missions with them than any other lead crew. On one mission with Johnson's crew, I was riding the right seat, having displaced the co-pilot, and the mission was relatively uneventful until a couple of minutes after we made our drop. Without the usual warning of a few bursts of flak at a distance, we were hit with a sudden barrage of very accurate heavy-caliber flak. Large red flashes and oily black puffs of smoke were all around, the closest ones

buffeting the plane and showering it with fragments.
After a particularly heavy bump and simultaneous tinny
sounds of flak piercing our plane's skin, the other waist
gunner called on the interphone to say that Sgt. Benson had
been hit, was lying down conscious, and didn't seem to be
in great pain. I told him to take care of him as best he
could until things quieted down, then someone would come
back and give him a hand. Soon after we ran out of the
flak, and started our scheduled let-down en route home, I
transferred my oxygen mask to a walk-around oxygen
bottle and crawled back through the bomb bay to take a
look at Benson. The tail gunner and other waist gunner
were crouched over him and worried because he was now
showing pain and blood was starting to flow from his
wound. They had administered to him very well, making
sure he stayed on oxygen, covering him as best they could
after his electrically heated suit had shorted out, and had
placed a tourniquet above the nasty looking wound on the
front of his right thigh. The bleeding was now becoming
more profuse as we let down and the temperature
moderated. I injected him with a syrette of morphine, and
decided to cut some of the clothing debris away from the
wound and apply a clean bandage. When the getting-
groggy Benson saw my trusty six inch switch-blade, he
protested vigorously, thinking I was about to amputate. I
sprinkled sulfanilamide powder into the wound, applied a
new compress, and redid the tourniquet as prescribed by
Doc Spivak in our every-rainy-day first aid training
sessions.

                    Upon return to base, we fired our
red flares which secured priority for us in landing, and
taxied to the nearest hardstand where a 'meat wagon' was
standing by. We transferred Benson to their care and
returned our slightly beat-up plane to its regularly
assigned hardstand. I felt quite pleased with my medical
performance and may have momentarily fantasized I
should have continued my pre-med studies. All I needed
was Spivvy's grudging approval of my doctoring. When he
returned from our station infirmary he reported that

Benson's wound was moderately serious, but expected he would be back on duty in a couple of weeks. Then he asked of me "How many of my first aid classes have you attended?" "Too many," I cracked. "Then how come you put the compress on upside down?" They were clearly marked: "Put opposite side against wound."

I was again flying with Johnson's crew over northern Germany, Benson back on duty, when a most unusual situation developed. I had heard rare reports of a German fighter slipping into the middle of a bomber formation in broad daylight—presumably to radio our exact altitude down to flak batteries, and possibly to gather some other intelligence. They were known to do this quite often in darkness when our planes were returning. On several occasions, they managed to slip into a formation and escape radar detection passing over the English coast, then jump our planes when they turned on their lights to land.

In broad daylight, this stunt can be pulled off in or near clouds and when the attention of crew members is focused on action in the opposite direction. Despite our persistent training and insistence that every man cover his zone in the sky, the curious eyes of all crew members tended to go where the action was. The Luftwaffe frequently staged major distractions on one side of the formation so that they could launch an attack unnoticed from the opposite side, or as in this case, slip an interloper in for a few seconds then split-S out without attracting a shot. Even if detected while there, he could position himself in such a way that any bomber gun aiming at him would find one of our own bombers just beyond in the same line of fire. This made the 'bandit' almost impervious to attack when positioned properly in a tight formation.

This day I had been looking left

(apparently everyone else had also) at some twin-engined German planes launching rockets at us, a very attention-getting scene. I just happened to glance to the right, and with the grand-daddy of all double-takes, found a F-W 190 sitting just behind the trailing edge of our right wing! I could see the pilot clearly, looking right at us. Benson spotted him from his waist position at the same time, and screamed "Bandit!" over the interphone. Because of the way this cool Kraut had sandwiched himself between us and our planes off the right wing, Benson couldn't shoot without endangering them. Since the Jerry was on my side of the plane, I took the controls from Johnson, and told Benson to take aim and when I called "fire," let him have it. With that I jerked back hard on the wheel causing us to rise sharply, then shoved hard forward dropping us suddenly back into formation. The German came up with us but was a little slow in reacting to the downward lurch and was left momentarily sitting up in the breeze all by his lonesome. I yelled and Benson fired a couple dozen slugs into the 190's fuselage —mostly in the cockpit area. The head of the pilot tilted down and his body slumped to one side, but his plane continued on.

It became apparent that this clever little maneuver solved one problem, but may have begotten a worse one! We then had on our hands, or more properly, our wing, an uncontrolled plane which with slight deviation in any direction but down could chew up one or more planes with its prop. Fortunately, the 190 started to veer slightly down and to the right, so that putting our formation into a gentle left turn we were able to distance ourselves from it. Gunners reported the fighter continued downward in a long and tightening spiral.

While there was some satisfaction in our handling of this unique episode, there wasn't much feeling of elation with the outcome. Our war had always been remote. From four miles up we dropped our bombs and wrought massive damage to property, and undoubtedly took many lives. We had seen many of our own die, but this was the first time we had seen, face-to-face, an enemy die. Our reactions to this were mixed, and would be difficult to describe, but were more on the somber than the happy side.

Benson had been very much in control of himself and his weapon, and executed beautifully this spur-of-the-moment maneuver. He had performed as well on several prior occasions and I believe had more fighter claims than any other gunner in the group. This was particularly noteworthy inasmuch as he was operating a single hand-held waist gun whereas most gunners were in power-operated turrets with twin fifties. On our recommendation Benson was awarded the Air Medal for this performance.

Not much later, Johnson's crew had a weekend pass. At check-in time Sunday evening, Benson was among the missing. Generally when a crew went on pass the enlisted crew members stuck pretty much together, and it was seldom that one got far out of range of the others. When Benson hadn't appeared by Tuesday, we called together Johnson's enlisted crew and told them that unless he were back by midnight he would be facing serious charges. A couple of the boys felt they could find him if they were given permission to go to London.

Our little farm boy had found himself (or been found by) a 'Picadilly Commando' and had discovered that there was more to life in the UK than shooting at German airplanes. He liked it so much better that he wasn't about to return to base. By the time his fellows found him, his money had run out along with his girl friend, or vice versa, which helped them to get him home before the deadline. We let him off the hook that time with strong words of fatherly and military advice, and warned him that should there be a next time, the results would be quite different. He had leaned on his good record as far as he could.

As feared, Benson turned in a repeat performance the next time the Johnson crew had leave. Again, fellow crew members picked him up and returned him forcibly. This time I yanked his stripes. I warned that this was the last time I would cover up for him, and if there were a next time he would face a court-martial over which we would have no control, and he could wind up with a stiff sentence. He appeared to be genuinely repentant and vowed it wouldn't happen again, but it did.

The next time he disappeared for such a long time he was no longer considered AWOL, but eligible for a charge of desertion. This time his buddies couldn't find him and it was some weeks before the MPs picked him up in London after he had again run out of money, and consequently, 'Commandos.' This time it was a court martial at division. I knew some of the officers who served on the court, so my testimony about his background, youth, and combat record may have had some favorable impact on the court. He got off lightly with six months in the guard house, loss of pay, and further reduction in rank to private. He realized he could have been sent to federal prison, and was grateful to those who appeared on his behalf. Maybe his gratitude and remorse were genuine at the time, but I felt that he was a Picadilly recidivist. His fellow crewmen begged, warned, and threatened him to serve out his sentence with good behavior. He tearfully gave them assurance that he would do so, get back his stripes, and return to combat status.

He wasn't in the guardhouse more than a couple of weeks when he disappeared from a work detail. We knew he would be headed back to London, without funds, and might try to contact some of the crew men for money. We warned them to not become involved and let the MPs know in the event. I wouldn't be surprised to learn that Benson did contact some of them. And while they didn't turn him in, I feel sure they didn't offer him any assistance. We all felt that our farm boy had let us down badly. We had gone out on a limb for him, and he had sawed it off.

Benson had become involved in black marketing or some sort of illicit activities to keep himself in funds, and was eventually he was picked up by the MPs in London. We understood they sent him away for a federal trial; we never heard any more of poor Benson.

1. My father had used a fictitious name here and for Sgt. Anderson, only to disguise somewhat the identity of this chapter's namesake. Closer reading of JJM's writing, however, makes clear the identity of the crew with which he crossed the Atlantic on the way to England, so I dispense with the device here.

2. A fictitious name. See first footnote to JJM's Introduction and Dedication.

18. General Johnson

Upon arriving overseas, the 492nd Bombardment Group (H) was assigned to the 14th Wing, of the 2nd Air division, of the 8th Air Force. The other two bomb groups in the wing were the 44th and the 392nd. The stations of the three groups were only a few miles apart, and the Wing Headquarters was at Shipdham, also the location of the 44th Group.

Brigadier General Leon W. Johnson was the Wing Commander.[1] In appearance and especially in manner, he would seem to fit more the stereotype of a college professor than that of an Air Force general. He was a good looking man of average size with a single distinguishing feature: a well trimmed mustache. His manner was pleasant, serious, and quiet. I never heard him raise his voice or become excited, even when conditions warranted it. Only once did I hear him give commands to a large military assembly. They were impressive, but still seemed to come from an unlikely source. This mild-mannered and surprising gentleman wore our country's highest military award, The Congressional Medal of Honor, for his leadership in the first attack on the Ploesti Oil Fields.

When we had wing operational staff meetings, recent missions were critiqued in detail, and the command pilots of those missions were called upon to describe the mission performance and respond to questions and criticisms. These sessions could get pretty warm, for example when someone felt the wing had been led poorly, or one group claimed interference by another, etc. When the problems of a mission had been particularly severe, the command pilot would be asked in advance to bring with him his lead crew officers for a complete 're-flying' of the mission. For the crew, this could be a lengthy and agonizing procedure. This was not an academic exercise, but a real post-mortem. When soneone felt that crews had been lost due to faulty leadership, the session could get rough.

The purpose of these critiques was, of course, to learn in the face of changing enemy counter actions. Decisions were made regarding assembly procedures, entry and exit routes for various parts of the Continent, formation changes against fighter attacks, etc. With this procedure, every mission could contribute something to the more effective performance of succeeding ones. It was a never-ending adapting and learning process. General Johnson chaired these sessions and did a skillful job of eliciting important information and screening out the superfluous. He kept discussion in the objective, contained tempers, and provided an atmosphere in which junior officers could challenge actions of their seniors without fear of recrimination.

After some of these meetings, the General would invite us to his quarters for a drink or two before returning to our bases. At one of these, I happened to comment on his extensive library, quite unexpected in a combat zone. I was to regret that comment later. He took that as indicative of a great interest in literature on my part, far greater than was the case. On that occasion and a few others, he gave to me a recently received book and asked that I give him a book report at the next meeting to see if it was worth his reading. This made another dent in what little free time I had, and cut into my Black-Jack table time at the Officers' Club.

Like the rest of us, the General lived in rather bleak and spartan quarters, and hadn't done much to dress up or luxuriate them. Other than his shelves of books he appeared to be enjoying only one small privilege—he had chickens! Because the only eggs we saw were not in shells, but powdered and not very appetizing in any form, the old-fashioned egg was a rare and highly prized commodity. He had a coop in back of his quarters with a few hens. His orderly fed them scraps from the mess hall and they were reasonably productive. When he had a good harvest on hand, we might come away from our meetings with one or two. These were more highly prized than the couple of belts of the General's better grade scotch.

One night very late after an Officers' Club party at Shipdam, a couple of friends from the General's staff and I got to thinking how good those

In his time at North Pickenham, Jim Mahoney passed countless times under this tree to his office in the Headquarters site, one of the few structures still standing. This is the location to which his son Brian was strangely drawn in June of 1999 before he knew what he was seeing.

eggs would taste in those wee hours. The more we talked, the more we convinced ourselves that raiding the General's ice box, while not advisable, probably would not be a death-by-firing-squad offense. After determining that the General was asleep and his orderly not around, we relieved his ice box of many of its eggs. We bound to secrecy (and a small share of the loot) the cook who prepared for us a sumptuous feast of scrambled real eggs, toast and ersatz bacon. We were never sure whether or not the General was aware of the theft, as he did not make any inquiries.

Before becoming the commanding officer of the 492nd, Gene Snavely had been a staff officer for General Johnson. When we arrived at our base at North Pickenham, the General spent a great deal of time with us during our pre-combat training period. He was also there to greet returning crews from our first several missions, concerned and puzzled as the rest of us when our losses started to mount. When it was finally decided to remove the 492nd from combat operations after intolerable losses, that decision hit him as hard as those of us in the group. He was visibly moved when he had to convey to us that decision from higher headquarters. He assured us that this decision had been made in light of circumstances beyond our control and the inexplicable loss rate we suffered in no way reflected on the ability or courage of our crews.

Even after we were disbanded and I had taken the newer of our remaining crews with me to the 467th Bomb Group at Rackheath in another wing, General Johnson's interest stayed with us. Whenever we met, he went out of his way to inquire about the later fortunes of the 492nd's crews and rehash the muddle and mystery of that ill-fated group.

I had great respect for the General as a man and as a commander. Much of what he taught served well not only in war, but also since.[2] One day when he learned that I hadn't been on pass for quite a while, he suggested I take a week at a 'flak shack.' I protested that I was not 'flak-happy,' and had too much to do on the base running my squadron. He insisted and said that two important factors in considering the performance of a unit commander were the function of his unit in his absence, and his training of a successor. Possibly a coincidence, but shortly after my return from leave he approved a combat promotion for me.

1. Johnson showed early leadership promise and went over to England as a member of the initial star studded 8th AF staff that included Timberlake, Spaatz and Eaker. As a Colonel leading the first operational B-24 group in England, the 44th ('Flying Eightballs'), he took through the hell of Ploesti in August 1943, earning him the Medal of Honor. When he became 14th combat Wing Commander in the fall of that year his group already had a reputation for bad luck, which some felt became the inheritance of two other groups in that command: the 392nd, and later the 492nd.

2. There is much evidence of mutual warm regard. Clippings in my father's album, 'Overseas I: North Pickenham,' followed Johnson's distinguished postwar career, entailing many major commands and distinctions.

It would seem that he was a 'man among men' type of leader; bigger than life yet approachable, blessed with 'the common touch,' and a role model for one admiring young lieutenant colonel, among many others. He died in 1997 at age 93.

19. Spivvy

Captain Seymour E. Spivak, M.D., had been with us since early anti-submarine days. He was an Elizabeth N.J. native, went to Rutgers and did his medical schooling, internship, and residency in New York City. Early in the war, Uncle Sam called and he was sent to Flight Surgeons' School at Brooks Field, Texas. From there he was assigned to us at Langley Field. Being only a few years older than other squadron staffers and gregarious by nature, he very easily and quickly became 'one of the boys.' He was equally comfortable with all ranks and ratings, and they were with him. He picked up the GI lexicon with ease and used it fluently, capable of going longer than most without a repeat.

In order to maintain his flight surgeon rating and receive flight pay, like all rated personnel, he had to put in four hours of flying time each month. A white knuckle flyer, this was the least favorite part of Spivvy's job. When we had B-25s in earlier anti-sub days, some of the pilots would 'wring it out' a little to tease Spivvy and cause him to blanche and sweat. He felt more comfortable with the B-24s for which such antics were prohibited and also inadvisable. After the first of each month he would start checking flight schedules at Squadron Operations for a local flight of four hours, and certainly no longer; under ideal (CAVU) weather conditions, in a non-war-weary airplane, with an able, and preferably senior pilot. It usually took a combination of several flights to satisfy his rigid requirements. Once the four hours were logged, Spivvy relaxed for the rest of the month.

Like most of us, Spivvy spent his evenings at the Officers' Club. He drank less than most because he knew better, and gambled less than most, even though he liked it, because he was uncommonly inept at it.

In poker, you could read his cards so well in his face and actions, that he might as well have laid his cards face up on the table. His fortune with dice was no better. The only way he ever made money was being my partner when I got the deal in blackjack. He would contribute half to the bank and take care of the collecting and paying-off, while I dealt.

His medical duties were pretty much routine and he handled them easily and well. Despite his wisecracking, he took his medicine seriously. On more than one occasion I saw other of our medical officers (we had five in the group) seek his advice and defer to his recommendations on professional matters. He felt that the war had interfered with his medical education, and to partially offset that, he accumulated military leave so that on his own he could take a course at the University of Edinburgh Medical School. When he complained too much about the war interfering with his career, I would remind him that at least he was practicing in his chosen field. I didn't feel that after the war there'd be much of a market for whatever skills I'd developed dropping bombs. Since I'd no intention of staying in the military or driving airplanes for a living, I really had something to gripe about, and he very little.

Spivvy had a keen sense of humor and was a leading candidate for squadron clown. Occasionally, German intruders would come over our base at dusk and head for the nearby major air depot at Watton to drop a few bombs and do some strafing. A couple of times we caught some of their first shots. The damage done was minor and it was more an annoyance than anything else. However, as soon as an intruder was known to be in the area and the siren sounded, Spivvy made a mad dash for his helmet and put on a Red Cross armband, all the while loudly calling the intruder vile names. He was always the first into the blast revetment. This was a roofless shelter with mounds of dirt piled high against interior brick walls. We could stand, look up and watch the attacking plane with little danger, unless it scored a direct hit.

As the Jerry passed overhead, Spivvy's head would tilt back to watch and his helmet would fall to the ground. He had once heard that combat infantry men never buckled their chin straps, so he didn't, and his small head and large tin hat always parted company. He would let out a few more original oaths and grovel in the near darkness to retrieve his helmet. We almost welcomed these ineffectual attacks to watch him go through his act. He would further ham it up by pointing to his Red Cross armband and yelling up to the attacker, "Geneva Convention! Geneva Convention!"

We kidded Spivvy about playing the additional role of squadron chaplain. Because he was well regarded, easy to approach, and older than most of us, many younger fellows turned to him for non-medical as well as medical problems. He was a pretty good counsellor at heart, for beneath his raucous voice and sometimes rough language, he was quite soft. He hated violence and it sickened him.

He had been close to our original crews, and as he saw most of them fail to return, he vowed that he was not going to allow himself to become involved with replacement crews other than in a strictly medical relationship. When they went down it would be just more 'flak fodder,' and not a bunch of fellows he had come to know and like. He was probably the most sensitive of our original squadron staff, and although he never flew a mission or saw any of the carnage in the wild blue over Europe, I believe the war took as much out of him as it did any of us. He did a great job with the physical and psychological hurts of the squadron, many of which left scars on the healer.

20. London Trips

I spent very little time away from base. It wasn't that I couldn't, but we were just too busy. My first trip off base when at North Pickenham, was two days to London with Jack Turnbull and a couple of others. Jack had been there many times on his pre-war athletic trips, and wanted to show us the town. The accommodations were difficult to come by, the ones you got were not very good, and the blitz was no fun. Stage shows and movies were good and the food at 'Willow Run,' the Junior Officers' Mess¹ at the Grosvenor House, was the best (and cheapest) in town. We did some shopping, ordered custom jodhpur-type flying boots made at Bunting's, battle jackets at Stone's, and lenses for my movie camera at Wallace Heaton's.

On a couple of visits there I had interesting chance meetings. One was very fortunate. Fr. Frank Sullivan, a Jesuit priest from back home, had become a lieutenant commander in the Navy Chaplain Corps, stationed in London. I enjoyed seeing him again, but the real bonus was that the Navy supplied him with generous rations of cigarettes and whisky, and he didn't use either, but offered me his rations whenever I could make it to London. Whereas on our base we were rationed various unheard-of brands of mongrel cigarettes, he could get Luckies or Camels in any quantity for the same price of 50 cents a carton. Our base Officers' Club was paying $18 a fifth for no-brand scotch diluted to half strength; Fr. Frank could get a fifth of any brand for one dollar! He got Johnnie Walker Black Label for me. The Navy really took care of it's own.

Another chance meeting was embarrassing, particularly for the one met. During an air raid, my flight surgeon Spivvy and I reluctantly obeyed the Air Warden's instruction to go down into the

Underground, which was always jam-packed with bodies, smelly, damp, and dimly lit. After much stumbling over sleepers, knitting ladies and crying children, we squeezed into a small opening on a backless narrow bench against the wall. As my eyes adjusted to the dark, I saw that sharing the bench to my immediate, left was a 'Picadilly Commando.' Even closer to her on her left was an American, his uniform amorously draped around the her. Curiously, I poked my head forward to get a peek at the uniform wearer at the same time that he wanted to get a look at me, the intruder upon his scene. There we were, almost nose to nose, and both incredulous. He had been a senior officer in my cavalry regiment in the late Thirties! We knew each other, I had met his wife and had given riding lessons to two of his children. Our eyes remained fixed for what seemed an eternity with neither acknowledging the other. He suddenly blinked, grabbed his girl friend, and they stumbled off into the dark.

Another time when in London for a couple of days of major dental work, I was billeted at the Dorchester with another dental patient, a colonel from Patton's armor.[2] After dinner and a late show, we were on our way back to the hotel, griping about the strict curfew rules making it too late for us to get a drink, when to our surprise we came upon a bar that was still open. It was crowded with uniforms inside, and a larger group outside trying to get in. It was unheard of for any bar, any day, any place in the UK to be open 'after hours.' There was a policeman standing right there. We asked him "How come?" He said he tried to close the place down, but couldn't with "those people in there." We asked, he answered: "The Prime Minister's daughter and the President's son!" Sure enough, we could see Sarah Churchill and Elliot Roosevelt at the center of a very festive group inside.

On a couple of occasions Spivvy and I took passes at the same time to London. We had the same interests—some good meals at 'Willow Run,' some shows, points of historic interest, and no pub crawling. Getting decent accommodations in war-time London was a problem. The rumor with Americans was that hotels there, particularly the better ones, gave preferential treatment to British Forces. The darker side of that rumor was that if you did manage to book a room, it would be on one of the top three floors—which proved most vulnerable to Blitz bombing!

          Spivvy stopped by my office one day to discuss a problem, and when finished suggested we take a couple of days in London. I preferred Edinburgh or nearby Cambridge. I was not too thrilled with London's V-1s and V-2s, and the closet-sized rooms with Water Closet down the hall we'd been getting there. It wasn't that much of an improvement over what we had on base. My senior clerk, Sgt. Brosseau, overhearing us, interrupted and asked where we'd like to stay in London if we had a choice, and ventured he might get a reservation for us. I gave him a disbelieving look, but having known him to pull rabbits out of a hat before, listed the Savoy as first choice and the Dorchester as second. He went back to his desk in the outer office and reappeared a few minutes later with a Cheshire grin and the pronouncement, "You have a room at the Savoy for two nights. When you check in, remember to use the English pronunciation of your rank and name." Knowing some chicanery was involved, I asked how he managed it. Switching from his natural Brooklyn accent to a very believable English one, he had represented me as a "Left-tenant Colonel in the Eighth" not specifying whether it was the famed British Eighth Army, or our Eighth Air Force, and followed with the English pronunciation of my name.

          When Spivvy and I checked in at the Savoy, while feeling a little apprehensive about participating in Brosseau' deception, I said to the clerk very positively, "You have a booking for Left-tenant

Colonel *May-uh-nee.* He checked his file and said "Yes, I do," then with a delayed but sizable double take, "But you are an American." I refrained from using any of several sarcastic replies that came to mind, said nothing, and stared him down. What he had said was out of surprise, but realizing I might take offense and create a bit of a row unbecoming the quiet dignity of the Savoy, he nervously summoned a bellman and sent us off to the lift. When we got to our room, the most luxurious we'd seen since we left home, and feeling very pleased with ourselves, we ordered up a couple of scotches—each. Next on the agenda was a hot bath in one of the Savoy's giant-size cast iron tubs! As we savored our drinks, letting the hot water flow, we were about to flip a shilling to see who'd get first crack at the tub, when there was a gentle knock on the door. It was a man wearing a cutaway coat, identifying himself as a house detective. He said he had passed our room several times and heard the water running continuously. He asked if we were aware of the restrictions on the use of water for bathing because of its need for fighting Blitz fires. He also wanted to check to see if we had exceeded the three inches allowed for a tub. He turned off the faucet, pulled a ruler from his pocket and plumbed the depth. Sure enough, we had substantially more than doubled the allowable. then, despite our vigorous protests, he did the unthinkable —he let that precious hot water go down the drain until it reached the three inch level on his ruler! "Rules, you know."

1. Likely this London trip antedates JJM's 6-20-44 promotion to lieutenant colonel.

2. *This* leave must have been taken while JJM was stationed at Rackheath, well after the breakout from the Normandy beach head in late June '44.

Capt. Charley Barrett was in charge of the Intelligence Section of my 859th Squadron. He was more than ten years my senior and had already had a full and interesting life. Son a of Mid-western itinerant preacher, he had left home in his mid-teens and joined a traveling circus. He learned to be a 'barker,' left that for door-to-door selling, then to sell for a major manufacturer of small appliances. He had been married at an early age, and by the time he entered service he had become national sales manager for his company, had seven children, and been divorced. I never asked why he divorced or why he volunteered for service. At his age and with that size family, he certainly didn't have to. To give you some flavor of his continuing active life style, after the war, Charley remarried and had several more children!

With the exception of Charley, all of the group's intelligence officers were college educated; like him, most were in their middle or late thirties. But Charley was well self-educated and could hold his own in any group. He had developed some expertise on subjects as diverse as astronomy and jewelry. He carried a jeweler's loupe with him whenever he went off base and checked out jewelry stores and pawnshops for 'buys;' he claimed to have made many. He handled his assignments very well, and was particularly effective on his feet giving the intelligence part of a mission briefing. Aside from his work, he assumed a fatherly role with many of the young crewmen, and they appeared to respond to it very well.

He was also an inveterate gambler, favoring dice over cards. He was a regular each evening at our Officers' Club craps tables. He claimed to be an over-all winner, but other regulars disputed that. He was essentially a non-conformist and enjoyed seeing how far he could bend a military regulation before it broke and got him into trouble. He had tested me a number of times before I made it clear that I didn't have the time or patience for his antics and expected him to toe the military line like everyone else. Once he 'borrowed' my jeep, somehow managed to get by our MPs at the gate, and

Charlie Barrett

was picked up by the MPs in town. (Officers were not allowed to drive off base.) I gladly let them throw the book at him. That shook him up a bit, and although I had him cornered, I never felt that I, or anyone else, could have totally contained Charley.

He was constantly asking

permission to go on a mission. There was no regulation against non-flying personnel doing so, but I felt very strongly, as did most commanders, that I didn't want any 'joy riders' or glory-seekers on a mission, only people who had a needed function to perform and for which they were trained. To let any added baggage fly would be a needless risk of life, probable interference with crew member functions, extra weight, use of more oxygen, etc. One day at interrogation following a mission, I was talking with General Johnson when Charley sidled up and put himself into a position requiring introduction. I obliged, not willingly, and he started his campaign on the General. The finale was to the effect, "General, don't you feel I'd be in a better position to understand crewmen and their reports to my intelligence section if I were to experience a combat mission?" The General could hardly disagree with that seemingly innocent, but unctuous rhetorical question, and unfortunately, didn't.

We waited until another milk run came up, then put Charley on to ride in the waist. It was over France, and when a sprinkling of flak came up, the crew waist gunner asked Charley to dispense the chaff. That involved simply ripping the paper wrapper off the bundle of aluminum strips and releasing them out the chaff chute, just below the waist window. The gunner reported later that Charley, in somewhat of a panic, was stuffing the bundles into the chute without removing the wrapper, rendering all his effort to no avail.

In our squadron officers' living area, Charley shared a hut with three other squadron staff officers. They complained that he would often sleep on his back and snore loudly. Added to the snore noise was a rattling sound caused by the vibration of an ill-fitting dental appliance of some sort. They asked Spivvy how they could get rid of Charley's snoring. After a few facetious suggestions, he explained that people snore only when the breathe through the mouth. If they could get Charley to breathe through his nose, to smell or sniff at something, their problem would be solved. One of the hut-mates had recently received a box of edibles from home, long delayed in shipment. Among the goodies contained was a package of cheese which probably didn't smell too great when it left home, but was now putrid and almost liquified. The next night as Charley got into his snoring, they dipped a cotton swab into the cheese and gently applied it to his mustache. The next morning I met Charley, half dressed, on his way to the ablution, holding his forehead and moaning. He said he had had a terrible night; his head ached and something smelled awful. No matter where he went, "...the whole world stinks!"

Charley was another of our memorable characters, and despite his antics was well-liked by all in the group. When our war ended, he offered jobs where he worked to a number of us on the squadron staff. Two accepted, and he launched both on successful business careers.

22. Private Spencer

Private Spencer was one of the two enlisted men assigned as orderlies, or as the RAF would say, 'Batmen,' to the staff officers of my squadron. He came from someplace deep in the hills of Kentucky and spoke with a characteristic mountain-country twang. He wouldn't break any IQ records, but as we learned as time went on, he was very shrewd. The other orderly was Private Olson from Minnesota. Like Spencer, he wouldn't have fared that well in IQ testing. Nobody ever defined the specific duties of these two, but it was assumed that they were to keep the staff officers quarters reasonably neat, and keep our 'ablution' (wash-up place) and latrine in presentable condition.

Spencer figured it was politic to spend most of his time on my behalf as I was squadron CO—a very obvious 'polishing job.' He gave me more service than was required or wanted. He kept my room in immaculate condition, and when I wasn't there, he was. He made the bed West-Point-perfect, and not only polished my shoes, but then laced them! It took me a couple of repetitions to convince Spencer that his lacing of the shoes and my unlacing them was labor twice lost, no matter how pretty they looked under the bed. Likewise with my shirts, blouses and battlejackets, which he kept brushed, cleaned and buttoned. They looked very nice, but somehow he failed to translate my lengthy discourse on lacing and unlacing shoes to buttoning and unbuttoning jackets. He rummaged through my things and knew where everything was better than I. I feel quite sure he also read my mail. None of this attention was lavished on any of the staff officers. They were wholly dependent on Olsen, and he managed sufficiently well that nobody complained. But there was much kidding about my prima donna status with Spencer, and the color of his nose.

Frequently at one or two in the morning, after participating in the preparation of briefings for that day, the briefing team would have an hour or two break before the lead crew briefing. We'd go to the mess hall (which ran 24 hours) for some powdered scrambled eggs, ersatz bacon, toast and coffee. We would then go to our huts and try to catch some brief shuteye before heading back for the pre-briefing of lead crews. Spencer, after observing this routine a few times, suggested that I'd save time by coming directly to my quarters where he could have ready some food from the mess hall. This would save me time to get a longer nap. Seeing the benefit of this arrangement for myself and not at that point sensing Spencer's ulterior and perhaps primary, motive, I agreed. The next time I had finished with my part in a briefing preparation, I called down to Spencer, and by the time I reached my hut, he had a tray of eggs, coffee, toast and a sampling of all the jams and jellies the mess hall offered. Spencer's idea worked out well and I complimented him on it. A couple of weeks later when in the mess hall for a regular meal, our mess sergeant Schultz commented he didn't understand how I managed to keep my waistline with the sizable regular meals I ate in the mess hall plus the very large midnight snacks Spencer procured for me almost every night. I told him that I had only a few such snacks. He then told me that Spencer was picking them up for me almost every night. I then noticed that it was Spencer and Olsen who were getting thick around the middle.

One night when he brought my snack, I noticed and commented that his greasy hands and fingernails were more like those of a line mechanic than an orderly. He explained that he had been working on his bicycle. By far the principal means of transportation on our base was the bicycle. We issued to qualified personnel 400 GI bicycles which were used going to and from work places and living quarters. Some were close to a mile apart. All of the crew chiefs, many of their helpers, ordnance people, etc. whose work was up on the line, were assigned the GI bikes. These were the English variety with handlebar brakes rather than our coaster brake type. Conditioning GIs to the English braking system involved frequent spills and a number of hospital cases. The official GI bikes could not be taken off the base, so many GIs and officers bought bikes for themselves. On our base there were about 1200 privately owned bikes. Used bikes had been selling for about fifteen to twenty dollars prior to the influx of Americans. With the massive demand our bases created, prices jumped to four and five times that figure.[1]

What Spencer and his buddy Olson came to realize was that while the prices of new and used bikes had gone through the roof, the price of bicycle parts had remained relatively stable. In their spare time (which was a large piece of the day) they started buying parts and assembling mongrel, but serviceable bikes. They had a ready demand for their product and the orderly room told me that within our squadron, they were sending home more money than anyone except our most successful gamblers.

1. On the micro-economic level, the sudden departure of several thousand Yanks from each of fifty airfields, unable to take their acquired bikes home, created inevitable stress in each locale. The hard decision made at Rackheath was to crush and then bury the bikes, perpetuating the waste of war in the peace which followed. David Hastings, a Norfolk teenager at the time, recalls that this left a bad taste in the mouths of natives. In competition with the invading GIs, they had already endured two years of a strong seller's market for bikes.

After VE, local bike dealers had apparently (and understandably) made very low offers on the potential supply glut, even though the individual cycles acquired piecemeal over the previous few years had commanded quite high prices. Wholesale giving of bikes to locals would have been chaotic and destructive to the local bike economy, if not so obviously wasteful.

At the macro level, one can draw easy parallels to the radical adjustments required when entire sectors of the war economy, such as aviation, practically shut down overnight.

23. A Fist Full of Pebbles

Ruth Register was the head Red Cross girl at AAF Station #143, North Pickenham, home of the 492nd Bomb Group. She had one American and one English uniformed assistant, plus several local English women who worked part-time in the kitchen and elsewhere in the base Aero Club. Run by the Red Cross, it was the exclusive domain of enlisted men and was strictly off-limits to officers. Ruth and her two girls lived, ate their meals, and spent most of their time in the club. Occasionally they would take a meal at the Officers' Mess, and usually attended Officers' Club monthly dances. On some bases the Red Cross girls were said to spend more of their free time with officers than GIs, which certainly was their prerogative. However, this did cause some to feel that those girls were more interested in the acquisition of a husband from the commissioned ranks than the current well-being of enlisted personnel. Such was not the case with Ruth. We were told she had been widowed or her husband was missing in action somewhere in the Pacific.[1] She was interested in doing her job for the GIs, nothing more.

In appearance, Ruth was no glamour gal, but a very wholesome looking all-American type. She was of medium height, compactly built— she might have been the captain of her school's field hockey team. Her hair was long, straight, and black, with a slightly olive complexion to match. She wore very well the somewhat mannish uniform of battle jacket and slacks furnished to the Red Cross girls. Not the type you'd immediately think of as being in a lacy evening gown. Her manner was quiet, and although very pleasant, she was rather slow with a smile. Because she was so reserved, it was impossible for us who knew her such a short time to know whether her demeanor was due to the relatively recent loss of her husband or whether she had always been that way.[2] My Squadron Executive Officer, Dana Smith, knew her very slightly several years earlier in their mutual home town, Bismarck, North Dakota. She was as he remembered her. Unlike most women on an air base in England, her social life was quite drab and uneventful, by choice. She made it patently clear that she was not interested in anything other than her Red Cross duties, and I never heard of any unwelcome advances being made by anyone on the base. When she did come to our Officers' Club functions she appeared to have a reasonably good time and joined in all the activities, although without perceptible enthusiasm. She always came and left unescorted.

After Ruth had been around the base for a few weeks, it appeared that she tended to become attached, in a motherly way, to certain types of our very young airmen—not the extroverts or the loudmouths, but the quiet, the sad, and the scared. She tried to conceal these feelings, and appeared to even resent them. It seemed that she might have promised herself initially to not become emotionally involved with anybody, but as time wore on, so did her resistance.

The officers saw her mostly upon return from missions when she and her assistant 'coffee-and-doughnut' girls set up their operation immediately behind the medical line in the interrogation room. As returning crews were brought in by the trucks, they first went through the medical debriefing to see who might have been hurt or shaken physically or psychologically. This was usually just a quick once-over, then a medic handed each crewman a 3 ounce shot of scotch in a paper cup. On some bases you were allowed to pass it up then and be given credit toward a full fifth. On ours we felt this eventually caused too much bookkeeping and other problems, so we insisted everyone drink it on the spot, or forfeit it altogether. Even the most fuzzy-cheeked novice who had no desire or taste for scotch would gulp it down with a thinly disguised expression of distaste, rather than let it be said that he passed up his scotch on the 'belt line' and turned it back to the 'pill rollers.'

After the medics came the Red Cross girls with the very welcome coffee and doughnuts, and occasionally some small sandwiches. More welcome were the friendly smiles with which the girls greeted the crews. Again, Ruth's smile was the slowest and quietest, but probably the most sincere. She tried to not show favorites, and I'm sure she didn't mean to, but from my vantage point it was becoming obvious that some of those very young pilots had special places in her heart, and she was particularly happy to see their faces come through the door after a mission. As more of those faces failed to return, her smile became less frequent and more forced.

My most poignant memory of Ruth was the mission return after the bombing of Bernburg, Germany. As was her custom, Ruth would join the hundreds of other base personnel who would come up to the flying field to 'sweat out' a mission. Word would get around when our returning planes had made landfall at Great Yarmouth, and all who could leave their work-stations would come up to the field. Officers and GIs would come by foot, jeep and bike from all directions. Each would hurry to his favorite spot to watch the landings. These carefully chosen spots were usually elevated, like the tops of vehicles or blast shelters, and provided a good view of the landing runway. This was a regular ritual, a sort of GI 'high tea,' an occasion for initiating and swapping latrine rumors while awaiting the arrival of the planes. Some would speculate and even bet on the number of planes that would fail to return, occasionally making long shot bets on individual planes. When the landings started, each touchdown was evaluated very critically—particularly by non-pilots. Rough landings would bring cries of anguish and a variety of GI expletives from members of the plane's ground crew.

Ruth had chosen the blast shelter nearest to the control tower as her habitual watching spot, and for every mission return would join her group of regulars there a few minutes before the planes reached the field. However, before so doing, she would come over under the balcony of the tower, call up to the control officer, and ask how many planes were dispatched that morning. She would then go to her usual spot atop the shelter, pick up a pebble for each plane airborne, and await the touchdown of our planes with her meaningful handful of pebbles. As each plane landed she would drop a pebble to the ground. On an exceptional day, she would wind up with an empty hand. Unfortunately those days were rare for the 492nd, and Ruth usually opened her hand to a sweaty palm with one or more pebbles. After all had landed, she would come over to the tower to check her count of the missing with theirs, and ask if the no-shows might have been diverted elsewhere. On such occasions she would hang around the tower hoping for some good word on the missing until she had to depart to her coffee and doughnut duties. As time went on and our losses became heavier, so did Ruth's hand and heart. She was obviously becoming sensitive to our loss of crews she knew, and was finding it increasingly difficult to muster a smile for those who did return. The worst of her 'pebble days' was one of the worst for the group, and the very worst for my squadron.

For a number of missions prior to July 7, 1944, the other three squadrons of the 492nd had been hit pretty hard, while my squadron losses had been relatively light. The other three were finding it difficult to put up their share of planes. This day, when the group had been asked for a very modest effort, I had put up seven of the twenty in our group formation. The mission was to an aircraft plant in Bernburg, Germany. As I stood atop the tower and watched our returning formation approach the field, I looked in disbelief as I saw no planes with my squadron markings! After the last plane had landed, Ruth came over under the tower, opened her palm to a fist full of pebbles, and asked if she could possibly be right. I assured her that not only was she right, but that all from my squadron had gone down. We had just received in the tower a phone message from an engineering shack out on the line relaying a report from the first plane to land, that there would be no stragglers, the missing all went down under a massive fighter attack over the target.[3] Ruth, without a word, left for her post mission duty, tissuing away a few tears and not attempting to disguise them.

Our Wing Commander, General Leon Johnson, happened to be in the tower that day. After the last touchdown, I went with him in his car to the interrogation room to meet the first crews coming in off the trucks. They elaborated on the phone message we'd received in the tower. Under extremely heavy fighter attack over the target, my lead crew pilot, Lt. Bernie Harding and the others, had all been shot down in less than ten minutes. Ruth was on the edge of the group listening, and that day, for the first time, failed to fill her spot on the coffee and doughnut line. Among the missing were several of her favorites. A month later, about the time our group was stood down from combat and disbanded, Ruth was transferred to a training base near the Wash. Whether her move was requested or directed, I never did hear.

It was shortly before Christmas, 1944, months after the 492nd had been disbanded and I had taken many of its surviving crews with me to the 467th, when I heard from Ruth again. I was flying Little Pete, observing the formation flying of some of our new crews on a training mission. Our tower called me saying that I had an urgent phone call and suggested I return to base. After landing, I went to the tower and they got the caller back on the line for me. I had assumed it must be an official and urgent call by the way the tower had handled it. I was greatly surprised to find that it was Ruth at the other end of a poor phone connection. Between that and her sobbing it took me a while to learn what her call was all about. Namely, her present base was an ATC (Air Transport Command) training base where crews were being checked-out in the transport version of the B-24, the C-109. Unbeknownst to me, two of my original squadron pilots, Lts. Ernie Haar and Danny Wolf, had been sent to this base as instructors. They had finished their tour months ago, and I thought had gone home. Both of these young pilots had been fond of Ruth, and she of them. It had been a happy coincidence that they all wound up at the same training base where nobody was being shot at.

The reason for her call was that there had been a tragic accident on December 18th, involving these two 492nd alums. As Ernie was had taken off with with a crew that he was 'flight checking' at the controls, Danny, already airborne, decided to fly in tight formation with them. The colonel in the left seat did not share Ernie's alarm, which was tragically vindicated when Wolf's plane suddenly and inexplicably crossed under, too close, costing Ernie's plane the props on engines 1 and 2 and destroying the tail of Danny's plane, which immediately plunged to the earth, killing all three aboard. Ernie quickly instructed the co-pilot on cutting fuel and ignition to the two engines on the left wing, which had already dropped 30 degrees. The plane was on fire and close to stalling at very low altitude over buildings on the base. Ernie quickly took the co-pilot's seat. He skillfully managed to let the plane slip left rather than continue its sharp bank into a stall or spin in the direction if the 'dead' wing. The engineer and co-pilot followed Ernie's instruction to stay against a forward bulkhead and survived the fiery crash landing in an open field. The pilot-colonel and the engineer in the rear did not.

An observant RAF ambulance crew were the first on the scene and got the survivors to the burn unit of their nearby hospital. Ruth's thought was that I should try to come over right away to see Ernie, although I wasn't sure why. Obviously, the only help he needed was medical.[4] Danny was gone and there was nothing I could do for him. We had a mission returning and I couldn't leave until it was wrapped up. By then it would be dark, and with the possibility of enemy intruders in the air and the British ack-ack shooting at everything that moved in the air at night, I wasn't about to make a night flight to Ruth's base.

I called the next day to ask her about Ernie's condition, with the thought that I might fly over there. One bit of good luck was that he had been taken directly to an excellent facility for treatment of his burns. Ruth had calmed down, and from our conversation I finally realized that she linked herself with the ill-fortune of the 492nd, convinced that no matter where she went, she was a bad luck token for our crewmen. That's the last I ever heard from one of The Red Cross's finest, Ruth Register.[5]

1. US Navy fighter pilot Lt. (J.G.) Frances Roland Register was the North Dakota's first ace. When he went MIA at Attu in the Aleutians in May, 1942, he had 8 Japanese 'kills' to his credit.

2. Dad's physical description of the young widow does not jive well with Ernie Haar's, and we have it from the subject herself that she always wore her hair up. In a telephone interview on Independence Day 2001, Ruth Register Coleman surmises that my father has conflated his recollecton of her appearance with that of Red Cross worker Ellen Burns, whom Ruth replaced at North Pickenham. With the additional minor correction that, as head of Red Cross hospitality she always knew as a matter of course, how many planes had been dispatched (and did not need to ask at the tower), she corroborates all the rest.
    As to her disposition, Ernie has pressed upon me that Ruth was, contra my father and despite everything, 'all smiles.'

3. My father's 859th BS lost seven of its 20 crews, the 492nd BG losing a total of 12 planes in minutes that day: 118 souls KIA, 18 MIA.

4. Ernie remembered feeling a need for 'tactical' support. The crash investigation and general tone at the base were not favorable to the 'newcomer' B-24 pilot. Ernie remembers asking Ruth to get Lt. Col. Mahoney to visit so that this ranking senior flier could assuage the ACT Group's CO

that Haar's dropping of the landing gear before the crash was the right procedure for that high-winged craft, with its notoriously weak fuselage. The C-47 men he was transitioning to the C-109, used to their very sturdy low-wing transport, would have bellied in. They wondered whether Ernie's action had worsened matters in the wreck that took two lives. After Dad's visit, the base CO actually posted a notice, vindicating Haar and specifying the dropping of gear as standard procedure in crash-landing the Lib (or its tanker equivalent).

5. In the course of research for this book, the younger author picked up the search. When I recently discovered that Ruth had registered herself (under her maiden name, Ruth H. Christianson) with the Women In Military Service for America Memorial as a charter member in 1991, but that mailings to her were returned as undeliverable after May 1993, I thought the worst. But there is a lesson here: I shared all of I had uncovered with a few other interested researchers, which inspired Ernie Haar to renewed and very clever efforts—in late May of 2001, he found Ruth to be vivacious and helpful in setting the record straight.

24. Threes

In the Air Corps the superstition prevailed that accidents occurred in threes. Of course, almost everyone would tell you that it was pure superstition and that he gave no credence to such nonsense. But deep down, even among the most intelligent, there was at least an uneasy feeling after two accidents in quick succession, and a sense of relief after the third.

In the 492nd, a sequence of threes in which I was unwittingly involved, became a case in point for those who openly supported the 'threes theory.' The genesis of these events dated back to our overseas training base at Alamogordo, New Mexico. The Air Corps had always provided parachutes in three sizes—24, 26, and 28 feet (the diameter of the opened canopy). Of course, the larger the canopy, the slower the descent. My weight qualified me for the 28 footer and I always insisted upon that prerogative. In the unhappy event that I should have to use it, I wanted the softest landing the government could provide, like the proverbial "butterfly with sore feet."

In the POM (preparation for overseas movement) instructions were very specific listings of materials we should take overseas, and others we could not. In a paragraph relating to parachutes, there was a clear prohibition which puzzled all, and disturbed me. No 28 foot chutes were to be taken overseas. But I wasn't about to give up my king-size chute. I asked my supply officer to provide me with an inventory of our chutes by size. He reported that we had five 28 footers and all the others were 24s and 26s. I instructed him to stash the 28s in large boxes of authorized materiel and hoped they would escape detection by any nosy POM inspector. They did, and when they arrived in England via surface transportation, I had the only large chutes on our base, and theoretically in all of the U.K.

It wasn't very long before it became an open secret in the group that not only was I wearing a 28 footer, but that I had a few additional ones stashed away. I was approached by some of the larger boys suggesting a swap of one of my big ones for the smaller ones they were forced to wear. The first time I yielded to such a request was at an early morning briefing when Jim Rogers, the Operations Officer of our 857th Squadron, told me that he was on the mission that day, that he had just learned that his chute had gone for repack and he didn't have another conveniently available. Jim was an old friend and one of our original group cadre, so I let him use one of my 28 footers. Jim failed to return that day; we were to learn soon thereafter that he was KIA. At about the same time, Luke Lutonsky, Squadron Navigator of the 857th and another of our cadre, approached me to borrow one of my chutes. Luke was a large, raw-boned and lovable character from Big Sandy, Texas, the best poker player on the base. He was a little older than most of us, and had a wife and a couple of children. Luke also failed to return from his first mission wearing one of my chutes, KIA.

Following Luke's loss and the realization that both he and Jim had been wearing my out-sized chutes, one night at a poker table, some one suggested that these might be the first two of another dreaded 'three.' It was a while before I was again approached for the 'loan' of one of my chutes.

This time it was one of the other squadron operations officers, Red Byrne of the 858th. Red was another of our original cadre, and also one of our group's outstanding 'characters.' A West Point graduate, he was known there for a rare combination of distinctions. He had been voted by his classmates as "Most Likely to Succeed," but also left the Academy with more demerits than anyone in his class. Again, I acceded to Red's request and he too failed to return. Red went down over the North Sea and was first listed as MIA. After an appropriate period of time and investigation, he was reclassified 'Presumed Dead.'

This completed the 'threes' series in the minds of those who had been openly worrying it, and undoubtedly, the many more who had never admitted to it. Nobody ever asked for any of the outsized chutes I still had left.

There was more to this 'tri-incidence.' Beyond being members of our original 492nd Group cadre, all were squadron staff officers, all about the same size, all had been good friends as had our wives. And sadly, all three had sons born within a few of months of their deaths.

25. Laundry Boy

One of the unexpected and annoying inconveniences of our everyday living was the lack of laundry and dry cleaning services. With the tens of thousands of Americans suddenly dumped onto that little island, it would have been impossible for the local establishments to have met our needs even if they had been adequate before we came—and we were given to understand by English friends that they were not. Our situation was further aggravated by location. Most of our bases were in rural farming areas of East Anglia. Very often, as in the case of our 492nd Bomb Group at North Pickenham, our military population was several times that of the nearby village.

To assist with our problem, and at the same time distribute our workload equitably among the few available laundry and dry-cleaning operations, an Air Ministry representative drew up a schedule for each base to send their stuff out. We went along with this arrangement for a while, but were unable, or unwilling to cope with the seemingly endless and insurmountable problems that arose. Some things took weeks to be returned. Some never came back, or you received someone else's stuff, always the wrong size. Anything that went white, though soiled, came back gray. Woolens were shrunk at least one size, and dress uniforms had been 'dry-cleaned' in gasoline or some other highly volatile petroleum derivative. The fumes were such that you didn't dare light a cigarette, and woolen shirt collars chafed your neck beef-red. It took a few days of outdoor airing to dissipate the fumes to a safe and wearable level.

However frustrating this arrangement was, it was not without occasional light moments. Apparently one or more of the ladies working at our designated laundry were desperate for dates. Several fellows received back in their laundry a lone sock to which was pinned a note saying, "I have your other sock and will return it to you next Tuesday evening at 7 o'clock in front of the Green Glove Pub. I am 21, five feet, three inches tall, blond, and will be wearing..." I don't know of anyone responding to such an invitation, but this unique proposal for matching a pair of socks did occasion some wild and humorous speculation as to how and why a particular sock was chosen.

For lack of adequate service, many had their things cleaned less often than they (and their hut mates) would like. Others wound up doing their own laundry, definitely a last resort. One of our squadron Staff came across a boy from a local village who said his mother would be willing to do laundry at a reasonable price. He also claimed that her work would be good and performed with great dispatch. Eric was thirteen or fourteen years old, respectful, intelligent, and very serious. We tried Eric's service with some of our less valuable apparel and within a couple of days he was back on his dilapidated bike with a handlebar basket full of thoroughly cleaned and neatly folded GI clothing. Very quickly he had more business that his mother could handle, so, enterprisingly he enlisted the services of neighboring housewives and his business expanded and flourished. The clothes were washed in a stream, then hung on outdoor clotheslines to dry. The latter function was often delayed by the same rainy and foggy weather that impeded our flying. Eric, his mother and helpers all did a good job at a fair price. He had a good thing going.

One evening in the Officers' Club after a few brews, Eric became a topic of conversation. We had come to know that he lived with his parents and a couple of younger brothers on a small farm at the edge of the village, and that his father was head clerk (pronounced 'clark') at the greengrocers in a nearby larger village. We speculated that our laundry business was providing more income to the family than the father's salary. Even taken together, the two hardly seemed adequate to support the family and provide for Eric's education beyond what was provided by the local school system. We felt that Eric deserved more than that with his keen mind and enterprising bent. Even after we had become fairly proficient with pounds, shillings, and pence, he was quicker than the best of us with his mental calculation of our laundry bills. One day after complimenting him on his facility with figures, I asked if he planned to develop this skill and become a mathematician or an engineer. Without hesitation, he stated that his goal was to succeed his father as head clerk at the greengrocer's as his father had succeeded *his* father.

Having been forever taught that if it was unnatural, if not un-American, to not want to out-achieve you forebears, Eric's answer was not easy for us to understand. We attributed it to his youth, or possibly his recognition that his family's meager circumstances could not afford him higher education. The subject was dropped for a while, but later that night, Eric's education again became a subject of discussion around the poker table. Ultimately, some well intentioned soul suggested that we tap each pot played at that table for a shilling to build an educational fund for Eric. It was agreed by all, and from that point until the group was disbanded a relatively short time later, unbeknownst to him and his family, the 'Eric kitty' was fed a shilling for every hand played at that table.

When the fateful time of our group bust-up arrived, the only pleasant chore we had to perform before leaving North Pickenham, was to surprise Eric and family with the 'kitty.' He was told only that a couple of our staff wanted to meet his parents to thank them for the fine laundry service, and to show our appreciation with a few little goodies from our PX. The story struck Eric as being strange, but so did so many other things we Yanks did, so he led the way to the family cottage.

Our envoys came back in a short while, puzzled, disappointed, and chastened. While Eric's parents recognized the spirit in which we had attempted to help the furtherance of the boy's education, they also felt that this was clearly an intrusion in a family affair and politely resented our presumption that we knew better than they what was best for Eric! They declined any part of the kitty. Eric's future was programmed in the traditional family mode and his life and living would be pretty much the same as those before him, with only the calendar changing.

However, the magnanimous effort was not a total loss. Eric's kitty provided an un-needed extra supply of spirits for our base farewell party, and the total experience served to point once more to our naiveté in dealing with people beyond our borders.

26. Demise of the 492nd

After only eleven weeks of combat and an intolerable loss rate, higher headquarters decided that it was time for the 492nd to give up the ghost.[1]   In that short period, we had 530 KIA and 58 MIA.   In addition to those appalling figures, we had an unknown number as prisoners of the Germans, as Internees in Sweden and Switzerland, and more we brought back wounded on missions.   Not all of those were from our original crews.   Replacement crews also contributed substantially to those figures.[2]

To us and to many others, it was such a paradox.   We had arrived with such a highly experienced pilot level, great things were expected of us

Flightless turkeys are now raised in sheds which incorporate the 150' wide 024 main runway ar North Pickenham as their foundation and access road.

by our wing and division—and by us!   Why such heavy losses?   Were we being picked on by the Luftwaffe?   Many then, and some still puzzle those questions.   Some theorized that because we were the first group to arrive in

Europe with all silver (unpainted) airplanes, we stood out in the bomber stream, inviting attack. That was highly unlikely.[3] Another theory offered was that because of our pilot experience level we flew such tight formations that we presented a very dense target for flak and offered attacking fighters a better chance for a hit. That is the only one of the many theories offered to which I can give even the slightest credence. On a couple of early missions I saw high frontal attackers ('12 o'clock high') fish-tailing their rudders as they fired and passed through our formation. They appeared to be spraying the formation rather than drawing a bead on a single plane.

But none of the many attempts to explain our hard fate truly satisfy. Even post-war interviews with ex-Luftwaffe pilots failed to uncover any inkling that the 492nd singled-out as a special target.[4] Most are now resigned to the simple conclusion that we were 'a tough-luck outfit.'

Our loss of any crew was tough to take, but the loss of so many original crews, the ones you knew longest and best, was particularly hard. They're the only ones still readily recognizable in the mind's eye—the same trim figures, unlined faces, and full heads of hair. They never had a chance to age.

1. In his album 'Overseas I: North Pickenham,' my father traces the strong lineage of camaraderie and *esprit d' corps* which began with the 104th Observation Squadron in Baltimore long before the war, then after a handful of designation changes and reassignments coursed through the *original* 492nd's 859th Bomb Squadron, transferred with them to the *second* 788th BS of the 467th BG, and died abruptly at war's end. This sensibility about continuity in human terms is in stark contrast to the formal, official record, concerned as it is with continuity of 'constituted units' as organizational constructs, quite independent of trivialities such as whether they have men or machines assigned to them.

    The hundred-plus pages you have now read of the fiery, bloody combat life, death, and nominal transmutation of the original 492nd, is reduced, in <u>Army Air Force Combat Units Of World War II</u>, to a single wooden technical sentence: "Transferred, less personnel and equipment, to another station in England on 5 Aug 1944 and assumed personnel, equipment, and the CARPETBAGGER mission of a provisional group that was discontinued."

"The Carpetbaggers" had formerly been the 801st BG, one of whose squadrons was formed out of the *original* 788th BS, sacrificed by the 467th in May 1944 to take on special training for dropping agents and special goods behind enemy lines, but you would only get the last bit of that by reading the official account.

Serving the OSS and General 'Wild Bill' Donovan with distinction, the 'second' 492nd was decorated by Free France with the Croix de Guerre, with Palm. That group's association has a web page which, as if to make the official expungement total, makes no reference whatsoever to the 'original' group. The web address may be found in the Bibliography.

2.   49 replacement crews flew combat with the original 492nd before disbanding. The phenomenal loss rate of the group is summarized in footnote number 2, page 74. Readers are referred to the Appendix, where "comparator: CASUALTIES" gives a more global ranking of the extreme hazard represented by fighting with this singularly 'hard luck' outfit.

3.   By the time the 492nd flew its first bomb mission in early May of 1944, all new replacement aircraft being fed into the 46 bomb groups of the Eighth Air Force had been 'natural metal finish' (NMF) for months; the 492nd happened to be the first group deployed to that theatre after the decision to eliminate the weight and drag of 'olive drab' had been taken.

That said, I share my father's wry notice of 'Little Lulu,' sporting olive drab and decorative nose paint, on page 10 of <u>Fortunes of War</u>. It maybe a different 'OD' Liberator which is the backdrop for a 5-30-44 photo in my father's album of the replacement crew of Lt. Kirkpatrick, one of the seven 859th BS crews which went down on 7-7-44.

4.   A common apocryphal legend in several bomb groups during the war was that they were 'marked' for special treatment by the most skilled Luftwaffe fighter squadrons as revenge for violation of the international air convention for surrender, signaled by lowering one's landing gear. The classic iteration has it that a bomber's hydraulics have been shot out, causing the gear to drop, but some inattentive gunner dispatches the enemy fighter which has come in close to escort the seeming ex-combatant plane to an enemy controlled field, and its crew to new POW digs. Other German pilots would have noted the group markings on the offending aircraft and the vendetta was on. Almost invariably, it is Goering's elite 'Yellow Nose' Squadron (so called for the yellow spinners on their F-W 190s) which is thereafter seen to effectively harass the marked group's planes, typically with the additional flourish that more ordinary German Air Force units were *called off,* just so that the elites could deliver an unmistakable, lethal message.

Dr. Harry Crosby, Group Navigator of the famous 3rd Air Division's "Bloody Hundredth," spoke to this during a presentation at the

National Air and Space Museum in Washington, on April 4, 1999. He knew of airmen who were told this story by their German guards in a *Stalag Luft*. He cited research done in another group which got to the bottom of 'their' story- a blowhard braggart making it all up. Crosby (as General Leon Johnson, in post-war correspondence with my father) was aware that the theory had been put multiple times to high ranking German fighter command officers, who would have had no reason to lie, who uniformly stated no knowledge, and in the case of Generalleutnent Adolf Galland, leading ace and commander of the Jagdverband 44 "Squadron of Aces," explained that fuel, trained pilots, and engagement opportunities were all so dear in the western air defense of the Reich, that holding an elite in reserve for a single limited target would have been ludicrous, even on the rare occasions it might have been possible.

It would seem that many who were attracted to one or another version of this red herring lost their taste for it over time, when serious research across different groups failed again and again to produce 'the' bomber, 'the' mission, 'the' crew, which behaved so badly. You have just read my father's final word on the subject, but into the 1960s he was still a believer in the 492nd's version. The portion of my father's lengthy letter laying it all out for the young Roger Freeman, written on the 18th anniversary of D-Day, is presented in the Appendix.

27. Black Al

When it was decided at some higher headquarters that the loss rate of the ill-starred 492nd was intolerable, it was "stood down" (taken off combat operations) and its personnel distributed to other 8th Air Force units. Only my 859th Squadron remained intact, and all other of the group's crews with less than 15 combat missions were assigned to it. We were then transferred to the 467th Bomb Group and redesignated as the 788th Bomb Squadron.

The 467th was located at Rackheath, on the estate of Sir Edward Stracey, a few miles east of Norwich. The 467th had been in business just a couple of months longer than the 492nd, and at that point was about an average performer in the division, but showing continual improvement. When we arrived there we were, of course, the new kids on the block, and as such were viewed variously with curiosity, suspicion, and disdain. Naturally, we reciprocated with apprehension, temerity, and some disdain of our own. Whereas we had been having the highest loss rate in the 8th, the 467th had the second lowest. We were hoping that their good fortune might rub off on us; they were fearful that our condition might be contagious.

The most significant difference in the operation of the two groups was in the group command function. At the 492nd, the squadrons enjoyed considerable autonomy in all activities, both air and ground. In the 467th, all air operations, and to some extent ground activities, were run from Group Headquarters. It was run as a one big squadron with the Group Commander operating as a super Squadron CO. This *modus operandi* was not by happenstance, but a direct reflection of the personality of the 467th CO, Col. Albert J. Shower, "Black Al."

In this new situation, I wasn't too pleased about surrendering some control over my crews, and made some noises about it. After a couple of months, Al Herzberg, the Deputy Group CO, was promoted to Wing Headquarters and I took his place¹ and then found myself on the opposite side of the fence, receiving from the four squadron COs the same gripes I'd been voicing. As his Deputy Group Commander (or Group Air Executive), I had to back up the Old Man in public and save my gripes for our private meetings, and there were a number of those. I spent the greater part of every day with the always dynamic, and sometimes difficult Al Shower. We shared an office in the Ops Block, and living space in a two-room suite in the group staff living quarters, "the White House."

Al was of Midwest German parentage, was appointed to West Point from Madison, Wisconsin, and was graduated in the class of 1935. He exemplified perfectly the stereotypes of his ancestry and training. He was a hard-nosed, tough, and sometimes rough military man. If Hollywood were casting for a WW II movie, they would very likely put him in a German rather than American uniform. If they knew him, they certainly would! Al was an imposing figure, big and raw-boned. He stood about 6'2" and weighed in at about 190 pounds without an ounce of fat. He was a handsome man with fairly out-sized ears and a narrow, almost pencil-line mustache. There was nothing else distinctive about his facial appearance, except that it was always very serious and seemed to be awaiting a reason to scowl. Everything about him and everything that he did, whether it was walking, saluting, or lifting a fork at the mess table, was determined, precise, and almost mechanical. Even when he smiled occasionally, it was like all his other moves, immediate and decisive— turned on and off like a light. In flying also he was deliberate and resolute in his manipulation of the controls, as if he expected them to fight back.

I never did learn when or by whom he was tagged Black Al; it happened sometime before my arrival at Rackheath. Frequently, commanders were given nicknames by their troops and many, like his, were not considered flattering. He was very much aware of his moniker, and understandably didn't like it. On a number of evenings as we walked back to our quarters from the mess hall or Officers' Club we heard "Black Al" cat-called from bushes at a safe distance and under the cover of darkness, followed by the clucking sound of a chicken, probably made by young crewmen fortified by a few too many brews.

The most definitive and loudest gripes the air crews had with Al were about practice missions and circling targets. We flew practice missions every flyable day we didn't put up a combat mission. Everybody flew them—command pilots, lead crews, experienced wing crews, as well as the new ones. This was especially annoying to our crews when they learned from contact with crews from other stations that none of the other groups flew practice missions with anything resembling our frequency and intensity. We might very well have used more fuel on practice missions than we did on the real ones.

Prior to my arrival at Rackheath, Al had led a mission where the heavily defended primary target was partially obscured by a low deck of clouds when they got there. He circled the target three times hoping for cloud movement which would give them a good shot at the aiming point. Their eventual drop was ineffective and a couple of planes were lost in the process. This became legend, and over drinks was transmitted to succeeding waves of replacement crews. On a couple of other lesser occasions he circled beclouded targets hoping, and usually getting, a better shot at the target. The dual dangers of doing this were longer exposure to anti-aircraft fire, and loss of position in the main bomber stream, leading to isolation and greater vulnerability to fighter attack. Al's philosophy called for relentless attack, taking your licking now, and not having to come back another day to finish the job, thereby doubling your exposure to losses. He was a dedicated subscriber to the George S. Patton school of aggressive tactics—and I didn't argue with that. Every partially-cloud-obscured target situation (there were many) was unique unto itself in terms of the degree of visual impairment, flak severity, fighter reaction, etc. If the briefed approach to the target was disallowed by these uncontrollable conditions, an on-the-spot command decision had to be made. Whatever it was, it could be argued many ways, and usually was. Critiquing such decisions in mission reviews evoked much speculation about what might have happened had the command pilot opted for courses other than the one taken. Only occasionally was this truly helpful.

The air crews also shared the gripes our ground personnel held for Al. Most of these stemmed from his being an unrelenting stickler for military formalities and discipline—somewhat of a rarity in the Air Corps, particularly in a combat zone. At Rackheath we exchanged salutes everywhere that didn't actually interfere with job performance, such as working on planes up on the line, even though most overseas bases seemed to have declared a moratorium on these rules. There were no exceptions or acceptable excuses. Each day, all who failed to render or return a salute were reported to the officer of the day, and that evening had to appear in Class A uniform at the main briefing hall for personal inspection and to listen to a boring speech on military discipline. The catch was that the senior person (officer or enlisted) reported for a military courtesy infraction that day was automatically elected speaker! It was bad enough to have to listen to the 30 minute lecture, but even worse was to arrive at the hall and find that you were the senior person present and had to deliver it, impromptu! While most drives for military courtesy eventually petered out, this one had a built-in self-perpetuating mechanism and continued effective until the day we left the base. For example, if a major saw a captain fail to report a sergeant for not saluting, or fail to return a sergeant's salute, the major was obligated to report the captain. On the other hand if the major failed to do so (and was caught) then he was reported and stood a good chance of being the senior person present that night and asked to deliver the half hour talk.

There were days when there might be only a half dozen reported violators and you would find an embarrassed, stammering non-com on the stage addressing a handful of junior enlisted men. One evening I dropped by and found a sergeant on stage, speaking to an empty hall except for the officer of the day sitting in the back of the room yawning and continually checking his watch, awaiting the end of agonies at both ends of the hall.

On many Saturday mornings, weather allowing, the entire base turned out in Class A uniform for inspection and dress parade up on the main runway. After the inspection of the troops and presentation of awards, the whole group passed in review led by our own little but mighty band. Following this all returned to the barracks area for inspection of quarters. Although there was some grumbling about this whole procedure, it was not resented as much as the casual visitor might expect. The personnel inspection and parade of the squadrons were enjoyed by most, if not all. Even the inspections of quarters were not really resented, and sometimes appreciated. They revealed a variety of ways in which we could and did improve living conditions in the huts. A GI might argue in vain with the supply sergeant for a new blanket to replace his worn-out one, but if the inspecting officer saw it, he could instruct the issuance of a new one.

In another instance, the only

source of heat in our nine-months-of-the-year cold and damp huts were some small coal-burning stoves, insufficient in number and inadequate in performance. And too, the soft coal allocated to us was less than satisfactory in both quantity and quality. Someone on base devised a relatively simple system for converting the stoves into oil burners. The problem was that the oil used was crankcase oil taken from engine changes on the planes, and we were under strict orders to ship this out for recycling. Knowing they were in direct violation of orders, the originators of this device would disassemble and hide it whenever they learned their hut was to be inspected. On an unannounced inspection we discovered the device, and they were amazed that we simply inquired about its operation and took no action. Word got around in a hurry that we were overlooking this violation and the oil burner business on base mushroomed. Ironically, we couldn't install them in our own living quarters because of the frequent and unannounced visits we received from wing and division brass. We knew of at least a couple who would not have approved.

Occasionally, there were other surprises during inspections of quarters, some humorous. One day when I walked into a hut, the senior non-com called the residents to "attention" as they stood by their cots. They were put "at ease" and I started my slow walk down between the rows of neat beds with footlockers in front, barracks bags tucked underneath. I noted one of the latter was jutting out a bit and spoiled the symmetry of the line, so I instinctively gave it a slight used-car-tire-kick to push it back in line. It responded with a high-pitched squeal of discomfort and an unlady-like expletive! To the obvious relief of the huts tenants, I continued my inspection seemingly ignoring the response to my kick, but outside I asked the first sergeant to prepare a report on the extra and unauthorized occupant. It was no surprise to learn that it was a diminutive Picadilly Commando who had gotten on base for an Aeroclub dance a week earlier, and with the whole-hearted cooperation of an untold and unidentified number, had decided to stay a while and ply her trade. She was escorted off base, and the medics and chaplains were asked to once again remind our participants of the respective medical and moral risks involved.

Some of Al's other edicts on very minor subjects evoked much griping—calisthenics three times a week for everybody, class A uniform in the evening for Officers' Mess and Officers' Club, etc. Another was the subject of much ridicule, the use of place cards at the 'brass' table in the Officers' Mess and in our theater and chapel. The brass table at mess had place cards for all invited to sit there; the group staff and the squadron commanders.   Al's place was in the middle, the air executive on his immediate right, the ground executive on the left, etc.   The best three seats in the theater and the middle three in the front row of the chapel were reserved for the same three top officers, with our names and ranks were indicated thereon.   Al really went overboard in insisting that these seats were not to be used by others even if we weren't using them.   On one occasion when we were busy preparing the next day's mission and had no intention of going to the movies, he asked the OD (officer of the day) to check on our theater seats and make sure they weren't being used!   That was really petty, 'chicken' and unworthy of him, and I told him so.

However, my most serious and continuing personal gripe with Al was his use sometimes of group punishment. A crew member might be late on return from a pass, so the whole crew would lose its passes for a period of time. A crew would screw up in the air or on the ground, and the whole squadron might be penalized. This was tantamount to an invitation to the use of old barracks discipline, wherein the group was indirectly pressured into taking whatever action it chose to insure that the offenders would not repeat an infraction. While there was something to be said for barracks discipline in some instances, it can lead to excesses. We never did come close to agreement on that subject.

As closely as we worked and lived together, we never did become 'buddies' or pals. Despite our complete agreement on such important matters as discipline, training, etc., we were different in the way we handled the command function. I had great respect for Al and felt (still do) that he was the most effective military commander under whom I served, or observed directly. I was not alone in this evaluation. In his "The Mighty Eighth," historian Roger Freeman points out that Al Shower was the only commanding officer the 467th ever had (most groups had several), and that it had the best bombing record of all the 46 bomb groups in the Eighth.[2] This evaluation was officially recognized when at the close of the war in Europe, the 467th was chosen to lead the final ceremonial flight of the Eighth, a massive fly-by of its High Wycombe headquarters by those same forty six groups.

1. Major John J. Taylor assumed command of the 788th BS.

Jim Mahoney was the only lieutenant colonel to serve as a squadron commander in the 467th. When Deputy Commander Lt. Col. Al Herzberg was reassigned to Horsham St. Faith in October 1944, Lt. Col. Mahoney, after just three months in the 467th, replaced him in this high administrative position.

The fact of the matter is that promotions were not sponsored under Shower's command nearly as often as they were at other bases, where it was not unheard of to have one or more lieutenant colonels commanding squadrons. It is this author's theory that the 2nd AD, in the very order which effectively disbanded the 'original' 492nd, also 'set up' Shower to accept as his deputy a secure natural leader with a more palatable style, to offset 'Black Al's' rigid ways.

Military writer Robert L. Dorr, having interviewed many 467th veterans, independently arrived at a similar conclusion. In the February, 2000 edition of Combat Aircraft he wrote:

"Lt. Col. James J. Mahoney, a less strident figure, was brought in as Number Two to 'mellow out' Shower's impact. Mahoney, who is now deceased, once recalled, "Discipline and training were essentials to our mission. Shower provided us with a full and continuing diet of both," while other bomb groups dispensed with formality. The 467th BG held inspections, dress parades, and relentless flying rehearsals."

2. The Appendix presents a letter written by my father to Phillip Day, editor of the 467th's newsletter in the 1990s. This warm and strong *apologia pro Shower* is the likely source of Dorr's quote in the footnote above.

28. Rackheath

Officially known as AAF Station #145, Rackheath was the home of the 467th Bomb Group and the military air base in England closest to Germany. It was just a couple of miles east of Norwich, and not far from the coastal city of Great Yarmouth. Because it was closest to the North Sea, Rackheath had more than its share of friendly visitors—and unfriendly ones too. During daylight operations of the Eighth, planes returning from the Continent and running low on fuel would stop at our station for refueling. About one night a week we'd receive an RAF plane low on fuel or damaged, returning from a mission over Germany. We accused those 'blokes' of stopping by just to have one of our hearty breakfasts of dehydrated eggs made with dehydrated milk, and flavored with dehydrated bacon bits. What they enjoyed most was to layer on to our 'home-baked' bread, several of the myriad of jams, jellies, peanut butter, marmalade, and apple butter found on each mess hall table. Occasionally, some of our GI blankets, warmer than the RAF issue, departed with them in the morning. During the last months of the war, when the OSS was busy parachuting agents into Germany, their unmarked, jet-black twin-engined bombers would stop by in the middle of the night to top off their tanks before heading out to drop their anonymous human cargo someplace deep into the Reich.

Our base was built on the estate of a local Baronet, Sir Edward Stracey. Sir Edward leased the land to the Air Ministry, who built the air base and in turn leased it to Uncle Sam. All the area flying fields looked pretty much alike. They were constructed by the Air Ministry along the same pattern, with minor variations to conform to the terrain, which in East Anglia was generally very flat. Most of the structures on base were Nissen Huts, which were the English equivalent of our Quonset Huts— heavy corrugated sheet metal arched over a concrete slab. They came in a wide variety of sizes, all the way from the very large mess hall size down to the smallest living quarters. There were some concrete block buildings, such as the control tower, some office buildings, etc.[1]

The highest ground on the base was reserved for the flying field, hardstands for the planes, and workplaces for all our flight-supporting activities. Our flying field area was known as "up on the line" or just "on the line." The field itself had one long runway, adequate for our planes, but we'd like to have had it longer for safer all-weather use. The shorter second runway could be used in an emergency, but rarely was. The even shorter third—I don't know why they bothered![2] The perimeter track circled the field, and off of it at various intervals were the hardstands, each of which could house two airplanes. The control tower was on one side of the field, opposite the hangars. The briefing rooms and all the facilities that serviced the aircraft such as armament for machine guns, ordnance for bombs, bombsight, radar, communications, photography, etc., were scattered along the control tower side of the field. For obvious reason, the bomb dump was tucked away all by itself on the farthest corner of the base.

Part way down to the base center was the group headquarters. It consisted of two buildings, the administration building for non-flying functions, and the Ops (operations) Block for all air related activities. The group commander, his deputy, the intelligence officer (or S-2) and the group operations officer (or S-3) and all had their offices and staffs in the Ops Block. Farther down the road, the base center was the hub for non-flying activities, the mess halls, theater, chapel, Officers' Club, Red Cross Aeroclub, etc. Surrounding this area were living quarters.

While the base had been officially

turned over to us by the Air Ministry, they left on the base a crew of civilians headed by the Clerk of The Works. He was responsible for furnishing us with utilities. The electricity was direct current and presented all sorts of problems in converting for use with our American-made alternating current equipment. He also furnished our ration of coal, and since that corner of England is cool and damp for a large part of the year, heating was a problem. The only source of heat in all of our buildings were small inefficient coal-fired space heaters. Each building was given a ration of coal. In the living quarters it was usually put to use in the early evening and was burned out before midnight. This meant that long underwear went on before the end of October, and didn't come off until after the first of May. It was usually worn for sleeping as well as waking hours and because of uncertain laundry service, inadequate bathing facilities, and a pitifully short supply of hot water (also coal-fired), they were not changed or laundered as frequently as we would have liked.

The Clerk of The Works was also responsible for the maintenance of the buildings, roads, runways, etc. on the base. While he was a fine fellow and well intentioned, he was also totally inflexible, his crew inadequate in number to handle the job, and painfully slow in performing what they did undertake. As a result we had to do many of their jobs ourselves, just to stay in business. The Clerk took indignant exception to our doing "Air Ministry work," and reported our violations to them through channels, forcing us to respond through our channels. We had serious run-ins on runway repair. It was essential that the only runway we had that could handle our mission takeoffs be kept in good repair at all times. Unfortunately, the runways had been constructed for bombers carrying less gross weight than ours. We were continually cracking slabs and chipping the surface. The clerk would dispatch two or three of his men with some shovels, picks, and wheel barrows. They would slowly pick away at the slab, hand-mix and pour some concrete that would require a long drying time. Fortunately for us there was a U.S. Army engineering unit not very far from us that had pneumatic hammers, mechanical mixing

Entrance portico to Rackheath Hall, under extensive restoration in 1999 for conversion to luxury condominiums. Tasteful redevelopment has rescued the beautiful Georgian mansion from neglect and dilapidation. (Photo permitted by Actionbond Building Company, Ltd.)

equipment and fast-drying concrete. They would start after the last plane of the day's mission landed, and the runway would be in good repair for the next morning's takeoff. The Clerk protested vigorously, but to no avail on this score.

Understandably, the advent of so many military bases to the area had put a great strain on local generating stations. We were allocated a fixed amount of current, and our actual usage was metered at the sub-station on the edge of the base. We had complaints from many of our technical support units about the shortage of power and how it adversely affected the performance of many of our electrical appliances. At the base dispensary, much of the AC medical equipment, did not function properly even when converted to DC. A memorable case in point was the dentist's drill. I first became painfully aware of it when I had to have some dental work done: they had gone back to the old-fashioned man-powered field drill with its treadle arrangement like grandma's Singer: one of the medics pumped away while the dentist drilled. That day, the electrification of that drill became a major project for our sub-depot repair group. And since we didn't have a saliva extractor either, I suggested that with all the vacuum pumps we had for our planes, they ought to be able to rig up one of those too. They had both ready for my next visit, and our very pleased dentist told me I would be his first patient to use them. The sub-depot boys had done a beautiful job with the saliva gadget except for calculating the amount of vacuum needed. When Doc turned it on it grabbed my tongue and almost pulled it out of my mouth.

One day we learned that, unbeknownst to us, someone had undertaken to solve our electrical problem. The Clerk of the Works came storming into the office reporting that somebody had tapped around the sub-station meter thereby giving us an additional quantity of power that was not being charged to our account! This resourceful bit of GI ingenuity   caused a lot of real trouble for us.   We never did unearth the culprit—we tried, but the Clerk never felt that we tried hard enough.

1. The typical 'schedule of buildings' for an 8th AF bomber base called for between 250 and 300 structures. The prototypic Class A airfield would have had three intersecting runways 150 feet wide, one of which was 2000 yards in length, the other two being 1400 yards each, or 1400 and 1200, oriented to compass points at even 120˚ intervals, but in practice there was wide variation.   A peripheral road connected all of the runway ends in a continuous loop, off of which were arranged hardstands for parking the planes. The peripheral road communicated directly with the hangars and shops of the 'tech site,' accommodating planes and their service vehicles.

Maps in the Appendix showing my father's two stations, give an idea of the range of variation, dictated by the particular terrain of each and intense existing land use in Norfolk. They also illustrate some interesting commonalities, such as the placement of headquarters and sick quarters closest to the airfield, and the communal site central among well dispersed living sites.

2. Rackheath's shortest runway (14-32) was approximately 1360 yards, or 4090 feet long, not quite to the 1400 yard standard. The B-24 operation manual called for a runway well over 6000 feet for a fully laden B-24 to take off. In practice, the Liberator was typically flown well outside the 'safe' recommended operating parameters, carrying far more fuel and bomb load than nominally allowed. At most airfields, the main runway was situated to make full use of the prevailing southerly wind in East Anglia.

29. Sir Edward

Our base was on part of Rackheath Park, the estate of Sir Edward Stracey, Baronet. Sir Edward owned a number of farms adjacent to the base. On several fields within our base, the farmers continued to plant and harvest their crops. Cattle were pastured on other fields next to our hardstands. We and the farmers conducted our very different activities simultaneously and without interference.

He was in his sixties, Lady Stracey (his second wife) in her thirties, their daughter Dureen in her early teens. He reminded me very much of C. Aubrey Smith, the English upperclass type Hollywood actor. He was of average height and girth with a fairly prominent nose, pointed features and dented cheeks. His manner was serious, but pleasant. The Straceys lived right on base in their manor house, Rackheath Hall.[1] It was a large box-type building of Georgian architecture constructed of stone and brick, and not in very good repair. Behind the house was an attractive lily pond and a clay tennis court which Sir Edward kindly allowed us to use. A favorite feature of the base property was a beautiful rhododendron drive. The enormous trees arched over a dirt road for a couple of hundred yards and created a fantastic tunnel of blossoms when in flower.[2]

Our contacts with the Straceys were rather infrequent. At Christmas, Easter, and Thanksgiving we would send a small representation to the Hall with a cooked turkey and a few other American dishes prepared in our mess hall. The Straceys were appreciative and cordial. The only other contacts we had were when a few of us were invited to some of Sir Edward's "shoots." His farms surrounding the base were overrun with game birds. Since only property owners were allowed to hunt game, it was incumbent upon Sir Edward to periodically organize a shoot to reduce the number of birds consuming the farm crops. The shoot was not only for sport; the birds we shot sold quickly the next day in the Norwich marketplace.

A shoot was a very formal and structured affair. It was preceded by a written invitation and followed by an elaborate accounting of the participants, weather conditions, number of birds taken by species—pheasant, partridge, quail, grouse, dove, etc. There were always seven participants, or 'guns,' one for each of the seven 'stations' in each of the fields we would shoot. As host, Sir Edward started as first gun in the first field. 'Gun number 2' was to his immediate left, then 3, etc. In the next field everyone moved one station to the left, so Sir Edward became #2, and #7 became #1. His selection of 'guns' was usually by formula as well: two civilians (usually friends and contemporaries of Sir Edward), two RAF officers, and two from the Eighth. One of his civilian regulars, Clare Van Neck, was a WW I vet, a fantastic shot, and also a frequent shoot guest of the King at the not-too-distant Sandringham Castle.

For equipment, the Americans were distinctly disadvantaged. All we had were semi-automatic GI shotguns intended for gunnery practice on a skeet field, and not field shooting of birds. Sir Edward had a beautiful matched pair of Belgian Brownings with his name etched in silver. While he fired one, his man Friday stood behind and reloaded the other.

On your first shoot, one was assigned the number 2 gun position in the first field, just to Sir Edward's left. In that way he could advise, coach and evaluate the neophyte's shooting. The 'beaters,' who were Sir Edward's tenant farmers, would start coming through the field toward our positions behind a hedgerow. Even as they came very close there was no sight of birds, just sounds of their rustling through the grass. Suddenly, they all erupted to a noisy and whirring low level attack on our positions. After the initial shock, I settled to a

Sir Edward recieves a Christmas cake from the 467th, 1944.

quick bead on an on-coming bird only to see the figure of a beater looming large directly behind it. (I noticed later that several beaters looked suspiciously pock-marked). I held fire, and as the birds passed very low and swiftly overhead, I spun around for a going-away shot, took aim at the tail feathers of one, and as I fired, another crossed behind my targeted bird. To my amazement, and even more so to Sir Edward's, both birds dropped stone-cold to my single shot. At the completion of that field's firing, he called all guns together to tell them of my 'miraculous shot.' After a few more fields we stopped for lunch at a tenant farmer's cottage where for others, he described my 'magnificent feat' in even more glowing terms.   On subsequent shoots, no matter how badly I shot, it mattered not. Whenever he had occasion to introduce me, he told of, and embellished on my single-shot of fame. In shooting, as elsewhere, first impressions are strong, lasting, and not always accurate! At the conclusion of the shoot, each gun would be given a brace of birds. A couple of days later, you'd receive by post the complete scorecard of the shoot.

When introducing me, Sir Edward also insisted upon pronouncing my name the way he said 'it should be,' as if it were spelled 'Mahney.' He claimed that to be the correct Irish pronunciation. When I questioned his authority on things Irish, he informed me that the seat of his baronetcy was some 300 years earlier in Ireland, that he still had property there, and that his name was also Irish.

Although he appeared to be somewhat stiff and formal in manner, he was a very pleasant gent and genuinely interested in people. He was well traveled in America, and upon meeting Americans would ask from which of the States they came. In my case, when I mentioned Boston, he related his having been there many years earlier for a New York, New Haven, & Hartford Railroad bond-holders' meeting. He stayed at the Copley Plaza and enjoyed it very much as its design and decor were "so continental." He recalled in great detail his Saturday evening meal before he was to board 'The Owl' (overnight sleeper train to New York City). As was his custom when abroad, he asked the waitress at the Copley what a favorite local dish might be. She told him that in Boston on Saturday night it was beans and frankfurters. He allowed that he had never heard of such a dish but

would like to try it. He not only liked it, but had seconds.
This epitome of English understatement later said of that
night on the train, "My, I was distressed!"

1.   The hall and its immediate surrounds, with the exception of the
stablehouse close, had fallen into a state of sad neglect when this writer saw
them for the first time in 1991, but it was being restored to former glory
and augmented with a dignified block of high value condominiums, under
construction during my 1999 return.
        Charming gate houses, in pairs at the former back entrance and at
the main, or "Golden Gates" entrance, are all smartly maintained individual
private residences. The extensive former estate is barely discernible today,
but its most charming elements survive in dignified use.

2. 'Rhododendron Grove' has survived in gloriously recognizable form over
the intervening 56 years, if not for obvious maintenance.

30. Innovation and Invention

About D-Day time, the 467th was slightly better than average in bombing effectiveness. At the end of European hostilities 11 months later, we ended up the acknowledged leader in the entire 8th Air Force. This performance drew the attention of brass at all levels, and the curiosity of other group commanders. When they realized that this was not a flash-in-the-pan type performance, but rather a continual and steady improvement with no relapses in performance, they started to ask questions. There were no easy or pat answers to their questions. This was an evolutionary process, involving many elements—chief among which was the unrelenting drive for better performance by our Commanding Officer, Col. Albert J. Shower.

Another significant contributor to our success was our Group Operations Officer, Lt. Col. Walter R. Smith, Jr. Smitty was an engineering graduate from Minnesota and exemplified very well the analytical and methodical characteristics of a good engineer. He was also a calm and unflappable—key requisite for his job.

After I was promoted to Deputy Group CO, I spent most of my working time with the Old Man and Smitty. We worked well as a team. Al was definitely the leader and the dynamic one, but Smitty and I held our own, and were the instigators of many of the organizational and operational changes made. We all worked hard and very long hours. Most of the few 'after hours' I had, I spent at the Officers' Club in conversation or playing blackjack. Al spent little time there, and Smitty even less. They were both readers. Smitty was not anti-social, but quiet, reserved, and a bit of a loner.

One important element in our

improved performance was the change in the way we handled lead crews. The conventional lead crew concept called for each squadron to designate a few of its better crews as *lead* crews, and subject them to additional training. From the standpoint of the crews selected, this was a mixed bag. It was an honor and a recognition of superior performance.   It also meant that they'd fly practice missions more often and combat less frequently, thus taking about twice as long to complete a tour as buddies flying on their wing.   Flying up in front you became a choice target for the Luftwaffe.   A couple of offset pluses for lead crews, were more opportunities for promotion and awards.

In the 467th we carried the lead crew concept farther than other groups.   We felt that splitting the care and feeding of lead crews among four squadrons was a dilution of the overall group effort.   By concentrating our training effort, talent and lead crews into one squadron we felt that we could achieve greater overall efficiency.   We then divided all of the 'wing' crews among the other three squadrons.   The initial impact was traumatic on the staffs of the three 'wing' squadrons, as expected.   They felt that they'd become second class outfits and resented it for quite a while.   It wasn't long before the positive benefits of this move showed up in our bombing effectiveness.   We'd always been above the 2nd Division average, but now we were running at the front of the pack—regularly.

A more subtle factor in our improved results was a substantial increase in our training staff.   The official Table of Organization for a bomb group did not provide for a training department. We built our own, a sizable one, as a function of our group operations.   From our own crews that completed their tours, we selected individuals from all crew positions who we thought would make good instructors, and offered to them the opportunity to stay on with us in that capacity—training others, and no more combat.   Most welcomed the offer, feeling comfortable with such an assignment there, versus not knowing what the next assignment would be if they went home.   As a result, we had an extensive and able staff of instructors to run a full-time daily schedule of both ground and air training. The program was not just for new crews; we had on-going training for crews already on combat status.

Some crews complained bitterly that they were worked much harder than crews in other groups.   But as time went by, they started to appreciate that it paid off and were proud to be a part of our achievement.

A major problem resulting from our comprehensive training program was the record keeping it entailed—e.g. to know which gunner had completed what courses—gunnery, first aid, ditching procedures, emergency procedures, etc.   The paper work became burdensome and unmanageable.   While discussing this problem one day, one of the ground officers assigned to our communications section came up with a suggestion which was our beginning of what today would be called operations research.   The term was unknown to us at that time, let alone the concept.   Lt. Keyes had worked for McBee before the war selling their Key Sort Card System. He thought that this system could be applied to record keeping for our training programs, and volunteered to write home to his company for some cards and accompanying equipment.   The company contributed the material and Keyes worked out a program for keeping track of the training status of our crews.   By pushing that long needle through all the punched holes in the cards, we were able to identify immediately the training status of any crew member.   This closed some gaps that had existed in our program and enhanced its effectiveness greatly.

We became intrigued by other possibilities afforded by this system. A number of base activities could visualize application of this system to their operations. For example, we were continually trying to analyze the patterns of attack by German fighters in order to arrange our formations for best defense against them. We set up a program to track the number of rounds fired, by gun location, against attacking Jerries. An analysis of these data together with consideration of our gunners' claims of 'destroyed' and 'probable' against the attackers, made evident what we'd long suspected: that the ball turret on a B-24 was of little or no defensive value against enemy air attacks. It was a rare occasion when this position had an opportunity to fire its weapons, and even more rare when a ball gunner claimed even a 'probable.' Looking at the ball turret then in realistic terms, we were risking a life, using up a lot of system oxygen, carrying his weight and that of a 2,100 pound turret, for nothing. He wasn't getting any effective shots because the most damaging attacks being made on us were from frontal and high positions. Adding the attacker's speed to our own, the rate of closure was at least 800 miles per hour. With a maximum effective range of about 500 yards, our top and nose turret gunners who could see the attacker coming in all the way had only a couple of seconds for possible effective fire. The ball turret, who couldn't see the attacker until after he had fired on us, had virtually no opportunity to position his guns for effective fire as the 'bandit' zipped by. After building up our case against the ball, we went to the Old Man with the recommendation that we should eliminate ball turrets from at least some of our planes and see what effect, if any, it might have on our vulnerability. We already knew it would increase the performance of the plane. Although he was a confirmed "do-it-by-the-book" West Pointer, and sometimes strenuously resisted our frequent attempts to do things otherwise, he readily recognized the significance of our case and gave a reluctant okay. We then removed the turrets from one squadron's planes and reassigned the gunners to a crew pool. We had checked pretty carefully what the effect of weight loss would be on the center of gravity along the MAC (Mean Aerodynamic Chord), and on the elevator controls. It moved forward the center of gravity, increased speed, reduced fuel consumption minutely, and made the plane less tail-heavy for landing.[1] We had just one worry. We had modified a piece of government equipment without approval. This was in violation of Air Corps regulations which clearly stated that all modifications had to be tested, then sanctioned and published in Tech Orders by Wright Patterson Field in Dayton, Ohio. The Old Man was taking a risk, and to a career officer this could be costly. Our test worked so well that within a couple of months you couldn't find a ball turret in any of our planes. Not long thereafter other groups started eliminating their ball turrets also. A significant and unexpected benefit from the ball turret elimination, was a new feeling among our people that we were open to explore better ways of doing things and were not hidebound by tradition or regulations. We started receiving suggestions from many quarters on ways for improving our equipment and our operations. One received from our engineering section and put into effect was the removal of all tail skids from our planes. On the rear underside, the B-24 had a retractable skid intended to protect the plane from harm when a pilot made a tail heavy landing and banged it on the runway. Our experience showed that when that happened, the internal bulkheads on which the skid was mounted became bent or distorted and it took at least one and usually two days to repair them. By removing the skid and the retracting mechanism, we took a little more weight out of our tail-heavy bird, but more importantly, any scraping of the skin in a tail landing could usually be repaired in an hour or two with some sheet metal and a rivet gun, and we did not lose the use of the plane!

Another recommendation from the engineering group was to remove the dust filters from all engines. In Africa and other dusty areas there was no question about the need for them. In our damp section of England they were eminently superfluous. Their removal didn't account for much of a reduction in weight, but every bit helped, and there was some feeling that air flow to the engines was improved. On another homemade modification made by one of our ordnance non-coms, we didn't dare bypass Wright Patterson. We didn't have any problems adapting the four B-24 bomb bays for any bomb we had in our bomb dump, except the 2,000 pounder. It took a full day to modify the bays of each plane to accept this bomb. This meant we had to know a day in advance when we were to carry them and we lost the use of those planes for a full day. This impaired the planning of 2,000 pounder missions. Our sergeant came up with a modification to an existing shackle which would allow the 2,000 pounder to be loaded as easily as any of our other large bombs. After checking out his arrangement by taxiing the plane around with an unfused 2,000 pounder hung in the bomb bay and determining that it would not shake loose, we decided to give it an air try. We wanted to see if it would shake loose in rough air, and if it would release properly when we intended it to. The Old Man was really enthusiastic about this idea. This could make a very significant contribution to the bombing operations of B-24s in all theaters of war. He decided to test fly the arrangement himself. He and several of our ordnance people and the sergeant-inventor took off for a practice bomb run on a yellow dye marker dropped off the coast in the North Sea. At the scheduled time, we in the tower strained to hear the 'bombs away' message from the Old Man and his experimenters. Unfortunately, he came on the air with some very unkind words about the experiment—he had a 'hung' bomb. It came loose from one shackle, but was dangling from the other, and he couldn't close the bomb bay doors. They tried to loosen it with tools, and they tried to shake it loose, but no luck. Col. Shower finally called in and said he was going to have to land with the bomb hanging down and asked that we have all emergency equipment standing by. This was a potentially dangerous situation, even with an unfused bomb, not because it would explode, but if it broke loose from the shackle on touchdown, it could get tangled in the landing gear and cause the plane to crack up, or it could go rolling somewhere at 120 mph and do all kinds of damage.

The Old Man set the plane down very gently, but the bomb broke loose (luckily missed the landing gear) and careened across the field like a mad rolling pin, heading for the tower. As its speed diminished it wavered more radically from its initial direction and fortunately wound up smashing harmlessly against one of our revetment bunkers. Before doing so it had cut a wide swath in the crowd of onlookers who had hurriedly gathered near the tower upon hearing of the hung-bomb landing attempt.

That failure did not deter our efforts and ultimately success was achieved and the sergeant's idea was sent to Wright Patterson for approval. As feared, they just sat on it, but because of its importance to every B-24 bombing outfit, we were able to enlist pressure from the highest level in Washington to expedite the approval process. They were still slow, but finally did publish modification Tech Orders on the sergeant's invention. He was decorated for his very important contribution to the effectiveness of B-24s everywhere.

Another nagging problem for all groups was the fast turnover of lead crews. A crew would probably have ten to fifteen missions under its belt before it would have demonstrated lead crew potential. With only ten or fifteen remaining before it completed a tour of 25 or 30 missions, that left little time for lead crew training, flying a few missions as a deputy lead, another couple as a squadron lead, before finally as a group lead. The problem of availability of lead crews was of course further aggravated by combat losses. Although I've never read or heard of any statistics comparing the loss rates of lead crews to wing crews, I would expect that for lead crews to be significantly higher. The lead crew replacement problem was roughly comparable to a college football coach having his best players with only two years of eligibility.

We wrestled with means for earlier recognition of lead crew material, and finally decided on a bold and unorthodox step—we would 'manufacture' our own lead crews. As it was, replacement crews received from home had been together as a crew for only a few months of transitional training in B-24s. They had been put together as a crew by a clerk/typist somewhere taking ten names in sequence from ten lists of MOS (military occupation specialty)—pilot, co-pilot, navigator, and so on, creating a crew on paper. While it was understandable that training schools didn't have time for a more studied process, this random selection seldom resulted in a crew strong in all positions. We decided that the crew created by the clerk/typist was not sacrosanct. When a batch of replacement crews arrived, our training teams went to work training and evaluating the crew members in the air and in class, as individual position performers, and not just as members of a crew. After extensive and multiple testing and evaluation, we ran that long needle through our 'Key Sort' cards and came up with our own ten lists of MOS with individuals listed in descending order of excellence. From those lists we created some new lead-crews-to-be, the number depending on our need at the time. Some crews remained as they came to us, others were transformed into balanced wing crews and assigned to the three wing crew squadrons. The 'manufactured' lead crews would go directly to lead crew training. After dozens of practice missions, and countless hours in class and trainers they would fly their first mission in a squadron deputy lead position. After all that training, they were happy to go on a mission in any position. With normal progression, after five or six missions they would be ready for a squadron lead, and after ten, for a group lead. This somewhat radical departure in the handling of lead crews paid off with dramatic results. Our home-grown production of crews was not without initial detractors among our peers, and screams of anguish by incoming crews when they learned they might be dissected. Having gone through stateside training as a crew, they naturally assumed they'd continue that way. Fortunately, after a few missions our re-formed crews achieved a higher degree of cohesiveness than they'd known in their original training school crews.

                    With the development of radar equipment, a number of lead crew changes had to be made. Lead airplanes were equipped with radar bombing and radar navigational equipment. This required the training and addition to the lead crew, of a radar bombardier and a radar navigator.   Eventually, through training and of necessity, we were able to combine the radar and DR (Dead Reckoning) navigational functions into one position.   The flight deck had become too crowded with two navigators. Also, to further assure correct target identification and assist the bombardier in picking up the target as soon as possible, we substituted a 'pilotage navigator' for the gunner in the nose turret.   He would have been originally trained as a navigator or a bombardier, usually the latter. We gave him the additional training in the operation the turret and its guns.   In the nose turret, he had the best seat in the house.   He could check ground points before they could be seen from the bombardier's or any other position.   Another reason for using mostly bombardiers as pilotage navigators was that we had quite a surplus of them as the result of more of our 'operations research' findings. We came to recognize that in a typical group formation of three squadrons of twelve planes each, we had three leads, and three deputy leads all capable of putting our bombs on target.   In the other thirty wing planes we had thirty bombsights and thirty bombardiers just along for the ride; they never got to do anything, except risk their lives.   It was unlikely that all six lead planes would ever get shot down—we never came close to that happening.   The result was that we eliminated bombardiers and their bombsights from all wing planes.   Our surplus combat personnel pool was already quite large with all the ball turret gunners we had taken off the crews and the lead crew copilots we had displaced with command pilots.   We then added to it most of the bombardiers in the group.   We had even given serious thought to the elimination of navigators and radio operators on wing crews.   They too, were mostly along for the ride, particularly after so many Allied air bases were established on the continent, and there were so many more safe havens to go to when in trouble, and not have to go back over the water to England.   However, all of our missions to northern Germany involved long over-water routes, and the navigator and radio operator were the key links to air/sea rescue of planes forced down at sea. We had reduced wing crews from ten to eight without sacrificing performance, and at the same time exposed two fewer lives to combat risks, saved on weight, oxygen, etc. Some of our planes were equipped with 'carpet blinker,' or RCM (Radar Counter Measures) equipment, and this required the addition of a trained operator to the crew. The function of the RCM operator was to pick up the frequencies the Germans were using to direct the fire of their anti-aircraft guns, then tune our transmitters to those frequencies, and jam them. On each mission, several planes were also equipped with cameras which were triggered by bomb release to start taking pictures every few seconds of the bombs falling, until and shortly after they hit ground.   These pictures were, of course, our immediate 'report card' on how well we did our job. In a few other wing planes, hand held cameras were given to waist gunners to record anything of interest.

Another change we discussed earlier was the replacement of co-pilots on some lead crews with command pilots. Generally, the group, deputy group, and squadron lead crews had a command pilot in the co-pilot seat. The squadron deputy lead rode with its own co-pilot in place. We didn't have enough command pilots to fill all those seats on all occasions. When our group was leading the division, we did furnish command pilots to the lead and deputy lead planes.

As with our lead crews, we had to worry about our command pilots finishing up their tours, going home and leaving us with a leadership vacuum. We had to bring along replacements. As for the more senior ranked command pilots, the length of a tour was indefinite. Once at a cocktail party at General Peck's quarters he asked how many missions I needed to complete a tour. I told him just a couple and added that I was looking forward to at least a respite at home. He responded only half-jokingly "There are just two ways you can go home. Screw up and I'll send you, or you can go in a box."

1. the Davis wing on the B-24 was comparatively narrow from front to back edge. It had very high 'wing loading,' that is, its surface area was comparatively small for the load it bore. Among its other defining characteristics, it was extremely sensitive to the loading of the plane—the performance and safety onus for getting the center of gravity situated on the center of lift was proportionate to its extreme difficulty. The interested reader is directed to Glossary listings for *Davis wing, mushing,* and *'on the step.'*

31. Ferguson's Crew

Evaluating replacement crews was an important and sometimes difficult job. The records and personnel jackets they brought with them indicated only the flight and ground training to which they had been exposed, individually, and as a crew. The information was all quantitative and did not contain any qualitative assessment of performance. It was up to us in our pre-operational training program to measure their proficiency and supplement the individual and crew skills as best we could in the limited time available to us.

Hard tp measure were the quality of leadership provided by the pilot, and his judgement in the tight situation. In the air he was both the pilot of the airplane and commander of the crew. On the ground he was still the latter. If a pilot allowed it, the informality of their air operations would degrade to a buddy-buddy relationship on the ground, eroding respect for the commander and with it, crew effectiveness. By observing crews on the ground during Saturday morning dress parades, quarters inspections, in briefing rooms and at the Officers' Club, it was not difficult to distinguish between pilots who were crew commanders and those who were just airplane drivers.

Very early in the screening of one bunch of replacement crews we spotted one of those 'Hot-shot Charley' pilots with his slouch hat, a big wad of chewing gum, and a generally sloppy appearance. Our immediate reaction to his sort was "My God we've really gotten to the bottom of the barrel when we're training the likes of him to fly." Initial checks on the ground and in the air proved to no one's surprise that Lt. Ferguson' and crew were indeed raunchy, and at best marginal. It was agreed that unless they straightened out very quickly, Ferguson would be replaced. After a couple of weeks, the squadron CO said he felt the crew was shaping up, that they deserved a chance, and he wanted to make them 'operational.' I was reluctant, but the Old Man was willing to give them a try. Sometimes a couple of missions did seem to drive home the need for training and air discipline more effectively than weeks of training room lectures and practice missions.

On his first three missions, Ferguson was reported to have performed reasonably well, though the missions were relatively uneventful. However, I was still unimpressed, having had occasion to dress down the officer crew members for clowning around and being inattentive at a mission briefing. If they acted that irresponsibly right under our noses on the ground, what could we expect of them in the air beyond our surveillance?

It was on his fourth mission that Ferguson justified my fears. It was an early morning takeoff and he had just cleared the field when he claimed he started losing power on one engine. He salvoed his bombs, feathered the engine, went to emergency power on the other three and started back to the base. The tower held the other planes about to take off, and cleared Ferguson for an emergency landing. He made a rough but safe landing. A subsequent engineering check could find no problem with the engine. Conceivably he might have lost a few RPMs, panicked, and did a lot of wrong things. However this was a judgment call, and it's easy standing on the ground to second-guess what a 20 year old with less than 400 hours of flying time should have done.

In the tower we heard his report of engine trouble, but we had been watching other planes after he took off and didn't realize—and he didn't tell us—that he had salvoed his bomb load! When we learned that, we drove to the hardstand, and there found out that there was another and more serious surprise associated with this abbreviated and aborted sortie: when Ferguson salvoed his bomb load, he dropped with it one of his gunners—sans parachute!

All bomb units were under strict orders regarding the arming of bombs in flight. While over the UK, all bomb fuses, both nose and tail, must be safety-pinned until an altitude of 10,000 feet was reached. This was not only for the protection of people on the ground, but also for the safety of the crew in the event of a crash landing. The established procedure was for one of the waist gunners to remove the pins from the fuses at 10,000 feet, before he went on oxygen. This meant some discomfort for the gunner working in the narrow confines of the bomb bay without a parachute or connection for his heated suit.

Ferguson's crew, contrary to prescribed procedure, had decided it would be easier to remove the pins right after takeoff, and unbeknownst to us had been operating that way. That day the gunner probably had his arm hooked though a tail fin reaching for a tail fuse safety-pin when the engine did whatever it did to panic Ferguson. He pulled the pilot's emergency salvo handle and sent the bombs with the entangled gunner right through the bomb bay doors. Not that it made any difference to the gunner, but fortunately for the people below he had not yet removed any pins. Consequently, none of the bombs exploded.

We jeeped our way to the location of his salvoed drop. Some farm folk already there were crouched behind a hedgerow, not knowing what to expect from those bombs barely sticking out of the soft freshly plowed ground. In the middle of the bomb pattern was an incredible and memorable sight. In a shallow puddle of water, the gunner was lying flat on his back, arms outstretched, unscathed, and looking as though he were enjoying a peaceful nap. Next to him was a deep impression of his body in the soft ground, as though someone had cut out a very large gingerbread man with a cookie cutter. Apparently he had landed flat on his back, then bounced a couple of feet to one side into the puddle.

In retrospect, it doesn't make any sense. Even though I knew he had to be dead, but didn't look it, and maybe I was hoping he wasn't, but I decided I ought to move him out of that water. I slipped one arm under his knees and the other under his upper back and tried to lift him, but stopped immediately. Despite his unmarked appearance, the fall had apparently shattered his bones so that when I lifted there was no rigidity and he draped over my arms in serpentine fashion like a length of wet spaghetti. The dispensary later confirmed that his skeletal system was smashed.

As we drove back to the base, having seen these results of Ferguson's misdeeds, compounded by my personal reaction to his limp gunner, I was determined that he had had his last flight as a pilot of a crew and possibly even as a co-pilot. When I filled-in the Old Man on what had happened, and my recommendation, I was amazed that he disagreed. He was usually the tougher disciplinarian, and I was the one who tried to soften some of the stiff judgments he made. He decided that Ferguson would be reprimanded and the crew 'stood-down' for additional training.

A week or so later, the squadron CO said that he was recommending that Ferguson be made operational again, and would I care to air-check him first. I agreed, and met the crew at their hardstand. They were still not very well organized in pre-flighting the plane and equipment. When we were at a safe altitude, I put them through some emergency procedures, from which they

This met the informal Air Force criteria for a 'good landing:' everyone walked away from it. Unclear whether it also met the Navy crieteria of a *damn* good landing: one where they got to use the airplane again.

recovered, but not easily, and not without a tinge of panic. Everything they did was barely acceptable. They gave me the feeling that they were not really a crew, just ten individuals of questionable expertise who were riding in different parts of the same airplane. Upon return, I told the squadron CO and the Old Man of my continuing concerns. The Old Man decided to air-checked the crew himself and returned it to operational status. This was the first and only time we had ever differed significantly in the evaluation of crews.

Two or three missions later, Ferguson came back with some flak damage. He called for priority in landing and was given third position behind two others who had greater problems. He acknowledged the tower's instructions without question, then without explanation, left our traffic pattern and headed for that of our sister-group at Horsham St. Faith, a few miles away. Their mission had not yet returned, so he probably felt that he could sneak in there for an immediate landing. He didn't contact their tower, and they were not aware that he was going to try a landing there. However they did have a plane taking off which apparently Ferguson didn't see until he rolled out of his turn to his final approach. He realized then that he couldn't land without a collision, so he gunned his engines and pulled up sharply—too sharply. The tower heard an engine sputter. True to form, Ferguson went for a feathering button and, as we later learned, the wrong one. Even with one engine feathered and another giving less than full power, the plane was now very lightly loaded having gotten rid of its bombs and most of its fuel on the mission. This would not have been a very difficult situation for most of our crews. For this one, though, it was too much. From his steep pull-up he stalled straight into the ground several hundred yards beyond the end of the runway.

Horsham tower called and told us what happened, no survivors— needn't hurry over, and they were putting out the fire. We got together an accident investigating team and headed for the crash scene. I had never seen so little left of a crashed B-24. They had gone straight down into a soft farm field and only the charred remains of the tail section were visible. The medics from Horsham had already removed the remains of crewmen who were probably in the rear of the plane. The front of the plane and its occupants were so submerged in the soft ground that they hadn't gotten to them yet. To check the Horsham tower theory that this might be another case of wrong engine feathering, our team engineering members dug around the engines trying to ascertain the positions of feathering motors and propellers. With the medical and flying members of the team, I was digging in what had been the flight deck area trying to find and determine the positions of the prop feathering buttons.

The ground had been soft enough at the time of the crash, but after the fire fighters poured thousands of gallons of water on it, each step took you almost half way to your knee in mud. There were the usual disgusting visual elements of a crash scene, and the nauseating combination of odors from burning rubber, hydraulic fluid, fuel, flesh, etc. Crash investigations generally, and this one specifically, interfered with the enjoyment of the next meal, and sometimes the complete digestion of the last one.

As each of us would stick a bared arm down into the quagmire where we thought the feathering buttons should be, we'd fish around and pull up something in grab-bag fashion and try to identify it. We didn't have any luck that day with the buttons, but we did bring up from that area quite an array of plane and people parts. The one that stopped me was a handful of soft, slimy gray matter. As I held it at arm's length, Spivvy, my flight surgeon informed me that that was exactly what it was—somebody's gray matter! This was one of those sensations which has endured and still deters me from eating a look-alike delicacy.

We finished enough of our investigation that day to confirm that the crash was due to a number of pilot errors, and returned to base for a couple of drinks instead of a meal. The Old Man didn't then, or ever again refer to Ferguson. It would have been pointless. We both knew that this was a singular case in which my judgment happened to have been right and his wrong. Those positions could be reversed anytime.

I imagine that on a bronze plaque in some town square or village hall, Ferguson's name appears preceded by a gold star, along with the names of other local heroic dead. That's the way it should be for family and friends, but despite efforts to at least forgive, if not forget, I still have some lingering resentment that he was responsible also for the names of nine other mothers' sons being gold-starred on memorial tablets.   And on a strictly personal note, I credit him with providing me with two repugnant memories of touch—the snake-like drape of his gunner's body, and the slimy feel of someone's brains, possibly his.

1. Ferguson is a fictitious name. See first footnote to JJM's Introduction and Dedication.

32. Dare-Devil Denton

Back at North Pickenham we had a psychological problem with nightmares which was never dealt with successfully. It wasn't surprising that some crewmen after a rough mission might have sleep problems and nightmares. Those disturbed the sleep of hut-mates. The problem fell under the domain of the medics, and their first stab at a solution was to put the chronic cases all in the same hut. That solved the problem for many huts, by concentrating it all into one. Most sympathized with the occupants of that hut, and left them alone, but it did pick up the tag "looney hut." Occasionally someone returning from a pub crawling trip with a skin full of mild and bitters and a warped sense of humor, would toss a handful of pebbles up onto the hut's tin roof—a near-perfect simulation of flak hitting the skin of a plane—and touch off some screaming within.

At Rackheath one day we received a replacement crew with a twenty-seven year old co-pilot. That was a rarity, as co-pilots were usually in their late teens or very early twenties. He was 2nd Lt. Denton,[1] or 'Dare-Devil' Denton to use his show business name. He had been a 'Hell Driver' for 'Jimmy Lynch's Hell Drivers' before the War. That was the first of those car-bashing outfits which played state fairs and exhibitions around the country. Denton had spent several years driving cars through brick walls, through burning barriers, rolling them over, cracking them up, etc.

We thought here was a man who would undoubtedly qualify for lead crew consideration within a very short time. With his maturity, experience, and unquestionable coolness in the face of all kinds of dangers, how could he miss? We assigned him as co-pilot to one of our up and coming young pilots, Ralph Sims. Sims and his crew were somewhat in awe of their new, unusual, and very senior co-pilot.

Denton was not overly modest about his achievements. He had brought with him a sizable portfolio of photographs and clippings about his activities on the race track and his associations with beauty contest winners, starlets, etc. He was a little on the cocky side and very interesting to listen to, without being obnoxious. He felt that combat was going to be a breeze for him, and couldn't wait to get his first whack at the Jerries. Inevitably that first whack came, and with it, "Dare-Devil's" bravado went. He became noticeably subdued. Sims was noncommittal when asked how his new co-pilot was doing. Finally, after three or four problem missions, Sims confided to Capt. Frank Green, his Squadron Operations Officer, that he had a serious problem with Denton: he was cracking-up. Whenever enemy fighters or flak were encountered, he would cover his face with his flak vest and start screaming. Sims had not reported this earlier hoping that Denton would get over it, but it was getting worse. On the last mission he had left his seat and had to be restrained from possibly jumping out of the plane. Sims was concerned not only about Denton, but his entire crew was becoming unnerved.

Frank and the Squadron CO, Jay Taylor, came up to us at group with their problem. We decided to confront Denton with Sims' report for verification and whatever explanation he might have for his conduct. To our surprise, he readily admitted to all that Sims had said, was totally humiliated by his actions, but could offer no explanation for them. He felt confident that this was a temporary situation which he could overcome, and wanted a chance to do so. He was obviously sincere, his braggadocio was gone and he sat there humbly, almost pitifully, asking for a chance to vindicate himself before others, and especially for himself. We let him try another mission, but things only got worse.

We grounded Denton and sent him down to the Eighth Air Force Psychological Board for analysis. Their findings were surprisingly simple and logical. They said here was a man who was accustomed to taking severe risks, but they were always calculable. He knew what he had to do to protect himself under any given set of circumstances. In combat he was faced with extremely dangerous situations of which he had no foreknowledge and over which he had no control. The fact that he could not anticipate or control these conditions upset him as much as the dangers themselves. The Board concluded that this condition would not change and recommended that he be taken off combat flying. Faced with these findings, Denton agreed that they made sense, but still pleaded for another crack at combat. When this was denied, he suggested that he should resign his commission, as it was based on his becoming a pilot. This appeared to be an honest gesture, but we reminded him that Uncle Sam had spent a great deal of money teaching him how to fly and still had a need for pilots in non-combat activities such as the ATC (Air Transport Command, sometimes referred to snidely by combat pilots as "Allergic To Combat"). He was transferred out of our group, to where I don't know, and that was the last I saw or heard of him.

Paradoxically, Denton came to us as a flamboyant and boastful character who was admired, envied, and almost worshipped by the younger fellows for his pre-service achievements, but left us humiliated in his own mind for having failed in his own boast. Sadly, we failed to convince him that he had in fact earned the respect of all for the manly way in which he faced up to his failure, tried to overcome it, took his lumps, and never tried to alibi his way out.

1. Fictitious name. See first footnote to JJM's Introduction and Dedication.

33. Trucking

After breaking out of Normandy, bypassing Paris and heading for the Ardennes, Patton's armor soon outran conventional resupply systems. The 'Red Ball Highway' was established to speed up his supplies, but soon it too failed to keep pace with his rapid advance. His tanks were being slowed and stalled for lack of fuel. Ordinarily such an assignment would be given to air cargo or transport units, but they were fully occupied flying supplies to all ground forces. The assignment was then given to the Eighth Air Force which had no cargo or transport types, only fighters and four-engined bombers. The job then fell to the 2nd Air Division whose B-24s were structurally better suited than the B-17s to accommodate bomb bay tanks and the 5 gallon "Jerry cans" of gas. The bomb groups of the 2nd Air Division then modified some of their planes (mostly old 'war wearies') for handling this unusual and undesirable cargo. In the 467th, we installed plywood platforms in each of the four bomb bays. By layering cans on these, each plane could carry about 200 cans. These almost constituted the maximum load for the plane, but because the trip over and back was so short, we could save a great deal of weight by cutting down on the fuel load carried in the plane's tanks for its engines. There were a number of other problems which could not be so easily resolved. Most significant of these was the fumes given off by the gas cans. They permeated the plane, especially the bomb bay. A spark from any of the plane's numerous electric motors could touch off a deadly explosion. Our solution to that problem was to have the waist windows open and crack open the bomb bay doors a little to ventilate the plane. That helped the fumes problem, but also made for a cool and drafty flight. Another major concern was the possibility of a load shift in flight. It was difficult to tie down all those cans securely. If they were to break loose in rough air, the consequences could be disastrous. A weight shift of that magnitude could throw the plane into a stall, spin and crash sequence. The cans crammed into the bomb bay also made the crew's entry and exit a chore, and a bailout in flight would have been extremely difficult.

Division asked the 467th to coordinate the 'trucking' flights for a number of the division groups and to find, establish and operate a base in France as close as possible to Patton's most advanced position. So while the planes were being modified to carry the Jerry cans, we were in the Ops Block secret room at the 'situation' map, comparing Patton's latest position reports with our aerial photos of the same area.

Our first base in France was a former Luftwaffe field near Orleans. Patton soon outran that so we had to go back to the situation map for something closer. Most of the Luftwaffe fields in that area had been attacked recently and were badly damaged. By far the best candidate for our needs was a major Luftwaffe installation called Clastres near St. Quentin. Its runways were concrete and long enough to handle our planes. We just had to hope that they were thick enough also to hold our load. Just a couple of weeks earlier our group had attacked that very field.[1] We had done a good job on the buildings and the runways except, unfortunately then, and fortunately now, one squadron's bombs were wide of their mark and left the longest runway unscathed. There was one slight problem with Clastres: Patton's latest position report indicated that it might still be in German hands.

I took off early one morning in our P-47 with a folder of maps and aerial photos to find us a base, hoping that Patton's boys would have captured Clastres by the time I got there. It was a beautiful clear day over northern France. I flew at sufficient altitude so as to be able to take a good look at the general area of our interest, and also to avoid small arms fire before coming down for close inspection of a couple of alternatives as well as Clastres. I expected that when I did drop down I'd be receiving ground fire from all directions.   I wasn't disappointed.

The nice neat 'front line' drawn on the situation map was meaningless here.   The ground situation was so fluid that it was impossible to be sure where our troops were and where the Germans were.   They just didn't stand out in the open so that you could identify them; one had to rely on the occasional spotting of a vehicle.   But that didn't help much because our armored thrusts had penetrated the German lines by several miles at some points.   Pockets of Germans were behind Americans, and vice versa.

After checking a couple of alternatives which appeared to be in friendly hands, but were not as close to the front as we wanted, I headed for Clastres.   Sure enough, just as our embarrassing strike photos showed, we had missed the main runway and it appeared very usable.   I circled at low altitude, did not receive any fire, and could find only one sign of life. That was a GI in the unbuttoned turret of a Sherman tank parked at the far end of the good runway. I kept my nose pointed away from him and exposed the side of the plane so that he could see clearly my friendly markings. After circling a couple of times, I dropped my wheels and landed on the runway toward the tank.   I rolled up to about fifty feet from him, shut off the engine and walked over to the tank. The sergeant tank commander immediately suggested I get back in my plane and get out of there as fast as I could. The Germans were leaving the field just as he arrived about twenty minutes ago.   He wasn't sure how far they had gone into the woods or whether or not they'd be back.   When I explained the purpose and urgency of my mission, he became less concerned about the Germans, and got on his radio to call for reinforcements. When he heard that they were on their way and not far from us, he relaxed, left his tank crew to guard the plane and we started across the field for a quick look at the base—he with his sub-machine gun and tin hat, and me with my little .45.

Earlier when he suggested I leave, he warned against going anywhere on the base as anything could be booby-trapped or mined. But now he walked us around with very little caution, assuring me that the Germans had left in too much of a hurry to have had time to booby-trap anything. We saw a couple of recently killed Germans, further silent testimony to the hurry in which they had left. Germans were known for not leaving their dead behind and unburied if they could possibly avoid it. I'd been fighting them for quite a while, but these were the first Germans I'd seen close up, alive or dead.

In an F-W 190 turned up on its nose was another recent casualty, the pilot dead in the cockpit. Apparently he'd been caught taking off by an Allied fighter. Other than a bent prop, the plane appeared undamaged. The sergeant, who was an old hand at this business, observed that the bodies we'd seen had all been killed by .50 caliber bullets, which must have been fired from the air as he didn't have any weapons of that caliber.

As more Shermans arrived at the field we extended our inspection and with greater confidence. In the German Officers' mess we saw plates of partially eaten food. It was well equipped with china, food, and wine. In the Officers' Quarters there were uniforms, weapons, cameras, etc. I have often looked back at that missed opportunity, rare for an airman, to collect war souvenirs. I was in a hurry to complete my check of the base and get out of there. Except for where we had messed up this place with our bombs a couple of weeks earlier, it was in adequate shape and good location to serve as our Continental trucking terminal. With the sergeant's assurance that their tanks would have the area secured before the end of the day, I took off for England.

Early the next morning, Al Herzberg (our Group Air Executive at the time) took off with a flight of planes loaded with personnel and equipment to start operations at Clastres. Several of us followed later with additional personnel and more equipment. When we arrived, the tanks were there in strength and, as promised, they had cleared a wide area around the base. They almost guaranteed we were safe from ground attack. The Engineers had cordoned off all structures and equipment declaring them unsafe until checked for mines, and booby-traps. My tank sergeant from the previous day had moved on. However I spent some time with his commanding officer, a Major in charge of all the tanks in the area. When I commented to him how foolish it was for me and his sergeant to have gone into those areas which were now roped off, he assured me that there was nothing wrong with his sergeant's judgment. He explained, not without sarcasm, that the Engineers' modus operandi was to move in quickly on an area that the infantry or tankers had captured, rope it off, even when they knew it was 'clean,' strip it of everything of value "...like a bunch of goddamned locusts," take down their ropes and move on with their loot. And that's what happened at Clastres. When they left, the Lugers, Rollieflexes, uniforms, fine wines, and other prizes I'd seen the day before, were all gone. The only thing left of interest to us was a very large supply of *vin ordinaire,* and we took a lot of that back to Rackheath.

By the next day our engineering and communications sections were sufficiently set up that Clastres could start receiving our planeloads of Jerry cans. We used half crews to make these flights; no bombardiers or gunners. Despite the unusual hazards of flying under these conditions, and knowing that these trips would not count toward completion of a tour, the crews were initially eager to make them. The novelty soon wore off after some days making two trips, helping unload all those heavy cans, and finding they had no opportunity to "see those French girls." The flight itself was simple—low level, easy navigation, short duration. Hundreds of flights were made by the division's planes with few mishaps.

Our most serious problem in starting operations at Clastres was the total lack of ground transportation. We didn't even have a bicycle, let alone a jeep or a truck. The more cans we brought, in the worse our problem became. We had to unload the planes by hand, pass the cans from hand to hand like a Chinese fire bucket brigade along a line of GIs to storage piles. Because we had no other way to move the cans, these piles were all close to and parallel with our one runway. They were not dispersed as they should have been and offered an easy and inviting target for Luftwaffe strafing attacks. We tried to beg, borrow, and even steal transportation from the ground forces, but they wouldn't give us a thing.

A few days after being at Clastres, Al Herzberg was promoted to our 96th Wing Staff. I took his place as Group Air Executive and Smitty replaced Al as head of our Clastres operation.[2] Someone in his contingent somehow made contact with a band of FFI (French Underground) and told them of our vehicle problem. They said they could help, and showed up the next day with a surprisingly large and motley array of vehicles to do some swapping for what we had, namely gasoline. The upshot of the bartering was that we wound up with a small French pickup truck, two German motorcycles, a Mercedes bus that had been converted into a flat bed truck, a couple of bicycles, and the prize—a Malford two-door sedan (made by Ford in France). This was a tremendous bargain for the price we paid in gas, blankets, K-rations, and a copious supply of the table wine we had liberated from the Luftwaffe.

Smitty was then able to move the newly arrived cans farther from the runway, but we still had a dangerous situation with the thousands that had already been stacked up in solid rows near the runway. Patton's tankers were no longer taking it away as fast as we were bringing it in.   This problem was remedied sometime later when equipment for off-loading bulk gas was set up at Clastres.[3]   We could then fly in the gas in bomb bay tanks and fighter drop tanks.

When we first started this operation, Patton's tankers were standing around waiting

Empty Liberators hauled a variety of souvinirs to England after taking gasoline to freshly freed France.

when the planes landed, helped us unload the cans and took them away.   We couldn't bring them in fast enough. On one of those days "Old Blood and Guts" himself arrived on the scene with a large entourage and blasted Smitty for not delivering fuel fast enough for his tanks.   He was as unreasonable as his detractors claimed he could be, having no understanding of, or interest in what we had to do in converting from bombs to his little Jerry cans. He gave Smitty a few typically Patton-esqe words for "the Air

Corps." A couple of weeks later while I was there visiting Smitty, worrying with him about the over-supply of cans and considering cutting back on the trucking operation, we heard a noisy entourage headed our way. It was another Patton parade replete with sirens, motorcycles, command cars, etc. He pulled up next to us and dismounted. We saluted, and before he could say a word, Smitty who was still steaming from their last meeting, looked him in the eye and almost shouted "General, there's your goddamned gas. Please get it the hell out of here before the Luftwaffe finds out about it and blows up this place!" I was more startled than Patton at usually mild-mannered Smitty. Patton frowned, hesitated, then half-smiled and with a mumbled "Well done, Air Corps," returned our salute, and turned on his own staff and chewed them out thoroughly in his infamous foul-mouthed fashion.

Soon afterwards we did start phasing out the operation. Patton's advance had slowed down, and his conventional supply means had caught up with him. When we pulled out of Clastres, we had delivered 646,000 gallons of gas. We turned over to some fighter squadrons, newly arrived at Clastres, all of our Maquis-acquired equipment—except the Malford. That we wanted to take home. Earlier we had made the mistake of asking permission to take home the FW 190 and were told that nothing acquired on the Continent was to be taken back to England. So, we just didn't ask about the Malford. We gave it a coat of official olive-drab paint, put on proper invasion markings, and faked unit numbers on the front and rear bumpers. While everyone else went home by air, our tower control officer, Lt. Galvin, a fast and smooth talker from Brooklyn, took off for Normandy with the Malford. There he learned that the American beaches were under strict orders to not return any vehicles to England. He almost had our car confiscated by some MPs who were very curious about his strange vehicle, but he managed to talk his way out of it. He was more successful at a British landing beach, concocting a story about it being the personal vehicle of General Doolittle.

They took him aboard, and the next day the Malford became the queen of our motor pool. Our mechanics put it in top shape and the Old Man drove it all the time on base. It was also a great conversation piece when visitors to our base saw it. When the war in Europe was over and we had to account for and turn in all our GI equipment But what were we to do with the Malford? After we in the flight echelon had flown home, I heard that one of our ground echelon, left behind to close the base, had "willed it" to his local lady-friend.

1. The 467th hit Clastres on August 8, 1944.

2. Lt. Col. Walter R. Smith was the group's Operations Officer, or S-3. (See Glossary.)

The Rackheath Aggies quickly settled upon an apt nickname for their French operation: Shower Expeditionary Force, a great parody of General Eisenhower's command, SHAEF (Supreme Headquarters, Allied Expeditionary Forces).

3. The ingenious and ambitious Pipeline Under The Ocean (PLUTO) project had gasoline flowing to distribution points in liberated France, all the way from England, by early October, 1944. But Patton's armor couldn't wait. The better known resupply operation on the ground, "The Redball Express," was augmented by "Operation Trucking" in the sky.

34. Ghost Ship

After our ground troops had captured many German air bases in France, Allied air operations enjoyed greatly increased flexibility.[1] These bases, built by the Luftwaffe, were used extensively by the RAF and our own 9th Air Force tactical units. Most were too small to safely accommodate the four engined bombers of the 8th Air Force. The few we did use were primarily as emergency fields for crippled planes that could not make it back across the water, or as alternatives when weather at home prevented our planes from getting back to England.

Up to this time we had been reluctant to send out a mission unless we were reasonably assured that the weather in the British Isles would be acceptable for landing when the mission was due to return. Once a squadron of fighters returning late to England found all bases within fuel range 'socked in.' All they could do was to get a radar fix on their position, head toward the North Sea and bail out, hoping the pilots would come down on dry land (which they did), and their planes on the water (which thankfully they did).

On Christmas Day 1944, while our planes were en route to tactical targets in the 'Bulge' area, Norfolk weather turned unexpectedly bad, and we weren't sure how long it would last. Division radioed this information to our command pilots suggesting they might have to divert to bases in France, and any planes crippled or running low on fuel should consider this alternative. Lt. Paul Ehrlich's plane from our group, flying as a squadron lead that day, qualified as a cripple. We had sent along as their Pilotage Navigator Lt. Challenger Witham, the bombardier from one of our top lead crews, that of Carl Johnson. Witham had fallen a mission behind his regular crew due to illness, so this was a chance for him to make up a mission and at the same time add some important experience to the Ehrlich crew.

Paul had been born in Austria. In the early Thirties his father had seen Hitler's handwriting on the wall and wisely headed for the U.S., settling in California. Paul had won a number of titles as a speed skater and had hopes to become a member of the 1940 U.S. Olympic Team, which never became a reality because of the war. Paul's co-pilot was a colorful Irish-American from Pittsburgh, Red Killmeyer. His bush of flaming red hair was only partly responsible for his being 'colorful.' Red was another of the group's 'characters.' Shorter than average, but sturdily built, Red had a great sense of humor, but his outstanding characteristic was a deep and booming voice. At the slightest provocation, especially alcoholic, he would break out in a superb baritone rendition of anything, frequently "Danny Boy." Late at night and well down into the bottle, many think they can handle that song, but Red was truly outstanding anytime. He was the self-appointed choral director around our twin-piano combo in the Officers' Club. Almost nightly, it was sing-along with Red and our two pianists until the Officer of the Day closed the place down. Red also contributed to our extensive and impressive repertoire of dirty ditties and bawdy ballads.

Soon after coming off the target, Ehrlich's plane took some flak which damaged rudder control. Later, under fighter attack, an inboard engine was hit and went out of control. Having heard the instructions from home that cripples were advised to land on the Continent rather than risk it across the water to the UK, Ehrlich left the formation and headed for an emergency field in France. He soon encountered a solid undercast, lost all reference to the ground, and the engine that had been smoking started to burn. Paul and Red decided that they were fast approaching that point where B-24s habitually blew up. The navigator wasn't sure whether or not they had yet reached our lines so that they could bail out to a friendly reception. That became academic as the increasing fury of the engine and wing fire made up Paul's mind for him. He decided that they should abandon ship.

Of the many air procedures a crew had to learn, that for bailing out was the simplest and the one which best commanded a crew's attention. Each position knew his primary and alternative exits, assuming the plane would be reasonably intact and under some control. Under less favorable conditions, everyone hoped that he'd somehow scratch or kick his way out.[2] The pilot's 'bail out' alarm button was connected to bells throughout the plane. When he pressed a rapid series of three rings, it was time for everyone to bail out 'on the double.' Paul put the plane on automatic pilot, rang several series of threes, then all on the flight deck took to the bomb bay and out into the breeze.

To anyone who hasn't been on a mission it might seem highly unlikely that all of this activity could have gone unnoticed by other crew members in the nose and tail. But it is not surprising, and happened in this instance. The bombardier and the pilotage navigator in the nose turret knew that they had a faltering engine and were headed for France, but were unaware of the fire and did not hear any alarm bells. The gunners in the rear were aware of the fire, felt it wasn't getting any worse, and assumed that it wasn't bothering the pilot either, as they too had heard no alarm bells. The tail gunner did see some chutes blossom out under him, and made an interphone comment about "some poor guys bailing out," not realizing it was his own flight deck crew! Sometime after the bailout of the flight deck crew, Whitham and the bombardier in the nose, not having heard from the flight deck for some time, looked back up through the slots in the floor of the flight deck and saw no feet on the rudder pedals! Failing to raise the pilot or co-pilot on the intercom, they decided they'd better go to the flight deck to see what was going on.

Finding the bomb bay doors open and the flight deck abandoned, they called to the gunners in the rear to come forward. Whitham sat in the pilot's seat and the bombardier in the co-pilot's as they contemplated their predicament. The gunners arrived and reported that there had been a bad fire in the dead engine but that it had burned out. Despite the loss of one engine, the plane appeared to be in good shape otherwise. It was trimmed up, on automatic pilot, and flying well. Whitham, being a bombardier, could fly the plane in the air with the automatic pilot, but wouldn't attempt to land it. While they were weighing their choices, all undesirable, a couple of P-51s snuggled up under their left wing and gave Whitham a questioning "OK" hand signal. Whitham responded with the same signal, and the 51s took that to mean that, except for the feathered fan, all was well within the bomber. They then pulled out and up to an escort position to safeguard the crippled bomber's flight home. At about that time, the navigator completed a quick position guesstimate which indicated that they were probably already well over northern France and could soon be out over water. If they were going to bail out, they'd better do it right away. All agreed, and the second half of Ehrlich's crew took to the sky, leaving a couple of dumbfounded fighter pilots all alone high up there in the blue.

An hour or so later back at the base, I received a call from a friend at one of our fighter groups who turned me over to one of his pilots, wanting to report about "...one of your planes." He related with great excitement how he and his wingman were on their way home from a sweep over southern Germany when they spotted our crippled B-24. They dropped down to offer protection. One engine was feathered but the 'pilot' acknowledged that everything was OK—then they all jumped! The fighters made a close visual check up through the bomb bay, through the waist windows, into the nose, and flight deck, but didn't find anyone on board. They followed the plane for a while, then headed back to their base.   When they left our plane, it was still flying beautifully, headed for England.

Not long after that call, our mission planes returned and the crews told us that Ehrlich had left the formation with a burning engine and was headed for France. Not very long after that, we had a call from the tower of an ATC base at Valley, Wales. They too, were excited about a plane of ours which had completed a rather good wheels-up landing in a bog not far from their base. Apparently it had run out of fuel. The plane was pretty well banged up and would be difficult to retrieve because of the soft ground. They speculated that with a few more gallons of fuel, it might have made it to their runway. "The strangest part is that there was nobody in it."

At that point we could account for the plane and five crew members —we didn't know which five, and where were the rest? That night we got a partial answer, from German Radio. We usually listened to Radio Hamburg; much to the annoyance of visiting stateside brass, we preferred it to our own AFN (Armed Forces Network). At night, they would cover air attacks of the previous night by the RAF and that same day by the Eighth. Although their accountings were flavored with their point of view, they were typically more accurate than the accounts of the same activities which appeared later in our own press. Also, some of their broadcasts would personalize the news by identifying groups that participated in the actions and even name individuals captured, especially high ranking ones. That evening they had a surprise for us. They had picked up Paul Ehrlich and told of his being a native German who emigrated to the U.S. That accounted for at least one of the missing five crewmen. The following morning we had a message from France that Whitham and his half of the crew had landed safely behind Allied lines, and after processing through a medical evacuation center would be returned to base.

When the war was over, Ehrlich, Killmeyer and the others who had jumped earlier, were released from prison camps and were sent home before we had a chance to get their side of the story.

Sixteen years later, I was with a group of business associates at a meeting in Toledo, Ohio. Out to dinner, one of the fellows who had heard me tell of this 'ghost ship' incident, asked me to repeat it for the others. I did so, and finished by saying that I still didn't know the full Ehrlich-Killmeyer side of the story, and probably never would. Precisely as I said that, I felt a hand on my shoulder, and my military rank and name were called out in that unmistakable baritone voice—it was Red Killmeyer!

Try as we could, Red and I couldn't convince my friends that this was pure happenstance, not a put-up job. Red was then living in Pittsburgh, and just happened to be in Toledo on business. Red filled in some of the gaps of my earlier information. He told how Ehrlich apparently had somehow been recognized and taken in a different direction from the others at the Luftwaffe Interrogation Center at Frankfurt, and he had not ever seen him since. As for the bailout, he said the fire in the engine and wing was raging out of control when they last looked, and they thought the whole crew had bailed out when they sounded the alarm. He and the others who became prisoners, assumed the others who didn't show up in Frankfurt had been killed or evaded capture.

Red was amazed and amused by the Whitham mini-crew experience, and that the only part of their mission to make it back to England was their pilotless plane.

1. Allied air superiority at the time of the invasion was so total in France

that only three enemy aircraft were sighted over the Normandy beaches on 'The Longest Day,' and none of these came close enough to shoot—or be shot at.

2. The visual imagery of air warfare over Europe during WW II offers a sickening array of horrors. Any who ever witnessed a stricken plane "spinning in" from over 20,000 feet, with less than 10 parachutes blooming, vicariously experienced the nightmare of being pinned against a bulkhead or the inside of the plane's skin by centrifugal force, helplessly contemplating one's imminent death for a terrible final 90 seconds.

   We are haunted by our inability to know, in any particular one of the thousands of instances a crew was shot down, what final acts of heroism or courage might have dignified their last minutes. But there are many anecdotes on record of crewmen who survived only because their plane exploded and they were able to open their chutes once freed from the spinning deathtrap.

35. zero/zero

The desperate Battle of The Bulge had been going on for several days under very heavy German-favoring fog that made air support of our troops absolutely impossible. Meanwhile, the skies over northern Europe were relatively good for strategic bombing and we continued our sorties against targets in Germany far behind the lines. However we knew that as soon as the weather cleared, we would be called upon for low altitude, close support missions for our beleaguered ground forces. Such tactical missions were infrequently asked of heavy bombardment crews, but were ones which they liked best, or more accurately, disliked least. They gave the feeling of being more involved in the war, seeing results at close range, and lending visible support to the GIs slugging it out on the ground. Also, at the low altitudes at which they were flown, there was little need for heated suits, and no need for oxygen masks. One negative however: low altitude brought you within range of every gun the enemy possessed. A partial compensation was the decreased likelihood of fighter attack at low altitude.

While we knew that in the long run, it wasn't as important to knock out a few trucks, convoys, ammunition dumps etc., on tactical missions as it was to blow up the factories that made them on our strategic missions, the results were observable and more gratifying to the crews. The gunners had a chance to exercise their armament against solid objects and enjoyed the rare opportunity of seeing their bullets and tracers kick up debris as they struck ground targets. This was in sharp contrast to four miles up where only the tracers were visible until they burned out into nothingness. Except for the rare occasion when a gunner hit an enemy fighter, there was a feeling that a lot of .50 caliber noise resulted in nothing more than a pile of spent shell casings around his feet. That his firing, even though off-target, may have distracted the attacking bandit's aim and spared us greater damage meant little to the gunner who missed.

When the weather finally lifted over The Bulge, we were called upon for a maximum effort to attack dozens of tactical targets along the nebulous front. Unfortunately at that time there was a variety of bad weather scattered over our bases. The basic weather condition was a dense and solid cloud cover with a base of about 1,000 feet. Although not ideal, this was not uncommon, and did not halt our operations. However there were also lower, intermittent and totally dense layers that hugged the ground and moved slowly in waves. In this stuff, you could not see more than 10 to 15 feet, which made walking risky, bikes and jeeps dangerous, and flying utterly impossible.

That day, between the time we had gotten our crews out of their sacks at 3 a.m. for feeding and briefing and when we sent them out to their planes, several of these waves had drifted slowly through the base. After the crews had been briefed, the Old Man and I went back to our quarters to catch up on some sleep. We had both gone to the briefing even though neither of us was directly involved in it. Smitty, our Group Operations Officer was the Briefing Officer. We had wanted to stress to the crews the importance of this mission to our ground forces and make sure their assignments and target approaches were crystal clear. When operating so close to our troops, any errors could be costly in Allied lives. Not a bomb was to be dropped or gun fired unless the target was unmistakably identified. Attentive crews left the briefing room with rare enthusiasm. Every crew man from nose to tail, and newest to most senior, was eager to get over there and do his bit for the 'Joes' below.

One aspect of tactical missions

was more complicated than our usual strategic efforts. We were usually assigned many small targets, none of which required many bombs or airplanes. We might put up six planes on a bridge, another six on a munitions dump, a dozen on troop concentrations, etc. It was really several distinct mini-missions within the total group effort. Very often, each target called for a different type of attack and a different bomb load. Anti-personnel bombs would be used against troops, something heavier for trucks and convoys, and still heavier for armor and rail targets. This also meant we had to use more lead crews—a leader and a deputy leader for each of these separate attacks. This day the group's bomb load ran almost the full gamut of our bomb dump's types. Some carried anti-personnel bombs, others incendiaries for fuel and munitions dumps, still others 1,000 pounders for marshaling yards.

After briefing, Smitty had gone to the tower to run the mission from there until it was airborne, when the Group Command Pilot Al Wallace, CO of the 791st Squadron, would take over. At the appointed time, the tower officer would fire 'start engines' flares, and later, 'taxi' flares signaling the planes to move from their hardstands in a predetermined sequence to the perimeter strip, and line up on both sides of the takeoff runway. Our group leader would take off with Al Wallace aboard, then the multiple leaders and their deputies, and finally the wing planes. This would be a low altitude assembly for a tactical mission.

Shortly after the taxi flares had been fired, someone called from the hangar on the far side of the field to report that a real 'pea-souper' was rolling on to the field and their visibility was absolute zero. Because it was dark, those in the tower had no way of knowing this. By the time the planes had lined up for takeoff, the fog had blanketed the runway and was moving toward the tower. With takeoff only a couple of minutes away, Smitty had a problem. Flying conditions had now become zero/zero (no ceiling and no visibility) and there was no way of knowing how long they would stay that way. His first move was to get word to the planes to hold position and cut engines. To do this and maintain radio silence, the tower phoned the caravan to dispatch runners with flashlights to pass Smitty's order down the line to the planes individually. Smitty then got on the phone to 96th Wing Operations to inform them of our situation and his decision. They were dubious about his description of the severity of conditions at our base, because nobody else in the area was reporting weather problems, but ours was the closest base to the North Sea, whence this fog sneaked in. They refused Smitty relief from the field order, but allowed him permission to appeal to 2nd Division Operations. He called division but got nowhere. They too had clear surface weather, and regardless of conditions at our base, because of the importance of this mission, there would be no exceptions to the field order.

At that point, Smitty rang my phone and made a very brief nap out of what was meant to be my half a night's sleep. He briefed me on his predicament and asked me to come to the tower and try my luck with wing and division. When I got to my Jeep, the fog still hadn't permeated the entire base, but as I approached the field I ran into it as suddenly as if somebody had thrown a bucket of white paint against my windshield. After much guessing about turns, many bumps and misses, some cussing, and still in first gear, I finally reached the tower. My urgent appeals met with even less results than Smitty's. The division operations duty officer that night was not known as being the most reasonable member of that otherwise very capable staff. Our conversation became quite heated, but I didn't have a prayer. He had the authority and rank, and used both. We were still not about to send our crews out in our peculiar brand of weather without giving the Old Man a crack at the division officer (knowing they were both West Pointers) and if need be, the division commanding general.

Just as we were about to call him, Al came through the door. Unbeknownst to me, having been awakened by Smitty's call to me and overhearing my end of the conversation, he decided to come to the tower also. He readily confirmed our judgment, then took his turn on the phone with division. He really struck out. No relief from the order, access to talk to the general denied, and a direct order to get our planes in the air immediately. A direct order is court-martial bait: it must be obeyed. The Old Man angrily ordered the caravan to send its runners again to have the planes restart engines and be prepared to resume the mission.

Under these conditions even our most experienced pilots would find it difficult to negotiate a takeoff. It had to be 'on instruments.' With so many of our wing crews so limited in total flying experience, and even less so in instrument flying, we were fearful that unless the fog lifted miraculously, we were in for trouble. We were already well beyond scheduled takeoff time, and delayed even further, hoping the fog would move out as quickly as it rolled in. It didn't. When division failed to receive a takeoff signal from us, they got on our phone with fury and threats. Reluctantly and bitterly, the Old Man gave the order for takeoff.

Al Wallace in the first plane, eased his throttles forward and traversed the runway in what sounded like a routine takeoff. Only by sound could we follow its progress down the runway and into the air. We were relieved and somewhat encouraged. But as soon as Al was safely aloft he broke radio silence, screamed to the tower that this was too difficult a takeoff for some of the young wing crews behind him. We feared he might be right, but did not acknowledge his transmission. After the 15 second interval, the next plane started its roll down the runway in what at first sounded like a normal run. However, about the time he should have been clearing the ground, we heard the engines surge. The pilot had obviously gone for emergency power, pushing the throttles beyond the stops 'to the firewall.' Something must have happened to take this drastic measure. Some of us thought we heard a snapping or crackling sound like the breaking of limbs off a tree. That's about all we heard as takeoff plane number three revved up and his over-riding sound was all that came out of the fog as he lumbered down the runway. He appeared to have taken off successfully. His engines sounded as they should, coming from the right ear, crossing to the left, then beyond and out of range. Number four was then the focus of our attention. Like number two, he must have been two-thirds of the way down his takeoff run when his props whined as he went for emergency power. This time there was no question as to his having hit something. We held our breath and waited for explosive noises, but the whine of the engines continued. Apparently he was in the air. As number five started to roll, he relieved us of the fading sounds of number four, but only momentarily. A tremendous explosion from the direction of number four left no doubt as to its fate. Although we felt sure that it had cleared the boundaries of the field, it could be lying at the end of the runway and subsequent takeoffs could go plowing into it. Once again we instructed the caravan to red light the planes ready for takeoff and pass the word down the line once more to cut engines and hold position. We had hoped for an acceptable reason to halt operations, and inwardly feared this might be it.

       The immediate problem now was to locate the crash. We no longer cared about what division might think, say or do about halting operations. We called the engineering shack closest to the end of the takeoff runway to find out if they could spot the crash by eye or ear. They reported that the last plane had passed very low overhead, hit some trees and obviously crashed at some distance from the base. The fire trucks, meat wagons, and an assortment of other vehicles started creeping though the fog in the general direction of the crash sound. While the Old Man took over control in the tower, Smitty and I got into my jeep and proceeded as fast as visibility would allow toward the base back gate. We got there before the others, and the MPs at the gate, based on the sounds they heard, suggested that about a half mile down the public road we try a dirt lane that separated some sugar beet fields.

Before reaching the MP gate, we had counted four distinct explosions and we knew that takeoff plane number four had been carrying eight 1,000 pound bombs. In approaching a crash, it was critical to know the number and types of bombs aboard. When a bomb exploded under these conditions, it was usually a low-order detonation. That is, the explosive material was set off by surrounding heat and not detonated by a fuse. A low-order release of explosive energy was far less potent than a fused detonation. The casing would rupture or split open, but not fragment and splinter like a 'high-order,' fused detonation. It sounded more like the softer whoosh of a shot gun as than the sharp crack of rifle fire. Nevertheless, it still presented a destructive force and frightening experience.

Following the dirt road the MPs suggested, we heard three more blasts which told us we were heading in the right direction. Soon we saw a tell-tale red glow in the fog, and started picking up the firecracker-like sound of exploding ammunition. When we reached what we thought to be the closest point to which we could drive, we climbed over a hedge into a sugar beet field. We could now see flames licking under the red glow and detect some silhouettes of objects at ground level as the heat of the fire began to lift the fog above it. We moved low to the ground and cautiously waiting for that eighth 1,000 pounder to pop. We didn't have long to wait. It let go with a thunderous roar and blew a massive puff of air against our bodies. With number eight heard from, we could now move faster between the muddy rows of sugar beets to the crash site where all hell was breaking loose.

There were the usual pyrotechnics and noises made by exploding ammunition, flares, sputtering hydraulic fluid, an occasional whoosh as another fuel cell burst and burned. And ever present at crash sites that nauseating combination of foul odors produced by burning.

Our attention was suddenly diverted from all this activity by another explosion, seemingly of the 1,000 pound variety, which literally stopped us in our tracks. We were blown to the ground and muddied, but not hurt. Where did that one come from? We must have miscounted. But, as we started to get to our feet, another one let go and flattened us again! We lay on the ground trying to figure out what was going on. Could we have miscalculated that badly, or were we wrong in our identification of the plane's bomb load? As we pondered that puzzle we also came to the realization that we were still the only people in the vicinity of the crash. There was no sight or sound of crash and medical vehicles which were needed more in this situation than we were. We decided we'd better locate them and direct them to the crash. Smitty started out in search of them and I inched a little closer to the fire.

I could now feel its heat, and when I came within a hundred yards or so, still another bomb let go. This time, being on my hands and knees, I didn't have far to fall but still wound up on my back, shaken, but no visible damage. As I lay there unhurt but completely stumped by this whole situation and looking for my hat which had been blown off, I spotted two figures silhouetted against the fog coming toward me like an apparition. They were walking more toward the wreckage than away from it. My first thought was that they were fellows from the base coming to help. As they got closer I recognized that they were crew members in full flying regalia—heated suits, parachute harness, Mae West, and helmets with oxygen masks dangling. When they came closer, I realized that both were in a state of shock with glassy eyes staring straight ahead expressionless and zombie-like. One boy appeared unscathed, his equipment and clothing not torn or even muddied except for his boots. The other had his arm around the neck of the first and appeared to be in pretty good shape too except for a lot of mud on his pants. However, when I got a closer look at the side of his head away from the light of the fire, I could see that it and his clothes were covered with blood from a fist-size hole in his left temple. Neither one spoke and only the seemingly unhurt one appeared to be aware of my presence. These two added to my confusion—going toward instead of away from the crash, not the amount of mud I expected to find on them, no evidence whatsoever of being burned, and yet they had to be a part of that accident. I started leading them toward my jeep, hoping that Smitty might have an ambulance there by now. I was stopped by screams coming from the wreckage. Up to this point I'd had no evidence of life from that scene. I told the two to continue across the field to the hedgerow and wait there for an ambulance. The unscathed one seemed to understand and I headed back toward the crash.

Forgetting the puzzling bomb situation, I ran toward the screaming and about 40 yards from the center of the wreck found an officer member of the crew. From the waist up he was muddy but otherwise appeared okay. However his legs were bloody, fractured and severely burned. I put my arms under his and dragged him a safer distance from the fire. There we were met by Lt. Kairis,[1] the Engineering Officer of the 790th Squadron, who had run down through the woods from the flight line. With his help, we got this officer to where the two crewmen were waiting, one sitting and the other prone. As we got there, so did the ambulance and a fire truck led by Smitty. They took over the wounded and Kairis, Smitty and I went back to the crash scene along with some medics.

By this time the heat from the fire had carved out of the still dense fog a dome of good visibility over the wreckage. We found another crewman who was just barely alive; before we could get him much farther from the fire, he 'checked out' on us. We worked our way around to the other side of the crash and found two more, both seriously hurt and burned. The medics put them on stretchers and took them away. Finding no more survivors, we were able to turn our attention to the wreck itself. The fire was starting to burn down and we could get a little closer. Our firefighting equipment couldn't get through the muddy field to the scene, but there was nothing left to save anyway, so it burned out.[2]

It was then that we got our first really good look at the scene as a whole and unearthed a very dramatic clue to explain the puzzling number of explosions. Sticking out of the very soft ground and twisted wreckage, I could count six propellers! We now realized we were looking at the charred carcasses of not one, but two airplanes. Further evidence then became apparent—the number of engines, turrets, some still unexploded bombs on the periphery, and worst of all, bodies. In addition to the five who had come from the scene in varying states of injury, we counted eight bodies, leaving another five to be found deeper in the pyre. Some were burned so badly that we'd have to rely on Doc Mason's dental impressions for identification. There was one I was able to eventually identify.

With my foot I rolled over what I thought might be a back pack parachute. Instead, it was the charred remains of the upper torso of Lt. Paul Kaminski.[3] Paul was a fine young Polish-American boy from a coal mining region of western Pennsylvania. He had been with us for a couple of months and we were bringing him along in our lead crew training program. He was an excellent pilot, intelligent and eager. This day, as part of his training, he was riding as co-pilot in a squadron lead plane. An hour or so earlier that morning as I left the Briefing Room headed back to my quarters for what I had hoped would be half a night's sleep, I had said a few words to him as he and some of the crew were about to receive Holy Communion from Chaplain Sharbaugh before boarding a truck for a trip to their hardstand. Then, they were vibrant and impressive individuals. Now, in that terrible mess and carnage their individual features were obliterated, and their remains shared the basest commonality—they all bled red.

The second plane to take off, the one that brushed the trees, had apparently lost flying speed in the process and made a reasonably good belly landing in the sugar beet field. Probably most if not all of the crew survived the crash and were getting away from the plane when number four, after hitting the same trees more severely, crashed directly on top of number two. It was this second crash that caused the explosions, the fire, and death to probably all of number four's crew, and those of number two who were still in their plane. The two wandering enlisted men probably had been in the waist of number two and had been thrown out of a waist window as the plane bellied into the field and before skidding to a stop.

Because of the severity of their injuries, the crewmen were not taken to our base dispensary, but to the 65th General Hospital several miles away. We never heard how all of the injured made out, but to my surprise I did learn that both of the two I encountered first had died, even the one who didn't appear to have a mark on him. I also heard that the lieutenant I found near the crash did survive but was crippled.

When we got back to base, the fog had long since rolled away and the group had re-launched its mission without further incident. We were of course very late and missed the DAL, but managed to reach and bomb our targets. We also learned that the last plane to take off before we interrupted the takeoffs, had also struck trees with one of his landing gear, which would not retract. Realizing he couldn't land without damage to the plane and possible injury to the crew, he climbed to a safe altitude, bailed out his crew, then with the help of his co-pilot and flight engineer landed at a base south of us which had good weather. The one strut collapsed on landing and the plane ground-looped, but he did a good job of holding down damage so that the plane was recoverable.

As happened so often after a tragically eventful day, that night we had an extra scotch or two to dismiss that sad and gory scene from our thoughts. And just as predictably, that ploy backfired: we became totally occupied with the subject we sought to dismiss. This was the second piggy-back crash I'd seen in a year. The other was on the flying field at North Pickenham. There was a sameness to such dramatic and tragic accidents. People were drawn to them like moths to a candle. When close enough to appreciate what had happened and was happening, they were repelled, frozen to inaction, more in awe than cowardice. They became gapers. The first ones on the scene were the ones to take action and seemed thereby to unintentionally acquire a sort of proprietary interest in the scene. It became "their accident." So too that day, while Smitty, Kairis, and I made repeated trips to the wreckage searching for and retrieving injured, many who had come down from the base, just watched from a distance, stunned by what they saw. Only the crash and medical personnel lent a hand. We didn't come up with any better answers to crash-scene behavior that night than we had on previous tries. This included a repeat of Spivvy's imponderable question: would the badly and permanently mangled survivors one day thank or curse the heroic efforts to save them? Probably both, at different times. The only matter resolved that night was that we would recommend an award for Kairis's deeds that day. He had run down through the woods from the flight line and was the first to arrive at the crash after Smitty and me. He made trips into the wreckage without hesitation and not without risk. Although the three of us had been together throughout, Smitty and I felt our situation to be somewhat different from his. As a ground officer he had very little opportunity to earn any recognition. For his actions that day he certainly deserved some. Also, under our complex but unwritten identity and loyalty structure, we felt that as a paddlefoot Kairis was not under quite the same obligation to assist those air crew members as were Smitty and I, fellow flyboys. The incongruity of it all was that the number of decorations Smitty and I had been awarded, stemmed mostly from situations in which we really had little choice. We were either fighting our way to a target to do a job, or having done it, were fighting our way home to save our own skins and those of our crews. This morning we could have waited for the trained crash and medical crews and would not have been censured for it. Whatever risks we took were not under orders, but personal compulsion, and were probably more deserving of recognition (not that we wanted it), than our involuntary combat actions. Because there was no enemy action involved the highest decoration we could recommend for Kairis was a Soldier's Medal—a very worthwhile award, but we would like to have gotten him more.

Our rehash of this tragedy and interminable discussions of its causes and effects ended with the simple recognition that this had been a costly day for us in men and machines. We were more than a little bitter about the giver of the "direct order." We could hope only that the 'eggs' we finally laid that day along the front line saved more GI lives over there than the number we lost back here. We had suffered greater losses, but handling injured and dead at home was somehow more upsetting than losing them over the continent where they were handled by others. We could conjure pleasant thoughts and memories of friends who failed to return, but our eyes and other senses left us with distasteful and very final images of those we picked out of crashes.

1. My father may be mis-remembering the name. The latest directory of the 467th BG lists no 'Kairis,' nor does Fred Holdrege, 790th BS CO, recall this name or find it in his records.

　　　　The directory, which is not claimed to be definitive, does list two plausibly close names; my efforts to contact those two have not yet borne fruit.

2. A haunting photograph of the scene as the fog cleared, can be found on historian Andy Wilkerson's web page. See Bibliography.

3. The 467th BG's latest corrected roster (©1997) lists no 'Paul Kaminski,' or any obvious homophone of that name, and none of the 15 names given in the casualty list for the 12-29-44 disaster are similar.

36. Flak Shacks

A number of these rest homes were run for the Eighth Air Force by the American Red Cross. They provided R&R (rest and recuperation) for combat personnel needing a break from missions. Because the average wing crew took only three or four months to complete its tour of missions, not all were qualified for a week at a flak shack. Most who went there were lead crew members and staff flying personnel who were on more lengthy tours of duty. Occasionally, a wing crew which had been through a crackup or other difficult experiences would be given a respite there.

After a couple of months, and very few days away from the base, General Johnson suggested I take a week at a flak shack. At first I questioned the suggestion wondering if I were being told in a polite way that I was getting flak happy and was in need of it. He convinced me that such was not the case, and I took off for a week at Moulsford Manor.

This was a small estate near Moulsford on the Thames, west of London. The Manor was a large private residence in English Tudor style with an exterior of bright yellow stucco between the oak beams. The inside was oak-panelled and tastefully decorated with an appropriate intermingling of oils and tapestries. Although it had many rooms, none were large, but all were comfortable.

The permanent staff at the Manor, under a Special Services Officer, consisted two American Red Cross girls and an English lady who supervised kitchen, housekeeping and groundskeeping staffs. They did a fine job providing great meals and keeping the place in tiptop shape, both inside and out. We found out that this lady was particularly well qualified for her job inasmuch as this at one time had been her home. After the death of her husband, as was the English custom, the property was passed on to her eldest son and she moved into the dowager cottage on the estate.

The first stop after arriving at a rest home was the supply room where, from a limited selection of well-used, loosely fitting, beat-up 'civvies,' you chose a couple of pairs of trousers, one for roughing it during athletic events and the other for dinner and evening best, a couple of T-shirts, a sweater, a dress shirt and tie matching nothing, a jacket and a pair of smelly sneakers. The next order of business was to change into these clothes and park your uniform and all military trappings in a closet where they would remain until about an hour before your departure a week later. One of the Red Cross girls would then give you a tour of the Manor and grounds, introducing you to staff and fellow guests as you went along. Introductions were by name only, with no reference to rank or military unit. At the next meal you'd be introduced to the group as a whole.

Because "Mouldy Manor" was small, it was friendly and intimate. It didn't take more than a day to know most by first name. The staff and the help did all they could to make living there as different as possible from 'back home' on the base. The day started with breakfast, in bed if you chose, or in the dining room any time until 10 o'clock. Most came down for breakfast, not because they were anxious to get up, but as elsewhere, you soon learned that the farther you get from the kitchen, the cooler the meal becomes. The meals were a pleasant surprise. They served real eggs and real bacon, plus a variety of breakfast foods and fresh fruits.

Between meals, the staff had us pretty well organized with softball, volleyball, hikes, or sightseeing trips to Oxford and other local points of interest. We had our 'high teas' at about four. This was done royally with fine china and silverware and a tasty assortment of goodies appropriate for that ritual. After that it was billiards, ping pong, and bull sessions until we started our cocktail hour. Although it had the appearances of an open bar, the bartender was under instruction to serve no more than two drinks to anyone. However he did have a pretty heavy hand so that although no one got bombed, everyone felt thoroughly relaxed by the time the dinner gong sounded. For dinner we wore the best of our sad lot of civvies. All meals were served in the dining room and at a very large table which could accommodate us all, the Red Cross girls, the lady of the house, and the Special Services Officer. The complete service of silver, glass, and china caused moments of quandary and great indecision for the guests about utensil function and selection, until they learned to follow the lead of the permanent staff. Each of us had an assigned place at the table, his own napkin ring, and a double-faced place card so that the others could learn your name more quickly. Concluding our meal with the finger-bowl-with-rose-petal ritual, we took our coffee in the library for more conversation, billiards, and three nights a week, movies. After that and a night-cap, we were expected to be in bed before midnight. We were also expected to remain on the premises—pub-crawling trips to town were strictly verboten.

The Red Cross girls on these assignments (at least at the two homes I attended) appear to have been carefully selected for their jobs. One was sort of a 'Miss Outside' who would organize the outdoor games, hikes, etc. The other was a 'Miss Inside,' who was more the hostess-type and worked with the lady of the house running everything within. The week at Mouldy Manor was enjoyable and relaxing, but a week was plenty. Your mind never left your base completely, and by the end of the week you just had to get back.

The other rest home I went to was quite different in many ways. It was called Knightshayes Court down in the beautiful rolling hill country of Devonshire. It was a very large estate with a huge castle-like main building. It was of classic Gothic architecture with gray stone, leaded windows, arches, flying buttresses and surrounding terraces. Inside it had many rooms of all descriptions, all large. It was the property of Sir John Amory, leased to the Americans for the duration. He and his Lady were living in one of the cottages on the estate.

Because Knightshays Court was so much larger than Moulsford Manor, it could accommodate about twice the number, and the staff was proportionately larger. And while at Mouldy most of the fellows were from bomber groups, here they were mostly fighter pilots. Possibly due to its size, this place was not as well run. There was less organization of activities, with a lot of just sitting around and 'hangar-flying.' Missions were reflown ad nauseam. Each time, particularly during cocktail hour, the missions became more difficult, our results better, and enemy losses heavier. The bartender here couldn't count very well, or lost count due to a generous sampling of his own concoctions. By the time we were gonged for dinner, some of the fuzzy-cheeked flyboys were bombed and trying to navigate on one wing. Despite the more elegant setting, nothing here was done as well as at Mouldy—not the food, service, linens, tableware, etc. Not withstanding, it was still several cuts above the mess back at the base. After dinner, on the nights when we had our movies, Sir John and his Lady would walk up to the main house to watch the movie with us then stay for the late bar following. They were a very charming couple, appeared to enjoy our company as much as we did theirs, and didn't seem to become upset by the occasional abuse their home suffered at the hands of the few who had more than they could hold.

Knightshayes Court offered two unique and outstanding recreational opportunities, both of which I enjoyed to the utmost and as frequently as possible. The large front terrace was surrounded by a magnificent privet hedge crowned with a topiary of hounds chasing a fox. Next to the terrace, Sir John had constructed a beautiful putting green for Lady Amory who had been a noted golf champion in England. The green had a full range of rolls, speeds, and cup placements, and she knew them all. Although help was short during the war, that part of the grounds didn't suffer in the least. It was trimmed regularly and meticulously.

The other unique feature was a 'court-tennis' court. Sir John insisted that it was properly called a "Canadian Sticky Court." He said there was only one other exactly like it and that was in India. He had played on it there when he was in His Majesty's Service, and built an exact duplicate when he came home. Inside a large building on a hill behind the house, it was a full size tennis court on a hardwood floor with one long wall and the two shorter ones (behind the base lines) rising vertically to the ceiling. The opposite long wall rose vertically for about six feet, then at a forty-five degree angle for about four or five feet, then vertically to a balcony with a couple of rows of seats for watching the game. The floor markings, racquets and balls were all the same as in regular outdoor tennis.

The ball had to be served along the 45 degree shelf running the length of the court. It had to bounce once on the server's side of the net then once again on the receiver's side before falling to the floor, hitting the back wall or whatever else you could do with it. Once the ball was in play, as in regular tennis you had to hit it over the net and it could bounce on the floor just once. Beyond that, no holds barred. You could use the walls, ceiling, and floor and any combination thereof. Sir John played with us every day and was delighted to have so many with whom to play, and to teach. He was probably in his sixties but ran us ragged. He knew all the combinations to drive his opponents head first into the walls and come out with few points and many bruises.

Knightshayes Court had another unique and picturesque feature, a flock of all black sheep. Not only picturesque, they were also functional as they kept the spacious lawns cropped down to fairway level. But in the process, they presented a hazard for our softball games. They had no respect for our baseball diamond layout and frequently lubricated the base paths—a slide into second sometimes wound up in left field.

The day I reported in at Knightshayes, a Red Cross girl invited me to join the other guests on the terrace awaiting a low-level air show. It seemed that one of the fighter boys who had gone home the previous day had promised that he would be back promptly at three o'clock to put on an aerobatics and low-level flying show. Sure enough, promptly at three, he came down through the valley in his P-51, up the front lawn toward the house almost shearing the sheep with his prop, and pulled up, barely missing the house. He then proceeded to 'beat up' the place a few more times and engage in his version of aerobatics. While I had often enjoyed both performing and watching precision aerial maneuvers, the sloppy exhibition we witnessed was sheer madness and an invitation to disaster. I was even more appalled by the comments of those watching as to what they thought was well or poorly done. They went on to promise how much better and more daringly they would perform the day following their return to base. Since it was obvious that I didn't share their enthusiasm for these goings-on, they kidded me about being a stuffy old multi-engine pilot who didn't appreciate the finer facets of seat-of-the-pants flying.

That evening at cocktails I spoke to the special services officer in charge, to get his reaction to this stunting. He said it was a tradition of the place, innocuous, the highlight of the day's activities, and that everybody, even the townspeople, looked forward to the arrival of the next challenger in this potentially deadly derby. I learned further that the Red Cross girls and even Sir John and Lady Amory felt that this was "good sport" and that I was in a distinct minority of one in disapproving these antics.

I beat a reluctant retreat that day, but after the next performance, which was equally bad if not worse, I told the officer in charge that if he did not report this activity to division, I would. He reminded me that he was in charge and he chose not to. I reminded him that I could get my uniform from the closet and outrank him. Regardless of what he chose to do I was going to call division, and did. The Division Ops Officer was surprised and angered by what I told him. He asked for names and their units of those who had performed and any who were planning to do so. I gave him the name and unit of the next scheduled performer. He said he would take action to have these violations stopped.

The word got around that I had squealed, and I was in no danger of winning a popularity contest that evening or the next day. That afternoon at the usually appointed time for the air show, there was no gathering on the terrace, as they figured the next contestant who was due that day, and who I had identified to division, would not be showing up. However, we were soon to learn otherwise, as the low-level reverberations from a P-47 prop dusted off the roof. This brought everybody to the terrace, and I joined the group with surprise if not pleasure.

After our hero of the day saw that he had his audience, he climbed to a couple of thousand feet and started his dive down the valley, up the lawn to the terrace, and a fast pull-up over the house. The consensus of the expert panel was that this was not as good as the previous day's contestant, and not nearly as good as any of those present could do. When he circled low to get his marks, he could see the waving of disapproval and you knew that his next pass was going to be more dangerous than the last. Around he came, down the valley, up the hill, tighter to the lawn than before. This time he delayed his pull-up too long, and wiped one of the chimneys off the top of the house with one loud crack, and the stones came tumbling down the slate roof. From there he crashed about 300 yards up the hill behind the house and just missing the tennis court building.

We ran through the woods to the plane, but by the time we got there it was totally engulfed in flames. There was no question but what our late 'little friend' had succeeded in his boast to fly lower than anyone else. When the special services officer meekly suggested that since I knew the division people, maybe I could inform them about the crash. I reminded him that he was in charge here, I was a guest, and didn't want any part in it. Shortly after putting his call through to division, he came out of his office quite shaken and said the division ops officer wanted to talk with me. He asked me for the details of the incident, and since I was the senior officer from the division near the accident site, would I be good enough to file an accident report? He asked this as a favor, recognizing that I was on leave. He said that they appreciated my warning call of the previous day, but didn't realize how prophetic it would become. He also informed me that the general was going to burn the hide of the boy's fighter group commander, who had been warned of his fledgling's intention.

Needless to say, this dampened the spirit around the place. Although I felt vindicated, I certainly was not gratified. I was once more angered by another needless waste of life due to stupid disregard of orders. For a moment you could almost feel that this young man got what he deserved, but only for a moment. I hoped that back home his loved ones were consoled in the belief the he died in defense of his country rather than spreading himself all over an English wood while trying to dust a few slates off Sir John's roof.

37. A Sad Exchange

During the perilous days of the Battle of the Bulge, when ground forces on the Continent were so severely pressed, we and all other air stations in the Eighth were called upon to send some people to serve with the ground forces at the front. This was obviously a necessary move, but a difficult one for us. The requests for personnel from our base came in several stages. Initially we called for volunteers, then had to supplement that number with the selection of some of our less skilled people. Eventually, after several calls, we were taking some of our highly trained personnel, who we sorely needed for our planes and equipment, and sending them to the front to fire an M-1; we sent over 300 people in all. We were promised that in return we would receive a like number of people who were no longer capable of serving at the front, but were not sufficiently impaired to be released from service.

After several weeks, the promised replacements started trickling in. We hadn't expected that they would be equal in skills to those we had sent to the front, but we were sorely disappointed in what we received. Most had just come out of hospitals and R&R centers. In terms of physical capability, a number had been severely wounded and could not perform anything but sedentary work. We objected vigorously and succeeded in having the more badly maimed (including one with an amputated arm) transferred out and back home. Most were short on even basic military training, and whatever they had was of little value to our operation.

Disappointed as we were with our 'replacements,' they were equally pleased with their new assignment. We lived in relative luxury compared to where they had been. They now had a bed, a roof overhead, three squares a day, and nobody shooting at them. Our cuisine may not have been the best, but it was hot and palatable, and better than K-rations. Many also saw an opportunity to learn a skill that might be useful in post-war days.

We felt sorry for these poor fellows, but their arrival did present a significant interruption to our base activities. Our training

Red Cross Captain Lindsay Rand (center in back), along with one American and one English helper, certainly brightened up many a gloomy day as they made rounds to Rackheath and a few other bases, serving hot coffee and doughnuts to the GIs from thier 'Clubmobile,' a converted old bus.

department which normally devoted most of its time to air crew training had to divert some time and attention to a quite different orientation and training program for these ground replacements. This started with a two week period during which each of the new arrivals was exposed to the major activities of the base. At the end of that period, each was asked to specify his first three choices of activity and he would then be interviewed by personnel from the chosen activities to see if they could use him. We reasoned that allowing these people to select an assignment, rather than being given one would make for better morale, easier training, and Uncle Sam owed them a break for what they'd been through.   Generally this procedure was successful.   It did backfire somewhat in that so many asked for assignments in technical areas such radar, bombsight, electronics, engineering, etc. for which most had not even basic qualifications.   After some give and take we had everybody reasonably happily assigned to a location and a learning program.

The problem underlying all of our training programs was the relatively low IQ level of these replacements.   Because the Air Corps had always received from voluntary enlistment and the draft those with relatively high IQs, we had not encountered this problem before.   Prior to their arrival, on our base of about 3,000 people we did not have a single case of illiteracy.   More than 20 percent of the 280 replacements we received could not read or write.   It became a lesson in patience for our section heads to recognize that some of these fellows had not been dealt a very strong hand and had to be judged in view of their limitations.   This also posed a new challenge for our training department because they had no aids so basic as teaching the three Rs.   A solution eventually evolved, and in an unexpected and gratifying way.   The top non-com of our base mess setup was Tech. Sgt., an ex-pug from Philadelphia.   His last few years before the war he spent fighting club dates, smokers, and the like for very few dollars and many hard blows, indelibly displayed on his face, nose, and ears.   Schultz did a superb job of running a 24-hour mess for the whole base.   He was a big man in every respect, and held in high regard by all.   As you might expect, a number of the replacements were assigned to his area.

Late one night I stopped by the

mess hall for a cup of coffee, and passing Schultz's office, saw him with a group of the replacements. They were standing behind him, looking over his shoulders as he was writing at his desk. I asked one of his assistants what was going on and he told me that Schultz was writing letters back home for these fellows. He was doing the reading and writing for an increasing number and was planning to start teaching them how. Schultz had already written for some pamphlets so that he could start giving lessons. The training dept. took over the organization of the material and provided space for Schultz to use. He started teaching several nights a week. Soon others joined his teaching staff, all on a voluntary basis. Before long, illiteracy was again becoming a thing of the past on our base, thanks largely to Sergeant Schultz.

Many of those ground forces GIs wound up in the motor pool, and mostly by choice. There we could use a number of people of varying skills for cleaning, driving and maintaining our extensive and varied array of motor vehicles.

One day shortly after all these assignments had been made, I found a smartly dressed infantry private sitting in a chair immediately outside of my office. We exchanged salutes and I walked to my desk wondering, but not asking, what he was doing there. After a while, curiosity got the better of me and I called in Sgt. Brosseau, the non-com in charge of the office, and asked if he knew what that soldier was doing sitting there. With a thinly disguised smile he replied "That's your driver, sir." "What do you mean, my 'driver'? You know I don't use a driver on base, and off-base I use Schleppy." "I know," he replied, "but he told the motor pool he wanted to be your driver. Since this is 'be kind to war-weary GIs week,' there he is." The motor pool officer apologized for not checking with me in advance of this assignment, but hoped I would go along with it inasmuch as this young man was so keen about the idea of driving my fancy jeep and wasn't really capable of doing much more. At least I learned that the attraction was not me, but my jeep, the jazziest vehicle on base. The sub-depot repair boys had taken some skin from a cracked-up B-24 in our 'bone pile' and constructed a complete metal enclosure - roof, side panels, and rear. They made of it a two-door sedan with sliding Plexiglas windows on each of the doors, and spray-painted the interior a light blue. The boys in the parachute section fabricated some comfortable cushions from old parachute seat packs, and stitched up some nylon curtains for the rear window. It was a pretty sensational looking GI vehicle and far more comfortable than in its original state for the cold and rainy weather we had so much of the year. Rather than tell this eager young soldier that I didn't need or want a driver, I 'chickened-out' and went along with the assignment, knowing it wouldn't last. With my irregular twenty-four hour schedule, the amount of time he'd spend cooling his heels, whatever glamour he now saw in that job would soon evaporate. After about a week it did.

Eventually, some of these replacements did establish themselves as useful members of our group, and had the war lasted longer, more would have. But, overall, we didn't fare well on this exchange. We sent to 'the Bulge' about three hundred men, all of whom were skilled, some highly so. We heard later that some of them were killed and others turned in outstanding performances at the front. Their replacements caused significant disruption to our routine that was not offset by their contribution to our operations. At least we had the satisfaction of knowing that our base went well beyond the call of duty for those GIs and afforded them many opportunities for self-improvement. The feedback we got from them indicated that our efforts were appreciated, and more importantly, successful.

38. Brooklyn Boys

Despite considerable experience which proved it folly, we still tended to prejudge what an airman's reaction to combat might be based on initial interview impressions. We were sometimes guilty of stereotyping the big and outgoing as being dependable when things got rough, and the smaller and quieter as ones to be worried about. Two of our errors in such judgments involved a pilot and a bombardier, both from Brooklyn. They had only one other thing in common—both were Dodger fans.

The pilot was David Klein,[1] a Jewish boy of average height, slender build, and fine features. He was quiet, seemed a little tense, and somewhat of a loner. He was also very intelligent, and had interrupted his college studies to serve. Initially we had wondered and worried whether he was robust enough to wrestle a B-24 around the skies, and assertive enough to be an effective air crew commander. Because of our concerns, we watched him carefully. He surprised us so well that eventually we put him in for lead crew training.

Klein's first mission as a lead crew was flying a squadron deputy lead on the morning of our tragic "zero/zero" mission. His plane hit some trees on takeoff, but managed to stay airborne. The right landing gear was damaged and left dangling. The right wing was also damaged, but the extent couldn't be assessed from within the plane. Klein calmly described his situation to ground control and indicated that in his judgment the most prudent course of action would be to bail out his crew, excepting the co-pilot and flight engineer, and try to save the plane with an emergency landing at one of our bases with flyable weather. He did so, all very effectively. As expected, the gear did collapse soon after touching down, but he maneuvered the plane skillfully so that no one was hurt and the plane was repairable.

The bombardier was Steve Rowe,[2] taller than Klein, heavy set, and rugged features—the kind who'd be picked first when choosing up sides for stick-ball in Brooklyn. Klein would have been chosen last, or nearly so. Rowe was outgoing and loud. Yet as much of a loudmouth and braggart as he was, he wasn't totally obnoxious and took a lot of kidding good-naturedly. Most new arrivals with big mouths became somewhat chastened and quieted down after a couple of missions, sometimes so quiet and introverted that they became cause for concern. Not so Rowe. The more missions he flew, the louder he grew. Despite his talk, he performed very well over the bombsight, which after all, was the name of our game. He had already become a lead bombardier when Klein and his crew were selected for lead crew training. Upon hearing of Klein's elevation to lead crew status, he was heard to say that he'd never ride with a Jew pilot, even if he did come from Brooklyn. He was subsequently told that he'd ride with whomever, whenever, and wherever he was told, and that further disparaging racial remarks would not be tolerated.

Sometime later on a mission to the Hamburg/Harburg area, I was Group Command Pilot and Rowe was flying as bombardier in my deputy lead plane. Our route in was over the North Sea, turning south just short of the island of Helgoland, following the Elbe river down to the target area. From the turn-south point to the target, the flak was heavy and intense. We were taking a beating, and yet by the time we reached the drop point, we hadn't lost a plane. As our bombs released, I looked out my window to see if the other planes had dropped with us. The deputy lead was tucked in tight under my right wing, and I was startled to see someone come out of the nose wheel door and drop clear of the plane, closely following our bombs. The individual was not wearing a chute, and although I did not get a look at his face, I knew it had to be Rowe. The only other person riding up front was the nose turret gunner, and I could see that he was still at his station. I became totally oblivious to all else going on around us as I watched and vicariously experienced Rowe's fall from 22,000 feet—undoubtedly the longest couple of minutes of his life. Paratroopers would facetiously refer to 'jumping to a conclusion,' and say "It's not the fall that hurts, it's the sudden stop."

After return, I had engineering check the nose wheel doors on that plane, because on some models of B-24s those door opened inward, and on others they opened outward. We were always concerned that the latter arrangement might open inadvertently under the weight of a crewman, if stepped on. This couldn't happen with those opening inward which turned out to be the arrangement in Rowe's plane. He had to open them to get out.

Why he did this we'll never know. I doubt that this was the scariest mission he was ever on. The consensus of those who knew him best was that his incessant boasting was a cover-up for fear, deep-seated and growing to a breaking point. One of those close flak bursts may have been his final straw.

From what we knew, we had to conclude that this was a suicide. We'd seen many of our people die, but this was the first to do so deliberately, by his own action. This occasioned some soul-searching on fear, that strongest underlying emotion of all crewmen. It rose dramatically on each take-off, and subsided only with the landing, but never went away until a tour was completed. Everybody had it. You wouldn't want anybody aboard who was so stupid as to not be afraid. It just had to be kept under control and not turn to panic. It was more obvious in some than in others. Sometimes I thought that like pain, some had a greater threshold for it than others. At other times it seemed more related to experience and intelligence. Those being more fearful were so because of their greater awareness of danger. Crews appeared more nervous on their last five missions than on the first five.

That sight of Rowe free-falling then, and the recollection of it even today, can cause those sudden muscular contractions in the lower abdomen, reminiscent of a first ride in a fast-descending elevator.

1. A fictitious name; see first footnote to JJM's Introduction and Dedication.

2. *Ibid.*

39. Ticket Punchers

Chaplains sometimes presented problems for unit commanders. It was not universally true that senior officers were dictatorial by nature, abusive of junior officers and GIs, and lacking in due regard for the spiritual well-being of their troops, but some chaplains took this as their starting assumption. Some also seemed to have difficulty in recognizing a point of demarcation between the spiritual and temporal aspects of GI problems. To them, *personnel* problems were frequently considered synonymous with *personal* problems and within their purview of their ministry. This situation may have been unique to air units where combat was engaged at great distances beyond the purview of 'paddlefeet' who lived in peaceful conditions and relatively comfortable surroundings. That was their assignment and they couldn't be expected to fully appreciate what the air crews went through on missions in the wild blue yonder. In ground forces, chaplains and other non-combatants were close enough to the front to share the hardships of their men and sometimes get a personal taste of it, giving them a greater appreciation of the necessity for command and discipline.

Our chaplains were good and well-intentioned men. We had a few who were a little too sanctimonious to achieve easy communication with GIs, and a few of the opposite type. In over-striving to communicate, these few out-did the GIs in language and/or drink and thereby lost the respect to which they were entitled by the insignia they wore. In the 492nd we had a full-time chaplain, a mid-western Lutheran minister by the name of Geitz. He was a little bit of a 'Holy Joe,' but a good guy and well respected by all on the base.

After the briefing team had done its best to present the target and all aspects of the mission in clear and positive terms, the mission command pilot or the group CO concluded the briefing with inspirational thoughts on the importance of the mission to the strategic effort of the Eighth, the overall effort in Europe, and the defeat of fascism, etc. Hopefully, at this point the crews would feel that the day's work ahead, though dangerous and difficult, was worth the candle. At this point Chaplain Geitz would be called upon to deliver his more-than-a-few words for the spiritual elevation of the crews.

His words may have been appropriate from the divine viewpoint, but not always from a military one. They sometimes served only to negate whatever uplift the command pilot's message had achieved. He gave voice to the single thought we all shared, that some of those before him probably had 'one way tickets' for that day's mission and would later that day face their Maker. Each time I yielded the platform to him to deliver his verbal Extreme Unction, I thought of the gladiators in the Roman circus being faced by the emperor and parroting "morituri te salutamus." He always wove into his little benediction some hint of the possibility of imminent death for some, and the absolute necessity for prayer and repentance by all. He concluded by reciting a brief original prayer in funereal tone and leading us in the Lord's Prayer.

Not that we expected our crews to go charging out to the planes with the same eagerness as starting a 48-hour pass to London, but at least we hoped that the mission objective would be paramount in their minds. After the good chaplain got through with them, the more sensitive ones might leave for the planes with their tails between their legs, alongside their parachute harness. Repeated admonitions to the chaplain regarding the gray area between our bombing mission and his spiritual one proved quite ineffective. It was not that he was defiant, but he felt (and it would be hard to argue) that ultimately his mission was more important than ours.

We insisted that he either tone down his requiem ritual, or we would eliminate his part in the briefing. He tried but seldom succeeded, and we never made good on our threat.

At Rackheath in the 467th we had two full-time chaplains, Father Sharbaugh, a Catholic priest who had come from a monastic order in Pennsylvania, and Chaplain Duhl, a Minnesota Lutheran. Father Sharbaugh was young and very military in appearance. Probably because he had come from a cloistered situation he seemed to take offense at even the mildest of the descriptive GI language heard around the work areas, mess hall, and barracks. He was a very admirable person with the best of intentions, but on the fringe of the 'Holy Joe' category.

Chaplain Duhl on the other hand was a big, good-natured oafish type. He was large in both height and girth, with an unkempt mustache which needed even more frequent wiping in the mess hall than it got. Quite in contrast to Sharbaugh, 'Chappie' Duhl enjoyed, or at least tolerated, the rough and ready language of the base.

Toward the end of 1944, the 467th attained peak efficiency in all aspects of our operations. We became the first B-24 Group to be the top bombing group in the entire Eighth Air Force. Until the war's end there were only a couple of months when we relinquished that lead. We were the lowest in loss rate of crews, highest in the percentage of planes kept in operation,and lowest in number of infractions by our personnel away from base (London, Edinburgh, Cambridge, etc.). We were receiving accolades from upper echelons for being at or near best in several minor measurable areas as well.

But we also led in a dubious

distinction—ours was the highest VD rate in the Eighth! Our people boasted that we were not only the best bombers but also the best lovers. 'Disgraceful' was substituted for 'best' by myself, the Flight Surgeon, the Chaplains, and the Old Man. The problem was damaging our effectiveness and image, and occasioned several meetings. It was generally agreed that most fellows leaving the base had no specific intention of getting into this sort of trouble, but circumstances sometimes developed which caused good intentions and virtue to fall by the wayside. Younger fellows especially would get to London and take on a skinful of spirits which would lower their resistance to the advances of the infamous 'Picadilly Commandos.' Some 19 and 20 year-olds didn't stand a chance against the onslaught of those old pros. Medics continually cautioned and lectured about what could happen, but since we couldn't go along and hold each one's hand or keep the Commandos' hands off them, the best we could do was to forearm them with 'pro' kits.[1] These were available at all medical stations, but Army regulations stated that a military person had to *ask* for one and that neither medical nor command personnel could force anyone to use or even accept one. Nevertheless, we decided that no one would be allowed to leave the base on pass or leave without a 'pro' kit. What he did with it, if anything, was his business. We just wanted to make sure that he was covered in the event that lightning struck.

Because our new homemade ruling constituted a distinct violation of regulations, it was never put in writing, but the word was passed around to all orderly rooms (where passes and leaves were issued) that no one would get through the front gate on pass or leave without showing or receiving there a 'pro' kit. Chaplain Sharbaugh's personal grapevine picked this up in a hurry and he came storming to our office to see the Old Man. Sensing his mission, Al let him cool his heels for a while, hoping he might go away, or at least calm down. He just waited outside and seethed. When he was finally let in he raged about our violation of all laws, moral and military.

He threatened us not only with the Inspector General for military infractions, but possible excommunication for moral ones. He eventually touched off the Old Man's fuse, whereupon he told Sharbaugh that this decision had not been hastily or easily made and was going to stand. Shower suggested the chaplain stick to punching tickets and leave the operation of the base to us.

Chaplain Sharbaugh didn't give up. The following Sunday with the Old Man and me sitting in the front row of our station chapel, he proceeded to lambaste the new rule from the altar, telling all present that they were under no military obligation to accept a 'pro' kit; rather, they were under moral obligation to *not* do so. The Old Man chewed on his mustache, I fumed as best I could without one. There was little we could do in the middle of the Mass to counter this overtly hostile act by our good chaplain. We learned later that he had been in touch with the 2nd Air Division chaplain and this spat was threatening to bust wide open. It looked very much as though we were going to have a major war within our minor one with the Germans. Of course we knew that we were wrong 'by the book,' but we also were sure that Wing and Division would understand our position and that no action would be taken unless the Inspector General became involved.

The Old Man chose to pick up the gauntlet and hit the chaplain where he knew it would hurt. Chaplain Sharbaugh, in addition to serving our base, volunteered as Catholic chaplain for a nearby POW camp run by the British for Italian prisoners. The camp was a couple of miles from our base and held several hundred "Eye-Ties" who had been picked up in the African Campaign. They were enjoying their confinement and often worked on local farms helping with the brussels sprouts and sugar beet crops. Unlike the penned German POWs, they were given a great deal of freedom. They had no interest in fighting, and most had never had it so good. In his work with his Italian POWs Chaplain Sharbaugh found some who were particularly artistic and bought a jeep-load of them to our base to decorate our Nissen-hut chapel. By the time they got through building an altar from bomb crates, painting and muralizing the altar, ceiling, and walls, and fashioning altar cloths from bed sheets, it looked more like the Sistine Chapel than the simple arch of corrugated metal over a concrete slab that it really was. The chaplain was good to his Italians and drove them around in his jeep on and off base. This never alarmed anybody. They got along famously with our GIs, many of whom had names like theirs and some could speak their language. However from a strictly military viewpoint, this was a pretty odd situation—allowing enemy prisoners freedom to roam about a highly classified combat base.

Rightfully and spitefully we clamped down on these activities and insisted the POWs not be allowed on our base or in our vehicles. The feud continued for some time before we were forced to back off a bit, and made it 'recommended' rather than mandatory that pro kits be taken when leaving the base. The words were different, but we made sure that the effect was the same. MPs recorded the names of those who didn't have one when leaving the base, to be used in the event that any of them wound up on our 'poison ivy' (VD) list. The following month we lost our top billing in the VD category. In succeeding months we never did regain first place, but despite mandatory viewing of VD horror films and our continued pressure at the MP gate, we always remained a strong contender.

Our tiff with Chaplain Duhl[2] was of a very different order. As noted earlier, his appearance was hardly military and bordered on being raunchy. Furthermore, he was gaining weight, and noticeably so. This was unusual; most of us were dropping pounds steadily on our diet of dehydrated *everything*—eggs, milk, orange juice, potatoes, etc. The fresh food we had most was locally grown brussels sprouts which were far too plentiful.   Meats were canned, and despite the valiant efforts of our mess crews, not very appetizing.   Most of our nourishment came from peanut butter, apple butter, and a variety of jellies and jams heaped on our own mess hall baked bread.   Cajun style coffee completed the list of mess mainstays.   Somehow, Chappie Duhl's battle jacket was straining its buttons, and his trousers were riding higher on the waist and further from the shoe tops.

The officers' mess was cafeteria style; food was served on steam tables along one wall. Along the opposite wall was the 'brass' table which was reserved for selected members of the group staff and squadron commanders.   The Old Man's place was in the center, I was immediately to his right, and Group Ground Executive Ion Walker was to his immediate left, nameplates at every place.   One evening at mess, Col. Shower watched with increasing displeasure as Chaplain Duhl proceeded along the chow line, loading his plate to the gunwales.   The Old Man commented in the direction of Major Joe Mann, our Group Flight Surgeon (but for all to hear), that the Chaplain was getting very fat.   Joe and the rest of us allowed that indeed he was.   With that confirmation, the Old Man took off on a lengthy and increasingly vehement tirade about how 20 years from now the Chaplain would be in a Veterans' Hospital someplace incurring a lot of expense for the government because his undisciplined appetite during the war had ruined his health! The upshot of this outburst was that he decided that the chaplain should be put on a strict diet to prevent him from gaining more pounds, if not rid him of some he had acquired.   He instructed Joe to prepare each week a daily diet to be followed by Chappie.   Joe would consult with the mess officer to develop Chappie's private menu, which was turned over to the Group Adjutant and published on official group orders over the CO's signature. That was probably a first for military orders.   Naturally, this generated all kinds of kidding about what could happen for violating a group order by taking an extra potato, etc. The chaplain was mildly chagrined by the whole procedure, but took it good-naturedly and tried his utmost to conform to Joe's diet. Chappie had to report each Monday morning for a weigh-in at the Base Dispensary. At lunch that day, Joe would give to Shower an oral report on the latest weight and girth figures. It worked! Duhl eventually divested himself of many pounds and inches, and looked and felt better.

Another area in which relationships with our chaplains sometimes became sticky was that of GI marriage requests. US Military personnel in England were required to receive commanding officer approval before marrying. The chaplains played a key role in handling such requests. With air crew members, we looked at such requests with a jaundiced eye. Most airmen were overseas for only three or four months. The amount of time allowed off base during that short period hardly gave an opportunity to meet, let alone really know, the 'right type' of girl.

The typical request would come from love stricken 19 or 20 year old naive airman involved with a less-than-naive local lady whose primary interest was an immediate marital dependency allowance, and a very possible subsequent GI insurance death benefit. Usually such motives could be brought out with a little investigation, and the request denied. The chaplain and fellow crew members could usually reason out this decision with the disappointed applicant. Such requests were infinitely more complicated when the girl was 'in a family way;' her family, friends, and clergyman all became tenaciously involved. They typically got support from our own chaplains. In those cases where a number of men from our base could honestly testify that any of them might be the father, acceptance of this hard resolution was less difficult.

In the absence of any negative indications as to the lady's character, some marriage requests were allowed. Our military and worldly points of view were at odds with those of our churchly representatives in some of these cases. Disagreements, which almost always related to the non-military actions of our people off base, were very time consuming and frustrating for commanders. This incongruity stuck me memorably one day—I went directly from the tower after dispatching a bombing mission, to a chaplain's-office meeting with an irate family and clergyman to discuss paternity and marriage.

1. 'Pro' is short for *prophylactic,* or condom—'rubber' in today's parlance.

2. My modest father, presently in no danger of embarrassment himself, had used fictitious names for all three of the chaplains in this story, which gave him the comfort to write plainly of matters which... well... we *never discussed.* I have taken the liberty of substituting the real names of Reverends Geitz, Sharbaugh and Duhl.

Reverend Geitz's sombre last words to five hundred men may have served to console some of them in their last moments. In the condom debate, the colonels and Father Sharbaugh each toed the line their roles required, and the conflict was inevitable. And Dad would certainly join me in my hopes that Reverend Duhl, having survived the Shower diet and open ribbing, went on to enjoy years of sweets without running up a big bill at the VA hospital.

40. Russians and Other Rascals

On our last trip to Berlin, the part of the FO which detailed the position of of Russian troops now just east of Berlin was unusually lengthy. It indicated the approximate location of Russian lines on the eastern outskirts of Berlin and cautioned against straying into that area. It also advised our crews to be alert for Russian fighters and the likely need for defending against them. The Eighth's relationships with the Russians had once been good enough that a U.S. air base was established on Russian soil. This allowed planes from England to bomb targets deep into Germany, land in Russia, refuel and rearm for a return mission to Germany then back home. Without that arrangement those distant German targets could not have been reached from England. These 'shuttle-bombing' missions were given great press fanfare as being ingenious and highly successful. After a short time they stopped abruptly with no official explanation or press notice. A senior officer who had been stationed there told me that the Russians, both military and civilian, made our operating there impossible and virtually drove us out. He said that Russian girls who dated GIs had their heads shaved—a lá French treatment of their women who dated Germans.

On early DPs (deep penetrations) to northern Germany we were instructed that in the event of plane problems which threatened safe return to England, our ranked choices were: 1. make it to Russia; 2. make it to Sweden; 3. bail out and try to evade capture. Later the options were revised: 1. Sweden; 2. Russia; 3. bailing out. Ultimately, and at the time of this mission, Sweden was 1st, bailout 2nd. The Russian alternative was omitted altogether; tacitly telling us we had better chances with the German enemy than with our Russian 'allies.' As the Russians moved westward, there were more frequent sightings of their planes over German airspace. There were a number of instances of their fighters attacking our bombers, but never our fighters! There can be no 'mistaken identity' excuse for their actions. The only four-engined planes over Germany were ours by day and those of the RAF by night. The Luftwaffe had long since lost the last of their few four-engined planes. A number of times our fighters caught their Yak 9s in the act of attacking our bombers, and made them pay dearly. One of our fighter pilots said that "Our 51s against their Yak 9s is like shooting fish in a barrel."[1]

The final FO item regarding the Russians was a reminder for crewmen to wear their 'blood chit.' A transparent plastic folder hung around the neck on a string, it contained a small American flag printed on silk cloth. Printed in Russian, one side declared "I am an American. Please communicate my affairs to the American Embassy in Moscow." On the reverse side were more detailed instructions for the Russian to follow in identifying and handling an American. We had also been taught to say "Yah Amerikanets" (I am an American).

The pilot of one of our Squadron Lead Crews that day was Lt. Chapman. His bombardier was a fellow of Slavic origin from Chicago, Lt. Yarcusko. His pilotage navigator was my old Squadron Bombardier, Capt. Ed 'Alex' Alexander. The takeoff and successive group, wing, and division assemblies were accomplished readily and on schedule. All went smoothly for our group until just before bombs away, when Chapman's plane took a direct hit near the bomb bay. Both engines on the right side were knocked out totally, and one of the others damaged. One crewman was killed outright, and the engineer was blown out of the hole in the plane. Not being able to hold the lead, Chapman called for his deputy to take over. His bombs were hung and he couldn't even salvo them. He was losing altitude rapidly and sliding off in an easterly direction. The flak followed him causing more damage and making the plane more difficult to control. Then a couple of Me.109s spotted his crippled ship, adding

more holes to the plane, but not the crew. They were
relieved as several Yak 9s happened along and drove off
the outnumbered Krauts, until these 'allies' then took
their turn at shooting up Chapman's plane. At that point
Chapman bailed out his crew, but the Russians continued
to attack them in their chutes. All landed safely behind
Russian lines, except for the killed crewman, who went
down with the plane. Alex's parachute came down directly
on top of him and a bunch of hysterical hens in a chicken
coop. When he rid himself of parachute and poultry, he
found he was nose-to-muzzle with a Russian rifle. When
he tried to reach for his blood chit, the Russian, probably
thinking he was reaching for a shoulder holster, batted
Alex across his already football-battered nose with the
rifle butt. He finally allowed Alex to get to his feet, but
Alex's repeated "Ya Amerikanets" made no impression on
the Ruskie , who pushed and shoved Alex along with his
rifle.

After a while, they came across
Yarcusko and his Russian captor. To Alex's great surprise
and relief, Yarcusko had his Russian under control.
Whatever Slavic language he had learned from his parents
back in Chicago was readily understood by his captor.
After being handled roughly earlier, Yarcusko blasted him
in the mother tongue and the Russian, possibly believing
him to be a Soviet flier and officer, backed off in a hurry.
In deference to Yarcusko's linguistic ability, he and Alex
received kid glove treatment until they arrived at a
Russian headquarters, where they were joined by the rest
of the crew. Yarcusko told their interrogating officer who
they were and what happened. The Russian officer gave
them a hard time and they were taken to a makeshift
detention area with no food or water, and no bandages for
their cuts and wounds. That evening they were brought
out, given an acceptable meal and treated hospitably by a
higher ranking officer and his staff. Yarcusko learned
that the reason for the sudden change in attitude was that
the officer who had interrogated them earlier was not an
army officer, but a member of a communist party group

that traveled with the army to make sure they toed the party line, not unlike the German SS. After he had left, the others felt they could be friendly to the Americans.

A couple of days later Chapman's crew arrived in Moscow, shortly after President Roosevelt's death. They were amazed at the state of public mourning they saw there. The American Embassy eventually arranged for them to fly back to England via Yugoslavia and Italy. More than a month after they were shot down they returned to base.

Crews returning from that mission gave a good indication of what had happened to Chapman's plane, and the following day we received from the Russians the names of crew members they were holding and the crewman who was killed. Because Alex and his wife Mary were very good friends, I wanted to let her know that he was safe before she might receive a dismal War Dept. MIA telegram. Since unofficial notification on my part was against regulations, that night I sent a simple cablegram to my wife asking her to "Tell Mary that Alex is visiting Uncle Joe." She correctly interpreted my use of Stalin's nickname and made the call.

The family notification for the dead crewman was quite another matter. His next of kin was a very pregnant, very young, and very recent bride living near the base. A few weeks before this mission, he told one of our chaplains that he wanted to marry a local English girl—in fact, he *had* to marry her! The chaplain discussed this with the Old Man, whose permission would be required. On further checking it was learned that the girl was very well known around the base and not the type we wanted to have any of our people marry. She decided to get her hooks into our crewman who was better paid as a flyboy than most of the fellows she'd been going out with. There was some question about his having known her long enough to be the father, but there was no doubt about her being pregnant. It could have been by him, or as one of our sage GIs put it, "...by any of many." The Old Man reluctantly caved-in, pressured by the girl, her family, her clergyman, a local official, our chaplain, and our crewman claiming he was madly in love and knew the child was his. In a nearby village church her minister and our chaplain performed the marriage.

Normally if there were to be any communication with next of kin after official War Dept. notification would be by a chaplain. In this case we felt we couldn't wait for a War Dept. notice, which would come long after the local grapevine would have informed the girl rather unceremoniously that she had become a widow. We felt she should receive official notice immediately by personal visit of his commanding officer, a chaplain, or a someone who knew both the crewman and the widow. One of the squadron staff officers fit the bill. After evening mess he took off with jeep and driver for his duty call. Before leaving he was reminded not to tarry as he was a member of that night's briefing team for the next day's mission. Late that night I was playing blackjack in the Officers' Club when a call came down from the Ops Block saying that the field order was in and completed, but the needed staff officer couldn't be found. A call to the motor pool revealed that he had sent the driver back to the base saying he'd call for him when he was ready to return. We found a replacement for the briefing team and I asked the MPs to let me know when our sad-tidings bearer returned to base.

Very early the next morning, the MPs reported that the missing officer had called the motor pool and a jeep was on its way to pick him up. I instructed that when that jeep came to the gate, the driver be told to drop his passenger at the Ops Block, with orders to report to me. He arrived there, pretty well hung over and uneasy, shortly after the Old Man and I reached our office. After much hesitation and several false starts, he came clean with his unclean story. While he had gone there with the purest of intentions to notify the pregnant wife of her new widow status, he wound up spending the night with her! This was some new kind of low, for both the girl and our officer. He received punishments for missing his Briefing Team assignment, but there wasn't much we could do about the reprehensible and despicable way he had delivered the official notification.

1. Richard Davis notes in his Carl A. Spaatz and the Air War in Europe (page 580) that one such dogfight was reported on 3-18-45, the the same fateful day that Bill 'Alex' Alexander had such a memorable welcome from one of our 'allies.' Six Russian fighters went down, but no Americans.

Returning from a mission, Lt. Roger Leister called in when a few minutes from the base, requesting priority emergency landing. The problems he described were such that there was good reason to doubt that he could negotiate a safe landing. With the rest of our planes just entering our traffic pattern, we didn't want our field closed by a crackup, so the tower instructed him to head for the special emergency landing strip at Manston. Leister, figuring he was a little closer to Rackheath, continued toward us. Crews considered being directed to Manston tantamount to a kiss of death. Even though it was designed for crash landings and was the best equipped of all the bases in the area to handle crashes and injured crews, pilots would rather go 'back to the barn' and take their chances in familiar surroundings, than go to a strange field.

In the event it made no difference; he was not going to remain airborne long enough to make it to either field. He was descending at a rapid rate, and barely cleared the little village of Kirby Bedon, belly landing in a field just beyond. The crash wiped out the plane and several of the crew. The others, including Leister, sustained varying degrees of injury.

Villagers who witnessed the final seconds of the flight felt that Leister had done a heroic job in avoiding their village and wanted to show their appreciation.[1] We were unaware of this until some weeks later when our chaplain received a call from the village's minister saying he would like to come over and have a few words with us. He then told that the villagers had collected a small amount of money and would like the names of the crewmen, both those killed and the survivors, so that they could be placed on a memorial plaque they planned to put in their church. Our chaplain thanked him for the kind thought and supplied the names. The minister said he would let us know when the plaque was ready for dedication. They would, of course want representatives from our base to attend.

When the minister finally called to say that the date of their dedication service in the churchyard was set, most of us had forgotten about it. The Old Man and our Protestant Chaplain were specifically invited; others were welcome. We asked if we could provide a bugler, a band, or a ceremonial firing squad. He thanked us for the offer, but said that all of those functions were being provided by the parishioners and the Home Guard.

It was a bright and clear Sunday morning when Chaplain Duhl and I, substituting for the Old Man, set out with my driver, Corporal Schleppy, to find Kirby Bedon. This turned out to be more difficult than planned. The village was not much more than a crossroad, and not in a direction any of us had ever traveled before. When the English removed all names and directional signs from the roads in this area so as to confuse any invaders, they had had the Germans in mind, but it turned out to be the American invaders who were ultimately victimized. By the time we arrived, the ceremony was just about to begin. The Home Guardsmen were a very senior and somewhat motley group with their tin hats, gas masks, and an interesting assortment of nondescript firearms. The band consisted of a bugler plus several other pieces, played by a mix of very young youngsters and very old oldsters—the males the war left behind in every village. It was a very touching sight.

The minister opened the ceremony with a brief and dramatic accounting of our plane being skillfully piloted to just miss the center of the village and crash in the outskirts. He went on to speculate as to what the thoughts and motivations of our crew might have been from earlier in the day performing their mission, being damaged, avoiding the village, then crashing, with some paying the ultimate price. He then drifted skillfully into

A network of common rights-of-way have criss-crossed Great Britain since Roman times. The farmer's deliberate 'two-track,' cutting diagonally across this new crop in the lower right, blazes one. From this viewpoint it heads east, over remnants of the main runway at Rackheath, to the hamlet of Salhouse.   Subtle but durable leftovers of invasions Roman, Norman and American, are to be found everywhere in the beautiful Norfolk landscape.

a dissertation on the bonds our countries shared, our common fight for freedom and against oppression. It was truly a beautiful and compelling piece of oratory. When he concluded with a prayer there weren't many dry eyes in the churchyard. 'The Star Spangled Banner' and 'God Save The King.' were played in turn. The Home Guard fired their volley of shots and the bugler blew 'Taps.'

I had managed to stay dry-eyed through the fine speech, the anthems, and the gun salute, but I was always a sucker for 'Taps,' even in Boy Scout days. Just as I was about to turn away, surreptitiously wipe a cheek, then thank the minister, he surprised everybody, especially me, with an obvious after thought:

"Now we'll have a few words in conclusion from the commanding officer of these gallant American airmen."

I have no idea what I said that day, or how long I took to say it. Apparently it was at least acceptable as I was warmly congratulated by the minister and some of his flock.

1. It was my distinct honor to meet Roger Liecster and his wife Dotti at the 467th's 1999 Reunion. I am compelled to include here the most telling part of the episode, which my father never recorded.

Leister recounted that he his confidence was badly shaken by the crash, and will never forget the way my father handled that discreet confession in the days before he was to return to flying duty. Dad arranged to 'check him out' again on the B-24, unobtrusively. The two alone took a Liberator on a flight in the Norwich environs, first with Roger in the right seat. He seemed comfortable enough, so my father put the Liberator down and put Leister in the left seat.

Roger had a few butterflies but was doing well, and glad for the opportunity, in privacy and outside the pressure of his next mission, to restore his comfort and confidence. But he still wanted to purge one last skeleton from the closet, and screwed up the courage to name his fear; that he might have a rough time flying low over bucolic English villages. Dad calmly told him that this was a fine and safe time to find out. With a heavy heart but perfect control, Roger made a low pass—over Kirby Bedon.

Leister finished his tour without substantial incident. With quiet honesty, he had faced his demons courageously. He is a perfect exemplar of the unsung hero, the self-sacrificing citizen-soldier who pressed on repeatedly, with all of his mortal fears and limits, in the face of gravest danger.

42. The Apple Farmer

Other than "Dare-Devil" Denton, I recall only one other case where an air crewman failed to complete his missions for other than physical reasons or incompetence. The circumstances in Denton's case, which required no forgiveness, were very different from these, for which forgiveness was beyond me.

We had a young pilot from the New York City area who had put in several missions, and had done a creditable job with no occasion for criticism or distinction. One day he told his Squadron CO that he would no longer fly combat missions, as orders were being cut in Washington to bring him home and release him from service. He explained that his father was a very close friend of a highly influential member of Congress, and the latter had arranged for his return to civilian life to manage an apple farm in upstate New York, which his father had just purchased in his name! Our initial reaction was one of disbelief. This hitherto quiet and conforming crew commander must have suddenly flipped. However it didn't take a psychiatrist to recognize that such was not the case. He calmly and openly stated that flying missions with a high probability of getting killed made no sense whatsoever to him. He knew that by refusing to do so he would be disgraced, but at least a few years hence he'd be alive, and many, if not most of those who continued to fly would be heroic dead. His cowardice would one day be forgiven, if not forgotten by the few who knew, and most of the people with whom he'd be associating in the future would never know. His argument, looked at from a purely objective position, had compelling logic. Suspending such intangibles as 'duty' and 'honor,' you could almost subscribe to his argument and its conclusion.

This was not a case for Psycho

Board deliberation, but for prosecution by the Judge Advocate's office. That didn't disturb our apple farmer in the least. He was grounded while waiting for the lawyers to decide on action to be taken. For his own safety and group morale, we kept his case under wraps as best we could and confined him to quarters except for meals at the mess hall. We also recommended that Division move him elsewhere while they were considering action to be taken. About the time they were to do so, orders were received from stateside reassigning him to a staff unit in Washington—with some ambiguous wording about consideration for release from the military for a "war-essential function."

This infuriated everyone Vigorous protests up and down the chain of command were to no avail. Our "apple farmer" took off for home, figuratively thumbing his nose at our whole effort and what we stood for. We never did hear the outcome of that political machination. Of all the failures and wrong-doings we ascribed to 'Washington,' this was the most bitter pill. And worst of all, I must admit our apple farmer was right: I'd almost forgotten the incident, and have *definitely* forgotten his name!

From the time the wheels lifted off the runway until they squealed down upon return, every mission entailed anxiety and tension throughout. The level varied greatly with the incidence of unpredictable happenings— most occasioned by the enemy, but some by our own miscues and equipment failures.

Mission assembly at altitude in the crowded sky over our corner of England was always an anxious adventure. In the dark, or through heavy cloud conditions, it was a perilous one as well. Collisions were not unheard of; near-misses were commonplace. After assembly the bomber stream departed the English coast and anxiety subsided until landfall over the Continent, when apprehension over what the Luftwaffe and the flak batteries had in store for us elevated the anxiety level again. The eventual appearance of the Jerries and flak drove it sharply higher.

At 'bombs away,' just as the plane seemed to heave a sigh of relief by rising a few feet upon release of its lethal load, crew tension dropped a little also. 'Til now we'd been "on government time." Now, having laid our eggs we were on our own time, and our only objective was to get ourselves and our big-assed-bird back to the roost in one piece. Not that we were home-free after bombing—some of our heaviest losses occurred then. Exiting the Continent and starting a gradual descent over the water, tensions abated markedly for most, but not for those with mechanical trouble or fuel problems and facing the immediate decision of whether to chance it over that long stretch of icy water, bail out over enemy territory, surrender, or limp to refuge in a neutral country.

Our missions averaged more than

seven hours, and could be a drain on the spirit as well as the body. I remember well my longest—nine hours and ten minutes to Munich and back. However during the course of any mission, even a difficult one, in the absence of severe mechanical or injury problems, there *were* periods of relative tranquility, when only an occasional radio or intercom message interrupted the steady soporific drone of the engines. Crews became quiet and pensive. The thought common to all was to get this one over with and have one mission less to go. Each had his own personal flashbacks to family and home and returning to both. There were wonderings about friends who were missing and imaginings about what could happen to you and your crew.

Random thoughts were triggered by the scenes around us. Sudden appreciation of the beautiful panorama below and surrounding majestic clouds—all of which you had been looking at but were only now suddenly *seeing*, reminded you that this was the way flying used to be. Mindful of the sharp incongruity of that peaceful scene with our far-from-peaceful intent, I even found myself recalling Sunday afternoons like this when we'd go out for a family ride with Grandma in the Reo Flying Cloud to see the fall foliage and be treated to a hot fudge sundae at Brigham's.

One day, snow-capped Alps jutting up through a gray layer of heavy undercast, hearkened me sharply back to our chaplain's message that morning. His biblical allegory was the mountain of life each of us must climb. I found myself wondering what the Luftwaffe chaplains might have said that morning to their charges; whose side was God on, anyway?

Out of necessity, we developed euphemisms for death, which was all around us and hard to keep far from our conscious thoughts. One day as I was entering the base, in the last days of the 492nd, I witnessed two of our planes returning from a mission entered the traffic pattern at the same time, both firing red flares. Each was calling for immediate landing. With both on final approach, and neither responding to tower control, tower asked the caravan at the landing end of the runway to fire red flares, intending both to abort landing. The lower of the two responded by pulling up and into the path of the higher. They collided about fifty feet above the surface and crashed just to the right of the runway. My driver sped cross-country to the field and the crash scene, arriving there soon after the fire trucks and meat wagons.

Scores of horrified ground personnel who'd been waiting for the mission return rushed across the field to the crash site. The planes were demolished and burning, their twenty crewmen in a variety of conditions from just badly banged-up to dying and already dead. It was such a helpless feeling to watch them die, checking out of the world the way they entered—very much alone.

It was a gory scene and I saw several of the emergency crew and medics lose their last meal. This accident and its losses had a much greater impact on base personnel than any of our much larger losses over the Continent. This they saw. The vast majority of our wounded and dead they never did see. These were cared for and buried by the enemy.

Death and dying became subjects of serious discussions in huts and drinking bouts in the clubs for the next few days. Some ventured that the badly mangled pulled from the wreck, might one day in their agony, resent or even curse their saviors. We could imagine that after a prolonged state of vegetation, we might prefer to have taken a quick shell in the chest. We all knew we had to one day die, and everyone had to do his own dying, but didn't know when, and that was a good thing. We knew only that from conception our days were numbered; that with each tomorrow the number would be one less.

While we were all now familiar with death, the word itself was usually avoided. The official written term was the acronym KIA (killed in action). The oral expression could be any of a number of euphemisms. 'Bought it' was probably the most commonly used. Legend had it that a soldier made his parents beneficiary to his GI insurance so that they could pay off their farm mortgage in the event of his death. In getting killed, he 'bought the farm.' Other euphemisms were 'had it' and 'checked out.'

Discussions of the 'when' of death frequently led to the deeper question of 'why' and ultimately the theme of that old spiritual song: "Why Was I Born?" No consensus on that question was ever reached among the many and differing theologies represented by our typical American assortment of Catholics, Jews, and all types and shades of Protestant. I didn't help to clarify the situation one iota by quoting the enigmatic statement of famed English clergyman John Henry Cardinal Newman: "Men are born only to die."

One thought that occurred to many after surviving passage though flak filled skies: what happened to all that stuff the Germans threw up at us? Those tons of shrapnel from air-bursts had to rain down on the Herrenvolk. And more lethal were the proximity-fused shells which hadn't come close enough to any metal to be detonated, and others which had failed to go off. These could create quite a bang when they returned to the Reich and the Krauts were 'hoisted on their own petard.' I imagine we were given credit for whatever damage they wrought—particularly on hospitals, churches, and orphanages.

Sometimes, looking out at the welcome and comforting sight of our little friends flying in close-support gave rise to Walter Mitty-like imaginings. How great it would be alone in a little P-51 or P-47 with six or eight 'fifties,' eager for targets. Picturing yourself in one of those little fighters in the "Keep 'em Flying" posters got you to sign up for the Flying Cadet Program in the first place. Then when you finished flying school everyone wanted to go into fighters (then called pursuit). You had no choice in the assignments; later I learned the rationale. A few from the top of the class would be kept on as instructors, the next batch of better fliers were assigned to bombers, where Uncle Sam had his biggest investment in lives and dollars, and the rest were sent to fighters, where only one life and a smaller investment were at stake. The better performers received the lesser desirable awards, one of many military paradoxes.

Peacetime life had its share of paradoxes, but wartime abounded in them. In nature a species is perpetuated and improved by the 'survival of the fittest.' In man's world we send our 'cream of the crop' out to kill the enemy's 'cream of the crop.' We put our best performers in lead positions where the danger was greatest, and those who performed unsatisfactorily we sent home where there was no danger. And while the fighters zoomed around spoiling for a fight, we lumbered along praying we wouldn't get one. Militarily, the fighter was classified as a defensive weapon (to defend bombers), and the bomber as an offensive weapon. The mental attitudes of their respective pilots were precisely the opposite.

Lone bombers which had become separated from their own groups struggled to join any available formation, to gain the protection it afforded. I often mused on my pre-war cavalry days, watching herd-bound riderless mounts gallop to join the nearest troop column. As if in a serial dream, on each repetition of this ritual I was struck by further analogies between my first military experience, horse cavalry, and my second, the Air Corps. Initial advisories given about the horse in Boot Camp and about the airplane in Primary Flying School were almost identical. I could see and hear Sgt. Gil Woodworth holding the halter rope, going through the military nomenclature of the horse and cautioning, "Never fear the horse. Respect it, and always be alert—it can hurt and even kill you." Some years later after an initial discourse on the operation of a Stearman (our primary training plane) Capt. Noel F. Parrish, the school CO, gave virtually the same caution.

Many times when running the gauntlet of flak-filthy skies and fighter attacks from all sides, Tennyson's "Into the valley of death rode the six hundred" came readily to mind. In our air formations, as in the cavalry we were totally exposed. In each case the highest ranking officers rode in the fore, were known by the enemy to do so, were prime targets, and consequently suffered higher casualties than their juniors who rode behind them. This was in sharp contrast to most other military forces where seniors usually direct from the rear and have lighter loss rates than their men. There was some telling common usage of terms between the two services—'squadron' as a unit designation, 'mount up' and 'bail out' as commands. Was it just by coincidence that a horse was always mounted from the 'nigh' (left) side, just as a single engine plane was entered from the left?

One comforting and comical musing was the bit of well-intended advice given to me by my mother when I left for flying school. As she pressed into my hand her mother's crucifix, dewy-eyed, she pled that I "Fly low and slow," the surest way to bust your butt in an airplane!

44. Dodging Flak

In our early instruction by combat veterans we received much information on Luftwaffe fighter tactics, but there wasn't much we could do about them except to maintain our tight protective 'box' formation and blaze away with every gun that could be brought to bear on the attacker. An individual plane could conceivably take some evasive action against such an attack, but a formation could not. You just had to take whatever they dished out and hope that your gunners might distract their aim.

As for flak, evasive action could be taken anywhere except on the bomb run (where the flak was usually heaviest). Changing heading or altitude on the bomb run could throw off the bombardier's aim. While we were told we could and should take evasive action at other times, no indications were given as to what kind of action to take, and when to take it. However that was an area in which I had some unwelcome training before the war.

On a number of occasions I'd been assigned to tow targets for Coast Artillery anti-aircraft batteries off the East coast at Sandy Hook, New Jersey, and Cape Henlopen, Delaware. Flying at 18,000 feet with only a 1,000 feet of tow cable between the tail of the plane and the sleeve target, you hoped those 'friendly fire-ers' down below knew what they were doing. You were asked to fly a predetermined course along the shore line and at level altitude. The initial bursts were tracking (or *predictor*) fire from a single gun trying to home-in on the target. After each round its aim was corrected until it converged on the target. At that point, the other guns of the battery, which had been silently following the aim of the tracking gun, joined in with a full scale battery barrage. As a matter of self-preservation, I learned to follow the progress and pattern of the tracking fire—on more than one occasion it closed in on my tail rather than the sleeve and I instinctively undertook what later became known as 'evasive action.'

Because the Germans employed so many batteries of guns in our major target areas, it was almost impossible to detect individual battery firing patterns on which you could base evasive action. But en route to and from targets we frequently encountered light flak areas where patterns of tracking fire were discernible. I figured that at our usual bombing altitude (circa 22,000 feet) I had about 10 seconds to maneuver between bursts—plenty of time to anticipate the next one and move away from its scheduled path. I can recall three times when I was able to put my tow target experience to good use. On two of those our fast evasive turn may have saved some damage or loss, but like the road not taken, you can't be sure. On the third, there was no question in my mind and the minds of accompanying crews that we saved ourselves a lot of serious trouble.

Returning from a mission in central Germany, we were at our usual 22,000 feet, high above a solid layer of undercast when suddenly we drew ground fire. The first burst was low and to our right, but the pattern developed quickly as succeeding individual bursts stepped up higher and closer to us. The progression was easy to spot with those oily black bursts with fiery cores silhouetted against the fluffy white cloud below. I warned the formation to be prepared for a quick and steep change of direction, and with one or maybe two more shots before I estimated they would have zeroed in on us, I turned the formation sharply down to the right. The sister group immediately behind did not follow my lead and ran into a massive barrage which cost them two planes and extensive damage to others. We didn't get a scratch. At our pilots conference after the mission, we reviewed how we calculated the enemy action and how when they zigged up and left, we zagged down and right.

I am satisfied that this one occasion fully compensated me for the misery endured towing targets over Atlantic Beaches.

45. Intruders

Napoleon and other military greats cautioned against underestimating the enemy. It seemed to me that most military commanders, lest they get caught violating that rule, tended to the opposite extreme of over-estimating the enemy and under estimating the impact of their own actions. Rommel and Patton probably were exceptions.

The enemy underestimated the effectiveness of three kinds of Luftwaffe 'intrusion' at our bases, all under the cover of darkness. The most modest of the three in terms of physical damage was bombing. Their attempts were infrequent and planes too few in number. Only a couple of small twin-engined planes were ever involved, and their bombs not usually well placed. Yet this meager effort caused some panic, much confusion, and provoked little effective counter-action. Just the sound of their non-synchronized props overhead touched off a lot of ridiculous scurrying about. No interceptors were sent up, and rarely was one shot down by the coastal anti-aircraft batteries.

The second type of intrusion happened at North Pickenham only once—if indeed it happened at all! At one point we were told that some abandoned German parachutes had been found nearby. It was speculated that they might have been used by saboteurs dropped in a desperate campaign to disrupt our operations. They were rumored to be wearing GI clothing. So, on those black and foggy nights, everyone was suspect. It was a pretty frightening thought that suicidal commando-types could be wandering around on base in our uniforms on those early spring nights, with their long hours of darkness.

A system of pass-words was inaugurated. We armed the base to its teeth. Figuring the planes would be a target, we manned the top turrets of all the planes on their hardstands. We set up a special guard around the bomb dump and other seemingly commando-attractive spots. Side arms and carbines were at-the-ready all over the base. Not to be outdone, to my personal arsenal of a .45 automatic and a carbine, I added a tommy gun.

Because the whole base was blacked-out and hundreds of people were back and forth all night, along hedgerow paths between the flight line, the communal area, and living quarters, the opportunities for mistaken identities and shooting from the hip were unlimited.

One night, an unknown someone thought he heard overhead the off-beat sound of Luftwaffe propellers. It didn't bomb or strafe, therefore it *must* be dropping chutists. In any event, one of the top turret guardians let go with his fifties, and a few others across the field, not sure where these low overhead shots were coming from, joined in the fray. Bullets and tracers criss-crossed the field, barely overhead. The only structure hit was, of all places, the MPs' hut. They came flying out and sounded the air raid alarm. Everyone with a firearm had it in hand, cocked, and finger at the ready. After several hectic and dangerous minutes, a wiser head sounded the 'all clear' from the tower and things settled down. Except for a few holes in the MPs' Nissen hut and a couple in the vertical stabilizer of one plane, there was no damage, but there were a lot of spent shells, and a lot of nervous people on base. That decided us to disarm the base and take our chances with intruders, imagined or real.

The third type of intruder wrought the greatest damage, directly as well as indirectly.

German fighters that joined in our bomber formations when returning in the dark during winter months could easily fly unnoticed in a formation and appear on British antiaircraft radar screens as just more of our planes.

When one of our planes on final approach would turn on his landing lights, a fighter would jump him. It was like shooting fish in a barrel. We would then get on the radio to call off the landings and turn off the runway lights. The planes that had already left the formation and were in the landing pattern were without a leader or course of action to follow and were on their own. Those still in formation were the responsibility of the leader. It became a real nightmare with individuals and formations from several local bases all milling about in the dark in the same small area with a troublemaker in their midst, and, even worse, the anti-aircraft boys now getting into the act. Meanwhile, the intruder gave those on the ground something to think about also as he made a couple of strafing passes low over the base.   On one occasion at Rackheath, we lost to the intruder one airplane on approach, a ground crewman killed in a strafing attack,[1] and two of our planes e friendly anti-aircraft fire.

We were thankful that the Germans apparently underestimated the effectiveness of their 'intrusions' and used them so seldom. Any night, a single plane could have dropped a bomb, and several opened parachutes, strafed a bit, and caused confusion and damage (mostly self-inflicted by us) on any number of bases, and still escape unscathed. This disproportion between small cause and potent effect was enormous.

By the same token, the Germans may have wondered why we didn't make more use of delayed fuse bombs.[2] We used that tactic on relatively few missions, mostly against railroad marshaling yards. To know that unexploded bombs were still lying deep under our target and not knowing when or if they would go off, must certainly have inhibited German repairs and made it a little nerve-wracking on their side of the water.

1. Pvt. Daniel E. Miney, 1229th Quartermaster Corps, was caught by a strafer on April 22, 1944.

2. Both Churchill and Speer (see Bibliography) give numerous examples where they were painfully aware of vulnerabilities that were inexplicably unexploited by the other side. In all cases, enemies failed to consider things from the opponent's standpoint. The overarching lesson this reader takes, is that in war one should spend a great deal of energy considering the way that the other is *different*, for their non-obvious vulnerabilities will be the greater ones.

But better: if half that energy is expended in *peace*, understanding how the other is both different and the same, we obviate the war.

46. Vengeance Weapons

Early in the development of both of these weapons, the Germans used the nearby city of Norwich as a test ground before turning their sights to London.[1] The reason given was that it was the major metropolis in the UK closest to Germany and on which they could get the best radar tracking of their missiles.[2] In any event, Norwich was the early recipient of both weapons.

At Rackheath, we were directly in the flight path of V-1s launched toward Norwich, and they were frequently overhead, very visible at only 4-500 feet, traveling at about 500 mph. The propelling engine had a very distinct and recognizable sound like the 'putt-putt' of a single cylinder motorbike. When the motor quit, it went into a glide and hit the ground in about 20 seconds.[3] As long as you could hear the 'putt-putt' you were OK. When it quit, take cover. None exploded near Rackheath while I was there, but I did see a couple hit in London.

One day while at noon mess there was an enormous explosion that shook the mess hall and fractured some windows.[4] Our backs were to the windows and some were showered with glass splinters, but nobody was hurt. We had no idea what had happened and knew for sure only the direction from which it came. Our bomb dump was in the opposite direction, so that was ruled out. We couldn't think of anything else of our doing which would cause such a blast. The Old Man and I got into his jeep and headed in the direction of the explosion. A short distance outside the base we came across an English woman who worked at the Aeroclub on our base. She was sitting next to her bike by the side of the road. The blast had blown her off her bike just where she was and she hadn't moved since, fearing whatever had happened might happen again. She was frightened and shaken but not hurt. She estimated that the blast occurred in a farm field about a half mile down the road.

We followed her directions and saw in a sugar beet field a crater about 50 or 60 feet in diameter. When we got close we could see that it was about 20 feet deep and was slowly filling up with water. We were the first ones there, and as we walked across the field had seen rabbits lying on the ground gasping for breath, but not moving, and pheasants running in circles with wings extended but broken. Closer to the crater we saw other animals dead, but not bloodied, apparently killed by concussion.

Although our experience had been dropping bombs and not evaluating results on the receiving end, this seemed to have been caused by something bigger than anything we carried. We spotted some metal parts around and I made the mistake of touching the biggest one and blistered my fingers—it was still white hot. We figured it had to be part of the engine of whatever device we were looking at.

The police arrived, cordoned off the area and before long, the site drew a crowd of military and civilian technicians. They told us they had been expecting this rocket weapon, and it was the reason we had been sent to bomb Peenemunde where Werner Von Braun and his rocket boys had developed it. It was tagged "V-2."

1. My father is wrong. The first V-1 and the first V-2 to make landfall in England each landed in London. Two weeks after each type premiered, each type also struck in the vicinity of Norwich. Although none landed within city limits, the clustering around this important center made it clear that Norwich was being targeted, albeit inaccurately. *See Glossary entries for V-1, V-2 in Appendix.*

2. Author Joan Banger in <u>Norwich at War</u> lays out the great interest the Germans had in targeting Norwich for conventional bombardment. 85% of all dwellings were at least partly damaged, 12% severely or completely.

Between 1940 and the end of 1943, Norwich's 1432 casualties represented 8.5 persons for every 1000 of her citizens.

Norwich's proximity to North Sea launch sites and Luftwaffe airfields made it their closest sizable British target.

In her introduction, Banger attributes to an unnamed German source their further interest in Norwich as a target owing to 'its beauty and unique historical interest.' See Bibliography.

3. An onboard gyro was supposed to keep the 'buzz bomb' on its set course, while a revolution counter driven by a tiny 'propellor' on the nose of the weapon was to determine range at which ignition would be cut and the tailplane tilted for the final plunge to earth and detonation. In practice, the inability of either 'Vengeance' weapon to hit precise targets made them terror weapons rather than strategic weapons. This is not to diminunize their substantial toll.

In his The 1,000 Day Battle, author James Hoseason indicates that the 1042 V-2s that made it to England took 2750 lives. 3531 of the 10,492 V-1s launched at England made it through defenses and took 6184 lives. (These figures do not include the loss of Allied airmen during nearly 16,272 bombing sorties against the V weapon systems, as cited by Freeman in The Mighty Eighth.) Approximately 2/3s of the effective strikes of V weapons fell in the populous greater London area. See Bibliography and Glossary listings CROSSBOW and Noball.

4. Banger lists six V-2 strikes in the Norwich area from 9-26-44 to 10-3-44. I suspect that the the the one from "...the general direction of Great Yarmouth" on 9-27-44 is that of which my father writes. Rackheath lies E-NE of Norwich; Great Yarmouth is just south of due east.

47. 200th
Mission Celebration

The completion of each 100 missions was an occasion for celebration. After the first 100, a Group was 'stood down' for one day, after 200, 'stood down' for two. The 100th involved just a small parade, a little speech making, congratulatory messages from headquarters, and a slightly freer flow of spirits at the three base clubs and nearby pubs.

The Aero Club was run by the Red Cross for the exclusive benefit of enlisted men. The Non-Com Club was of course for non-commissioned officers; on a base in the Eighth that included a large percentage of our enlisted combat personnel. We did not send anyone on a combat mission with less than sergeant's stripes, because the enemy, according to the Geneva Convention, could not force anyone at or above sergeant's rating into slave labor.

The third club on base was the 'O' Club (Officers' Club). This was the center of most officers' social life. While large numbers of enlisted personnel would go into town or to a local pubs when they had a night off, most officers, especially combat personnel, tended to stay on base and at the 'O' Club unless holding two- or three-day passes to London, Edinburgh, Cambridge, etc. Actually, the GIs had a better deal on base than the officers. Everything was supplied for them by the Red Cross- snacks, coffee, lounges, game rooms etc., and a dance every Saturday night, not to mention the congenial hospitality of the Red Cross girls. The 'O' Club, on the other hand, had no feminine touch, no female presence except for the monthly Officers' Club dance. As in the other clubs, the gaming tables and the bar drew the most attention. But the liveliest corner of our 'O' Club,[1] was where we had our *two* grand pianos.

The bars were not as busy as the concerned folks back home seemed to think. The *mild* and *bitters* (ale and beer, respectively), were pretty heavy for American taste. For unbelievably bad bootleg scotch, we paid $18 a fifth, to a man who must today be one of the wealthiest in England. Although its nondescript label claimed 86.3 proof, we had batches tested at the 65th General Hospital lab, and it registered less than half that. The only prohibition at the bar was that those alerted to fly the next day's mission were not to drink once a mission was 'on.' Over the bar were three colored lights to remind an imbiber of the group's combat status of the moment. Green, of course meant that we were 'stood down;' the bar was open and unlimited to all. Yellow signified that we were 'standing by,' and the red light meant that the field order was in and a mission was on. The alerted crews were very good about respecting the meaning of those lights, and I recall only a couple of occasions when we had to take somebody off a mission crew because we felt he was alcohol-impaired.

Originally, we had just one piano, one player. Dick Grey, a pilot in his late 20s, was a tremendous jazz pianist and a very good honky-tonk type plunker. After finishing his missions, he was one of those who offered to stay on with us in a training capacity. He welcomed the opportunity, and that 'O' Club piano, no doubt, played some part in our offer and his acceptance.

Some time after Dick was well entrenched as our virtuoso of the 88, along came an excellent navigator, Johnny Gile, who, although trained in classical piano, soon became an accomplished jazz player. Johnny also was added to our training staff upon completion of his tour. After having them share the same bench and instrument for a couple of weeks, we managed to acquire another piano, and placed the two back-to-back. Our musical repertoire expanded significantly, and Johnny introduced a more classical element. They picked

up on some of English and Empire songs heard at
neighboring RAF and Royal Navy installations. Some of
these had stronger lyrics than we were used to, and it took
a little time before our amateur choristers could deliver
them unabashedly with the same raucous irreverence that
our Allies did. We had some great voices to carry the
tunes and lead the group sings. Red Killmeyer was a

Generals Kepner and Peck, Colonel Shower at Rackheath Officer's Club,
listening to the 1944 Army-Navy game on the radio. Commanders,
respectively, of the 2nd Air Division, The 94th Bombardment Wing, and
the467th Bomb Group.

baritone, and Tom Goodyear was a basso-profundo.[2] A
number of original lyrics were developed to be sung with
popular tunes. Our fight song was "Rackheath Aggies,"
from our group's nickname, alluding to some of the plowing
our errant bombs did in farmers' fields.

        The most popular of the local
productions described a mission to 'Big B' led by the 'Old
Man.'[3] He was the central figure in the lyrics which poked
fun at him, and which he never did appreciate. It was

never played in his presence until one night when General Peck was visiting the Officers' Club. He had heard of our twin pianos, joined in, made a series of requests, and enjoyed himself thoroughly. When he requested that they play our "Rackheath to Berlin" original[4] about which he had heard so much, with the Old Man present, there was a long silence. All smiled except the two pianists. They stalled, the general insisted, and Dick and Johnny started their original and most popular composition, but without the usual gusto. As they went along they picked up moral and audible support from the more venturesome around the twin pianos. By the time they got to the final and most devastating stanza, the walls were reverberating in customary fashion. The delighted General Peck asked for successive replaying until he got the hang of the lyrics and gave out with full voice! All of this was quite frustrating for poor Al; he couldn't leave and he couldn't stop the exuberant general. He just stood there, glowered, and chewed on his mustache.

By the time our 200th mission rolled around, we had acquired among our new crews two more pilots who were very fine pianists, Dave Nash and Jerry Squire. Along with our two originals they became a significant and much-appreciated part of our celebration.

The celebration itself was prepared as diligently and meticulously as a combat mission. We had committees for dances at all three clubs. Prior to the dances we had combination beer parties, picnics and an air show. At the beer parties and picnics, the officers reversed roles with the GIs and did the serving. After the refreshments there were volleyball and softball games, then everybody converged on the tower to watch the air show. We had invited two fighter groups from our division to send over their aerobatics teams to put on a show for us.

Unfortunately, it was a misty day with a low ceiling—too low to allow the vertical airspace needed for the more spectacular maneuvers. I was very concerned about the ceiling and suggested to both fighter team leaders that they omit from their programs any maneuvers which could not be performed with reasonable safety under such limited conditions. They did cut out a few, but also extended themselves on some that I would not have undertaken. The P-47s from the 56th Fighter Group put on a stunning show, and after a final very low fly-by returned to their base. Then came the P-51s from the 479th Group under the leadership of Major Robin Olds. They took off to do their stuff and naturally felt that it was incumbent upon them to outperform the boys from the 56th. Their entire show was practically 'on the deck,' with barrel, slow, hesitation, and snap rolls, Immelmanns, chandelles, and an extensive variety of tight and spread formation maneuvers. After they made one of their low-level formation passes over the base, we spotted a lone P-51 tagging along behind and trying to catch up. At first some thought he might have been part of Olds' contingent, but his plane's group markings were different. He decided to join in the fun and when the Olds team came across the field in trail doing hesitation slow rolls, the newcomer, in the tail-end Charlie position, decided to try his hand at it. It was obvious from the moment he pulled his nose above the horizon to start his roll that he didn't have his plane under control. He approached the field low, inverted, and losing altitude. He narrowly missed the tower on which we were standing, and crashed up-side down near our mess hall. Even though he was right in the middle of our living area, he hit no buildings, and took no lives but his own. Olds called off his show, sent his team home, and came in to land. I picked him up at the hardstand and assured him that it was not one of his boys. He hadn't had a chance to see that extra plane in the air. We inspected to the crash site together. Though maddened and saddened by what he saw, Olds was relieved not to have lost one of his team.[5]

We learned later that the pilot was

a bomber pilot who had finished his tour and asked for a shot at fighters. He had very few hours in the 51, was on a local orientation flight, and certainly should not have involved himself in aerobatics which were well beyond his limited experience in the plane. It was another of those most frustrating and depressing instances where lives and materiel were so needlessly destroyed. Looking at a body battered and bloody as a result of error, the first reaction is one of anger. You would like to be able to give them a good tongue lashing or a kick in the pants. The only service he had performed for his country was to provide an object lesson to the young pilots who stood looking on in absolutely silence.

On reflection, all felt sorry for the poor guy. This was a helluva way to 'check out.' It cast a crushing pall on our celebration.

1. The officer's club at Rackheath was sometimes referred to as 'The Sword and Chain;' the nickname issued naturally from the insignia of the 467th BG. The motto *Liberamus* is Latin for *"We liberate."*

2. Tom's love of song took the form of substantial philanthropy years later. He heavily endowed the Glimmerglass Opera Company, summer home of New York's Metropolitan Opera. The land on which it sits was part of his substantial family estate on Otsego Lake, near Cooperstown, New York. When our family moved to nearby Norwich, New York in 1963, Dad soon reconnected with his affable old friend, who was our enthusiastic and gracious host many times.

3. The term 'Old Man' is found throughout the literature of the American fighting man of WW II. It seems to have been capable of implying the full range of regard for one's commander, from endearing and warm to the opposite. By its universal tolerance, it would seem that wise military leaders understood the power of an informal title for high authority, to cultivate *esprit de corps.*

In the case of the 467th, the application of this 'fill in the blank' moniker to Colonel Albert J. Shower could not have been more apt. This larger-than-life CO was very often held in contempt and respect at one and the same time. To this day, through the now relaxed ribbing he endures about the very tight ship he ran 57 years ago, there is an abiding and unmistakable high regard for 'Black Al.' His strict style was not just coincidentally linked to the superior performance and low casualty rate that are the historical hallmarks of the 'Rackheath Aggies.'

4. See Appendix for "Rackheath to Berlin" lyrics, unearthed from JJM's footlocker in 1999.

5. My father got some of the details wrong. From Robin Olds' letter to me, May 14, 2000:

> "I did not lead the fighter demonstration. That was some other P-51 unit. As fate would have it, I happened to be flying over the base just as that lone P-51 pilot attempted his maneuver. You see, some very brave and very foolish bomber guys had volunteered for a tour in fighters after having completed their own. I have no idea what idiot in headquarters approved the idea, but of an unknown number, four were sent to our group. By then I was commanding the 434th Squadron and gave silent thanks that none of them were assigned to me. I couldn't imagine changing from a two-dimensional world to one of three dimensions just on a whim. Those of us in fighters had spent hours and months learning our trade, and in fact, we learned something new each time we flew. I am not suggesting any mystique or art that could not be learned. What I am saying is that you don't just step into a fighter aircraft and become qualified to operate it as a weapon of war.
>
> In any event, I landed to check out my suspicion. Sure enough, the markings on the wreckage identified the plane as belonging to one of the other squadrons in my group. It wasn't easy reporting what happened when I returned to my base.
>
> Sadly, only one of the four assigned to us managed to survive the war."

48. B-17 vs. B-24

The Eighth Air Force used only two types of heavy bombers, the B–17 "Flying Fortress" and the B-24 "Liberator." Of the Eighth's three Air Divisions, the 1st and 3rd flew 17s and the 2nd flew 24s. Each division had about a thousand airplanes.

Most pilots felt strongly that the type of plane to which they had been assigned was the better of the two. Only the very few who had flown both types could be objective in making that assessment. I had too few hours in the 17 to qualify as one of those few, but I'll make some general observations anyway.

As indicated by its lower numerical designation, the B-17 was considerably older in date of design and original manufacture than the B-24. Its conventional wing and semi-monocoque type fuselage construction made it a stable and sturdy aircraft. The B-24's modified Davis Wing and boxy fuselage made if faster, but less stable and less sturdy. In Europe, where the premium was on altitude to distance yourself as far as possible from anti-aircraft fire, the 17 could fly significantly higher than the 24. This was a major advantage even though the 17 flew slightly slower and carried a smaller bomb load. Also, because of its greater stability at altitude it made for a better bombing platform. In theaters of war where bombing altitude was not a critical factor, the 24's greater load capacity and superior speed were real pluses.

Both planes had roughly equal

firepower to defend themselves, and fuel capacities to remain aloft for about the same length of time. The 17 was powered by four Wright engines and the 24 by four Pratt & Whitneys. My personal experience with engines of both manufacturers favored the latter.

The basic construction of the wing and airframe of the 17 were unquestionably superior for the types of trouble we generally got into. When hit by fighters and flak the 24s, because of the fuel system layout, burned and blew up more readily than the 17s. When power was lost, the 17 was a pretty good glider, whereas the 24, due to its type of wing and higher wing loading (ratio of weight to square feet of wing lifting surface) went down more like an elevator, giving rise to some cracks about the manufacturer being Otis. Most importantly, the 17 could crash-land relatively safely on land or water. The 24, because of its flimsy underside, collapsed very readily when crashed on any surface. Many fewer crew members walked away safely from crashes of B-24s than B-17s.

Because it was less stable than the 17, the 24 required more control attention to keep it in a desired attitude or position. To achieve optimum performance, you had to get the wing "on the step," like a power boat in water. The slightest jockeying of flight controls or even rough air, could throw you "off the step" at a cost of 8 to 10 mph of flying speed without changing power settings. While formation leaders could get their planes on the step and maintain them there, wing men, constantly maneuvering to stay in formation, could not. Consequently, they had to use higher power settings and, use more fuel than the leaders—a major consideration for command pilots, particularly on long missions. They had to consider that their wing men had less flying time left in their tanks than the leaders did.

Despite a strong sentimental attachment to the B-24, and gratitude for its getting me home in one piece, I'll have to go with the judgment of those with many hours in both types: the B-17 was the better and safer vehicle for the job we had to do in Europe.

49. Trolley Missions

As our troops advanced into Germany and the Russians closed in from the East, there were very few strategic targets left in the narrowing corridor remaining in German hands, and none that had not been visited before. Our business was drying up,

467th's meteorologist Roy 'Cloudy' Lindstrom in Clastres, France with the prized Malford.

thankfully. That was a very good thing as the Luftwaffe, reinvigorated by the advent of their new Me.262 jet fighter, was threatening to take back control of their own airspace. They were shooting down our bombers at an alarmingly increasing rate and could easily out-perform and shoot down any Allied fighter plane.[1] They had plenty of airplanes, but were short on fuel and pilots. The only tactic our fighters employed successfully was to catch them in the vulnerable positions of take-off and landing.

As we had more down time for lack

of targets, we started to close up shop gradually. Rumors were rampant that we would be re-deployed to the Pacific. Nothing was official or certain, but we were advised to get ready to move someplace. When V-E Day did arrive, we were pretty well packed, and started our move for home a couple of weeks later. Before doing so, someone at higher headquarters had a commendable and popular idea for 'Trolley Missions.' The paddlefeet who had watched us go out and return for so long and made our efforts possible, were now going to have a chance to see where we went and what we had done. All the bases set up schedules to load about a dozen paddlefeet into each bomber, and take off singly for a conducted low level tour of many of our target areas and the Rhine Valley. They had box lunches and beverages, and most took their cameras. They didn't need heated suits or oxygen masks as they flew at about 1,000 feet and got a good look at the countryside and some of our bombing results—so much of a good look that our air crews wanted to fly these missions and see for themselves what they had missed on their missions, from more than four miles up. To help control the heavy traffic, differing routes were assigned to each group, and senior pilots were sent out to monitor the traffic and keep the 'Trolleys' on track. I made a couple of such policing trips in 'Little Pete' and also enjoyed getting a clasp look at many points of interest that I had wondered about from high above. Trolleys were a tremendous success with our paddlefeet, and greatly appreciated by all.

1 This remarkably advanced twin-jet fighter, thankfully mis-deployed as a bomber in small production numbers by Hitler's orders for more than three years, was finally appropriately and effectively used against Allied bombing when it was too late for Germany. By the time the Me.262 *Schwalbe* (Swallow) menaced daylight bombing of Berlin starting in late 1944, the desperate shortage of aviation fuel had profoundly curtailed pilot training. The Luftwaffe defenders were able to deal out more attrition than they could take.

German Armaments Minister Albert Spear, on the receiving end of Allied strategic bombing, kept looking for signs of careful and clever target selection by his enemy, and urging the same approach on Goering and Hitler. In his postwar writings and in cooperating with the work of the US Strategic Bombing Survey, Spear indicates that his enemy's efforts seemed marked by misdirection and missed opportunities until the very effective targeting of fuel production beginning May 12, 1944. "On that day, the technological war was decided." Thereafter, daily production seldom exceeded one third of its previous value, and "it meant the end of German armaments production." See <u>Inside the Third Reich</u> in the bibliography.

50. Above
and Beyond

Every Tuesday the Second Air Division Awards Board met at Ketteringham Hall (Division Headquarters) promptly at 8:30 a.m. The board consisted of seven field-grade flying officers (major rank and above) on active combat duty with the bomber and fighter groups of the division. Each board member served for seven consecutive weeks. Every week was the seventh and last for one member, and the first of seven for another. This device facilitated continuity in the board's operations and consistency in its approval of awards. Captain Lewis, a ground officer from 2nd Division Headquarters, served as the permanent (non-voting) secretary. His function was to present recommendations received from the units of the division, and pass on to the division commander those approved by the board.

Award recommendations started with group commanders. Typically written up by an intelligence officer, a commendation described the meritorious performance and indicated the award which he felt it warranted. This was generally given perfunctory approval at wing headquarters and sent on to the Division Awards Board. The Board could turn it down or recommend its approval as written. On rare occasions, it used its authority to approve a different award. The division commander usually accepted the board's recommendations.

There were few established guidelines or parameters for the operations of an awards board. This was one of the very few military functions for which the Army didn't have minutely detailed procedures and regulations. We had no definition of heroism or "above and beyond the call of duty," or, for that matter, just plain 'duty.' The only medal with specific and unarguable qualifications was the Purple Heart—it was automatically awarded when enemy action occasioned a show of blood.

A resultant lack of consistency early in the war led to critics that the Air Corps and the other armed services devalued awards by presenting them too freely. A large number were given more for an action's political or headline significance than its military value. Over-generous awards engendered some criticism in civilian circles, even more in the military. In conscious attempts to repair the system after early extravagances, our board was constantly trying to upgrade our standards. This tightening process inevitably occasioned confrontations within the board; were we over correcting for past practice, and making it too difficult to earn an award?

Against the criticism that the 'who' involved in a deed was sometimes more important than the deed itself, our board designed some rules regarding the preparation of award recommendations. The individual's name, rank and unit were not read to the board, only his position in the crew and his deed. At one point we tried having a board member abstain from voting when he recognized the recommendation concerned him directly or someone in his outfit, but this tended to defeat the anonymity and even tempted other board members to vote favorably in deference to the abstaining member. We were all well aware of recent notable incidents and missions, and the most carefully prepared write-up could not always conceal the identity of the unit or individual involved. Nonetheless, with our compensations for these skewing factors, a high degree of objectivity prevailed.

Our biggest challenge was to distinguish between a truly noteworthy achievement, and a spine-tingling write-up of something commonplace. This was a recurrent problem with one group, whose award writer had been a successful detective story writer before the war. After a few Tuesdays on the board, one came to recognize his writing not only by its flamboyant style, but also by the annoyance with which Captain Lewis read it. Attempts to separate the wheat from the chaff led to some fairly warm arguments. Newer members, not yet inured to the writing style, tended to be more favorably disposed than the longer term members.

In one of my stints on the board, my last couple of sessions overlapped the first few of Jimmy Stewart. In awards philosophy I was the conservative; he the liberal. In voice and cadence so familiar to moviegoers, he intoned, "Anybody flying those missions over Germany deserves everything our country can give him." One Tuesday, shortly before our lunch break, Captain Lewis, with a slight curl of the lip, started reading from a new batch of recommendations. A couple of us recognized the products of the detective story writer. I settled back uneasily for the intellectual abuse and snow-job which followed. After the first award reading, I protested that we were being conned by clever writing to give an undeserved award. Stewart took the opposing position. On the vote, my side lost five to two. After the reading of the second from the same writer, same arguments, our side gained one convert, but still lost. During our lunch break, the discussion of extravagant prose versus meritorious deeds continued. After lunch, the next recommendation by the same writer failed, five to two. When it was moved to reconsider those approved just before lunch, over Stewart's howling protests, those approved earlier were also disallowed. Even Stewart agreed that we were then being consistent, though he insisted we were being consistently wrong.

I recall one rare occasion when we upgraded an award recommendation. We had received recommendations for the same award to several fighter pilots all participating in one incident. All had multiple 'kills' except group commander, Col. Dave Schilling who had only one. After thorough consideration, all awards were approved as requested except Schilling's—his was upgraded. Based on the number of kills it might appear that we were 'polishing some brass,' but not so. After completing an escort mission at altitude and not meeting any 'bandits,' on the way home Schilling took his group down to deck to find some targets-of-opportunity. They came across a Luftwaffe air training base where young German pilots were being given final pre-combat training. There were dozens of planes taking off, landing, and in the air. Several flak batteries were strategically arrayed around the field.

Rather than turn his boys loose for an uncoordinated free-for-all, Schilling surveyed the situation and assigned specific targets to each of his flights. He circled above observing, advising, and dodging flak. When the air targets were dispatched, he coordinated approaches for strafing ground targets on and around the field with minimum exposure to flak battery positions. While his Mustangs were clobbering the ground targets, a lone FW 190 started taking off. A couple of our boys tried to bounce him as he became airborne. He skillfully avoided their attack, whipped around and shot one of them down. This was no student pilot! Sensing that this last angry hornet to come out of the nest could give our newer boys more than they could handle, Schilling dove down from his traffic-directing spot to join the fray. He and the lone Jerry tangled from ground level to 5,000 feet, skillfully employing the whole gamut of offensive and defensive maneuvers. Other action—even the flak batteries—came to a near halt for this spectacle of two highly skilled fighter pilots going at it like jousting knights of old. At the end of the pitched fight, Schilling succeeded in disabling the 190 and pilot bailed out. German Radio that night described the action, identifying both Schilling and their pilot, a leading Luftwaffe ace then commanding that flying school. They acknowledged that our man won, but noted that theirs was unhurt and hoped to have the opportunity to meet Schilling again.

When the recommendations had been prepared at his group, Schilling had insisted that his be no higher than that of any of his pilots.   Our decision to upgrade Schilling's award was vindicated by its enthusiastic approval at his base.[1]

Twice during my tenures on the awards board we were over-ruled by higher headquarters. In the first instance, a moderately sized effort was sent to a factory near Paris. The mission was short, the resistance light, and the bomb results excellent. After reviewing the results an enthusiast from higher headquarters recommended that the command pilot should receive an award. Nobody in the division agreed. We felt that this was the kind of work for which we were being paid, it was an easy mission and that no bonus was called for. Laughably, it was fairly widely known in the division that the command pilot, a high ranking officer, had been partying very heavily the night before, and had gone along for the ride on what was expected to be a 'milk run.' He had fallen asleep not long after takeoff and didn't wake up until touchdown upon return to base. Both our division commander and the board declined to recommend an award, but it was made anyway at higher headquarters. The embarrassed officer   jokingly referred to it as his "sleeping award."

The other instance engendered considerable hard feeling and even bitterness toward higher headquarters. The mission involved a major effort into Germany. The air executive of the lead group was flying as command pilot for the 2nd Air Division. The weather forecast called for heavy cloud formation en route and over the target area. We were warned that the clouds might rise to an altitude that could prevent the bomber stream from topping them and reaching the target. Two major prohibitions in our operations were taking a formation into dense clouds, and taking fully-loaded B-24s above 24,000 feet. A B-24 could stall out at that altitude, in contrast to the B-17 which was more stable at altitude and could carry its lighter bomb load quite a bit higher.

As the division made landfall over the Dutch coast at 22,500 feet, they ran into a gradual up slope of dense cloud. The division command pilot put the formation into a slow climb. It soon became obvious to all the other wing and group command pilots that they were not going to be able to top, or even go around this massive dense cloud formation. Despite their insistent and repeated radio requests for a decision from the division command pilot, he procrastinated until it was too late. With planes hanging on their props and near stalling, he dragged the first groups with him into the dense clouds. He made no attempt to get them out in an orderly fashion, abandoned his responsibility, and left the groups to their own devices. The other command pilots reacted quickly: to lighten loads and regain flight stability, bombs were salvoed and they communicated arrangements for separation of altitude and non-conflicting turns back out of the soup. In a massive panic situation such as that, things seldom work out that smoothly. Crisscrossing collisions in the cloud cost the division *thirteen* planes, and none ever got close to the target! Strangely, reconnaissance photos take the next day showed extensive target damage. Upon seeing these, some soul at higher headquarters, presumably oblivious to the fiasco, sent down to the division the recommendation that a Silver Star be awarded the division command pilot—this while the general was considering what kind of punitive action would be appropriate for this grievous failure, so costly in lives and materiel. Our division general protested vigorously, and refused to initiate any award recommendation.

It turned out that the overly media-conscious higher headquarters had already released to the press the recon photos with a 'mission success' story, naming the command pilot and indicating that he would be decorated appropriately for his achievement. They weren't about to retract their fiction. Eventually, a write-up was prepared by them and sent down to the division for the regular approval process. After it was disapproved by both the division awards board and the commanding general, the award was made at the 8th Air Force headquarters. Someone there even made a feeble attempt to cover their tracks by suggesting that one or more of the planes that failed to return had somehow made it to the target and completed our mission for us. This we knew to be absurd. Our pre-mission target photos were not very recent, and there may have been an explosive accident, or a saboteur might have blown it. The culpable command pilot was never seen wearing his award overseas. Home after V-E Day, we happened to meet on Fifth Avenue. He was wearing his Silver Star, which seemed badly tarnished in my eyes.

This single gross error in award-making was unique in my experience. Our division procedure worked well and fairly. Whenever someone rises above the crowd and is recognized, though, there are bound to be detractors. The most cynical I met was a colonel from Patton's armor. He and I happened to be in London at the same time for major dental work, and were billeted together at the Dorchester Hotel. His experiences on the ground were quite different from mine in the air. He'd seen a great deal of action and awards in Africa and France. Heroics, in his view, often came as a result of someone having to fight his way out of a situation into which he had stupidly blundered. His heroes were the unsung guys who intelligently analyzed the situation and accomplished their mission with the most gain and least loss.

My experience with the awards board didn't bring me any closer to a clear-cut definition of heroism, but I came to understand that it manifests in the heart and/or gut of the doer, not the eye of the beholder. Overcoming fear in order to act is the first and most important element. Individuals have differing thresholds of fear just as they do for pain; an act that might be heroic for one is taken in stride by another.

Awards board members were constantly nagged by our inability to know about or proclaim the heroics of the thousands who didn't make it back. Opportunities for courageous action in crippled planes, for whom there was usually no one to speak, certainly abounded even more than in the ones that returned. But I know of one case where the story made it back.

In the closing months of the war in Europe, Allied forces overran a number of German prisoner-of-war camps. The German Air Force operated the Stalag Luft camps for the containment of captured Allied airmen. Americans released from these camps were funneled into Camp Lucky Strike in France, the initial rehabilitation center, from which they were to be shipped directly back to the States. Many were strongly motivated to check back with their outfits in England first, and a few succeeded. Some wanted to check on possessions left behind, some longed for reunion with their old buddies, some were compelled to make known heroic efforts of fellow crewmen and obtain appropriate recognition for them.

Shortly before we were to leave for home, Sergeant Brosseau stepped into my office in the Ops Block to inform me that I had an enlisted visitor accompanied by two medical corpsmen. Normally, no one at my rank or below crossed the threshold to my office without a cool and comprehensive screening by Brosseau, so it was unusual that he had no idea who the fellow was or why he wanted to see me. Rather than waste time by asking what had rattled him so, I told Brosseau to bring in the group.

The enlisted man was wearing tech sergeant's stripes, but beyond that there was no way I could identify him. He was being led by the medics because obviously he couldn't see. Where his eyes had been there was mainly burn-scarred skin. Most of his facial features were obliterated; there were few remnants of his nose or ears. Small and irregular patches of hair on his head separated big areas of scar tissue. Below the nostrils of his truncated nose was a lipless slit where his mouth had been. He certainly was a pitiful sight; I felt guilty that I found it a revolting one also.

The medics offered no information. They walked their charge to my desk, saluted, retreated a couple of steps and said nothing. The sergeant spoke almost inaudibly, barely understandable. He identified himself as the radio operator on Newman's crew.[2] This was one of my original 492nd Bomb Group crews that had gone down on the Bernburg mission more than a year before when we were still at North Pickenham. Understanding his exceptional case, they released him from Lucky Strike and took him to North Pick looking for us, where he was redirected to our second station at Rackheath. When I suggested he sit down and relax, he recognized my voice, and apparently feeling he was finally 'home' with his old outfit, choked up and became even more difficult to understand. His obvious physical problems were then further complicated by emotions.

He explained that Newman's plane received some sort of a direct hit up front. He thought it might have been a fighter cannon shell. The bombardier and nose turret gunner were killed outright, and everybody on the flight deck injured. The sergeant and the co-pilot helped the more seriously injured navigator and flight engineer out of the plane while Newman was trying to keep it under some control. The sergeant wasn't sure about the condition of the engines, but the plane was burning furiously and losing altitude fast. His oxygen source caught fire and a flash of flame came through to the mask on his face. He ripped off his mask and helmet, only to be showered with burning gas or hydraulic fluid -he wasn't sure which. Newman ordered him and the co-pilot to jump. Before he could, an explosion blew him into the bomb bay and out of the plane. While free-falling he was able to beat out the fire on his clothing before pulling the ripcord. He spent all of his time in captivity in German hospitals. He never got to a Stalag Luft, and didn't know what happened to the others on his crew. He was sure that Newman had forfeited all chance of survival by staying at the controls long enough to ensure the evacuation of his crew. The sergeant asked that we do what we could for a posthumous award for Newman. It was too late for us to process and follow up on the customary award procedure, but we did record the sergeant's narrative, sent it up through channels, and hoped that something deserving would happen for Newman and his pitifully disfigured sergeant. I never heard, as we came home a couple of days later. But I've never forgotten that faceless face and have wondered whatever happened to that poor guy and the many others like him. Where did they go; where are they now?

Service on the awards board was looked upon as an administrative chore for which ranking combat personnel had little time or taste, and initially it was. After involvement in several all-day meetings, I began to look upon it as a welcome change from the everyday pressures of combat operations and a chance to exchange ideas with peers from other bomber and fighter groups. Importantly, it provided an opportunity to back off briefly from the forest of large aerial formations, and take a close look at the astounding mettle and resiliency of the individuals riding within those planes.

1.   Roger Freeman's <u>The Mighty Eighth</u> (pp 272-281) gives extensive *curriculum vitae* of our top aces; Schilling was ranked fifth. His 56th Fighter Group, base at Boxted for the last year of the war, was the first USAAF group issued the P-47 Thunderbolt, and the only fighter group in the 8th to keep this equipment throughout the war.

He remained in the service as a fighter leader then staff officer, but was killed in an auto accident in England in 1956.

2.   Russell Ives' <u>89 Days</u> records the radio operator for Newman's crew as T/Sgt. Wm. F. McLaughlin, KIA. If that designation came after my father's meeting with the severely injured crewman and JJM correctly rembers the man's crew position, then it would seem that McLaughlin eventually died as a result of his extensive injuries.

51. Operation HOMERUN

The brief, hot, brilliant, colorful burn of signal flares against a suitably grey Norfolk sky, shot from the tower of USAAF Station #145, seemed like the right metaphor for 13 months that had snuffed out too many young lives and changed every survivor forever. It was mid June, 1945, and we were just getting used to the unfamiliar look of England at peace, the first it had known in six years.

The flares called for engine starts. Alex, J.J., Frank and I, last remnants of a proud lineage which so strongly compassed so many lives, broke off our reminiscence, and we headed to our assigned planes. For the last time as comrades is arms, we lifted off of English soil, just going for a ride now, passengers in 'Operation Homerun.'

The return movement of our adopted 'good luck' 467th BG to the States was by a northern route: the Azores; Goose Bay Labrador; Dow Field in Bangor, Maine to Windsor Locks, Connecticut. From there we were taken by rail to Camp Miles Standish in Plymouth, Massachusetts. We were assembled in an auditorium and given the shocking news, in an incredibly insensitive way by a truly stupid major: our group, squadrons, and crews ceased to exist as of that moment!

And so it ended. We were now a random collection of individuals of various ranks, ratings, and specialties, all in a replacement pool and responsible to the camp commander only. Without so much as a run of the flag up the pole, blowing a bugle, a salute, or even a 'thanks' for its effort, the 467th was no more. Not that we expected a ticker tape parade, but this and some subsequent stateside receptions left a bad taste in the mouths of all.[1] We felt that we had done our bit and were justifiably proud of it. The Germans had tried long and hard to do what this stateside chairborne so-and-so had accomplished in seconds—knock the 467th out of the sky. Obviously he was acting under orders, but he couldn't have delivered them in a worse way.

When the A-Bomb was dropped, I was parked on an air base in Sioux Falls, South Dakota, along with some 30,000 other flyboys from the Eighth who nobody knew what to do with. I applied for immediate discharge, but with the sudden ending of the war in the Pacific, everybody was caught off-guard, and paperwork, which had always moved at a snail's pace, moved that much slower. My next-door neighbor in the BOQ (Bachelor Officer Quarters) was the Base Commander, Col. John "Killer" Kane. He was another of the Medal of Honor recipients for his part in the original Ploesti raid. To get in my flying time, I made a couple of flights with him to his home base at Barksdale Field, Louisiana, in the only multiengine plane we had at Sioux Falls, a B-25 Mitchell. I asked to use it sometime for a cross-country trip to visit family in New Jersey and Boston. He added my name to the lengthy list of others who had asked for it. Finally, I was next on the list and really looking forward to my junket East, but it was never to be. The fellow ahead of me banged our B-25 into the side of the Empire State Building![2]

That's my last 'war story.' There is nothing particularly special about this one among all the others. It just happens to be my last *war* story, before I got on with the rest of my life. It is actually typical of so many of them: it connects me personally with a bigger event in a fateful way, with me living to tell of another close brush with death. I certainly do not mean this to sound blasé. These are the words of a grateful and lucky man, one who has had a long full life in a basically peaceful world, one who remembers, every day, those who never got to see what their sacrifice secured.

1. The repatriation of the beloved hardware of the 467th didn't go any better.   Uncle Sam's impolitic agents charged with 'repossessing' the legendary *Witchcraft* from the equally legendary ground crew of Sgt. Joe Ramirez, nearly opened a Home Front.   Having nursed 'their' B-24 through a record 130 missions without an abort, the celebrated "League of Nations" team was honored to escort her home.   After the receiving crew insulted the war-weary plane, Ramirez, Dong and Betcher saw to it that they became blooded troops and that the MPs at Bradley Field, Connecticut, would not soon forget their names.

The Witch was sent on a bond-selling tour, but they had seen her for the last time.   All but a handful of the 18,000+ Liberators built, were scrapped.

2. At 9:49 a.m. on July 28, 1945, Lt. Col. William Smith crashed into the 79th floor of the Empire State Building in dense cloud.   Three in the plane and 11 in the building were killed in the fiery disaster.

Nature inexorably reclaims the airfield tower at Rackheath.

part II

Apocrypha

Apocrypha Introduction

The preceding 51 chapters have presented my father's own written stories, only edited for style. Because he was a participant or observer in all of the episodes, he qualifies as an historic source. By contrast, this small section consists of stories which come to the reader through the filter of this younger author. Although I may be a serious student of 'the war,' I am a generation removed from the action described. Dad is my prime (and in some cases, *only*) source for what follows, but problematically so in every case. In some instances I rely on his writing in a form with which he was not yet satisfied; in others where I rely on his spoken account, you and I must trust my memory.

Regarding the unwritten accounts: academic integrity, if not humility, requires me to plainly state their limitations as *history:* these are my recollections of my father's stories, or worse: my *rehearsed* and beloved versions of *his* versions, subject to all the glories and pitfalls of true 'oral tradition.' In the present context, it is a confession, not a boast, to state that I am my father's son, and he sure loved a good story.

The article *'Neutrality' and Internment* was partly compelled by my father's rough typescript, full of marginal notations and cross-outs. I surmise that his hesitation to develop it fully was because much of the information he had was second-hand to him, garnered from acquaintances who, unlike himself, were actually interned by the Swiss during the war. I have found two definitive sources (see Bibliography) for corroboration and refinement of his draft, last worked on more than 20 years ago. I am glad that he did not throw it away, but instead successfully baited me to investigate further by leaving it in a folder he marked "Do not use."

My article "Terror Target" goes well beyond my father's original vignette (which he named 'Target Templehof'). His written account is not reconcilable with his compelling oral account, which he told me nearly 30 years ago, and which scored a strong moral point on an obviously impressionable collegiate. The official record of the mission *as flown* corroborates neither version. At times during my research I felt as if my Holy Grail were within grasp, that I would find another who could testify to the night the teletypes stopped and higher command thought better of its deadly plans. But the dissonance between the three versions has only sharpened, so I present the reader with the whole paradox, which continues to engage me as no other subject in this entire project.

Not all are weighty stuff—some are here just because they are so funny.

These really *are* 'war stories,' in the sense that they resist, probably for the rest of time, all attempts to definitively substantiate them. Their truth value, at the level of representing the flavor of a time and place, a glimpse of the human condition, or the occasional profound moral lesson, is quite independent of their elusive *factual* parentage.

If the inclusion of stories in this section impels more talented researchers to unearth critical facts, I will be grateful that my incomplete task—realizing the maximum value of my father's memoirs *to the historical record*—will have been more fully achieved.

BHM

Blackjack's Last Mount

Dad told of one special charge given to his cavalry unit in the Massachusetts National Guard, during his collegiate days and at the very beginning of his military life. Somehow, it had fallen to them to care for the aging black horse that had been General John J. Pershing's last mount, probably with him in Europe at the end of WW I. The animal would have been at least twenty at this time.

The veterinarians had a simple prescription for comforting the arthritic steed: three bottles of beer a day. After light exercise in the yard and a good brushing, the cadets would return the horse to its stall, where all seemed to look forward to the medicating routine. In turn, three bottles of Narragansset were opened and placed on the floor just a foot outside the stall door. The horse needed no prompting to lean over, grab the top with his teeth, raise his head up and back, draining the contents in one smooth chug and setting the bottle back down in the same spot. As soon as a full one was substituted for the empty, he would repeat.

Getting In

To get into the Air Corps in 1940, one had to be able to get into the equipment of the day, and the 23 year old who reported for his flight physical at an armory in Boston was, for his day, quite tall. But he was sure at the time that it was just a case of the random hazing a recruit had best get used to, when the doctor who stood between him and basic flight school interrupted the physical, right at the point where they were measuring his height.

Inwardly irritated, Dad shrugged it off, ran around the field house five times as commanded, on that hot summer morning, and reported back. No sooner had he resumed his place on the scale, than the flight surgeon congratulated him on narrowly passing. The droll doc's explanation: Dad was 1/4" over the strict 6'2" height cut-off limit when he first stepped up on the scale after a good night's sleep, but a little real-world spinal compression exercise did the trick and allowed an interesting military career to proceed.

'Neutrality' and Internment

Note for this article: passages appearing in quotes are as found in the JJM rough draft, which he relegated to his 'do not use' folder some time prior to his retirement in 1980. All other attribution of views to my father in this article are from my memory of our conversations on this broad subject. I have long taken an interest in the particular issues of Swiss 'neutrality,' and as much of this conversation was in the last few years it is quite 'fresh' for me.

Allied bomber crews who judged their damaged craft to be unfit for the return to England could strike out for nearer havens in neutral Sweden, across the North Sea from northern Germany, or Switzerland, proximal to targets in southeastern France, Southern Germany, and northern Italy. After the Normandy invasion, emergency fields were also available in liberated areas of the Continent.

The concept of internment is that a combatant who presents himself to a neutral power is 'out of action' for the duration, absent some particular arrangement between the combatants, along the lines of an internee/prisoner exchange. A crew with stricken vessel and all of its equipment, surrendering to an interning host, are to be treated as guarded guests, non-combatants. But entering the territory or airspace of a neutral with no intention of submitting to asylum is a violation for which one should expect lethal retaliation. In practice, the Germans rarely had trouble returning to territory they held, so we can only guess whether they would have fudged these simple internment conventions as often as we did.

"It was generally assumed that the likelihood of evading capture when shot down within Germany proper was very remote. There were a few who did manage to get out of Germany and into Holland, Belgium and France and then via the underground back to England—but they were very few. On the other hand, landing in the low countries or France, chances of avoiding capture were reasonably good. We were given general instruction on the best steps to take once you hit the ground. Dispose of your parachute and any unwanted equipment, seek cover until darkness, avoid metropolitan areas, and try to find a railroad or waterway for orientation with your escape map. Where and when and to whom you should identify yourself for best chances of contacting the underground was the $64-thousand question.

Interestingly, the best chances for contacting the underground in occupied countries were said to be in red-light districts. It was said that most links in the underground chain for getting Allied airmen out of Europe were brothels.

There was some conjecture that more crew members entered the many tributaries of the underground system than ever reached the terminals through which they could pass to Allied hands. While some may have disappeared due to a breakdown in the system for passing evadees along, it was suspected that a few might have elected to stay in the system and opted not to be passed along, possibly in fear of being caught during moves between underground stops, and possibly a few were enjoying the bawdy-house.

After the liberation of Paris, the MPs made considerable effort to round up any such malingerers. Rumor had it that they did harvest quite a crop, but nobody (including the MPs themselves) felt that they succeeded in uncovering all. We all had a lingering suspicion that a few MIAs might have 'gone native' in France and elsewhere."

The buzz during my father's time in the ETO was that sometimes Swiss treatment of the Americans was rough and hostile, though by no means consistently so, while the Swedes rolled out a consistent red carpet. This had the possibility to become a discipline and morale issue, luring 'cripples' to Sweden that might have had a decent shot at making it 'home' to England.

"In this vein, Sweden was more of a problem than occupied Europe. From the time we started making fairly deep penetrations into Germany, especially the north, landing in Sweden became the recommended alternative to attempting a return trip home over the North Sea with a badly crippled airplane. Word got around fast that the Swedes were treating our boys extremely well. They were well fed and well clothed. They had complete freedom, and found that the Swedish girls were very attractive, amiable, and anxious to please. Notions about the desirability of Sweden as a place to sit out the war in comfort were prevalent enough that we made a special point in briefings regarding the conditions under which an airplane would be considered legitimately eligible to seek sanctuary in Sweden."

As more scholarship and letters came out in the two decades since he wrote those words, my father became convinced that the frequency of unjustified landings in Sweden was not significant. Nonetheless, high command at the time took note of the steady rise of asylum seekers, even when safe continental landings became an option, as indicative of a morale problem among air combat crews with ever lengthening tours of duty, and took steps to better identify and treat instances of combat fatigue.[1]

With the increasing Allied hegemony in the European airspace from May 1944 onward, fighters were deployed in strafing runs on transportation targets when returning from bomber escort, or even as their prime assignment. These were not as risk-free as might be assumed: it was with justification that fighter command began to allow 'ground kills' in tallying a fighter pilot's career record. With intense antiaircraft defense of airfields and defensive 'ak-ak' from specially disguised 'boxcars' on trains, this kind of work entailed loss rates similar to dogfighting skilled defenders aloft.

My father recounted seeing gun-camera footage from an American fighter strafing a freight train just entering Germany from Switzerland. Per standard operating procedure of the day, the pilot avoided not only the series of cars bearing the International Red Cross symbol on top, but also immediately adjoining unmarked ones as buffers protecting the relief supply goods. In the plane's first pass, one saw an ammo load detonate spectacularly as one of the 'fair game' cars was raked with .50 caliber rounds. The pilot went around again and the film showed that a chain reaction of explosions had gone all the way through the train, revealing that the Red Cross markings were bogus. After this, fighter pilots were, unofficially of course, given a freer hand, and met with similar results on many occasions.

Realists then and now would understand that a neutral country, completely surrounded by the territory of a combatant, could hardly avoid trading with them, nor does neutrality require such abstention. And a casual glance at the map reveals the impossibility of wartime Switzerland conducting any commerce with the Allied side.   But solid evidence of Swiss war materiel trade with the Third Reich, abuse of the protective symbol of the International Red Cross, and instances of needlessly stern treatment of Allied internees, made my father and other knowledgeable contemporaries wince at the phrase 'neutral Switzerland.' The present-day reader, mindful of recent revelations of the complicity of Swiss banking interests with the murderous and plundering Reich, and of the sad tales of widespread dealing in palpably ill-gotten art treasures by Swiss dealers and collectors, who asked none of the appropriate provenance questions of their Nazi *nouveau riche* clientele, may still be astounded to learn that at one point it actually came to blows between Swiss and American fighter planes.

It would be simplistic to dismiss all of the instances of Swiss hostility toward American internees as German partisanship; our own conduct could be less than ingratiating. On three different occasions,[2] poor navigation coincided with poor judgment to accidentally put lethal US bomb loads on Swiss territory, certainly engendering suspicions and resentments. And as the account of the American-Swiss dogfight makes plain, Americans in the air and on the ground were capable of breaking rules and baiting our 'hosts.' Accounts of the reasonable Swiss reception of official, high-level US apologies right after two of these incidents,[3] suggest that the Swiss government was not hostile toward us, at least once it was clear which way the wind was blowing.

I do not know whether the Germans or the Swiss knew it at the time, but the US had ceded some moral high ground in its own adherence to the understood conventions of neutrality; note the blasé way my father delivers this shocker: "There was a night-time shuttle service between England and Stockholm.   Unmarked American planes retrieved our internees, and at least some were returned to their units and combat status."

Engineers and technical personnel were cycled in to Sweden to evaluate whether particular decisions to seek refuge there were justified by the damage to aircraft, and air crew were cycled back to England. A scratched out portion of my father's typescript alludes to an unnamed womanizer who made for Sweden when, it was later determined, he might easily have made it back to England to continue his combat tour. "Either that night or the next one he was on the shuttle flight back to England and a court martial."

"...the feedback to us was that the [Swiss] reception [was] quite unlike that in Sweden. The Swiss were viewed as openly pro-German and hostile to Allied personnel. Our internees felt that the Swiss as individuals were arrogant, unpleasant, and a little on the slow side. All of these characteristics [were] somewhat in contrast to what we heard about the Swedes.

At least it made it easier for us in deciding or evaluating the necessity for a plane to take sanctuary in Switzerland. It was obviously a case of necessity, as in the combat crew members' minds, this was the last resort next to being captured by the Germans. However, on missions to Munich and in that area, we always lost at least a few to Switzerland."[4]

He described the elaborate (and occasionally successful) German ploy to lure refuge seekers to a field on their side of Lake Constance, built to mimic the Swiss field opposite. Then he describes conditions within:

"The Allied airmen who landed on the Swiss field were interned in a small town a short distance from the field. Most of our internees were housed in one of two inns on opposite sides of the same street in this town. The officers were on one side on the street and the enlisted personnel directly opposite. They were closely guarded and given little freedom by the Swiss. With little freedom and much time on their hands, our boys spent much of their time thinking of ways to irritate the Swiss.

Every morning and every evening and at other times it suited them, the Swiss had everybody fall out in front of the inn in which he was billeted for a roll call. Much to the annoyance of the Americans, these were conducted in a strict military fashion and involved much more time and formality than they felt necessary to count heads. They used these occasions for schoolboy pranks and practical joking to annoy the Swiss, whom they found to be devoid of humor... the discovery by some of the internees that there was a long abandoned secret passageway under the street between the two inns... provided all kinds of intriguing opportunities to confound the Swiss during morning and evening roll calls. Whenever the spirit moved them, the internees would have one of their number take the tunnel under the street and join the roll call of the other group. When the Swiss found that they were one man short on one side of the street, they would sound alarms to search for the escapee. They were furious when they discovered that the 'missing' individual was lined up on the other side of the street. Since they were unable to extract an explanation of this phenomenon from any of the internees, the Swiss doubled the nightly guard on the street to make sure that no one crossed. Variations of the underground switching continued to the total annoyance and frustration of the Swiss guards."

As my father's script proceeds, one infers that he had at least one source, likely an officer, who was privy to the boasts and bravado of Swiss flying officers, but no names, Swiss or American, are given for corroboration in his written account.

"Every day that an Allied mission was flown near the Swiss border, the Swiss fighters would take off and cruise around the German-Swiss border, waiting for someone to violate their airspace. When that occurred, they would take up close escort formation and lead the plane to their airfield. On such occasions, the whole town would turn out to watch the Swiss fighters go out and see what they would come home with. On most occasions it was an American bomber, frequently under escort to the Swiss border by an American fighter protecting it from German attack. Our fighters would then give way to the Swiss escort and return to England or Italy.

Somehow or other the Swiss felt that taking off of the American fighter escort in some way symbolized his fear of becoming entangled with their Swiss pilots, whom they were sure were better than anybody else, even though they had never been combat tested. This feeling on the part of the Swiss did, of course, very little for improving the already strained relations between the interned Americans and their guards. There was one point however that did rankle.

Among their extensive and varied collection of allied aircraft, they did not have a single P-51.[5] They had heard that it was the best Allied fighter and boasted that they might one day have the opportunity to demonstrate their superior fighting ability by engaging a Mustang in aerial combat. That day did arrive to the chagrin and wrath of the Swiss, and the delight of all the Allied internees."

My father's written account has a few factual errors, underscoring the danger of relying on his second hand recollections, at least for specific details if not for 'flavor.'[6] According to Roy Thomas' Haven, Heaven, or Hell (see Bibliography), on September 5, 1944, two P-51s from the 339th FG were escorting 1st Lieutenant John Fanelli's 389th BG B-24 to refuge when they were engaged by two Swiss fighters, with the result that both went down and one pilot was killed. My father's account admits that the American escort violated the Swiss airspace and was menaced by the Swiss when they did not surrender as instructed, but returned fire instead of meekly retreating to German airspace.

"The Americans stood cheering loudly [while the Swiss were] beside themselves with anger. After completing [their] relatively easy task, [they] added insult to injury by buzzing the Swiss field before heading home. This day was the highlight of the many miserable ones spent by the internees in that Swiss town. But they never forgot it, nor did they ever let their 'hosts' forget."

My father's rough typescript on these subjects goes on to relate the escalating clash between opportunistic Yankee gumption and the 'rules' of internment in a neutral country. 'Escaping' from asylum before the end of hostilities compromised the neutrality of the host, unlike a prisoner of war's true escape from the control of one's enemy.

> "...there were very few attempts made to escape internment there until the closing months of the war, when French underground troops started to wrest control of the French Alps from the Germans. At that point, the Allied internees did organize and accomplish many large scale breakouts from Swiss internment into France. When General Patton made his famous flanking run around Paris in pursuit of the Germans, he encountered one large French underground force which counted in its number a substantial number of 492nd [BG] combat crew members who a few months earlier had escaped internment in Switzerland and resumed their combat careers on the ground... harassing Germans. One of our alums became a leader of a large underground unit."[7]

1. For a fine treatment of this complex issue, readers are referred to page 379 of Carl A. Spaatz and the Airwar in Europe, see Bibliography.

2. On April 1, 1944, one group, separated from its formation in dense cloud, with malfunctioning radar and navigation equipment, thought they were bombing Freiburg, Germany, as a target of opportunity, but in fact hit Schaffhausen, Switzerland, 60 miles away, killing 40. On March 4, 1945, separate navigational debacles resulted in bombs falling on Zurich, killing 5 and injuring a dozen, and on a rail yard in Basel. During a court martial in connection with the Schaffhausen incident, two low ranking USAAF officers were acquitted on severe charges, but American reparations were negotiated and paid to Switzerland at the end of the war. (See The Day We Bombed Switzerland in the Bibliography.)

3. At the strong urging of General George C. Marshall, General Carl Spaatz, then Commander of the United States Strategic Army Air Forces (USTAAF), went to Bern and met privately with high Swiss officials to convey personal and official apologies for the incidents and to outline stringent control measures to prevent future accidents, which appeased them. (See Carl A. Spaatz and the Airwar in Europe in the Bibliography.)

4. The 467th had two planes interned in Switzerland, which arrived on 5-11-44 and 7-12-44. JJM might have had access to their crews upon repatriation, but he was not with that organization when these crews took refuge. The 492nd had five planes there. As JJM was one of that group's bomb squadron COs, it is a little more likely that he knew some of these crews well and had contact with them after repatriation. But his notes and correspondence files do not specify any of his sources for what he wrote about Swiss relations, internment conditions, or 'the incident.' I now regret that I never thought to press him for names.

5. Eventually they acquired at least one Mustang, a P-51B from the 4th Fighter Group, seen in Swiss markings on the cover of <u>Strangers in a Strange Land</u> (Vol. II); see bibliography.

6. Or maybe JJM *did* get it right. His 'incident' involved a *single* Mustang jumped by two Swiss fighters while escorting a *B-17*. My correspondent, 44th BG veteran and Swiss internee Forrest Clark, stated in an e-mail on 2-25-99, "The incident is very similar to what you related so it is likely this could be it and the B-24 was confused with a B-17. At any event it is worth checking. There were several accounts and confirmed reports of Swiss fighters attacking American bombers over the border so there may have been other incidents."

7. Again, no corroboration is to be found in JJM papers. The intrepid escape of these 492nd personnel, if it predated Patton's movement around Paris by months, would have been around the time of D-Day, long before the rout of German forces on the French-Swiss frontier.

Dad had a reputation as a very successful poker player. In his day, he also won a few bets, solidly based upon what today might be called 'good front-end analysis of risk.' He was rather proud of one where he suckered other hotshot pilots (on more than one occasion) by taxiing a B-24 *backwards*. I have caught a few present day pilots in a 'dry run' of this one myself, after informing them that the pitch of the prop blades was *not* reversible on a Lib.

The trick was to run up one of the outboard engines while the main gear brake on that same side of the plane was set, the opposite side free, and the nose gear free to pivot. Because the powered engine was *outboard* of the pivot point (that is, the one locked gear), when it thrust forward it pivoted the rest of the plane *backwards*.

Once the plane had pivoted back thirty degrees or so, the procedure was repeated, using the opposite combination of outboard engine and main gear brake.

Dad claimed to have been able to do this fairly smoothly, and reported no balking at collection time over whether one should really call the resultant backward lurches of a 60,000 pound bomber 'taxiing.' I presume all of this took place in the wide open spaces of the American West, before they went overseas. The combination of rigorous training programs and bright young men with bits of unstructured time and powerful machines on their hands, was a crucible for high-jinks.

What I find more remarkable is

that he managed to put considerable wear and tear on a quarter of a million bucks worth of Uncle Sam's machinery, just to score a point and a few brews, without getting chewed out by a crew chief or a CO! But then, he got away with a lot—I've got the films to prove it.

*   *   *   *   *   *

One of Dad's compatriots from the same period, name unfortunately not noted, never had to buy himself a beer if there was a betting man on the premises.

His routine was to start by betting the bartender that he could *completely consume* a draft, *glass included.* Incredulous others were invited to put their money down before his dramatic start. After downing the beer, he would crack the rim with his teeth and crunch the pieces very deliberately and carefully into shards no more than half and inch across—then swallow! Dad saw him do it once but found it difficult to watch on successive occasions.

He assured Dad that his pre-med schooling on the wonders of the alimentary canal had proven, so far, correct. He had been taught that the autonomic nerves and smooth muscles of the system were 'programmed' to handle sharp and rough stuff, so long as it was not very big. Dad never knew this fellow to cut his mouth or report any other bad 'outcomes.'

In the years since hearing this, it has inspired me to come up with scores of easier, if less dramatic, ways to con someone out of a beer. I have also wondered if Dad's friend finished school after the war. Specialized in proctology, no doubt.

Daring

Cinematographer

Dad's interest in photography manifested itself in his military days and continued throughout his life. He devoted considerable energy to recording, in a variety of media, his wartime experience and then the growth and principal passages of his family. He was an almost compulsive record keeper, allowing me to tell you that on March 25, 1944, Capt. Mahoney paid $195 for his Bell & Howell 70D 16mm movie camera, and for another $44.40, Don Thompson Photographic Supply in El Paso threw in two lenses for same.

To this day, the 2200 feet of film he shot overseas, most of it in color, is recognized as historically significant by researchers and veterans alike. His short narrated video conversion of the highlights, first issued in 1990, is still being produced by popular demand, and three prominent museums have incorporated his footage in their presentations of 8th Air Force history.

Dad was showing the family some of the film about twenty years ago when I noticed, for the first time, a pronounced lurch in a 'bombs away' sequence. By this point, I think I had come to appreciate that he was violating procedure by being in the bomb bay during a drop, and that it was probably against a handful of regulations for him to be carrying a personal camera on a mission. When I asked if he could remember what the 'lurch' was about—nearby flack, perhaps?—he shot me a look that said "drop it," so I did, until a reel-change break when Mom went to the kitchen to refresh her drink.

In a low voice, he allowed that he was *really* pushing it: an observant waist gunner also broke the rules that day by coming onto the bomb bay catwalk during a drop, and grabbed Dad's suspenders and pulling our absorbed John Ford back to balance after he started to follow the bombs he was filming. Dad had not been wearing an oxygen mask or parachute, and was not even saftey-lined to the plane. As the full 'impact' of this revelation sunk in, and I imagined my unborn life figuratively passing before my eyes onto der Vaterland 20,000 feet below in vivid color, I blurted out that he hadn't even stopped filming the sequence. His retort: "Do you have any idea how much Kodachrome cost in 1944?"

Floral

Flag

Dad told of flying over Northern Holland, before its liberation at the very end of the European war, low enough to clearly make out a tulip field planted in the colors and form of the Stars and Stripes. In an instant, all on board knew that the careful planting of this defiant symbol in the previous fall represented terrific courage and sacrifice. This occasioned no conversation at the time because there was not a dry eye among the crew. Unfortunately, neither was there a camera.

By the fall of '44, conditions in the Dutch areas bypassed by Montgomery in his push eastward were extremely harsh, worsening by the month. Tulip bulbs had become a food of last resort as tens of thousands starved to death, and Nazi crackdowns on the underground (and all able-bodied Dutch males generally) included forced conscription, forced labor, and summary executions on the slimmest of pretexts.[1] The liberators in the Liberators had an appreciation of the context in which the rebellious and grateful tulip growers had designed and planted this very moving symbol.

My attempts to corroborate this story have unearthed one poor aerial photo of what a believer could imagine was a horticultural American flag,[2] but no witnesses, Dutch or American. But the strength of my father's account and my admiration for the dignifying choices made by an oppressed people will keep me on the scent of this 'apocryphal story.'

1. See The Hunger Winter in the Bibliography.

2. Col. Arie P. de Jong, Royal Netherlands Air Force (Ret.) has been a helpful correspondent to me and many researchers, particularly as concerns wreckage of 8th Air Force aircraft that came to rest in Holland during the war.

The history books will tell you that the sound barrier was first broken on October 14, 1947, when USAF test pilot Chuck Yeager flew the Bell X-1 rocket ship to just past Mach 1 over Muroc Dry Lake (from present-day Edwards AFB) after being dropped from the B-50 mother ship. That is the first officially sanctioned, documented and well-recorded instance of a piloted craft exceeding the speed of sound in controlled level flight.

The obsession with speed, and generally with 'pushing the envelope' of all flight performance characteristics, was not restricted to laboratories, test facilities, or the dreams of futuristic air-war planners. It coursed through the veins of all who ever flew or wanted to. During war, this interest in a few extra miles-per-hour top speed, or the ability to 'pull a few more Gs' in a turn, is not for mere thrill or glory. It defines the life-or-death critical competitive edge over one's enemy. It is natural to assume that German fliers, like Americans, pushed each new fighter model, with or without official sanction, often past the breaking point. It is understandable that the more extreme uncontrolled tests would have been explicitly forbidden, but also that these prohibitions would have been in vain. Given the number and types of rocket and jet aircraft produced toward the desperate and chaotic end of the war on the German side, is likely that they also have 'apocryphal' stories on this subject.

The heavy, big, radial-engined Republic P-47 Thunderbolt was appreciated for its ability to take amazing punishment and its ability to dive. My father told of two incidents where 'Jugs' were put into power dives over East Anglia from high altitude, with the intention of exceeding the speed of sound.[1]   The first ended in a crash, but not before the stricken pilot radioed that his control surfaces had gone from functioning with increasing effort, to being totally ineffectual. The pilot in the second attempt pulled out *literally* at ground zero, but was never named in Dad's telling. Wheat stalks were wedged into sheet metal seams on the underside of the stress-deformed wings, and the pilot's boots had cracked the bezels on the instrument panel as he used all of his strength to pull the stick back in the instant when his plane went supersonic, restoring extremely dense airflow to the control surfaces, and at the very last possible instant.

By the time Dad was stationed in England, the 56th Fighter Group was the only one still flying the Jug, so I surmise that their equipment and personnel were involved. I have the impression that Dad was present at the non-fatal demonstration, and that this activity was regarded with strong ambivalence by higher-ups. While the tests proved nothing of immediate military utility and put men and machines in extreme peril, all involved were fairly inured to mortal danger, intrigued to know the full potential of their sturdiest fighter, and aware that supersonic flight was the next design and performance challenge looming on the aviation horizon.

This high-stakes experimentation would have made even more sense to them in immediate terms. Our best and fastest, the P-51 Mustang, was no match for the approximate 540 mph level cruising speed of the Me.262 *Schwalbe*, the Luftwaffe twin jet fighter which started to appear in numbers over Berlin in late '44. All knew at that time that if the Germans could find fuel and enough skilled pilots, they would severely menace our bombers and fighters. The closest thing we had, the P-80 Shooting Star, would not be available in production quantities for months. In the meanwhile, several things were required for the Allies to maintain clear air

superiority and press for a quick end to the European war:
keep hitting aircraft production, fuel and airfield targets,
and develop fighter tactics for dealing with the latest
German planes.

One clear Columbus Day weekend
in the early 1970s I was home from college, helping Dad
rake leaves as the Air Force's Thunderbirds happened to
be performing over the Chenango County Fairgrounds, two
miles away and a few hundred feet lower than our perfect
hillside vantage point. Their routine had them flying at
our eyelevel, down the narrow valley in front of our house
leading toward downtown Norwich, New York. On each pass
they did a different aerobatic display. Their finale had
the outermost F-4 Phantoms peel outward and a bit upward
as another went a little less outward but up much more
steeply. The last plane pulled up extremely sharply, hit
his afterburner, and before breaking the horizon of hills
on the far side of the valley, made a thundering crack of
the sound barrier *going straight up.*

Having returned to civilian life
after the war, my father had been 'out of the loop' of
military aviation for nearly 30 years, and his personal
vivid memories of attempts on the speed of sound could not
have been in starker contrast. Dad's reaction was as
stunning and memorable as the latter day demonstration.
This staid Bostonian, whose vocabulary was less obscene
than Mother Superior's, let himself fall backwards into a
large pile of leaves and exhaled "Holy shit!" with what
little was left of his breath.

1. British Author James Hoseason had a source on some of the same
information. He writes: "It was one of the 56th's pilots who diced his P-47
to achieve a supersonic speed of 728 MPH." (Page 162, Thousand Day
Battle)

'Characters'

Dad's text affords the reader a few glimpses into the character of several 'characters.'[1] It seems appropriate here to share a few more. There was in fact a genre my family called "Charley Barrett stories." Even if these anecdotes did not already illustrate the high caliber of GI antics, or how war finds one improbable friends, they would deserve recounting because they are so funny.

shy in the shower

Every time a soldier gets assigned to a new military organization—basic training, flight school, advanced flying—there will be occasions when new acquaintances see each other in the altogether for the first time. The slight inherent unease of the shower, and the fact that as a kid Charley had lost a toe in a hunting accident, were 'material' for this master of hard-hitting dark humor. At several points in their parallel military careers, Dad would brace himself for the scene in the quiet, full shower room when Charley would pointedly look at some innocent and intone "I know you are looking at my toe." Protests were in vain, and none could resist the urge to steal their own look, even at the peril of being singled out for the same treatment.

cool or cruel?

As fate would have it, Charley and his second bride lived close to Mom and Dad right after the war. Both had young children, making it hard to coordinate a night out, but they settled on a plan where my parents would get a sitter and go to the Barretts' after dinner one night for dessert.

Mrs. Barrett was upstairs feeling unwell when their guests arrived. My concerned mother could not eat dessert without asking just how sick she *was*—to which Charley answered straight faced: "She was so sick, I had to hold her up while she did the dishes."

Doc Spivack

<u>*callous conductor*</u>

At one point before going overseas, Dad and Doc Spivak were jointly charged with getting a troop train full of airmen from the Norfolk area to Trenton. Dad, possessed of excellent instincts in these matters, remembered being more apprehensive about the high-jinks of his 'assistant' than of the numerous nominal charges.

The train was very slow, smoky, and crowded. Doc's complaints about the Army, their assignment, and their legroom, were surely building to something when the train lurched to a halt at a water stop miles from anywhere. Before Dad could react, the damage was done: Spivak had gone to the vestibule at the end of the car and impersonated a Penn Central conductor most effectively with his bellowed "Trenton, Trenton!"

In the comfort of a now half-empty car, Dad had plenty of time to contemplate the chewing-out he would get for failing in this inane mission, knowing that Doc would be of even less help then.

1. Please see my father's chapters 'Charley Barrett' and 'Doc Spivak.'

The philosophical, stylistic, practical and moral valuations that differentiated the US and British contributions to the combined strategic air assault on the Reich have been discussed incessantly since the fledgeling Eighth came on the scene in 1942, intent upon proving the value of precision daylight high altitude bombing. The joint bombardment of Dresden on Valentine's Day 1945 is typically cited as exceptional for the Americans, eschewing for once their goal of hitting precisely identified strategic targets with as little collateral damage and waste of ordnance as practicable, and going along with the Brits on an 'area bombing' mission.

As penance for the heat that I generated in countless sophomoric discussions on this important subject, I will now try to reflect some light. To German civilians on the ground in Berlin late in the war, the practical distinction between American 'precision bombing' by day, and British area-bombing by night, for all our various intentions, was nil. The US conceit that we could hit a tank factory in one urban neighborhood and somehow not take out half of the residences within 2,000 yards, *even on a good day,* was belied by the statistics. The British were in the vanguard of developing and implementing myriad radar and navigational systems which, though still very crude at war's end, rendered their over all bomb aiming more accurate than the American.[1]

The Yank who would persist in apologizing for Dresden will find a sliver of succor in Richard Davis' scholarly treatment,[2] for indeed the Americans were not carrying just incendiary loads, and were actually *aiming* for (and did hit) rail targets of strategic importance. But the same book goes on to cast serious doubt on the proposition that noble US intentions of always avoiding the civilian or terror target persisted while a vanquished foe's capital kept showing up on an ever-shorter prioritized list of thing left to bomb. American military leaders who hewed to the high ground had to defend it forcefully and often at the end. Davis quotes Eighth AF Commander James B. Doolittle, appealing to USSTAF General Carl 'Tooey' Spaatz to cancel a round-the-clock massive terror bombardment of Berlin: "We will, in what may be one our our last and best remembered operations regardless of its effectiveness, violate the basic American principle of precision bombing of targets of strictly military significance for which our tactics were designed and our crews trained and indoctrinated." It is arguable that ultimately only caprice and pragmatic considerations prevented Operation Thunderclap from achieving one of its stated goals, the "...killing or wounding of 275,000 people." The strident 'morality play' within Allied high command at the end of the European war is recapitulated in my own difficulties sorting out the riddle of conflicting versions of a story which goes to the very heart of the subject.

By dint of the story's important moral lessons, it is deserving of all the digging needed to give it sound factual underpinnings and a place in the historical record. Alas, as of this writing, the riddle still resists my attempts to deliver a resolution. In its place I offer the reader my exposition of the conundrum and a synopsis of my research odyssey. This is not a perfect substitution, but I offer what follows, confident of its engaging quality and hopeful that publishing this much at this time may yet flush out a helpful witness.

I. Three conflicting versions

1.   The oral version   (Brian Mahoney's recollection of what his father told him approximately 30 years ago)

Dad, in his role as Deputy Group Commander, was in the Ops Block at the secure teletype machine on the night of March 17, 1945 with 467th BG Commanding Officer Albert Shower, and possibly one or two others there who were allowed to see *in toto* the lengthy secret 'field order' for the next day's operations. Specification of long-delay fuses and the absence of a visible military objective in the target photos piqued my father's curiosity, and he asked an intelligence officer to bring a civilian map of Berlin. It was instantly clear that the direction of the bomb run, oriented with a prominent boulevard and subway beneath, meant that the big bombs were intended to blow when they had reached the depth of what was serving as bomb shelter.

Dad felt that a line had been crossed, and that USAAF command was now soiling its hands with targeting of previously forbidden non-military targets. He was willing to take some personal risk to register his discomfort with the order, and with his commander's acquiescence, phoned either 96th Wing or 2nd Division headquarters with a request for clarification, citing all of the telling specs and, in effect, tipping his own hand. His succinct message was taken by a junior officer who told Dad to expect a direct reply from the man in authority. Dad and Shower had been waiting in a cold sweat for five minutes when the teletype fell silent in the middle of the long field order transmission. It resumed with words to this effect: "Disregard previous field order. Retrieve and destroy all copies. New order to follow." And so it did; one which cited a military objective, albeit in the heart of Berlin.

2.   The written version (as presented in James Mahoney's latest typescript dealing with the same episode)

In Dad's ultimate evolution of his

book, the vignette he titled 'Target Tempelhof' relates this episode with a disturbingly different outcome. Perhaps the written version should be regarded as more authoritative, having been continually refined and polished by him over the many years since he told me the oral version. But it can be argued that the recollections of a man still in his early fifties and looking back a quarter century, can be trusted as a more direct and reliable primary historical source than his long-considered and possibly over-polished written version, influenced as it was by accounts of others and his ever growing collection of derivative research.

In the written version, my father removes himself as a factor in the turn of events, and then asserts that the thinly-disguised 'terror raid' went ahead unchanged:

"The last mission to Berlin was not as difficult as previous trips to 'Big B' had been, but had some unusual aspects and unexpected consequences. The night before, after the target section of the field order had been decoded, I was called to the Ops Block and told that our target was the Templehof rail station in Berlin. That was a little surprising—it had already been badly damaged and didn't appear to have any significant military value. As more information ticked off the teletype, we became more puzzled. We were being told to carry eight 1,000 pounders, unusual ordnance against a lightly constructed, spacious frame building. Even more unusual were the fuse settings given for the bombs. Normal nose and tail fuses settings of one-twentieth of a second detonated the bomb just after it had buried itself. This field order called for both fuses to be set at one-tenth of a second: the bombs would be well underground before exploding.

The AP (aiming point) given for the bombardier was in the center of the building. The AP was usually designated short of the target, so that the first bomb would hit there and the following ones would trail through the target to the far edge. What made this AP even more unusual was the intervalometer setting given. Normally, after the first bomb dropped, the others would follow in sequence at an interval of one or two seconds. The lengthy setting given for this target would mean that if the first bomb were placed precisely on the given AP, the following seven would drop well beyond the 'target' area. We started to wonder, what was the real target? Then came the angle-of-attack instructions. For a square or rectangular shaped target such as this, we usually flew diagonally across the target so as to give us the longest dimension of the target to hit. Following this field order, we would be taking the shortest distance across the target and also flying down-wind, contrary to our usual up-wind approach to a target. Intrigued by these unusual instructions, we dug through the target folder and found the answer to our many questions. Leading out from the rail station was a major boulevard, and running for some distance under it was a bomb shelter! In effect, the FO called for the first bomb to hit the station and the remainder to punctuate the length of the boulevard, penetrating to the depth of the shelter, qualifying this as a terror raid. This was a first for us and to our knowledge for the Eighth, excepting a limited participation in the highly publicized one against Dresden sometime earlier. That caused quite a howl from some quarters because Dresden supposedly had nothing of military interest. But most German air attacks against England by the Luftwaffe, and later by the V-ls and V-2s, were made against populated areas with no military value—all unabashed terror raids. Some RAF night area-bombings over Germany could also be characterized as indiscriminate, but the Eighth had stuck to precision bombing of military targets usually well removed from densely populated areas. When there were non-military institutions such as schools and hospitals in the vicinity, we were cautioned to avoid them. Just to be sure we were reading the same script, we got on the scrambler phone to Division to verify these unusual FO specs. They confirmed that the information teletyped was correct, and without so stating recognized that we understood the real target. Neither they nor we cared to admit that we were about to engage in a type of warfare about which we felt a little uneasy, even though it was widely and freely practiced by all other combatants on both sides."

A bit later, his writing simultaneously negates and trivializes the moral of the earlier, oral version:

"At no time during the following morning briefing of the crews did we reveal our suspicions as to the real intent of the mission. We presented the information as it was given in the FO. We made no reference to the air raid shelter, as that was not mentioned in the order. Some crewmen may have recognized possible implications of the mission and were not bothered by them. One officer crew member did ask the medical officer to be excused from the mission on some vague pretense. The medical officer told us later that he sensed the real reason, but rather than risk a confrontation, grounded him as being 'psychologically indisposed' or something similarly cryptic."

3. the official record

In The Mighty Eighth War Diary, Roger Freeman accurately summarizes the original mission report pertaining to field order #1779, exactly as I have read it in the microfiche collection at the Air Force Support History Office at Bolling AFB. Specifically, the third force of the March 18, 1945 Berlin raid consisted of 35 squadron formations (347 B-24s) from the 2nd Air Division. 80 of the 174 assigned to the 'Berlin/Henningsdorf Tank Plant' hit it with "good" results, using 110 tons of general purpose, and 74.5 tons of incendiary bombs. The 'Berlin/Tegel Tank plant' was hit by 225 of 173 assigned aircraft,[3] with 258.8 tons of general purpose bombs and 162.1 tons of incendiaries, with "excellent" results. Freeman runs a photo with a caption indicating a 467th BG plane and smoke markers "...dropping toward the Tegel armored vehicle factory..." and summarizes that "...railway stations and tank plants in the Berlin area were attacked visually or by H2X as weather permitted." The 467th's beautiful post-war book by Alan Healy is consistent with Freeman and the USAF records, describing the Berlin mission with some comment on losses but none on objectives.

II. Reconciling the conflicting accounts

The assertion that a thinly disguised terror operation was ordered and executed would require for corroboration either: a) the testimony of another involved and credible individual, or: b) a damning FO or annex thereto.

The assertion that there was an 'earlier version' of the FO for that day could also be corroborated by human or paper witnesses, but with the understood constraints that *at most* only a small number of persons would have been privy, and that there would have been overpowering cause (a direct military order) for the entire paper record to have been destroyed at the time.

Credible damage reports by either German or Allied authorities, if strongly suggestive of *deliberate* and *particular* action, rather than random misses or even generalized area bombing, would support the former assertion. (Specifically needed to rise to the level of evidence: a very long bomb pattern, reported on or closely paralleling a principal boulevard, and bomb cratering consistent with the use of very heavy GP bombs with long delay fuses.) Absence of any such report would not disprove the intent to do such damage.

For present purposes, I accept it as a given that the official account, so far as it goes, describes the mission as flown that day. It was often the case when all three divisions and more than a thousand bombers were launched on a day late in the war, there would be smaller targets that received the attention of a single bomb squadron, and it would be unusual for such details to survive in the gross summaries.[4] It is quite possible that some of the 467th's planes were assigned to a Berlin target other than the Tegel or Henningsdorf tank plants, and there would be nothing 'suspicious' *per se* about the absence of its specific mention in the sources I have examined. That is to say, the available record, while failing to substantiate JJM's written assertion that a civilian shelter *was* targeted in a mission that *was* flown, does not disprove it.

As a minimum condition for the tenability of *either* of JJM's versions, there needs to have been in Berlin a rail station which had been previously hit and was of little apparent military value, at right angles to which ran a boulevard, underneath which Allied intelligence might have reasonably thought there was a long air raid shelter or subway station(s). This minimum condition is met; my extensive map study suggests three plausible 'candidates.'

1.   *F r i e d r i c h s t r a.*
Hauptbahnhof. This was and is a busy and important
commuter rail station; it lies on the north edge of what was
the inmost heart of 1945 Berlin, and running south from it
is Friedrichstrasse itself, underneath which runs—and
ran—one of the main U-Bahn lines. The intersection with
Unten Den Linden, perhaps *the* principal intersection of
the city at that time, lies a mere 400 meters from the
station's main entrance. Two more subway lines and two
tram lines intersect Friedrichstrasse by the time it
reaches Hallesches Tor, a scant 2,000 meters away, across
the most built-up (and bombed) real estate in the Reich.

For this candidate to fit, we have
to discount JJM's use of the name 'Tempelhof' and allow
that the briefed wind was out of the north on that March
day in one of the most severe winters of record, which
would have been neither typical nor implausible.[5]
Suitably, the station hall is at right angles to the bomb
run, and a pattern of bombs approximately a half mile long
would have nailed four subway stations, one of these a
main intersection station.

2.   Potsdammer Hauptbahnhof.
This station was on the west side of the dense inner heart
of the city, oriented N-NE toward the nearby Brandenberg
Gate. It was a terminus for long- and short-distance
passenger and freight lines and at the foot of a very
substantial marshaling yard, pointing into the city center
from the S-SW. (Following its utter obliteration, the
barren no-man's land of the Berlin Wall and 'Checkpoint
Charlie' displaced this station during the Cold War. Post-
war reconstruction of a smashed and divided city restored
only a fraction of the medium and heavy industry and
attendant rail service, and no longer would these be found
in a substantial concentration inside Berlin's girdle of
service railroads. Today this spot is 'ground zero' for the
exciting redevelopment of a politically, culturally and
economically significant capital city, but the contrasts

between its feel and look in 1940, 1989 and 2001, could
not be stronger if it had first been Times Square, then the
surface of the moon, and were now the Garden of Eden.)

In front of the wartime station,
prominent Leipziger Strasse led east. Three hundred
meters distant lay Hitler's official office
(Reichschkanzlerei) and Wilhemstrasse, on which were
arrayed all of the principal ministries and organs of Nazi
power. One more long block east lay broad and busy
Friedrichstrasse with its U-Bahn beneath. A bomb run as
described would have crossed the axis of the station and
aligned with a rat's warren of subterranean tunnels and
shelters serving the entrenched fascist functionaries.
Perhaps that realization should disqualify this candidate,
as such targeting could be considered strategic and
military rather than civil and 'terror.'

3.   Tempelhof   Bahnhof.
Reunification has allowed the reconnection of an old S-
Bahn line running E-W along the south side of the old
airfield, crossing prominent Tempelhoferdamm which
defines the field's west side. Four kilometers south of
Potsdammerplatz, the station served two intersecting
passenger lines, with freight lines of the south part of the
city's 'rail ring' running through, and substantial
marshaling yards less than 2 kilometers to the west.
Although these yards were associated with the 'Anhalter
Guterbahnhof' (freight station), the authors of the official
USAAF damage report from March 18th, could
understandably have been referring to them when they
wrote of "...Tempelhof M/Y [marshaling yard] and A/F [air
field]."[6]

A half-mile long bomb pattern
going northward from that station would have encompassed
three subway stations serving a densely populated
residential neighborhood. This candidate's name fits, but

as with the other two, nothing yet unearthed suggests that it was *targeted* in the mission as flown.

If the oral version is true, then my substantial efforts to recognize the 'terror target' in either an order or a damage report should have proved fruitless. But, of course, that I have yet to turn up any thinly disguised anti-civilian targeting barely suggests anything, and proves less.

I have not succeeded in finding another living soul who remembers this 'substituted' field order episode. Colonel Shower, when I interviewed him in early 1999, was already a frail 87 years old and, by his own admission and a few tests I inserted into our interview, 'selective' in his memory of lot of specifics from his Rackheath days. I tried contacting leadership in the other two bomb groups in the 96th Wing (the 458th at Horsham St. Faith and the 466th at Attlebridge would likely have gotten the same transmission) but was able to locate only one among any of the high ranking officer who might have been at the teletype that night. Colonel Alan Herzberg had been made Group CO of the 458th by then, having recently moved up from the deputy position at the 467th and a position at 96th Wing headquarters.

When interviewed Herzberg by telephone on 11-27-00, he seemed in full possession of his faculties and most insistent that what I described to him certainly would have been memorable, and that he had no such recollection. He was skeptical that it could have happened without his being informed at the time, and hence skeptical that it happened at all.

I have discussed that mission with a half dozen men who flew it. None recall an unusual briefing or, for that matter, anything inconsistent with the official summaries.

When I encountered the jarring 'modern' written version a few years ago (months after my father's death), it felt like I had caught him in a most uncharacteristic lie, but it was too late to challenge him. The old oral version, beloved by me, and last written one could not both be true. Lying was not in his character, so both my personal feelings and intellectual integrity spur me to account for how his story shifted, as a completely separate matter from (trying) to prove what bombing 'went down' that day.

The interpretation most consistent with his character would be that the 'lie' is in the last version—that he backed off from what he might have seemed a self-aggrandizing tall tale if he could not also deliver the smoking gun. When it came to the hard work of scholarly research, the aging retiree-author cut himself a little slack. In his introduction he promised memoirs, which require no apology, rather than history, for which he clearly understood that unusual claims would require strong proofs. He did not go too far afield in his research. His many correspondences with soldiers and researchers spanned decades, and he amassed a comfortable home library of a few hundred relevant titles and complete sets of the association journals of his bomb groups and the the Second Air Division. His 'War Room,' as we liked to call it, was certainly adequate for confirming most factual details but too limiting for historical research of things that 'go against the record.'

Here, on a discussion of Jim Mahoney's character, the argument will rest until more evidence comes to light. It was *in character* for him to remember things vividly. While it is hard to dismiss the possible 'Target Tempelhof' naming problem (his friends and family will attest to his amazing recall, especially for names and faces), his memory of the overarching story, his consistent maintenance in both versions that an anti-civilian target was at least planned, *cannot* be dismissed. I incline toward trusting his memory (and incidentally my own) to have correctly offered up the strange and unusual, while forgiving it in the matter of less exciting particulars, such as specific place names, for which a diary or contemporaneous journal would have served so well.

In the circumstances, it would have been *in character* for him to quietly, courageously and effectively make a stand on principle. And, finally, it would have been just as much in character for him to grow circumspect about taking credit for it.

reverse italics?

There is no evidence to suggest that a terror mission was *flown* by the Eighth that day, and plenty to suggest it was not.

There is a very strong character-based argument for believing that the unusual targeting information my father offered was neither misremembered nor a lie.

I have persuaded myself, therefore: that such a mission was ordered; that that mission was *not* flown, and thus: that the oral version is the truth.

One person *can* make a difference.

1. This is a gross simplification, which knowledgeable readers may forgive if I at least point out an important difference in American and British bomb aiming. Each RAF heavy bomber did its own bomb aiming. American lead crews did the bomb aiming for the multiple planes in their squadron or

even an entire group. All were good or bad together, and the damage area was expected to be big if the bomber formation was big or loose.

The paradox is that the British method would have better served the American value of *precision,* and the American tactic of plopping down an often big footprint of destruction would have sufficed for British 'area bombing.' American bombing, in striving for precision often failed to be accurate, and the British might as accurately have bombed 'the central part of Munich' without expending lots of training and fancy equipment in precisely putting *this* plane over *this* block.

2.   From Carl A. Spaatz and the Air War in Europe, page 556. (See Bibliography.)

3.   The careful reader will have noted that the 'extra' planes hitting the second target in the official account roughly match the number of 'missing' planes hitting the first target. It was unremarkable for entire groups to become separated in the confusion over a heavily defended target, and tag along with the nearest well-ordered formation, dropping on their lead, benefitting from their navigation, and assisting in mutual defense against fighter attack.

But what is even more important to note is that this amount of confusion went unremarked in the official summary of the day.

4.   On the official AFHRA microfiche roll covering this period of operations, one frame shows an index to the folder containing orders for the heavy bombing of Berlin on 3-18-45. This index lists fourteen different field orders. But only a small portion of the overarching order itself (FO #1779 from 8th AF Hq.) was saved in this record. That order makes clear that the Second Air Division had four principal targets, and the same microfiche roll includes damage reports relating to each of these. Each of these targets would have entailed lengthy and very detailed orders.

5.   Frame #1000 on the same microfiche roll depicts actual paths flown by the planes attacking the Tegel tank works, with an indication of wind from 327 degrees at 54 mph, presumably at bombing altitude, at the time of the attack.

My friend, Berlin resident Heidi Birgfeld, has concisely summarized the 'prevailing wind' in *Deutschlands revereinigte Haupstadt:* "März ist in Deutschland nicht Winter sondern springtime. Meistens kommt der Wind aus dem Westen mit Regen und Wolken. Wenn es kalt und sonnig ist, dann meistens aus dem Osten. Oft kommt der Wind auch aus dem Nordwesten, meist mit Regen und Kälte. Du siehst, es gibt viele Möglichkeiten. But normally the wind comes from the west." Their weather (rather like language choice in our correspondence) tends to be highly variable, but when it is rainy or cold, March is associated with a northwesterly wind.

6.   The Appendix reproduces the portion of 'INTOPS SUMMARY NO. 322' which gives a summary report of damage to Berlin from the 3-18-45 raid.

THE MORAL OF THE WORK
In War: Resolution
In Defeat: Defiance
In Victory: Magnanimity
In Peace: Goodwill

-Winston S. Churchill's <u>Memoirs of the Second World War,</u>
frontice

appendix

Glossary

Note: words appearing in glossary entries in *italics* are themselves glossary entries.

<u>Aeroclub</u> Recreation and socializing facility on base for use of the enlisted personnel operated by the Red Cross; officers not allowed.

<u>aileron</u> Airplane control surface on trailing edge of wing, used to control *roll* as when banking for a turn.

<u>Air Medal</u> Award which commends good performance of duties in a flight crew position; established by Executive Order of President Roosevelt on 5-11-42.

<u>ak-ak</u> Anti-aircraft fire from ground guns. *see:* *flak*

<u>AP</u> (aiming point) The exact ground spot on which the (lead) bombardier 'released.' As other bombardiers in the same group 'toggled,' (flipped a switch) to release their loads when the leader did, the train of bombs in principle would have an impact pattern centered somewhat *beyond* the AP. *see:* *IP, MPI, RP*

<u>APU</u> (auxiliary power unit) 2-stroke gasoline engine-powered generator on a cart, it was started with a rope and provided electrical energy to start engine #3 on a B-24. Electric energy from #3, in turn, was available for starting the other engines, sparing the plane's batteries. Also known as 'putt-putt.'

<u>ASI</u> (air speed indicator) Instrument which shows a plane's speed relative to the air through which it flies. Air speed determines an aircraft's flight characteristics, regardless of whether that air mass is moving relative to

the ground.   Two scenarios illustrate the important distinction between *air speed* and *ground speed*:

i) Bets have been won by pilots who 'landed backwards' by heading a low stall speed plane, such as a Stearman biplane, into a *faster* headwind.

ii) Extreme headwinds aloft have been known to be so close to the air speed of bombers, that their relative *ground speed* was very nearly zero, giving plenty of time for both bombardiers and enemy anti-aircraft gunners to perfect their aims, wind compensations and all.   This was a frequent bane to B-29s over Japan. *see: pitot tube, wind sock, IAS*

ATC Air Transport Command. Comprised troop carrier and other groups, which flew cargo planes such as the C-46 and C-47, generally out of the forward battle area; not to be confused with airborne combat units.

AWOL Absent without official leave. A first offense of leaving one's station without permission, or not returning from a permitted leave on time, did not necessarily lead to court martial, but typically entailed restrictions, forfeitures, or extra duties.

bandit Aircraft thought to be enemy. *see: bogey*

barracks discipline The unsupervised punitive or disciplinary action of service members to keep one of their own rank 'in line.' Officers are broadly aware of the group morale and issues of the men under their command, and can control this aspect of 'the military culture' by selectively turning a blind eye on this practice when it serves their purpose, but at the constant hazard of individuals being bullied unfairly or punished excessively.

barrage, -artillery This tactic fills a target area with lots of shells, as opposed to trying to aim at particular targets (aerial or ground) with each shot.

barrage, -balloon The tactic of using lighter-than-air balloons, tethered to the ground by strong wires, which made an airspace very hazardous for aircraft. This defense was used effectively by the British at several strategic points along the Channel coast. Barrage balloons are visible in may photos of the D-Day invasion.

blast revetment A raised earthwork around a depressed trench, often lined with masonry, metal or timber, into which personnel can quickly leap for protection against explosions of shells. These were strategically located around USAAF air stations in areas likely to be attacked by the Luftwaffe.

blinker see: carpet blinker

blood chit Identification device used by downed airmen for presentation to Russian troops upon first contact, in hopes of avoiding rough treatment. The concept originated with the Flying Tigers prior to the US entry in WW II. Printed on fabric alongside a Chinese flag were the Chinese term for 'life token,' and a promise of reward for the safe return of a downed aircrew member. Blood Chits are now routine, adapted for the area of operation.

bogey Plane not yet determined to be friend or foe, as picked up visually or by radar; contrast with bandit. see: IFF

bomb dump Munition storage was typically situated at the end of the airfield farthest from the tech site and well away from the other base sites. Unfused bombs were arranged in rows, separated by earthworks to theoretically inhibit chain reactions in the event of an accident. Metfield, Station #366, had a spectacular accident on July 15, 1944, which killed five bomb handlers. (Tellingly, the squadron assigned to this very undesirable but essential work was comprised of Black men.) The detonations destroyed several planes, broke windows for miles around, and was heard and seen at North Pickenham, 26 miles distant, where dust fell from the rafters. The first home of the 491st was not economical to fully repair; when the original 492nd was stood down and broken up, the 491st took over North Pickenham.

bomb run The precisely defined straight path in space which planes were to fly without deviation, from the *Initial Point,* through the *Aiming Point* and then to the *Rally Point.* The lead bombardier typically put the plane under control of his bombsight for the bomb run, giving him time to accurately compensate for all relevant factors, such as drift, relative ground speed and direction, altitude, and intervening winds in airspace below. The tightly grouped bombers were at their most vulnerable during the bomb run. Accomplishment of the primary objective, an accurate bomb drop, precluded the possibility of any evasive maneuvering while on the bomb run. Enemy flak installations had plenty of time to dial in the altitude and direction of their 'sitting ducks.' Enemy fighters backed off and let the anti-aircraft guns do their worst in flak zones. *see: Norden bombsight*

briefing team Group of flying and staff officers, including navigator, pilot and bombardier, serving their roles in rotation, were charged with carefully studying a *field order* and making all of its technical points clear to the crews which were to fy the mission. *see: S-3*

-Bulge, Battle of the Last significant German offensive operation of the war, began in late December '44 in Belgium. Allied planners were caught off guard and in poor command of intelligence that suggested a large concentration of enemy armor in the area between Luxembourg City and Liege. Hoping to push west to The River Meuse then the sea, to take the deep harbor of Antwerp and isolate the Allied troops in the Low Countries, Gen. Model led Army Group B. Bad flying weather in the first week of the battle greatly favored the enemy, but allied air superiority was restored after very spirited fighting upon the return of better weather. Coordinated bombing, close support and especially resupply from the air, played key roles for Allies.

bunchers Approximately two dozen fixed radio beacons around East Anglia, each operating on a unique medium frequency, allowing navigation in poor flying conditions and darkness.   After D-Day landings, truck-borne bunchers improved navigation over the Continent. *see: splashers*

buzz To fly very close to the ground, usually to get the attention of people there, often showing off or celebrating. Synonymous terms: to 'beat up' a place, to 'mow the grass.'

buzz bomb *see V-1*

BTO Bombing through overcast. *see: H2X, Mickey, PFF, visual bombing*

cadre Core group of leadership personnel from which an operational unit is built.

caravan Trailer that could be towed to different locations on the airfield to direct taxiing and lineup for takeoff. Painted in bold black and yellow checkerboard pattern, the caravan used a phone line to communicate with the airfield tower, and visual signals to communicate with planes, obviating reliance on interceptable radio transmissions.

Carpetbagger Clandestine operations using 'stealthy' methods, such as tree-top flight and night flying, which gave direct aid to partisans behind enemy lines, dropped infiltrators, etc. *see: OSS*

carpet blinker Plane-borne radio equipment used to jam enemy gun-laying "Wurtzburg" radar. Three hemispheric plexi bubbles behind the nose wheel doors of a so-fitted B-24 protected the antennas, which operated over multiple frequency ranges simultaneously.

CAVU   Ceiling And Vision Unlimited   This acronym spelled good flying conditions, in a word.

chaff   Bundles of metal foil strips, of a specific length determined to wreck havoc with particular wavelength used by German radar-directed antiaircraft fire.   Chaff could not hamper visual range-finding in clear daylight conditions, but may have served the secondary purpose in those conditions, of detonating some proximity-fused ordnance.   Strips were released into the air via a purpose-built chute under waist gunner window.   Fine filament version still in use today against air and surface launched antiaircraft missiles. *see Window*

chandelle   Aerial acrobatic maneuver consisting of a sudden, steep climbing turn.   As execution requires deft transition to 'opposite rudder' when plane approaches stall speed, it is considered an important coordination exercise for student pilots.

Class A uniform   One of the more formal uniforms issued to a WW II Army officer, and likely the most formal one found outside of higher level headquarters.   Typically reserved for special occasions such as dress reviews and awards ceremonies.

CO   (commanding officer)   At any military organizational level, the most responsible person.   Phrase typically applied at squadron and higher levels.

command pilot   At the group, wing and division levels in the bomber formation, specially designated leaders flew in the respective lead crew planes and were responsible for mission completion by all 'beneath' them in command.   At each of these levels, a deputy command pilot, on the commander's *wing*, was ready to assume responsibility in an emergency. Ranking flying officers served in these special roles in rotation.

contrail The visible trail left by an aircraft engine when low atmospheric pressure and/or low temperature of the air causes water vapor in the exhaust to condense. More pronounced with altitude, contrails from a four engined bomber in daylight operations were most helpful for visual spotting and ranging of anti-aircraft fire, and a hazard to navigation for all but the lead planes in close formation. On the 'plus' side, gunners on the *'heavies'* could more easily spot a *bogey* overhead if contrails were forming there.

CROSSBOW, Operation A joint British and American project begun in 1943 to curb or eliminate the threat of German *V-1* and *V-2* missiles aimed at England by targeting the mysterious looking coastal installations, manufacture and assembly facilities, and mobile launchers. Before these weapon systems were operational, their ability to disrupt British fighting ability and morale was overestimated, resulting in considerable diversion of strategic bombing assets to work for which tactical bombing would have been better suited. *see: Noball*

DAL (division assembly line) A definitively specified line in time and space along which the *wings* of a division (having been formed up out of their component *groups*) were to assemble in proper relative position as last step in formation before heading to target.

Davis wing When the Consolidated Aircraft Company proposed its design to the Department of the Army in 1939, the B-24's innovative wing promised superior load carrying capacity and a higher cruise speed than the B-17 already in the inventory. Operationally, this was not without its price. Loaded Liberators became progressively trickier to fly safely at altitudes over 23,000 feet, where the *Flying Fortresses* were fine and further from enemy flak batteries. It is this author's view that, looking in cross-section at the *Davis wing,* the severe break on the top surface (where the high point transitioned to the start of the sloped rear plane) made it very difficult for airflow to adhere to the wing surface. In the *mushing* attitude, laminar flow immediately behind the substantial 'hump' of the wing was replaced by turbulence, with palpable loss of lift and 'slipperiness,' effective displacement of the center of lift forward, and a consequent perpetuation of the 'nose high' attitude itself, which made it very difficult to correct. Indeed, if the center of gravity of the plane was not at, or forward of the 'correct' center of lift, the one intended by the designers and experienced when the B-24 was 'on *the step,*' the Lib could not be be wrested from 'mush mode.' The slightly disorderly airflow cavitation on the top surface of the wing was the ever-present seed of a high-speed stall, an unforgiving disposition, twitchily waiting for a only a momentary high-attact angle or bit of well-placed battle damage, to put 30 tons of men and machine into the dreaded flat-spin of death. *see: mushing, on-the-step*

dead reckoning Navigation based upon accurately tracking one's progress from a known location, relying on instrument information rather than direct observation of ground points (pilotage navigation) or star-fixes (celestial navigation). Good dead reckoning required good instruments and maps, and great skill and diligence on the part of the navigator. Radar assisted navigation, and especially coordination of this with dead reckoning and pilotage navigation in group leads, increased overall bombing accuracy as the war went on. *see: BTO, H2X, Mickey, PFF, pilotage navigator*

drop Informal term for the putting the bombs (or other payload, such as an infiltrator) on the target.

East Anglia Eastern most part of England, comprising Norfolk, Suffolk, Essex and Cambridge counties, which housed most of the fighter and bomber bases of USAAF and

RAF.   Supply and recuperation facilities tended to be situated more to the rear; often in the Midlands, Scotland and Northern Ireland, off of the crowded deck of the 'unsinkable aircraft carrier.'

element   In formation flying, the most basic combination on which successively larger groupings were based.   For the fighters, and element consisted of two planes: the leader and his wingman, typically flying somewhat behind and to the right, somewhat above.   For the bombers, the element was of three or four planes: leader, deputy and wingman, the deputy being to the right, the wingman to the left of the leader, both behind, with deputy a little high and wingman a little low.   The 'slot' position, last in a four-plane grouping, was in line behind and a bit lower than the element lead plane.   *synonym: flight*

elevator   Flight control surface on the trailing edges of the horizontal tailplane of an aircraft; controls pitch, affects roll control.

escapee   Variously subscribed-to international conventions governed the definition and acceptable treatment of a *POW* who got away from enemy control. Unless one clearly surrendered, he was effectively a combatant, even if unarmed.   In practice, it is not thought that escapee surrenders were treated as such; they were frequently shot on sight regardless of 'Hande hoch!' or unarmed status.   *see: evadee, internee*

evadee   Under international military conventions, a combatant in enemy held territory who is neither captured nor surrendering, but trying to return to their side while evading capture.   *see: escapee, internee, POW*

ETA   estimated time of arrival

ETO   European theater of operations during WW II

ETR estimated time of return *see: Sweating Out*

field order (F.O.) Order sent to groups' headquarters from division headquarters, specifying in detail a combat operation to be carried out.

flak (from the German 'Fliegerabwehrkanone') Anti-aircraft artillery fire. Shells could be fused to explode by proximity to metal, by altitude attained, or both. German flak became heavier and more accurate as the war progressed. There were limits to the evasive tactics bombers could take, especially while on the *bomb run*. Countermeasures were limited to disrupting the radar used to 'lay' the flak, and use of armor, flak vests and helmets. Flak overtook enemy fighters as the leading cause of bomber loss after June '44, when approximately 150 heavy bombers were lost to each cause. *see: chaff, carpet blinker, window*

flack shack Nickname for rest facility to which airmen were remanded as deemed advisable, especially after harrowing combat. Fresh air, civilian clothing, simple recreation and good food at a remove from the the base constituted good medicine for many.

flak happy Psychologically suffering from the effects of combat exposure, analogous to the World War I phrase 'shell shocked.'

flaps Flight control surfaces on trailing edges of an aircraft's main wing, which substantially enhance lift characteristics at the cost of greatly increased drag. Deployed to take off and land.

flight *see: element*

flyboy One whose service was in an aircrew, as opposed to a ground support unit. *see: paddlefoot*

<u>Form 1</u> Pilots used this to make a report of the plane's performance, for maintenance purposes, after each mission, combat or otherwise. *see: plane's log*

<u>GAF</u> German Air Force

<u>Gee</u> (also called 'Gee-H' or 'G-H') British-developed navigation and bombing aid; the 'G-box' on plane sent pulsed signals on two discreet frequencies to 'master' and 'slave' reciever-transmitters (responders) on the ground. Ranging from the two fixed points and displayed as illuminated 'blips' on a cathode ray tube, these gave plane location to within 6 miles at the 400 mile limit. By war's end, majority of USAAF heavy bombers were equipped with Gee, but by then its functionality for bombing and navigation over the Continent was greatly reduced by effective German jamming by 'Heinrich' transmitters. It remained very helpful, however, for accurately navigating up to the European 'entry point' when outbound on a mission, and simplified precise navigation back to one's airfield afterward. *see: bunchers, H2X, Mickey, Oboe, splashers*

<u>GP</u> (general purpose) <u>bomb</u> Available in gross weights of 100, 250, 300, 500, 1000 and 2000 pounds. The 100s were considered an uneconomic payload unless potholing airfields or marshaling yards.

<u>grade</u> Any of the official ranks or ratings of officers or enlisted personnel. Commissioned officers, by increasing seniority, are in three categories. Company grade: 2nd Lieutenant, 1st Lieutenant and captain. Field grade: major, lieutenant colonel and colonel. General officers: brigadier general, major general, lieutenant general and general. These grades correspond to pay grades O-1 through O-10. Additionally, in wartime the five-star grade may be authorized (general-of-the-armies; general-of-the-air-forces; fleet admiral). *see: rank*

ground speed   Aircraft's speed relative to the ground beneath it. Often very different from its speed in the air mass in which it flies, owing to wind speed and direction. *see IAS, ASI*

group   The USAAF organizational unit made up of *squadrons* and included in *wings*. There were various bombardment and fighter groups and very specialized squadrons, such as for photo reconnaissance or weather scouting, serving within the Eighth.

H2X   Downward-looking radar, bombing/navigation aid operating in 3cm wavelength. Built up areas and water were more clear than other targets on the primitive screen. Used for bombing when visibility was limited, 'Mickey' was a follow-on to earlier British-developed H2S (which used 10cm wavelength), and by war's end most bomb groups had two or more planes so-equipped. The system had no range limitations as it did not rely on ground-based transmissions. *see: PFF, BTO, Mickey*

headquarters site   The area of a base concerned with administration and intelligence, usually situated very near to the airfield and the sick site. Arrayed at greater distances from the airfield were living, mess, and communal sites, the last being the location for the post exchange (PX) and recreational facilities.   *see: bomb dump, Ops block, tech site*

'heavy'   During WW II, a bomber was classed as light, medium, or heavy. Twin-engined Bostons and Havocs (also classed as 'attack' aircraft, e.g. 'A-20') tended to be used with smaller ordnance at lower altitude in smaller numbers, often in relatively close support of ground operations. Medium twin engined bombers (Mitchell B-25 and Martin B-26 Marauder) had more defensive crew positions and flew in large formations, with the latter seeing significant deployment in the Eighth. 'Heavies' were four engined; the Boeing B-17 'Flying Fortress' was the primary tool for the 1st and 3rd Divisions of the 8th; the Consolidated B-24 'Liberator' was the defining offensive weapon of its 2nd Air Division. B-24s, limited numbers of B-36s, and substantial numbers of Boeing B-29 'Super Fortresses' were deployed in the Pacific. The letter at end of a bomb group's number indicated how it was classed, e.g. 44th BG (H) or 323 BG (M), equipped respectively with Liberators and Marauders.

<u>hardstand</u> Paved parking place for an aircraft, typically situated on the *perimeter strip*. 'Loop-style' could accommodate two heavies, while the earlier 'frypan' type could only handle one.

<u>HE</u> (High Explosive-) <u>bomb</u> The normal payload of strategic bombers, available in weights from 50 to 2000 lbs. and capable of being fused in a variety of ways for safe handling and detonation at widely variable intervals after impact. Contrast with *incendiary bomb*. *see: GP bomb*

<u>IAS</u> indicated air speed. *see ASI*

<u>IFF</u> (identification: friend or foe) An interactive radio system designed to positively recognize friendly aircraft by their correct discrete frequency response to electronic query. Often the only way of preventing aircraft loss to friendly ground fire, but hardly foolproof.

<u>ILS</u> (instrument landing system) <u>beacon</u> Navigational aid located in line with main runway extended, on several of the Class A airfields.

<u>Intercom, Interphone</u> Hard-wired communication system connecting every manned station on a bomber. Personnel had earphones and mouthpiece or throat microphones in their headgear; no radio transmission involved.

internee A combatant who finds their way to neutral territory, where, absent a particular agreement among the warring countries, they and their combat equipment are supposed to remain 'interned' for the duration of hostilities. A state which allowed the return of evadees to their side could be considered to have thereby given up its claim to neutrality. In practice, there were several effective clandestine schemes for repatriation of key Allied personnel (and others who were marked for discipline) from Sweden. *contrast: evadee, escapee*

intervalometer Instrument used by bombardier to control the time between release of the individual bombs. The *field order* specified intervalometer settings or, infrequently, called for ordinance to be *salvoed* on the target.

IP (initial point) The precise point in space at which the *bomb run* began. *see: AP, RP*

jamming Process of identifying an electronic signal by frequency and broadcast method, then transmitting a signal which covers or renders useless the 'jammed' signal. Tactic implemented to block enemy communication, navigation, radar tracking.

J-type hangar More permanently constructed type of hangar found at handful of 8th AF bomber airfields, 300 x 115 feet with masonry construction lower walls. *see: T-2*

KIA (killed in action) Official status of a combatant known through compelling physical evidence to be dead as a result of combat. It was the fate of many airmen, especially lost over the sea, to be listed as missing in action, and perhaps at a much later date be 'upgraded' to "*MIA*, presumed dead."

KILOD (killed in line of duty) For example, death in a

training accident.

left seat   Pilot's position in aircraft; sometimes by informal extension, the person 'in charge.'

Little Friends   Allied fighters. A successful rendezvous with friendly protective escort, whether by plan or good luck, improved a bomber's chances against enemy fighters, especially the damaged or lost straggler that was out of protective formation with other bombers.

magneto   Electrical generation apparatus fitted to an internal combustion engine to power its ignition system.

MIA (missing in action)   Designated status of combat personnel not returning from combat, but not *definitively known* to be killed or captured. Many downed fliers who finished the war as *POWs* were so rated until Red Cross or diplomatic channels passed official notification from the enemy of their capture alive. Others, still unfound after passage of reasonable time for such notice, were pronounced "MIA, presumed dead." Next-of-kin could then receive death benefits from the military. *see: KIA, KILOD*

Mickey   Slang for H2X radar equipment, or the specially trained navigators who operated it in lead-crew aircraft on missions where visual bombing capability was in doubt. Operated in 3cm wavelength. *see: BTO, H2X, PFF*

milk run   A combat mission thought to be easy. Many experienced warriors considered it folly, if not bad luck, to dub a mission this way until after it had been completed.

MOS (military occupational specialty)   All active duty personnel, enlisted or officer, received specialized training in order to do a particular type of work in their service.

MP (military police) Charged with enforcing military law and, in the environs of many foreign military installations, civil lawfulness of active duty personnel while off-base too.

MPI (mean point of impact) Theoretical center of the target, around which all bombs would ideally cluster. Practice of making careful analysis of the percent of bombs which exploded within 1000 feet of MPI revealed that accuracy was hard to achieve, collateral damage virtually unavoidable in urban industrial areas, and the notion of putting "bombs in a pickle barrel" from 20,000 feet under combat conditions a complete whimsey. For much of the war, a drop which put 50% of the payload within 2000 feet of MPI was considered *good*.

MTO Mediterranean Theater of Operations. The 15th Air Force operated from bases in North Africa, and later Italy. With long range bombers, they struck targets in southern and eastern Europe, notably the Ploesti natural oil refinery targets in Romania.

mushing The undesirable flight-attitude of a B-24 when it was a bit 'nose high,' sluggish on the controls, consuming excessive fuel, and not capable of it's top-speed. If the center of gravity was not at or forward of the center of lift, it was very tricky to keep the plane in the preferred attitude, *'on the step.' see also: Davis wing*

Nissen hut The most common metal prefab building type at bases of the Eighth- came in variety of sizes, saw supply, repair, residential and storage uses. Corrugated metal arches were available in spans up to 30 feet. On older installations in England a higher proportion of service buildings were made of masonry with asbestos tile type roofing, preferred for greater comfort in hot or cold weather.

NMF (natural metal finish) Plane without olive drab paint. As allied air supremacy reached the point (spring '44) when threat of German attacks on airfields in UK diminished, the need for camouflaging parked aircraft was outweighed by the 5-10 mph increased airspeed and improved fuel efficiency of the lighter, slipperier planes. There is endless speculation, with basis, that silver planes, especially when first introduced into European combat, 'stood out' as easy marks for the enemy. *see OD*

Noball mission Bombing mission targeting launch sites of the V-weapons. These were considered relatively easy, in that the coastal targets did not involve long flight or time over enemy held territory. Demarcation of water against land showed relatively clearly in radar scopes, making coastal 'Noball' targets a regular choice on days of cloud undercast on the continent. Tremendous resources were diverted to 'Operation *CROSSBOW*' from Fall '43 up to D-Day to stave off the threat. *see: milk run, V-1, V-2*

Norden (M7 or M9) bombsight Sophisticated analog computer device directly integrated with plane's flight controls. Compensated for all variables affecting bomb aiming from altitude. Despite extraordinary security measures, it was found out after the war that the Germans were very familiar with it.

Oboe Electronic navigation/bombardment aid worked on the opposite principle of *H2X*. One ground-based beam provided the aircraft with directional information (in the form of audible pulses telling the crew whether they were to left, right, or 'on' the beam) and another beam with range-to-target information. Oboe was supplanted in the heavies, but the equipment continued to be developed and techniques refined for use by medium bombers in the 9th Air Force. Beam-type systems were subject to limitations of range and vulnerable to enemy *jamming* of the radio signals upon which they relied. *see: H2X, PFF*

OD   Olive drab; the ubiquitous paint color on US Army equipment. *see NMF*

Officers' Club   On-base facility for socializing and entertainment; enlisted men had their separate *Aeroclub.*

officer of the day (OD)   In one of several duties rotated among officers, the OD acts for the commander in routine administrative matters.

officer promotions   During WW II there was a dual-track promotion system where commissioned officers (regular and reserve) held both a 'permanent' and a 'temporary' grade. This structure allowed for a substantial increase in the size of the military during times of war or national emergency, without impeding the ability to conduct a reduction in force (RIF) at the end of the mobilization. As a result, many officers served in (and were paid at) a 'temporary' grade that was one or more grades above their 'permanent' grade, to which they would revert in the event of a RIF. The Defense Officer Personnel Management Act (DOPMA) eliminated this distinction in the mid-1980s, and all officer promotions are now 'permanent.'   *see: grade, rank, regular officer, reserve officer*

on the line   Refers to the area of the airfield ('flight line') where the aircraft and their support facilities were.

on the step   The ideal cruising flight attitude of a B-24, at times tricky to maintain.   The effective center of aerodynamic lift of the *Davis wing,* when 'on the step,' was supposed to coincide with the plane's center of gravity. If the COG was slightly rearward, the plane was prone to flying a little nose-high, or *mushing.*   *see also: Davis wing*

Ops Block   The principal building within the *headquarters site* on a base, near to the airfield. Windowless, guarded, fitted with a positive pressure air-lock against potential chemical warfare threat, this building was the planning center for the missions. Large status boards tracked readiness/availability of crews and equipment.

OSS (Office of Special Services) Precursor to the Central Intelligence Agency of post-war era, founded by colorful General 'Wild Bill' Donovan and charged with top secret espionage and coordination with underground organizations in enemy held areas. The *Carpetbagger* crews that dropped operatives to rendezvous behind the lines with the underground, knew better than to ask the names of their special passengers.

perimeter strip Paved ring road encircling the three runways of an airfield; connected with *hardstands* and repair facilities at the technical site, allowed all-weather movement of heavy planes, fire, rescue, tow and fuel vehicles, fast trucking of aircrews to and from their plane, etc.

PFF (pathfinder force) General term for specially trained crews and their specially equipped aircraft, which were used to lead poor weather bombing missions with the latest versions of electronic navigational and bombing aids as these evolved during the war. First activated Pathfinder group was the 482nd at Alconbury, August 1943. Before radar sets were widely available, Pathfinder crews were established in each of the divisions, and later in the wing organizations. On typical PFF missions through Fall '44, the group or wing commander (and sometimes his deputy) would go to the base housing Pathfinders to 'pick up his plane' for the mission, or the special crew would fly in to the host base in time for mission briefing *see H2X, Mickey*

"Picadilly Commando" London prostitutes were found in abundance in the neighborhood of Picadilly Circus.

pilotage navigator Navigator trained to recognize ground features to determine the plane's location and route;

dependent on adequate visibility. *see: dead reckoning, Mickey, PFF, radar navigation, zero/zero*

<u>pitot tube</u> Small forward-facing pipe on the outside of an aircraft, connected to a gauge so calibrated as to indicate *air speed. see: ASI*

<u>plane's log</u> In the tradition of ship's log, a legal document which records crew, passengers, basic flight information. *see: Form 1*

<u>POM</u> (preparation for overseas movement) <u>Inspector</u> Bomb groups were not assigned to combat theatre duty until a host of conditions were met, governing state of equipment, crew training, medical and group records and accounts. This process was at times a traumatic hurdle for a group; enough so for the 467th that they named their assembly ship 'Pete the POM Inspector' and the executive staff P-47 'Little Pete.'

<u>POW</u> Prisoner of war. *see: internee, escapee, evadee*

<u>'pro' kit</u> Condom, prophylactic, 'rubber.' *see: VD*

<u>propwash</u> Air turbulence left in the wake of a propeller driven aircraft. An invisible but substantial hazard to aircraft flying in train, as in formation flying or short-interval takeoffs. Heavy bombers taking off at 20-second intervals used alternate sides of the 150' wide main runway to minimize the danger. Skilled RAF pilots in fast single-seaters used propwash effectively against *V-1 'Doodlebugs'* by flying in their path and destabilizing them over less populated areas.

<u>PRU</u> (Photo Reconnaissance Unit of the Royal Air Force) By extension, term used in both USAAF and RAF for reconnaissance photo taken under favorable conditions after a bomb strike to assess results. *see: SAV*

rank   The relative seniority of a service member. All majors outrank all captains. Members serving in the same grade are ranked by seniority within that grade. No two service members have the same rank, even though they may serve in the same grade. Even where their promotion dates are identical, other objective criteria are established to determine who is senior (time in service, alphabetical by name; order of birth). NOTE: In common parlance, 'rank' is often used imprecisely to refer to *grade*. For example, 'rank insignia' is the insignia authorized to be worn by members serving in a particular *grade*.

RCM   Radar counter measures. *see: jamming, chaff, 'window'*

Red Ball-Express   Massive re-supply operations in early Fall of '44 which were needed to keep up with fast advances of General Patton's armor. The intense, short term diversion of strategic bomb groups for airborne 'Trucking' operations flew 2.1 million gallons of 80 octane gasoline to Normandy. *see: Trucking*

regular officer   Leadership of the 'standing army' maintained during peacetime. All graduates of the U. S. Military Academy (West Point) were commissioned as regular officers. Some reserve officers (on extended active duty) were offered 'augmentation' into the 'regular' officer corps on a merit basis. In more recent years, only the top graduates at the service academies and from the ROTC (Reserve Officers Training Corps) programs are initially commissioned as regular officers. Almost all, however, are augmented as regular officers by the time of their selection for major. *see: reserve officer*

reserve officer   An officer commissioned in the military reserves, assigned to a reserve unit (or to a state national guard unit when federalized in emergency or wartime). Reservists serve training periods, and short periods of active duty either individually or with their units. When called up in wartime, reservists serve on extended active duty. Prior to enactment of the Defense Officer Personnel Management Act (DOPMA), reservists could also serve on extended active during peacetime. Sources of reserve commissions during WW II were: Officer Training School (OTS), the Reserve Officer Training Corps (ROTC) at colleges, the Aviation Cadet program, and direct appointment. All still function, except for the Aviation Cadet program, which ended shortly after WW II. *see: regular officer*

right seat   Crew position of the co-pilot. *see: left seat*

RP   (rally point)   Specified place in space and time where elements of plane formation come together as a group formation after the bomb drop. *see AP, bomb run, drop, MPI*

rudder   Movable vertical control surface which affects a plane's left and right turning, or yaw. In planes of conventional layout this is in the rear (tail) of the aircraft. The B-24, the B-25 and the P-38 each had two. *see: aileron, elevator, needle-and-ball* not in glossary

S-1   A WW II bomb group's administration officer, sometimes called executive officer or ground executive, was broadly responsible for personnel, discipline, base maintenance.

S-2   Group intelligence officer. Responsible for the secure and safe keeping of all target and communication information, central role in mission briefing, responsible for collecting intelligence from returning crews and forwarding summaries up to the wing level. *see Ops Block*

S-3   Group operations officer. Logistician for getting the planes in the air for combat and training missions; important role in briefing about weather conditions, escort, anticipated enemy resistance. *see: briefing team*

S-4 Group supply officer. Provisioned base with combat and living stores for as many as 3500 souls at a time.

salvo, salvo lever In the event of an emergency, the pilot could cause all of the bombs to be immediately dropped at once. The bombardier on occasion would salvo the bombs, but normally adjusted the *intervalometer* to release them with a timed separation as specified in the *field order*. The intentional dispersal of ordinance over a more extended ground area increased the odds of hitting a smaller target or distributing damage over a larger one.

SAV (strike attack: vertical) Photograph taken from aircraft in a bombing formation to show impact and detonation of bombs, conditions at time of the attack. *see: PRU*

SBA (standard beam approach) Landing aid which used four discreet, directional transmitted signals, each covering a precise 90 degree sweep from the center point of the runway in use. Pilot to left of intended glidepath heard Morse Code 'a' (dot-dash), to right of runway extended he heard Morse Code 'n' (dash-dot). When right on the mark, he heard a steady tone, as the two synchronized signals combined.

signals square Paved area near control tower emblazoned with basic information useful to incoming planes—landing direction, base name, runway in use, etc. Reference to visual aids, when practical, reduced reliance on radio transmission, intercept able by the enemy.

splashers Powerful fixed radio beacons useful for longer-range radio triangulation to 'fix' a plane's location. Approximately 12 splashers were erected across East Anglia. *see: buncher, H2X, Mickey, Oboe*

squadron The most basic military organizational unit in the Air Force having a command staff; during WW II a *group* typically comprised four squadrons. There were fighter, bomber, reconnaissance and other combat squadrons, as well as specialized supporting ground squadrons attached to the groups. *see: group*

strike photo Generically, a photo taken on a bombing raid; some were by crew members using hand held cameras, most taken automatically by special cameras at intervals after 'bombs away.' *see: PRU, SAV*

sweating out Waiting for aircraft and crews to return from a combat mission. In the relatively 'close quarters' of the European air war, both sides observed radio silence as much as possible, and news of losses, about which nothing could be done, came home with those who did return. *see: ETR*

T-2 Large standard hangar structure on WW II USAAF heavy bomber bases; one or two per station. Interior dimensions of 240 x 115 x 29 feet made it possible to accommodate 3 heavy bombers at a time. Many of these serve to this day in a variety of functions and their distinctive profile is often the only, or strongest, indication of an old 8th AF airfield. *see: J-type hangar.*

tail-end Charlie The undesirable last position in a bomber formation. Successive and cumulative reactions of waves of aircraft trying to follow the movements of the leader were greater and greater toward the rear of a formation. Difficulty of flying was compounded by *propwash* and often *contrails* left by preceding aircraft. Lead aircraft were somewhat more vulnerable to fighter attack, but many attacks were from behind. Also, in a large formation, aircrews toward the rear could anticipate that the aiming of *flak* had been refined by the time they flew into its range.

tech site The array of hangars, specialized shops and storage structures on the airfield of a base. *see: J-type hangar, Nissen hut, T-2*

<u>V-1</u> ('Vergeltungswaffe 1,' or 'Vengeance Weapon 1')
Subsonic pilotless flying bomb, the original cruise
missile, usually launched from inclined 'ski ramps' in the
Low Countries and coastal France, mostly against British
targets, starting the night of June 12-13, 1944. Later also
directed at European cities liberated by Allies in the
west. When the ram-air induction pulse engine cut out,
the 'buzz bomb' or 'doodle bug' would dive to earth with its
1,800 pound payload of high explosive. *see: CROSSBOW,
Noball, V-2*

<u>V-2</u> (*Vergeltungswaffe 2*, or 'Vengeance Weapon 2')
World's first liquid fueled supersonic ballistic missile
with range of 200 miles, top speed of 3,355 mph, payload
of 1,650 lbs. of high explosive. Inertial guidance better
than on V-1, but still poor enough that both of these are
properly thought of as terror, rather than tactical
weapons. First one hit London September 8, 1944.
Absence of audible warning made this weapon more
terrifying if no more potent than the *V-1*. *see:
CROSSBOW, Noball*

<u>VD</u> Venereal disease; sexually transmitted disease. *see
'pro kit'*

<u>visual bombing</u> Bombardment of visible targets using
optical aiming devices. The rapid early advances in beam-
guided navigation and plane-based radar never got to the
point, during WW II, of consistently exceeding the results
achievable with bombardment by visual sighting with
sophisticated analog computer sights, but the
foreshadowing of all manner of 'smart' weaponry and
electronic navigation, communication and weapon-
directing systems was unmistakable. *see: BTO, Norden
bombsight, PFF*

<u>war weary</u> An aircraft which, by dint of long hours and/or

rough service, was considered no longer fit for combat operation, but perhaps available for transport, training, assembly or other utility missions outside the combat zone.

<u>Window</u> British term analogous to *chaff.*

<u>wind sock</u> Large, light colored fabric 'sock' which can freely pivot on a pole at an airfield, giving pilots simple visual indication of wind direction.   The historically changeless importance of landing 'upwind' is multiplied when a runway is short or a returning plane's hydraulics (for the brakes) are shot out.

<u>wing</u> 1. Organizational unit in US Army Air Forces below *division*, above *group.* The 467th Bomb Group was one of three groups in the 96th Combat Wing, and there were five wings in the 2nd Air Division.
2. Position to right of, and slightly behind 'leader' in a flight *element.* Typically, a deputy group command pilot would fly *wing* to the command pilot's lead.

<u>zero/zero</u> By convention, visibility from an observer's position was rated in terms of the distance one could see upward/forward;   this   particular   extreme   rating (zero/zero) is reserved for cases when the observer's view is completely limited, as in a dense ground fog or in a cloud while flying.   Cloud cover, as distinct from visibility, was judged in 'tenths.' A pilot reporting "ten-tenths undercast" was unable to see the ground. One-tenth overcast reported by a ground observer meant that 90% of the view overhead was free from cloud. *see: pilotage navigator*

Worl War II

Timeline

1-30-33	Adolf Hitler made Reichs Chancellor of Germany
3-7-36	Remilitarization of Rhineland by Germany in open defiance of Treaty of Versailles
3-12-38	Anschluss (weakly contested accession of Austria by Third Reich)
9-26-38	Germany starts illegal occupation of Sudetenland (Czeckoslovakia)
9-29, 30-38	British Prime Minister Neville Chamberlain enters Munich Pact with Adolf Hitler, declares "Peace in our time"
11-9-38	Kristallnacht (Night of Broken Glass) burning of synagogues, widespread looting of Jewish property in Berlin, police and 'Brownshirts' fan flames
9-1-39	Blitzkrieg invasion of Poland; England and France declare war on aggressor Germany
9-23-39	Soviets and Nazis make Non-Aggression pact and secretly plan the partition of Poland
10-14-39	German Navy sinks HMS *Royal Oak* at anchor in Scapa Flow North Sea
5-10-40	Claiming that Britain and France were planning to attack through neutral Low Countries, Germany invades these and France, ending the 'Sitzkrieg,' or 'Phony War.' Chamberlain resigns; Churchill assumes Prime Ministership
5-14-40	Germany bombs Rotterdam, killing 980; Dutch government flees to

	London.
6-4-40	Emergency evacuation of retreating British troops from continent at Dunkirque completed
6-21-40	Free France capitulates to Germany, collaborating Vichy government set up under Marshal Pétain
7-10-40	Battle of Britain begins; German high command intends to follow defeat of RAF with cross-channel invasion by end of summer
8-24 to 9-6-40	Battle of Britain enters its "Darkest Hour" with daily engagements of all available day fighters; attrition favors RAF 2-to-1, who remain resolute at the brink; "Never in the field of human conflict has so much been owed by so many to so few" (Churchill)
1-6-41	President Roosevelt proposes Lend-Lease program to give material aid to beleaguered England, makes "Four Freedoms" speech
2-7-41	Australian and British forces rout last of Italians from Cyranaica (Libya) in North Africa
5-10-41	Incendiary night bombing of London destroys empty House of Commons
5-27-41	British Navy sinks German capital battleship *Bismark*
6-22-41	Operation BARBAROSSA steps off: Germany invades Russia
7-7-41	protective cover of US convoy escort extended east to Reykjavik, Iceland
8-12-41	From their first summit in Placentia Bay, Newfoundland, Churchill and Roosevelt issue the Atlantic Charter
9-3-41	In experimental first use of poison gas in Nazi deathcamps, Russian POWs murdered at Auschwitz

9-8-41	Leningrad virtually encircled by von Leeb's Army Group North; long siege begins
10-19-41	US merchant vessel *Lehigh* sunk by German U-boat off west coast of Africa
10-30-41	Repulse of German forces 50 miles from Moscow begins, siege of Sevastapol starts
11-12-41	British capital battleship *Ark Royal* sunk by U-boat 25 miles from British colony of Gibraltar at mouth of Mediterranean
12-7-41	*"Nacht und Nebel"* decree issued in Germany: military authorized to summarily execute dissenters, who effectively disappear into 'night and fog'
12-7-41	Japanese Navy sinks much of US Navy's Seventh Fleet at Pearl Harbor, destroys 66% of Air Force planes stationed in Hawaii in Sunday morning surprise attack, "...a day which shall live in infamy." (Roosevelt)
12-8-41	US declares war on Japan, Germany, Italy (the *Axis*)
12-8-41	At Chelmno Nazi death-camp in occupied Poland, mechanized murder first becomes operational: Jews from Lodz Ghetto and gypsies are the first gassed
1-14-42	Panamanian tanker *Nordness* is sunk by German U-boat off Cape Hatteras, beginning open warfare in western Atlantic
1-20-42	Wansee Conference—Nazis formally plan the 'Final Solution' to 'the Jewish question'
1-8-42	Russians break German siege of Sevestapol

1-28-42	8th Air Force created
2-15-42	British garrison at Singapore, owing to impossibility of reinforcement by British or American forces, falls to Japanese
3-11-42	Japanese conquer Philippines, retreating US Gen. Douglas MacArthur vows: "I shall return."
4-10 to 4-22-42	Bataan Death March begins - Japanese force-march 76,000 British and American prisoners 60 jungle miles without food or water; this and conditions in the camp at San Fernando lead to death of half the prisoners
4-18-42	In bold Doolittle Raid, 16 B-25 Mitchell bombers launched from USS *Hornet* put US bombs on Japan's home island—great boost to US morale
6-4-42	Battle of Midway is stunning turning point for US in Pacific war
6-12-42	15th Air Force makes daring, effective but costly low-level first attack on oil refineries at Ploesti (in Rumania) from bases in North Africa
6-29-42	Unofficial first 8th AF sortie: American crew in one of 12 RAF Bostons hit Hazebrouk marshaling yard 30 miles S of Dunkerque
7-4-42	Yankee Doodle puts a feather in his cap: 6 USAAF crews join RAF Squadron 226 in sweep of enemy airfields in Low Countries; first official US air operation against Hitler's 'Festung Europa'
8-4-42	Roosevelt and Joint Chiefs declare to Churchill their intention to open a European western front in Spring 1943 if at all possible

8-17-42	under RAF fighter protection, twelve B-17s commanded by Ira Eaker strike marshaling yards at Rouen without loss, in first American led raid of Europe from England
8-19-42	German General Paulus' 6th Army begins extremely costly attempt on Stalingrad; battle will take 600,000 Axis and 1,000,000 Russian lives
11-7-42	in 8th AF's first all-B-24 effort, 2nd Bombardment Wing (later called the 2nd Air Division) Commander General Hodge leads the 44th BG to Cap de la Hague, France
10-23 to 10-26-42	Japanese navy suffers unrecoverable loss of 34 ships in Battle of Leyte Gulf, to US loss of 6 vessels
11-8-42	Operation TORCH: combined US and British landings in North Africa
11-23-42	German siege of Stalingrad is broken; Paulus' 6th Army, encircled between the Volga and the Don Rivers begins retreat
1-12-43	Start of Casablanca Conference; cross-Mediterranean and cross-Channel invasion plans set for '43 and '44; Roosevelt announces US commitment to fight until *unconditional* surrender of all enemies
1-27-43	8th's 31st mission puts 'heavies' from the 1st and 2nd Bombardment Wings over Germany (Wilhelmshaven) for the first time
5-13-43	last Axis forces driven from Africa at Tunis
5-26-43	German Admiral Dönitz withdraws U-boat fleet from North Atlantic; anti-submarine measures have

upper hand on menace which cost Allies 2,600 vessels, 15,000,000 tons of goods and 5,500 merchant marine sailors against German loss of 785 U-boats by end of European war

7-10-43	Invasion of Sicily
7-28-43	P-47 Thunderbolts fitted with range-extending 'drop tanks' perform first deep-penetration escort into Germany
7-25 to 8-2-43	RAF 'thousand bomber raid' on Hamburg over three nights claims between 60,000 and 100,000 lives, severely rattling German high command
1-5-44	operational range of escort fighters extended with introduction of P-51B Mustangs, flying this day to Keil; successive experiments with auxiliary fuel tanks continue to increase effective operation to Berlin and beyond, greatly reduces loss of bombers to enemy fighters on deep penetration missions
1-27-44	Leningrad: 900 day siege fully broken after death of 640,000 by starvation, German shelling and bombardment
2-20-44	'Big Week' begins; strategic targeting of German aircraft production and aerial combat reduce Luftwaffe fighter strength by a third ('Operation Argument')
3-4-44	first US led daylight bombing raid to 'Big -B' (Berlin)
3-26-44	353rd FG begins first strafing attacks after specialized training; increasing use of this tactic through 1944 helps to secure, then increasing symbolize, Allied

	hegemony in European airspace
5-22-44	RAF hands over North Pickenham to USAAF; station #143's first tenant is short-lived original 492nd BG; last of 77 such ceremonies
6-6-44	D-Day; largest naval invasion in history. 'Operation Overlord' on Normandy beaches begins Allies' land campaign in western Europe
6-12-44	First German 'Vergeltungswaffe-1' (Vengeance Weapon) V-1 buzz-bomb falls on London
6-21-44	First problematic 8th AF 'shuttle' mission; bombers hit targets deep in the Reich, land in Russian-controlled east to refuel, reload, strike enemy on return trip
6-27-44	Russian Army crosses Dnieper River; its lurching hegemony on the *Ostfront* is inexorable and undeniable
7-17-44	Russian Army sweeps into Poland; driving west, the rout of the Germans accelerates on a broad front
7-20-44	unsuccessful attempt on Hitler's life by high-ranking Germans
7-29-44	Rocket-powered Messerschmidt 163 Komet first seen in combat
8-5-44	2nd Division stands down 492nd BG ending still-unexplained slaughter of US 8th AF's hardest-luck group
8-12-44	PLUTO pipeline between Isle of Wight and Cherbourg becomes operational; aids in fuel crunch created by Allies' advances after Normandy breakout
8-26-44	Liberation of Paris
9-5-44	Liberation of Brussels
9-8-44	First German V-2 supersonic ballistic missile with payload of

	1,650 pounds lands in Cheswick section of London; over 1000 will make it to England by end of war
9-20 to 9-30-44	'Operation Trucking;' B-24s of the 96th Combat Wing deliver 2.1 million gallons of 80-octane gasoline to three improvised terminals in France to fuel rapid advance of General Patton's 3rd Army
10-20-44	General MacArthur's forces return triumphant to Philippines
11-27-44	Antwerp opened as a deep water port for Allies, under heavy V-weapon assault
12-24-44	Largest bombing operation to date hits transportation targets across western Europe
12-26-44	Battle of Bulge turned in Belgium; last German advance of the war is routed
1-30-45	Hitler gives last defiant radio address as Soviet forces move to within 70 miles of Berlin
2-13,14-45	RAF and US bombers conduct incendiary raid on Dresden; 35,000 civilians killed in what is decried a terror raid with limited military objective
2-23-45	US Marines raise victory flag on summit of Mt. Suribachi, Iwo Jima, 4 days after landing and enduring extremely heavy fighting
3-7-45	Ludendorf Bridge across Rhine (at Remagen) is taken intact, allows US armor to pour into *der Vaterland*
3-9,10-45	Nighttime incendiary bombing of Tokyo takes 83,000 lives, wounds additional 45,000, leaves 1 million homeless—more casualties than in either of the atomic bomb attacks

4-12-45	32nd US President Franklin Delano Roosevelt dies in office, succeeded by Harry S. Truman
4-15-45	KZ Bergen-Belsen liberated by British, who find 40,000 alive and 10,000 dead
4-16-45	General Carl 'Tooey' Spaatz calls end to all strategic air operations in Europe
4-25-45	Russian and American forces shake hands at Torgau near Leipzig
4-30-45	Adolf Hitler and his bride of one day, Eva Braun, take their lives in Führer's Bunker in besieged Berlin
5-7-45	Colonel General Alfred Jodl renders unconditional German surrender to Allies at Eisenhower's headquarters, Reims, France
5-8-45	V-E Day declared
5-13-45	467th BG leads entire 8th AF in victory flypast at High Wycombe headquarters
5-28-45	'Lord Haw Haw,' traitorous radio propagandist for Nazis, captured at Flensburg; Queen Wilhelmina returns to Holland; American and British navies jointly announce that merchant shipping in all but Pacific waters, may now "...burn navigation lights at full brilliancy"
6-26-45	UN Charter signed in San Francisco
7-16-45	'Big Three' begin final war conference in Potsdam, Germany- seeds of Cold War mistrust are strongly evident
7-25-45	Allied leaders warn Japan to surrender or face "utter destruction," Stalin has just been informed of US possession of and intent to use the atomic bomb
8-6-45	8:15 a.m.: B-29 *Enola Gay* drops

first	atom bomb on Hiroshima, Japan; kills at least 78,000
8-8-45	Russia declares war on Japan
8-9-45	Casualties of 35,000 in Nagasaki as second A-bomb dropped
8-15-45	V-J Day proclaimed by Allies, Japanese emperor uses radio for first time to order his subjects to lay down their arms
9-2-45	aboard USS *Missouri*, General-of the-Army Douglas MacArthur, for the Allied powers, accepts formal unconditional surrender of Japan, leaving Emperor Hirohito enthroned but supervised; WW II is over

Biography of

James Jeremiah Mahoney

I. Early Years

-2-4-1917 Born in Newton, Massachusetts.

-11-4-1918 Father (Jeremiah) dies, leaving
mother (Margaret) to raise 3 step-children
plus JJM and 2 older surviving brothers,
one of whom dies 2 years later.

-1923-1935 Attends public schools, is altar boy,
Boy Scout, caddy. Completely ambidextrous
and a 'natural,' shows athletic prowess in
golf, tennis, shooting, baseball, hockey. (A
lifelong low-handicapper, he was a much
sought after golf partner. Rarely did he
give up a tennis game to one of his kids.)

-Fall 1935 Matriculates Boston College, makes
varsity hockey squad, enlists in Troop B,
Massachusetts National Guard's 110th
Cavalry

-Spring 1940 Graduates college.

-8-13-1940 Honorably discharged from National
Guard to enlist in US Army Air Corps as
aviation cadet next day.

II. Military Years

-8-14-1940 Reports to Basic Flight Training at
Gunter Field, Alabama.

-5-29-1941 Order #126 JJM awarded 'Pilot'
rating as graduate of basic pilot training
program.

-5-29-1941 Spec. Order #127 2nd Lt. JJM to
report 5-30-41 to USAAC (that is, US Army
Air Corps, later called US Army Air
Forces) Advanced Flying School, Maxwell
Field. Effectively a call-up to active duty
service. Commissioned as reserve officer in
the grade of 2nd Lieutenant.

-4-24-1942 Graduation, advanced flying school.

Temporary promotion to 1st Lieutenant.

-5-25-1942 Spec. Order #137 permanent promotion to 1st Lieutenant. (Also his mother's 56th birthday, and exactly one year before birth of his oldest child.)

-5-1942 to 9-1943 Anti-submarine patrol over the Mid-Atlantic coast with Maryland National Guard's old 104th Observation Sqn., redesignated ultimately as 12th Anti-Submarine Sqn., based at Atlantic City Municipal Airport then Langley Field, VA. On a double-date in this period, met the 25 year old Mary McKenna, date of his friend Bill Hall. Hall later married Barb Woodward, JJM's date.

-8-22-1942 JJM and Mary McKenna wed.

-9-8-1942 Temporary promotion to Captain.

-2-18-1943 Spec. Order #49 permanent promotion to Captain.

-4-8-1943 DECORATION: Air Medal, upon completion of 200 hrs. of patrol flying; Gen'l. Order #7. (JJM logged over 1500 hours by June 1945)

-4-17-1943 Appointed member of Instrument Flying Proficiency Board, first assignment as instructor pilot (on the antiquated B-18).

-5-25-1943 James Jeremiah Mahoney, Jr. (Jerry), born, Langley Field, VA.

-9-17-1943 Movement order from Langley Field, VA, to Blythe Army Air Field, CA.

-10-1-1943 12th Anti-Submarine Sqn. officially redesignated as the 859th Bomb Squadron, cadre of the 492nd BG, created on same day at Clovis AAF.

-10-27-1943 Movement order to Clovis Army Air Field, NM (present-day Holloman AFB) for B-24 transition training.

-12-3-1943 Movement order to Alamogordo, NM.

-3-18-1944 Promoted to temporary Major.

-4-10-1944 Overseas movement begins; Air

Echelon of the 492nd Bomb Group heads to North Pickenham, (Station #143) Norfolk, England. JJM is Squadron Commander of the 859th Bomb Squadron within this group, under command of Col. Eugene Snavely.

-6-20-1944 Under Spec. Order #194, promoted to temporary Lt. Col. USAAF. (At 27, one of the youngest in WW II.) 492nd BG's single worst loss day: 14 planes shot down, 138 KIA on its second Politz raid. All seven planes put up that day by JJM's 859th BS shot down.

-6-21-1944 DECORATION: Second Oak Leaf Cluster to the Air Medal by Gen'l order #105, Headquarters of 2nd Bombardment Division.

-8-10-1944 492nd BG 'stood down' from active combat and completely reorganized. 29 surviving aircrews having less than 15 missions are put under command of Lt. Col. JJM and reassigned as 788th BS, attached to 467th BG at Station #145, Rackheath, located 5 mi. N-NE of Norwich, England.

-10-3-1944 DECORATION: Distinguished Flying Cross (DFC) by Gen'l. Order #258.

-10-14-1944 (approx.) JJM promoted to Air Executive (and Deputy Group Commander) of 467th BG under Col. Albert J. Shower, Group Commander.

-6-10-1945 Operational order #63: JJM to command movement #7 of aircraft and personnel of 467th BG back to US ('Operation HOMERUN'). At this point in time, he anticipated new orders to retrain in the Boeing B-29 'Superfortress' and be sent to the Pacific Theatre... none of this happened thanks to a decision by President Truman.

-9-14-1945 Lt. Col. J. J. Mahoney officially separated from active duty.

Military awards and decorations
>   Distinguished Flying Cross with Oak Leaf Clusters
>   (two times)
>   Air Medal with six Oak Leaf Clusters
>   Croix de Guerre, with Palm (France) Group award to
>   the successor 492nd BG (the Carpetbaggers)
>   by French Government in Exile,
>   widely considered to be retroactive to the
>   original organization
>   Campaign Ribbons for Battles of the Atlantic, the
>   American Theatre (with Battle Star), the
>   Middle Eastern Theatre (with 6 Battle
>   Stars), Northern France, Normandy, Air
>   Offensive Europe, Central Europe,
>   Ardennes-Alsace, Rhineland

III. Postwar

>   -1945-1949 Salesman, then sales Mgr. for Vick
>   Chemical company, living in Clifton, New
>   Jersey then Wellsley, Massachusetts.
>   -1949-1958 Business consultant with McKinsey,
>   first in Boston, later in NYC.
>   -7-26-55 Fifth and last child is born.
>   -1958-1963 Advertising Manager, Miles
>   Laboratories, Elkhart, IN
>   -1963 Moves to Norwich Parmacal Company,
>   Norwich, NY as VP of Marketing, advances
>   ultimately to President of Norwich
>   Products Div., Proctor and Gamble.
>   -late 1960s Begins, quite privately, to start
>   writing down his 'war stories.' Sought after
>   by historians and veteran groups for his
>   knowledge and documentation of 8th AF
>   operations in England. His 2000 feet of
>   16mm Kodachrome movies constitutes some
>   of earliest Allied color footage of combat in
>   European Theatre of Operations (ETO).
>   -1980 JJM is last of the original Norwich
>   Pharmacal Co. mgmt. to finally be
>   separated, in an early retirement at age 63.

Final project was to supervise construction
of the first automated warehouse in New
York (North Norwich Facility of Proctor &
Gamble/Norwich Pharmaceutical Division,
still in use). P&G hires *three* men to
replace him.

-3-31-1989 Mary McKenna Mahoney dies after
long illness, during which JJM was
constantly in attendance.

-June, 1990 Marries Polly Roberts.

-August, 1990 Moves to Hamilton, NY.

-Spring, 1992 Makes last of half dozen return
trips to Rackheath and North Pickenham
bases in England, visits son Jerry, then a
USAF colonel serving at Rhein-Main AB,
Germany.

-1980-1998 Continually refines and expands his
war memoirs, corresponds extensively with
veterans, researchers.

-9-15-1998 Dies after 6 month illness at age 81,
survived by widow, 5 children, 18
grandchildren, one great-grandchild

JAMES JEREMIAH MAHONEY

Whom neither shape of danger can dismay

Nor thought of tender happiness betray.

8 Wetherell St., Newton Upper Falls

Mousie, Jim; Language; Weeks; Boston College; Junior Varsity
Basketball, 2; Intermediate Hockey, 3; Aviation Club, 2,4;
Legislature, 4; to be generalissimo of the US Army.

(from the 1935 "Newtonian," yearbook of the
Newton, Massachusetts, High School)

Aircraft Types Flown by JJM

Air Corps / USAAC

PT-13
PT-21 (postwar, John Tupper)
BT-9
BT-13
AT-6
BC-1A
AT-10
O-46
O-47
O-49 (L-1)
O-52
A-19
A-20
A-29
B-17
B-18
B-23
B-24
B-25
B-34
P-42
P-47
P-51
C-45
C-47

Royal Air Force (England)

Oxford Trainer (twin)
Mosquito
Spitfire xxl

Royal Canadian Air Force

Norseman

Civil Air Patrol as liaison from Air Corps
(some privately owned)

>Stinson Reliant
>Stinson Voyager
>Stinson 105
>Bellanca
>Fairchild Ranger (Wyant Farr)
>Fairchild Warner (Hugh Sharp)
>Grumman Widgeons (Tom
>>Eastman, Bill Zelser)
>Cessnas
>Aeroncas
>Cubs
>Kinner Bird
>Beech -negative stagger
>>(Ig Sargent)
>Luscombe (Ed Davis)

flown right-seat only

military
>A-26
>B-26
>C-46
>B-29
>DC 5
>Constellation

civillian
>Ford Tri-motor
>Sikorsky Amphibian

(Source: list typed by JJM)

Germany's second and last Fuehrer, Grand Adm. Karl Doenitz, said the air power of the Allies was the decisive element in the failure of the Nazi submarine war. Field Marshal Gerd von Rundstedt listed air power as the first of several ingredients in the triumph of the United Nations. Col. Gen. Alfred Jodl said the winning of air superiority altogether decided the war and that strategic bombing was the most decisive factor. Field Marshal Wilhelm Keitel assigned to the Allied air forces the chief credit for the victories in the west. Of a dozen German generals who surrendered in Italy, all but one regarded air power as chiefly responsible for the defeat. Albert Speer, the redoubtable minister of armaments production and by far the most valuable source for the effects of strategic bombing, emphatically stated his opinion that such bombing could have won the war without a land invasion. The list of interrogated German generals and industrial officials was long, From Goering and Doenitz down to division commanders and factory managers they praised the achievements of Allied air power. Most of them regarded it as the decisive factor in Germany's defeat.

The Army Air Forces in W W II, v. III, page 786

comparator: CASUALTIES

people killed worldwide in WW I	21,000,000
people killed worldwide in WW II, 9-1-39 to 8-16-45	53,469,000
US casualties, total, Korean War	54,000
US casualties, total, Vietnam conflict	58,000
US Marines killed in WW II, mostly Pacific theatre	19,733
US Army killed in WW II, mostly in Europe	182,701
86th Infantry Div. killed in WW II (a hard-luck group in Europe)	3,620
USAAF personnel KIA WW II, Pacific theatre[1]	19,500
USAAF personnel KIA WW II, Europe	31,914

deaths per 1000 combatants, select WW II organizations

all US Army Air Forces	.016
US Army (not including USAAF)	.020
US Marines	.029
US 8th AF 467th BG[2]	.091
US Army 83rd Infantry Div.[3]	192
US 8th AF 492nd BG[4] (original organization)	442

1. Source for this and next item: 8th Air Force News, Summer 2000.

2. The denominator of this equation, 2700 air combatants, is an estimate based upon the known number of leaders of ten-man combat crews (276) and consideration that a small number of these were promoted to group command duties before their crews finished tours. Numerator is KIA plus KILOD, officially 248.

3. John Ellis, WW II: A Statistical Survey, p. 254 (see Bibliography)

4. Denominator is based on 70 original aircrews of 10 men each plus 49 replacement crews which flew in combat, plus 10 men to allow for group staff who flew combat but were not crew members. Numerator is KIA plus KILOD, officially 588.

comparator: TONNAGES of bombs dropped by US

WW II total, all theatres	2,050,000
European theatre, WW II	1,600,000
Pacific theatre, WW II	502,781
Korean War	476,000
Vietnam	6,200,000
Gulf War	88,000

comparator: US AIRCRAFT

model (production years)	total production	unit cost
DeHavilland DH-1 (1917-18)	1,213	
Boeing P-26 Peashooter (1933-36)	136	$9,999
Boeing B-18 Bolo (1936-39)	473	
Grumman F4U Corsair (1940-51)	12,571	
Republic P-47 Thunderbolt	15,579	
Boeing B-17 Flying Fortress (1935-44)	12,731	
N. American P-51 Mustang (1941-45)	14,490	
Consolidated B-24 Liberator (1939-45)	19,203	$750,000
Lockheed F-80 Shooting Star (1944-58)	1,715	
McDonnell F4 Phantom (1958-79)[1]	5,000	$18.4 mil
Boeing B-52 Stratofortress (1955-63)	744	~$30 mil
Lockheed Martin F-16 Fighting Falcon[1] (1979-01)	2,216	$26.9 mil
Northrop Grumman B-2 Spirit Bomber (1993-present)	16+	~$1.2 bil
Lockheed F-117 Nighthawk (1983-90)	54	$122 mil

1. Unit cost given is for *end* of production run.

comparator: GROWTH OF THE US AIR ARM

date and circumstances	personnel	aircraft
1911 Aviation Section, Signal Corps	120	6
1917 as US enters WW I (4-6)	56 pilots + ?	250
1918 Armistice Day (11-11)	197,338	~10,000
1939 Germany invades Poland (9-1)	?	2,422
1941 Pearl Harbor attack (12-7)	3,304	6,777
1944 at WW II peak	2,400,000	80,000
1953 at Korean conflict peak	?	23,212
1968 Viet Nam build up	?	16,784
1991 during Operation Desert Storm	506,000	8,510
2000 current peacetime level	351,000	6,205

Sources: Air Force Personnel Center website and others. See Bibliography.

Aircraft inventory figures for 1939, 1941, 1953—2000 include Air Force Reserve and National Guard unit aircraft, but do not include classified planes such as the SR-71 Blackbird.

JJM LETTER TO PHILLIP DAY, December 3, 1986
on the character of Albert Joseph Shower

Dear Phillip,

In belated response to your note of several weeks ago, there are some comments I'd like to make for your "POOP from Group 467" newsletter, and these concern our group's 'Old Man,' Col. Shower.

As I reflect on our days at Rackheath, I feel there are some things that should be said, and said now, not held for the inevitable eulogy and obituary notice when everyone but the subject learns how much his existence was appreciated.

When Col. Al Herzberg left the 467th to join the 96th Wing Headquarters at Horsham St. Faith, I succeeded him as our Group Air Executive. From then until the end of 'our war' in Europe, some nine months or so later, I shared an office with Al Shower in the 'Ops Block,' we shared a suite of living quarters in "the White House," my designated place at the "brass table" was to his right, etc. In short, I worked longer and more closely with Col. Shower than anyone in the group and thus justify my self-appointment as the one to make these comments on the man who steered and drove our group to top performance in one of the most skilled and complex fighting machines of WW II—the Eighth Air Force. The ultimate recognition of this achievement being the selection of the 467th to lead the Eighth's farewell fly-by over its headquarters at High Wycombe before departing the U. K.

Everyone in the group was aware of the Colonel's total dedication to the reason for our being where we were—to put bombs on the target. Nobody, in my experience, approached his unrelenting intensity in pursuing that objective. Many crews can recall (and not kindly at the time) Al circling the Group in flak-filled skies over a cloud shrouded primary target, hoping for a visual drop after all other groups had opted for secondaries or targets-of-opportunity. But, even when inevitable griping was most vociferous, no one ever accused the Colonel of asking more, or even as much, of his men as he did of himself.

Discipline and training were the absolute essentials to the accomplishment of our mission, and Col. Shower provided us with a full and continuing diet of both.

We had plenty of use for our Class A uniforms, personal appearance was checked before leaving the base, no flight jackets allowed at evening mess, we had our regular dress parades on the main runway with awards ceremonies and passing in review behind our marching band. This was followed by inspection of personnel in their barracks, We saluted and returned salutes at all times, anywhere, to anything that moved, As our Wing Commander, General Peck once complained, "I wear out my G__ d___ arm saluting whenever I come to this base!"

We flew training missions whenever the treacherous East Anglian weather allowed. I suspect we burned as much fuel on training as on combat missions. Then there were the ground trainers and ground school—always fully scheduled. Our high levels of discipline and training were considered more demanding than at other bases, and not surprisingly, generated a fair amount of GI griping. Paradoxically, the fruit of those two rigid program, our bombing results, provided the bragging rights for these same gripers.

Less obvious, but very important to the success of our group was the Colonel's willingness to innovate. This is a characteristic not usually associated with Service Academy graduates, at least by reserve officers. For four years as cadets they were thoroughly indoctrinated in doing things 'by the numbers' and checking 'regs' before making decisions. Al recognized that the Army Air Corps Tables of Organization, Technical Orders, manuals, etc. when written, didn't and couldn't contemplate the conditions under which we were operating, From our air operations standpoint we found it more efficient to reshape the squadrons into one lead-crew squadron and three wing-crew squadrons. In so doing, we took much of the control over crews from the squadrons. Initially this was not well received, but eventually accepted when the advantages to our overall effort became obvious. Also, not everyone was happy with our combat crew modifications: dropping co-pilots from lead crews; replacing bombardiers with togglers in our wing crews; eliminating our ball-turret gunners, etc. Some of our equipment changes were major. The elimination of ball turrets saved 2200 lbs. of what we found to be ineffective weight, and risked one less life. The development of the 2000 lb. shackle by one of our own non-coms allowed quick loading, as opposed to the 24 hour stand-down previously required for modification of a plane to accept the 'big ones.' Our many other innovations encouraged by the Col. often represented departures from 'regs' which wouldn't have gladdened the heart of someone from the Inspector General's office, but were carefully considered and did make positive contributions to our effort.

Even less known was Al Shower, the man. Colonel Shower was hard, he was tough, he was single-minded. This sometimes made him hard to get along with. He and I had our disagreements—but never on objectives, only on ways of implementing them. Despite his rather stern appearance, he was softer inside than generally believed, and he kept it that way. He was not insensitive to his personnel's problems and needs and made sure that were given the required attention, Our KIAs and MIAs were more than just statistics to him. As with us all, they left scars that don't show.

The Colonel was a God-fearing man and a regular church-goer, but more importantly, his daily military and personal conduct conformed to his beliefs. In summary, and to me most important of all, he was a man of integrity.

We should all be grateful to Al's forebears for having the good sense to depart Deutschland for the wilds of Wisconsin, otherwise he might have been on the other side! Due largely to him, the 467th's bombing performance was among the highest. Due at least in part to him, our crew loss rate was among the lowest. This very large and favorable divergence between these two vital measures of performance provide mute testimony to the outstanding combat leadership of Colonel Albert J. Shower.

Jim

excerpt, JJM LETTER TO ROGER FREEMAN, June 6, 1962
on the 'marked group' theory

"There is an extremely long story to be told and I shan't attempt it in full, but it became apparent after not very many missions that we were being singled out by German fighters. It was so obvious that at one time, an 8th Fighter Group was assigned to us exclusively. I believe it was the 352nd Fighter Group stationed at Bodney. During this period of special chaperoning of our group many pilots of the Fighter Group ran up an impressive string of victories. I recall that one of their squadron commanders, Maj. George Preddy (later shot down by U. S. ground forces when defending the Remagen bridgehead against Luftwaffe dive bombers), shot down eight or ten fighters during the period when his squadron was assigned to close support of our Group.

There was much discussion and considerable bewilderment at all echelons as to why the Luftwaffe was obviously singling out the 492nd for special and unwelcome attention. I have already touched on two of the possible causes which were advanced: (1) That the pilots of the 492nd flew the tightest formation on missions and therefore presented a very closely knit and solid target for fighter guns. I personally doubt this theory, although I do recall seeing F-W 190s on twelve o'clock high attacks going through our formations with the pilots kicking the rudders ("fish-tailing")—obviously spraying the formation rather than singling out an individual plane as a target; (2) The second theory was that our all-silver-plane-formations were much easier to spot and keep in the German fighter gun sights when attacking from a high position with the sun at their backs. I rather doubt the significance of this factor, also. (3) I tend to go along with the third possible cause—and this takes a little telling. It starts with the action of one or our aircraft under heavy fighter attack during an early mission in the Berlin area.

We had identical twin pilots in our group—they were George and Frank Haag from Philadelphia, Pennsylvania.

None of us ever did learn to tell them apart and to this day I can't tell you which of the two was involved in this incident. In any event, on this mission when the plane piloted by one of the Haags was attacked and hit by enemy fighter fire, the landing gear dropped. This, of course, was considered in aerial combat to be a sign of surrender. Knowing both of the Haags and that the plane itself was not badly shot up, I feel that an intention to surrender is a very unlikely explanation for the wheels dropping.

A more logical or plausible explanation is that the landing gear, when retracted after take-off, had been raised but not fully latched in the "up" position. The gear was kept "up" due to hydraulic pressure and not the mechanical latch. When eventually the plane was hit with fighter gunfire, any puncture of the hydraulic system would allow the pressure to dissipate and the wheels would drop. I must admit, however, that this was not a common malfunction of the B-24 landing gear system.

In any event, after the gear dropped and the plane had fallen a bit behind and below the formation, several of the Goering squadron (yellow-nosed F-W 190s) closed in, not to fire, but to escort this plane to a landing field in Germany. When they pulled up alongside the B-24 the gunners opened up on the fighters and according to some witnesses, knocked down at least two and possibly three of these F-W 190s.

Even though our information on this event was never fully substantiated and was always a bit hazy, it did appear to be the most logical reason that could be advanced for the singular interest of the Luftwaffe in the 492nd Bomb Group. On many missions I personally saw the Goering squadron go down the bomber line until they found our Group and then dive to the attack—completely ignoring the Groups ahead and behind us."

S E C R E T

HEADQUARTERS EIGHTH AIR FORCE
AAF STATION 101
APO 634

INTOPS SUMMARY NO. 322

PERIOD: 0001 hours 18 March to 2400 hours 18 March 1945

*   *   *   *   *   *   *

4.   Damage to Enemy Installations

Berlin/Schleisischer Station - H2X - Unobserved
Unable to pin-point any concentrations on this
target.   Total of 23 partial concentrations plotted, most
of which fell on various parts of Berlin including
Templehof M/Y and A/F.   Installations in northwestern
corner of A/F could be seen burning late in attack.
Friedrichshain Park flak battery hit, as well as built-up
areas adjacent to the park, where damage should be severe.
3 partial concentrations each plotted in Neukoln and
Rummelsburg sections of city.

Berlin/Hennigsdorf Tank Plant - Good
1 squadron blanketed south end of the plant; most
of the bursts were 1 to 2 miles east in a partially built-
up area.

Berlin/Tegel Tank Plant - Excellent
Total area seen burning upon leaving target. Bursts
seen on tank assembly plant, large assembly type
buildings, engineering buildings and auxiliary works as
well as adjacent city areas.

Oranienburg - Fair
Bursts seen in partially built up areas.

Berlin North Goods Station - Unobserved to Fair
Most of the plotted bursts hit average of two miles
from MPI.   A number of visual strikes within the built up
area were plotted but the extent of the damage could not
be assessed.

-7-
S E C R E T

(BHM transcription from original, showing report heading and one telling page.)

"Rackheath To Berlin"
to the tune of 'Wreck of the 99'

Oh, it was a long rough ride, from Rackheath to Berlin,
And the flak was bursting high,
And the P-38s and the P-47s
Were guardin' us high up in the sky.

We were half way between Lake Dummer and Hamburg
When all Hell broke loose in the Blue,
For Jerry had spotted us from five o'clock under,
And was coming up to see what he could do.

The first pass was made at the 467th,
Colonel Shower in the lead.
Oh, he pissed and he moaned,
And he shit and he groaned,
When he looked and saw that he was all alone.

Now the Colonel, he called his Brave Navigator,
"Can you give me a short heading home?"
But with his hand on the ripcord, the Brave Navigator
Said, "Al, boy, you're going home alone."

Then the Colonel, he called to his Brave Bombardier,
"Do you know the right way home?"
But the Bombardier had already scuttled,
And there was silence on the Colonel's interphone.

With his crew all gone, he chewed on his mustache,
And his balls drew up in his sack,
And he munched on his candy at 22,000,
For he thought that he was never coming back.

Now with four engines feathered
He glided to safety at his home base.
And it's with great pride that he tells this story
With a shit-eating grin on his face.

Bibliography

Air Force (US), Department of, *Air Force Combat Units of World War II* (Washington, 1961) The dry and official statement of the lineage of particular military organizations. Of interest for illustrating how military bureaucracy finesses the decimation and dissolution of a group, for the historical record, behind a short declarative sentence about 'relocation of command without personnel or equipment.'

Ardrey, Philip *Bomber Pilot* (Lexington, KY, 1978) Personal memoir of an articulate young man, paying attention to the big picture and his own role. Builds clear picture of America going to war, individuals committing to important service, experiencing specialized training, adventure, senseless loss, etc.

Banger, Joan *Norwich at War* (Norwich, England, 1974) collection of contemporaneous reports and personal accounts of travails of often raided British city and well organized and heroic response of her citizenry. Makes good use of newspaper photos, headlines, articles; gives statistical picture of the loss and destruction suffered.

Bastien, Charles R. *32 Co-Pilots* (pre-publication draft, 1994) Author has collected the stories of his colleagues, co-pilots in the original crews of the 492nd BG. Through their training, movement to England and their various fates, reader has a window on short and turbulent life and death of the 'original' 492nd.

Birdsall, Steve *Log of the Liberators* (Garden City, NY, 1973) Enjoyable account of the B-24 and its variants and services to around the world. Well illustrated; special color plate section shows representative identification markings.

Blue, Alan G. *The Fortunes of War* (1967, '87) Author grapples with the myriad theories and ultimately unanswerable questions that are the legacy of the ill-fated 492nd Bomb Group.

Bowman, Martin *Fields of Little America, an Illustrated History of the 8th Air Force 2nd Air Division 1942-45* (Norwich, England, 1977) Well researched and illustrated narrative.

_____ *The B-24 Liberator 1939-1945* (Norwich, England 1979) Full of previously unpublished b & w photos, author gives the general audience a very accessible historical and technical introduction to history's most-produced aircraft.

Bryant, Arthur *The Turn of the Tide* (New York, 1957) A unique war history taking as its basis the diaries of Churchill's Chief of the Imperial Staff, Lord Alanbrooke.

Churchill, Winston S. *Memoirs of the Second World War, an abridgment of the six volumes of 'The Second World War'* (Boston, 1990) Riveting, penetrating, persuasive, passionate and logical all at once; in this brilliant work, the spellbound reader feels personally escorted through all of the shadings and stratagems of politics and power from personal to global in scale, by the man himself. The complexity and richness of the individual character, of the historical episode, and of the grand mortal themes; all are taken up with an enthusiastic courage, with an infectious and indomitable intellectual curiosity.

Craven, Wesley F, and Cate, James L. *The Army Air Forces In WW II , Vols. II and III* (Chicago, 1949) Long regarded as the 'Bible' for thorough and incisive analysis of the performance of the air arm, this series is still an important cornerstone in military and airpower scholarship

Davis, Richard G. *Carl A. Spaatz and the Air War In Europe* (Washington, 1993) Scholarly, comprehensively researched biography of the man who implemented the American contribution to the combined strategic bombing of the Axis powers in Europe. Evolution and implementation of strategic bombing doctrine and the organizations and leaders that carried it out.   Draws effectively on correspondences and interviews to lay clear the tremendous stylistic, moral, pragmatic and political differences amongst the leadership, the difficulties and foibles in this most consequential of the war's theatres.

Ellis, John   *World War II, a Statistical Survey*   (1993) Rich resource for quantification of production, destruction, mobilization, conquest and loss around a world at war.

Freeman, Roger A.   *The Mighty Eighth, a History of the US Army 8th Air Force*   (Garden City, NY, 1970, multiple subsequent impressions)   First of three companion references which, taken together, give a comprehensive account of the history, purpose, challenge, travail, methodology, tools and ultimately success of this huge fighting organization.   This volume lays out the overall history, includes unit histories, stories of the most decorated.

_____   *The Mighty Eighth War Diary*   (London, 1981)   A daily chronology of 8th AF operations, peppered with interesting incidents and framed by a lucid discussion of the theory and practice of daylight strategic bombing.   Every caption offers memorable irony or basis for awe; every page is packed with information in a digestible form.

_____   *The Mighty Eighth War Manual*   (London 1984)   The engaged reader of this most readable textbook will become a well-rounded and well-grounded student of the operational methods, procedures and equipment used by the main organizations of the Eighth.

Goldstein, D., Dillon, K. V., and Wenger, J. M.   *NUTS ! The Battle of the Bulge*   (Washington, 1994)   In photos, maps, tables and narration, authors lay out entire orders of battle, conditions, aftermath of battle as seen from both sides.

Goralski, Robert *World War II Almanac* (New York, 1981) Terrific collection of facts and statistics paints the large and gruesome picture of the world war in chronologic narration.

Granholm, Jackson *The Day We Bombed Switzerland* (London, 2000) Author recounts his service in a bomb group and insightfully sets scene for his successful defense of two men court martialed in connection with one of the three erroneous bombings of Switzerland.

Healy, Allan *The 467th Bombardment Group* (1947, '80, 85, 93) Deservedly popular group memento piece of stunningly high quality, with deft treatment of complex issues, superbly accessible exposition of the story and spirit of the group in prose and photo.

Hoseason, James *The 1,000 Day Battle* (Lowestoft, England 1979) Enthusiast's compendium of wide variety of facts, photos and anecdotes of the Eighth, with heavier emphasis on the story of the 448th BG near author's boyhood home.

Ives, Russell *89 Days, The 492 BG (H) at North Pickenham* (Huddersfield, England, 1998)   Compilation of remembrances, diary entries, clippings, photos, reports.

Jablonski, Edward *Airwar* (Garden City, NY 1971) A most engaging 'big picture' look at the air arm as deployed globally during the Second World War. Two volumes, illustrated.

Kaplan, Philip, and Smith, Rex A. *One Last Look* (New York, 1983) Stunningly beautiful photographic and literary collaboration in which remnants of USAAF bases in England are lovingly presented 40 years after the war. Interwoven with individual recollections. Appendix with telling statistics, glossary. Foreword by Andy Rooney, who cut his journalistic teeth with the Eighth.

Lindbergh, Charles A. *The Wartime Journals of Charles A. Lindbergh* (New York, 1970) Author makes good account of himself, the often misunderstood globalist and non-interventionist, who had entrée to the halls of the enemy. Reveals the bases for his unpopular darker and pessimistic pronouncements and gives the thoughtful reader pause to reconsider relative 'morality' of American conduct in warfare in particular instances.

Polmar & Allen, Eds. *WW II: the Encyclopedia of the War Years 1941-45* (New York, 1996) Readable populist work focused on period of American participation.

Shilts, Randy *Conduct Unbecoming- Gays and Lesbians in the U. S. Military* (New York, 1993) In-depth look at history of military policy concerning homosexuals, full of examples of effective and valued careers halted by uneven, costly implementation of policies rooted in increasingly archaic notions.

Speer, Albert *Inside the Third Reich* (New York, 1970) Written post-war by the introspective imprisoned Armaments Minister of the Third Reich. A compelling and lucid examination of issues of personal responsibility attending position, however gained. An authoritative exposition of the overwhelming and inexorable power of the Allied air campaign, seen from the receiving end.

Stapfer, Hans-Henri, and Künzle, Gino *Strangers in a Strange Land, V. II: Escape to Neutrality* (Carrollton, TX 1992) Rich with period photos and reports from Swiss, German and American sources, a chronological presentation of the story of internment of various combatants, mostly American heavy bomber crews in neutral Switzerland. Pragmatic to political, the paradoxes of the period are not lost on the authors, who thankfully waste no energy trying to separate devils and angels.

Stewart, John *Forbidden Diary* (New York, 1998) From contemporaneous journal of a young navigator, a personal look at a bomb crew member's operational experiences over a tour of 31 missions. Pedagogic presentation of dead-reckoning navigation principles and tools is a treat for the curious.

Thomas, Roy *Haven, Heaven and Hell* (Monroe Wisconsin, 1991) Tabulation of records and experiences of USAAF crews interned in Switzerland.

van der Zee, Henri A. *The Hunger Winter* (Lincoln, Nebraska, 1998) Detailed account of political, military and civilian situation in occupied Holland, with power vacuum and struggles among collaborationist, left and right-wing underground organizations, in context of unliberated North Holland, bypassed by the Allies in extremely painful last winter of war.

Watts, W. P. S. *The Parish of Rackheath 1066-1997* (privately printed, Norwich, England, 1997) Lovingly researched monograph seamlessly integrates the WW II inhabitation of the town by the 467th Bomb Group, into its long history.

OTHER SOURCES

2nd Air Division Association *'The Journal'* Newsletter 1962-2001 virtually complete; BHM continuing JJM's subscription.

467th BG Association *'POOP from the Group'* Newsletter 1981-2001 complete, plus two immediate post-war numbers edited by Capers Holmes.

492nd BG Association *'Happy Warrior'* Newsletter 1992-2001 virtually complete.

Dorr, Robert F. *'Rackheath Aggies: Missions of the 46th Bomb Group'* Article in Combat Aircraft, pp 582-6, Vol. 2 No. 7 (February, 2000)

Dzenowagis, Joe *Video History Project* Videotaped interview series. James J. Mahoney interview by Dzenowagis while attending reunion of Second Air Division Association. (Dearborn, Michigan, 1991)

Gruen, Adam L. *'Preemptive Defense—Allied Air Power Versus Hitler's V-Weapons, 1943-1945'* (Washington, 1998) Monograph in Air Force History and Museums Program.

Kurtz, Clarence P. Personal WW II album, unpublished.

Mahoney, James J. *'Overseas I: North Pickenham, Overseas II: Rackheath, Overseas III: Rackheath'* Three substantial annotated albums covering the period of his military service in England, including correspondence, combat, attack, and reconnaissance photos, personal mementos, base photos, news accounts, organizational charts, touristic photos, etc.

_____ Correspondence files, personal papers and effects 1944-1997 covering matters related to his military service years.

_____ Films. 2200' of original 16mm color and black and white film covering overseas movement, base and combat scenes of 492nd and 467th Bomb Groups. Portions of this footage regularly displayed at The Mighty Eighth Air Force Heritage Museum, Pooler, GA.

_____ *'467th BG (H) 1944-45'* (Norwich, NY, 1991) Videotape showing selections of films (above) relating to operations and scenes around Rackheath, with JJM narration.

McFarland, Stephen L. *'A Concise History of the U. S. Air Force'* (Washington, 1997) Monograph in Air Force History and Museums Program. Includes excellent 'suggested reading' list.

Turnbull, Robert Bruce   *'Born to Glory- a Biography'* (Privately printed 1987) A nephew's lovingly researched and compiled story of the remarkable Lt. Col. John I. ('Jack') Turnbull, KIA 10-18-1944

Warnock, A. Timothy   'Air Power Versus U-boats-Confronting Hitler's Submarine Menace in the European Theatre' (Washington, 1999) Monograph in Air Force History and Museums Program.

SPECIAL RESEARCH

Cartography. Map Reading Room of the U. S. Library of Congress, with its helpful staff, proved invaluable in my visualization of the war-ravaged Berlin of March 18, 1945.

Official Records. Air Force History Support Office (AFHSO) at Bolling AFB, Washington, DC, houses a complete set of the 14,000 microfiche reels, giving indirect access to the actual hard-copy collection, accessible at the Air Force Historical Research Agency (AFHRA), Maxwell AFB, Alabama. National Archives Records Administration (NARA), College Park, MD, houses a wealth of partial collections of papers and photos grouped coarsely by military groups, plus a copy of the same microfiche film set.

Worldwide web. (This short list of key sites will give the interested reader, by navigation to linked pages, entrée to numerous more particular sites. As site addresses (URLs) tend to change with great rapidity, page *owner* is given below so that by simple search these valuable sources may be easily found into the future.)

<http://www.obycity.com/2admemorial/index.html> *2nd Air Division Memorial.*   The Memorial is a unique, endowed educational and intercultural bridge, established at war's end by 2nd AD personnel before leaving Norfolk. Housed within the Norwich (England) Library. Their web site features picture gallery of Norfolk area bases and air force operations, explanation of their living educational mission. Links to sites of various WW II bomb groups.

<http://www.siscom.net/~467thbg/index.html> *467th BG Assn.* Group history, bulletin board, photos, links to related sites.

<http://www.maxwell.af.mil/au/afhra/> *Air Force Historical Research Agency.* Official AFHRA site gives overview of collection, tells how to access it and get research assistance.

<http:///www.afhpc.randolf.af.mil> *US Air Force Personnel Center.* Offers information on demographics of this military branch going back a quarter century.

<http://www.anesi.com/ussbs02.htm> *Anesi, Chuck.* As the war drew to a close in Europe, the US Army wanted to determine precisely what aspects of the huge investment in lives and materiel were most effective in the prosecution of the war. Leading industrial, civilian and military minds were enlisted, enemy authorities interviewed, etc. The resultant United States Strategic Bombing Survey (USSBS) is a cornerstone for the academic understanding of airpower; this very helpful site makes the official summary of the immense, multi-volume survey immediately accessible.

<http://www.aviation-history.com> *Aviation Internet Group.* A 'virtual museum' of historic military aircraft, rich with information.

<http://www.fas.org> *Federation of Amercan Scientists.* Information on aircraft in the current US military inventory.

<http://www.mighty8thmuseum.com/> *Mighty Eighth Air Force Heritage Museum.* Introduces institution near Savannah, GA which memorializes the sacrifices of the members of the 8th. Gives sampling of its educational films, programs for school and other groups, displays, tours by veteran-docents, etc.

<http://www.nara.gov/nara/nail.html> *National Archives and Records Administration (NARA).* Site is a window on their holdings, in form of an interactive catalog searcher, based on some of their holdings; full online interactivity

with the collection will be the eventual result. Very useful for predetermining utility of a research trip and organizing requests before going to College Park.

<http://paul.rutgers.edu/~mcgrew/wwii/usaf/html/> *Rutgers University.* Listing of all USAAF strategic bombing missions in all theatres, by date, during WW II, from official records.

<http://www.usaaf467th.org.uk/> *Wilkerson, Andy.* One of the Group Historians of the 467th BG Assn. offers extensive photo galleries, crew photos and histories.

<http://www.af.mil/news/biographies/> *U.S. Air Force.* Searchable listing of articles and biographies of prominent personages, wealth of links.

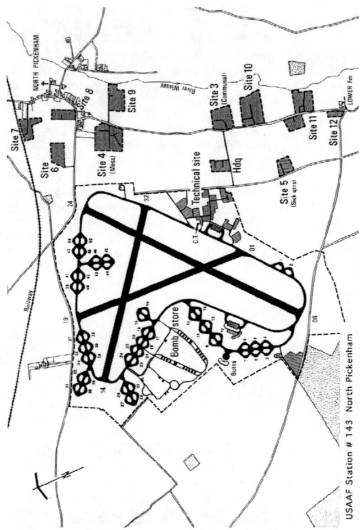

The two station maps are by the late Norman Ottway, reproduced by permission of Roger Freeman.

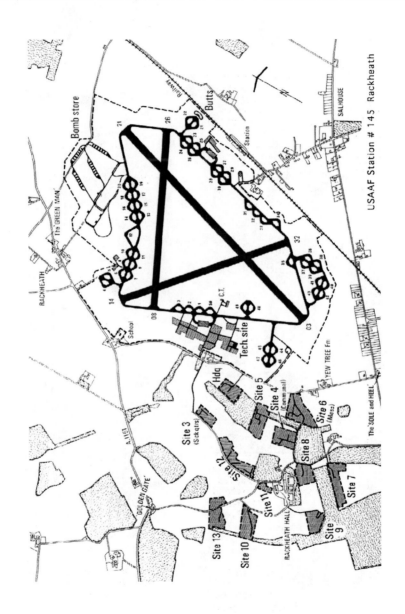

USAAF Station # 145   Rackheath

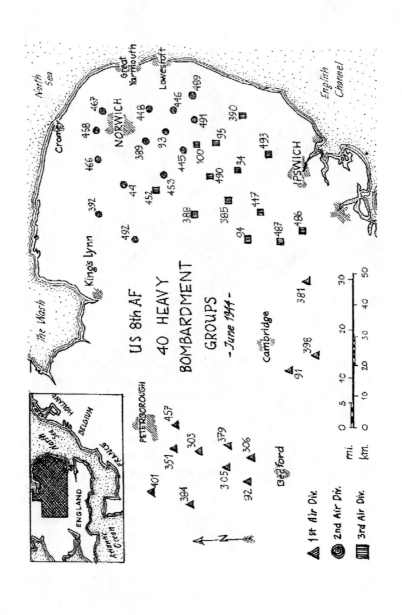

US 8th AF
40 HEAVY
BOMBARDMENT
GROUPS
— June 1944 —

1st Air Div.
2nd Air Div.
3rd Air Div.

Index

30 tons   *50 dials*   *150 swiches*

-'<u>planes & eqpt,</u>' section in JJM's
original book outline; description
of a B-24 Liberator

Forward P.1
Typeset P.14, 15, 37, 51, 65, 101, 120, 130, 140, 213, 226, 228, 240, 269,
P. 27, 48, 51, 52, 60, 64, 77, 97, 99, 102, 109, 136, 139, 143, 145, 159
160, 163, 168, 172, 173, 176, 178, 181, 185, 189, 229, 231, 234, 237, 238,
241, 250, 252, 255, 266, 272, 276, 278, 282, 295, 298, 314, 323, 335, 341,
349, 358, 361, 364, 367, 382, 401, 433, 450, 455, 459, 460, 461, 467, 471, 473,
474, 475, 976, 479, 487, 488, 497, 501, 510, 515, 516,

Typeset P.294, 296, 314, 316, 334, 363, 400, 408, 426, 434, 457, 458,
484, 490, 491,

ISBN 155212875-X

9 781552 128756